PELICAN BOOKS

A 358

CHINESE ART · VOLUME ONE

WILLIAM WILLETTS

中國藝術

魏禮澤著

吳世昌題

CONTENTS

VOLUME I

3. BRONZE

4. LACQUER AND SILK

INTRODUCTION   174

LACQUER   188

CONTENTS

VOLUME II

CONTENTS

LIST OF PLATES

LIST OF PLATES

(c) Perforated tube, *ts'ung*, amber jade with brown splashes, probably Chou dynasty. H 2⅝ ins (6·6 cm). *British Museum, London*

7 (A) Bird, green jade, perhaps Neolithic period; said to have been found near T'ai-yüan, Shansi. L 5½ ins (14 cm). *William Rockhill Nelson Gallery of Art, Kansas City*

(B) Perforated disc, *hsüan chi*, greyish-white jade with corroded surface, Shang-Yin dynasty. D 7¾ ins (19·6 cm). *Francis Hopp Museum of Eastern Asiatic Arts, Budapest*

8 Pendants and amulets:

(A) Tortoise, dark green jade with grey clouds and brown veins. L 2⅛ ins (5·4 cm)

(B) Turtle, cream jade with dark blue-green clouds. L 1⁷⁄₁₆ ins (3·7 cm)

(C) Water buffalo pendant, opaque grey-green jade with black markings on back. W 1⅝ ins (4·1 cm)

(D) Bird pendant, translucent grey-green jade with brown to tan areas. H 1¼ ins (3·2 cm)

(E) Bird pendant, ivory jade. L 2¹¹⁄₁₆ ins (6·8 cm)

(F) Bird pendant, translucent grey jade with white clouds. L 3 ins (7·5 cm)

(G) Dragon-bird finial, translucent green jade with white clouds. L 3 ins (7·5 cm)

(H) Bird pendant, translucent pale yellow jade with brown markings. L 3⅛ ins (7·9 cm)

(I) Bird pendant, translucent grey jade with brown markings. L 3⅜ ins (8·5 cm)

All probably early Chou dynasty. *C. T. Loo, Frank Caro successor, New York*

CHAPTER THREE: BRONZE

9 Ritual wine vessel, *ku*, bronze, First Phase (c. 1300–900 B.C.). H 13 ins (32·7 cm). *City Art Museum of St Louis*

10 (A) Ritual food vessel, *ting*, bronze, First Phase (c. 1300–900 B.C.). H 9¼ ins (23·5 cm). *Mr and Mrs F. Brodie Lodge, Flore, Northants*

(B) Ritual food vessel, *ting*, bronze, First Phase (c. 1300–900 B.C.). H without handles 7 ins (17·8 cm). *City Art Museum of St Louis*

11 (A) Ritual wine vessel, *yu*, bronze, First Phase (c. 1300–900 B.C.). H 10¾ ins (27·3 cm). *A. E. K. Cull Esq., Abergavenny, Mon.*

(B) Ritual wine vessel, *chüeh*, bronze, First Phase (c. 1300–900 B.C.). H 8 ins (20·3 cm). *F. G. Macalpine Esq., Clitheroe, Lancs.*

12 Cart-pole end in the form of an ibex head, bronze, early Chou dynasty (c. 1000 B.C.). L from muzzle to ear-tip 2⅝ ins (6·7 cm). *Academy of Arts, Honolulu*

13 Ritual wine vessel, *tsun*, in the form of an elephant, bronze, First Phase (c. 1300–900 B.C.). L 38 ins (94 cm). *Musée Guimet, Paris*

xiv

CHAPTER FOUR: LACQUER AND SILK

CHAPTER FIVE: SCULPTURE

CHAPTER SEVEN: PAINTING AND CALLIGRAPHY

41 Unknown Artist (10th century A.D.), *Monk with a Tiger*, ink and colour on silk. 31½ by 20¾ ins (80 by 52·5 cm). *Musée Guimet, Paris*

42 Attributed to Tung Yüan (*fl.* A.D. 947–970), *Festival for Evoking Rain*, ink and colour on silk. 61¾ by 63½ ins (156·3 by 161·1 cm). *United Museums and Libraries, Palace Museum Division, Formosa*

43 Attributed to Hsü Tao-ning (*fl.* A.D. 1030), *High Temples in Snowy Mountains*, ink on silk. 65¼ by 34¾ ins (165·2 by 88·9 cm). *Municipal Museum, Ōsaka, Japan*

44 Attributed to Kuo Hsi (*c.* A.D. 1020–1090), *Winter Woods*, ink on silk. 60¼ by 39 ins (153 by 98·8 cm). *United Museums and Libraries, Palace Museum Division, Formosa*

45 (A) Mi Fei (A.D. 1051–1107), *Valedictory Poem*, ink on paper. 12⅝ by 25½ ins (32 by 64·5 cm). *United Museums and Libraries, Palace Museum Division, Formosa*

(B) Mi Fei (A.D. 1051–1107), *Landscape with Mountains*, ink on paper. 20⅛ by 19¼ ins (51 by 49 cm). *Fusetsu Nakamura, Tōkyō*

46 Li Lung-mien (*c.* A.D. 1045–1106), part of the hand-scroll *Picture of Five Horses*, ink and slight colour on paper. L of complete scroll 72 ins (182 cm), H 11 13/16 ins (30 cm). *Formerly in the collection of Sanji Suenobu, Sendai, Japan; now reported destroyed*

47 Attributed to Emperor Hui-tsung (A.D. 1082–1135), *Quail and Narcissus*, ink and colour on paper. 10⅝ by 16½ ins (27 by 42 cm). *Nagatake Asano, Odowara, Japan*

48 Li T'ang (*c.* A.D. 1049–1130), *Autumn Landscape*, ink on silk, 42 by 17⅛ ins (106·6 by 43·5 cm). *Kōtō-in Temple, Kyōto, Japan*

49 Liang K'ai (*c.* A.D. 1140–1210), *Li T'ai-po Reciting his Poems*, ink on paper. 31⅛ by 11 13/16 ins (79 by 30 cm). *National Museum, Tōkyō*

50 Attributed to Hsia Kuei (*fl.* A.D. 1180–1230), part of the hand-scroll *Ten Thousand* Li *of the Long River*, ink on silk. L of complete scroll 36 ft 6⅝ ins (11·14 m), H 10⅝ ins (27 cm). *The Palace Museum, Peking*

51 Ch'ien Hsüan (*c.* A.D. 1235–1290), *Squirrel on a Peach Bough*, ink and colour on paper. 10¼ by 17¼ ins (26 by 44 cm). *United Museums and Libraries, Palace Museum Division, Formosa*

52 Kao K'o-kung (A.D. 1248–1310), *Mountain in Rain*, ink on paper. 48 by 32⅜ ins (121·8 by 81·7 cm). *United Museums and Libraries, Palace Museum Division, Formosa*

53 Attributed to Wu Chên (A.D. 1280–1354), *Bamboo Shoots*, ink on paper. 9 by 8¾ ins (22·8 by 22·5 cm). *British Museum, London*

54 Ni Tsan (A.D. 1301–1374), *The Jung-hsi Studio*, ink on paper. 28¾ by 13¾ ins (73 by 35 cm). *United Museums and Libraries, Palace Museum Division, Formosa*

LIST OF FIGURES, TABLES,
AND MAPS

FIGURES

xxi

CHINESE ART

INTRODUCTION

Definition

'ART', says Croce, 'is what everyone knows it to be.' That granted, to embark on a long explanation of what I have in mind when I think about art would be neither here nor there, even if I could persuade myself it was anything at all easily put into words. But what is meant by 'art' in the present context is merely a matter of summary definition. To begin with, we do not mean art, the aesthetic expression of feeling and emotion, but rather the vehicles of such expression – that is, the art-forms themselves. And whereas a writer on European art might properly confine himself to the *arti liberali* – the 'free' arts of painting and sculpture – he would be telling only part of the story were he to do so in the case of the arts of the Far East. For all who have come into contact with Chinese art will agree that its masterpieces were no less frequently wrought in materials such as jade, bronze, and pottery than in those of painting and sculpture. Each is an art-form in its own right.

Painting and sculpture came to maturity only relatively late in the wide span of Chinese history. So that were we in fact to confine our survey to painting and sculpture alone, we should find ourselves with practically nothing to say about a period of two thousand and more years of China's prehistoric and early dynastic culture. Is it antiquarian bias that makes us unwilling to ignore this vast tract of ancient time? Such a bias may well be the result of what might be called a contemporary education in Chinese art history. During the last fifty years or so, Westerners have come to realize that the picture of Chinese art as a whole is not at all what Europe of the eighteenth and nineteenth centuries took it to be. The Chinese then showed us only a small part of their artistic inheritance. It was no fault of theirs that the brilliant *œuvre* of the eighteenth century – the lacquers, textiles, porcelains, and so forth then being made in China – should so completely have satisfied contemporary European taste for the decorative, the exotic, or the merely quaint; or that during much of the last century European fancy was for articles valued chiefly as curios or objects of *vertu*. But they were at no great pains to create a better-informed taste on the part of the West; one doubts whether they believed such a thing possible. Then, about the turn of the century, a very few Western scholars began to realize that Chinese art extended back into a scarcely credible antiquity. Compared with what was now coming to light, the *chinoiséries* of the eighteenth century began to seem trivial and effete. Lacking critical standards by which to judge so completely unfamiliar an art, those who did not turn their backs on it were forced to see it largely through Chinese eyes, and from much the same historical standpoint as did the Chinese antiquarians who compiled the great Imperial catalogues of Sung and later times (p. 133). Hence a possible prejudice on the part of the writer for art-forms, other than painting and sculpture, whose interest lies to some extent in their association with China's distant past.

Yet a picture of Chinese art including what we would call 'applied' as well as 'fine' art is, beyond doubt, the only one we can paint. Even for European art a distinction between the two categories is not easily made; in the case of Chinese it breaks down more or less completely. Sculpture, for example, has never in China won for itself the exalted position of sculpture in Europe. So that the distinction, if one insisted on making it, would have to be between painting and calligraphy on the one hand, and the remaining art-forms on the other. Yet the same thread of artistic genius, married to technical mastery of a very high order, runs through them all. It is a vague awareness of this common quality that emboldens us to think and speak of Chinese art as an organic whole.

And the physical elements out of which this picture is built up are almost as complete as they are ever likely to be. It is, of course, true that some phases in the history of each art-form remain still to be discovered, while others are irretrievably lost. The architecture of the early dynasties, for example, can only be reconstructed from indirect evidence, for not a single building from before the time of Christ is known to survive. That, I dare say, is the greatest single loss; although others, such as that of most of the textiles and wooden objects of the same period, are almost as deplorable. Nevertheless, the range of materials and media in which the aesthetic impulse manifested itself, over a period of upwards of 4,000 years, now seems to be permanently established.

Stephen Bushell, writing his *Chinese Art* in 1904, apparently knew little or nothing of any art in China before the beginning of our era, except from literary sources; the centre of gravity of his book is still the eighteenth century.[1] Despite the great advance that *Chinese Art* undoubtedly marked, and despite Bushell's erudition, one scarcely gets the impression that Chinese art as we know it to-day was a living reality for him. Credit must go to men such as he; to the great school of French sinologists, among whom Édouard Chavannes, Paul Pelliot, and Henri Maspero were outstanding for their scholarship and catholic taste in art; to explorers such as Sir Aurel Stein and archaeologists like Gunnar Andersson; to collectors like George Eumorfopoulos and Oscar Raphael; to the Chinese archaeologists of the Academia Sinica headed by Dr Li Chi; and to many, many others who helped to build up this immense structure of knowledge and taste, and bequeathed it to the world. In the West the climax was reached with the International Exhibition of Chinese Art held at Burlington House during the winter of 1935–6. This was undoubtedly the finest display of Chinese art objects ever brought together under one roof, and it proved once for all that Chinese art was equal in magnitude to that of any other of the great divisions of mankind. At the same time it gave an opportunity for measuring the dimensions of each art-form in relation to Chinese material culture as a whole; no major revaluation in this respect has since been made, and, as we have already said, probably none ever will.

Scope

In this book we intend to discuss eight art-forms; namely, those of jade, bronze, lacquer, silk, sculpture, pottery, painting and calligraphy,[2] and architecture. Of them, bronze, sculpture, pottery, and painting and calligraphy are, we suppose, automatic choices; and so also would be architecture, were it not for the fact that its theoretical and actual accomplishments are as yet scarcely known to the West. And if the others – jade, lacquer, and silk – seem to us minor arts by comparison, they no longer appear so when placed in their proper contexts in the history of Chinese civilization. If the reader will presently accept the list as it stands, we shall try to explain, in each

1. S. W. Bushell, *Chinese Art*, 2 vols, London 1904–6.
2. For reasons that will be discussed later (pp. 562–3), these two will be treated as a single art-form.

chapter, the reasons why the art-form there discussed is entitled to its place in a history of Chinese art.

Method

The method of this book will be descriptive. We shall not pass aesthetic judgements on the objects discussed, but shall allow the illustrations to speak on their behalf. Nor shall we try to evoke in the reader the sort of intellectual excitement that Roger Fry and Laurence Binyon were able to stimulate by the compelling force of their prose. Not that 'exclamatory' criticism is necessarily bad. Whatever leads people to explore where they might not otherwise have gone has a value of its own, even when it is very little more than an infectious enthusiasm. But word magic is deceptive, and even if one had the power to perform it, the reader might yet be in danger of confusing verbal imagery with the objects it is meant to embellish. The art historical approach is better suited to our purpose, although the methods of European art history admittedly will not as yet reap comparable rewards when applied to the art of China; we still know far too little about it. But a start has been made – for example, by Swedish archaeologists working on Bronze Age art – and part of our task will be to hand on to the reader some of the results yielded by these first attempts at handling the data of Chinese art history.

Everybody is aware of a close connexion between art and the society of which it is an ingredient. A major art-form grows up in response to a social need which it alone can satisfy, a need that can be traced to the nexus of cultural factors that makes up the history of its day and age. Like an organic growth, it contains possibilities of variation. And its coming into flower, should that happen, is the result of a selective process working along a definite line and is not, so to speak, a sudden and unpredictable mutation. The question then occurs, how much meaning can a work of art have for us if we know nothing of the social forces that govern its growth and maturation? I think we would agree, not very much. Binyon himself begins an essay on painting and calligraphy by remarking: 'If we are truly to appreciate any work of art it is idle to approach it from the outside, bringing with us all our prejudices and preconceptions. We must try to enter into the mind of the man who made it, discover what his aim was, and consider how

4

far he has achieved his aim.'[1] Two comments are perhaps called for here. First, before we can get an idea of the artist's aim, we must have at least some idea of the nature of the society in which he lived and worked. Second, and connected with the first, we *cannot but* approach Chinese art from the outside, however hard we try. For most of us there simply is no means of intuitive *rapport*. With European art it is different; ignorant as we may be of its detailed progress, however little aesthetic significance it may have for us, the content and conventions of European art are part of the tradition in which we grow up. For we are ourselves members of the society of which it is a historical ingredient. I do not think there is any need to stress how foreign are the content and conventions of Chinese art; our approach to it must, in the long run, be analytical.

By this we do not imply anything impersonal, or emotionally sterile. The spirit that lives in a work of art can never be merely a matter for sober intellection on the part of the beholder. Were there no first liberating shock of pleasure on sensing that spirit, one would have no heart to consolidate and deepen the aesthetic experience. But the shock in this case is surely inevitable. However hidebound we may be with 'prejudices and preconceptions', we cannot encounter a thing so fresh to our eyes as an object of Chinese art without experiencing altogether new reactions. But if an experience is to go beyond mere novelty, if it is not to fade into indifference or even revulsion, it must be deepened by understanding; and part of the process of coming to understand Chinese art necessarily involves understanding the conditions that give rise to it.

In the following chapters our attention will quite properly be concentrated primarily on the art-forms themselves, rather than on the society that gave them birth. But this is not to say that we are interested in the latter only for the sake of what it can tell us about the former. The two cannot be considered apart from each other; together, they form a complex quite distinct from any other art and society the world has ever known.

In writing a book on the material arts of any civilization, one or other of two approaches is possible. The theme may be unfolded in chronological and historical sequence, each chapter being made to

1. Cf. L. Binyon (edit.), *Chinese Art*, a collection of essays on various Chinese art-forms by Laurence Binyon, Leigh Ashton, R. L. Hobson, Una Pope-Hennessy, and A. J. Koop, London 1935, p. 1.

correspond to a major historical era. This method has the practical advantage of establishing continuity, but its drawbacks are no less great. In a case like that of China, where several art-forms can be shown to have flourished during successive historical periods, the treatment of each necessarily becomes discontinuous, and the reader cannot hope to gain a clear picture of any single one unless he sifts material from all over the book. Again, with such an approach, emphasis tends to be placed more on social and political history and less on material culture and art.

Following the second method, each chapter may be devoted to a single art-form, whose whole known history is traced therein. Chronological continuity is now forfeited. Dates and names of dynasties have to be repeated over and over again, and so does the description of that great unifying quality common to all the arts of a given period – its historical style. And the social and political background tends to get ignored in the effort to describe technical, typological, and stylistic developments in an art-form with a history of perhaps 2,000 years within the limits of a single chapter.

Both methods suffer from a further defect. Both lay the writer under the necessity, unless he clearly states an alternative intention, of discussing the progress of each art-form over its whole life-span. To do this at all properly is quite out of the question in the present case; for Chinese art, like every other dimension of Chinese culture, is of appalling magnitude. Nor do we think the reader would be at all grateful if we attempted this task. After all, the progress of each art-form is quite uneven; there are bound to be long periods in its history scarcely worth mentioning, and the best comment on mediocrity is perhaps silence. Such omissions, in fact, may in themselves help to make for a sort of overall evaluation, leaving our attention free to concentrate on the best work that was being done in each successive period.

With these considerations in mind, we have tried to effect a compromise between the two methods just outlined. Chinese history can be made to fit, very loosely, into phases represented here by chapters two to eight. The first known phase of Chinese civilization belongs to the late prehistoric period, roughly 2500–1300 B.C., and forms a natural background to chapter two. The Bronze Age, between about 1500 and 500 B.C., forms another distinctive social and political phase and is dealt with in chapter three. The social and political character of the period covered by chapter four, roughly 200 B.C. to A.D. 200, is in turn quite different from those that precede it: and so on. The historical phases thus follow each other in more or less strict chronological sequence from about the third millennium B.C. down to modern times; and chapter one, which forms an introduction to the others, takes the story back to the earliest traces of man in China.

But again, each main historical phase has at least one art-form – sometimes only one – which is for one reason or other especially characteristic of that phase; in the case of the period 1500–500 B.C., for instance, bronze. True, we know next to nothing of other material arts during this time. But what we *can* claim is that bronze art, represented by the sacrificial vessels with which we mainly deal in chapter three, is absolutely characteristic of the social outlook and aspirations of pre-Han dynastic China; and furthermore, that at no later time did it reach greater beauty or expressiveness. And the same is true of the period between the Han and T'ang dynasties (A.D. 220–618), corresponding to chapter five, when sculpture reached its *floruit* under the patronage of Chinese Buddhism. For other historical periods the issue is not always so clear, and we have then had to make arbitrary decisions, the correctness of which is no doubt open to question.

The advantage of this approach is that while retaining historical continuity it also gives to each art-form a more or less self-contained chapter of its own. Such a combination seems so desirable to the present writer that I am prepared to encounter criticism to the effect that important phases in the development of some of them – especially perhaps those of pottery (chapter six) and painting and calligraphy (chapter seven) – have unwarrantably been left out. To this objection the only effective answer is perhaps that an even more unsatisfactory result might have ensued had they been included. Apart from the obvious danger of overburdening both book and reader, we would have had to forgo the advantage of combining historical continuity with separate treatment of each art-form, as discussed above. Bibliographical references in the footnotes will help the reader to gain a more complete picture of the historical development of each art-form.

Romanization

This is the means whereby Chinese words, for each of which a distinctive character exists in Chinese, are rendered alphabetically, so that the Westerner can get some idea, at least, of how they are pronounced by at least *some* Chinese. There are almost as many systems of romanization as there are Western scholars of Chinese; we use the modified Wade-Giles simply because it is that best known to English readers and has the widest circulation. But consistency in such matters is quite impossible, and I am afraid that more than one system will find its way into the text. The Chinese Postal Guide spellings, for instance, have been adopted for the better-known place-names both in the text and on the maps – and we have had to decide in each case whether a place-name is familiar, or less well-known; if the latter, we have fallen back on Wade-Giles. Nor is this all. Here and there, in quoting a passage from some other writer, we have necessarily had to give his romanization, however far removed from Wade-Giles. In such cases, where ambiguity is at all likely, we have added the Wade-Giles in square brackets.

Notes on Cross-references, Bibliography, Index, and Appendices

Where brief reference is made to a topic more fully discussed elsewhere in the text, a cross-reference usually follows in brackets. Where no cross-reference is given, the index should lead the reader quickly to the main reference. All bibliographical material will be found in the form of footnotes. Wherever an author's actual words are quoted, or when for any other reason it has seemed proper to acknowledge an author's work, a superscript numeral appears in the text at that point, and refers to a footnote which either itself gives full bibliographical details, or else, if the publication in question has already been cited in an earlier footnote, refers to that footnote by means of a cross-reference. To facilitate indexing, pagination has been made continuous through both volumes.

To save space, we have followed the convention of abbreviating the names of periodical publications referred to in footnotes, and have omitted their places of publication; full bibliographical details of periodical publications are given in a special appendix. Another appendix provides a table of Chinese dynasties.

Chapter One

GEOGRAPHY AND EARLY MAN

WE propose to begin this chapter, and this book on Chinese art, by discussing those geographical factors that can be shown to have affected the course of Chinese history. We shall then give some account of early man in China down to the time about 4,500 years ago, when Late Neolithic communities with distinctively Chinese traits flourished in the northern part of the country; a stage at which we shall take up the story of jade. But a slight overlap hereabouts is inevitable, and for this we ask the reader's indulgence. Nor should he ask for anything like a complete account of prehistoric cultures in north China and nearby areas; our knowledge of them is hazy in the extreme, and what we have been able to piece together indicates no more than a general pattern. As for the physical environment, this is constant or changes only very slowly indeed. A distinctive culture emerges out of a distinctive setting, and no apology need be made for examining, as a preliminary, the environmental forces that have helped fashion Chinese society. Let us glance first of all at China viewed as a political unit.

The Eighteen Provinces (Shih pa shêng)

It is never very easy to say at what point in a nation's history national consciousness comes upon its people. We have ample archaeological evidence to show that advanced societies were living in north China well before the historical period; and no doubt some of these conceived of themselves collectively as a 'We' group united by common social, cultural, and linguistic traits. But there is no reason to suppose that their effective political authority was at all widespread. Nor are political conditions during the early dynastic period at all easily imagined. Judging by the state of affairs late in the Chou period (c. 1000–256 B.C.), the centres of higher society were scattered, and were separated from each other by pockets of unassimilated barbarian tribes whose society, culture, and speech were relatively foreign.

9

Orthodox Chinese history leaves us with the names of two over-lordships preceding the Chou; namely, the Hsia and the Shang-Yin.[1] That the first of these ever existed is archaeologically unproved; the Shang-Yin certainly did (p. 109). At any rate, the term 'Hsia' is used in Chou times not only to name the alleged dynasty, but also to designate the 'We' group in a cultural sense; for the expression *chu Hsia* – 'all the Hsia' – has precisely this meaning in Chou texts, when the superiority and exclusiveness of Chou society *vis-à-vis* the barbarians are being asserted. And if, as some have thought, the Hsia dynasty was a mere myth created by the Chou after their conquest of the Shang-Yin in order to equip themselves with a legitimate civilized ancestry, this is surely the best possible reason for concluding that they acknowledged the China of their day as a distinctive, self-contained, and adult society and culture. They were simply securing title-deeds to their newly-won inheritance. The term *hua Hsia*, in which *hua* means something like 'flowering', 'cultivated', or 'cultured', is still in use to-day as an epithet for China.

The area of effective Chou rule was never very extensive, and within three centuries it had been reduced to a tiny royal domain surrounded by powerful independent States sprung from fiefs originally granted by the Chou to its military aristocracy. These States were of two sorts. All were at loggerheads; but those lying in the region of metropolitan China, around the Yellow River valley, were continually being forced on to the defensive by their powerful and aggressive neighbours in the west, south, and east. Collective security never took practical form; but at least the notion was current that *chung kuo*, or 'the Central States', in some way formed a distinct polity whose traditions and institutions were older and more valid than those of outlying societies. This expression, too, has come to stand as a designation for 'China'. We often translate it, wrongly, 'the Middle Kingdom'.

In 221 B.C. an aggressor State in the west, Ch'in, succeeded for a time in bringing all China north of the Yangtze under one rule. The

---

1. For reasons given by W. P. Yetts, *An-yang: a Retrospect*, London 1942, pp. 9–10, it seems proper to adopt the rendering 'Shang-Yin' for this dynasty. The term 'Yin' does not occur in contemporary inscriptions, but seems to have been used first by the Chou to name both the dynasty and the people. There is some disagreement as to whether the word 'Shang' was used by the 'Yin' peoples to name themselves, but certainly it designated their last capital and very probably the last but one as well. In Chou times it *did* name the dynasty, as is proved by its occasional appearance in contemporary bronze inscriptions.

dynasty then founded was not destined to endure, but various measures aimed at unification of the country were set on foot (p. 565), and the Ch'in Empire marks a definitive stage in the growth of a politically integrated China.

The northern States had long since thrown up defensive walls on their northern frontiers as protection against the horse-riding nomads of the steppes and deserts of what to-day are Mongolia and Manchuria, peoples who were definitely *not* Chinese either by race or by way of life. Ch'in now undertook to join these walls into one long, defensive chain. This act of integration, whatever its military value may have been (see footnote p. 24), had important political consequences, for the Great Wall (plate 58a) served to point the contrast between the peoples living inside it – 'south of the Wall' – and the nomadic tribes who lived beyond. Not only did the Great Wall help to weld the Chinese into a nation; it had an equally formative effect on the outsiders. It helped to unify the peoples of the steppes into a great political and military power, and so marked a turning point in the political history of Asia as a whole.[1]

The map of China was still not such as we would recognize to-day. The 'Chinese' world still stopped more or less at the Yangtze. But the tradition of a centralized government was thereafter never broken; and during the succeeding dynasty – the Han (205 B.C. to A.D. 220) – Imperial control gradually extended until it reached into south Manchuria and Korea in the north-east, Tongking in the south, and Chinese Turkestan in the west. The normal, or 'optimum' limits of China Proper had been established for posterity. And, in recognition of this fact, the Chinese still speak of themselves as 'Han', using the word to signify a racial and cultural comity differing in these respects from the many minority peoples within the Republic.

To-day the country is variously named. We in the West speak of 'China' – and this word probably has a long descent from the name of Ch'in State – 'China Proper', 'the Middle Kingdom', and 'the Eighteen Provinces'. We almost always mean the whole area south

1. Cf. O. Lattimore, *Inner Asian Frontiers of China*, New York 1940, p. 452, where the author agrees with a contemporary Chinese account of the nomads suggesting that 'the appearance of a nomad ruler who was a kind of crude equivalent in the steppe of the new Chinese kind of supreme emperor was not only contemporary with the Ch'in unification of China but in some way attendant on it'.

of the Great Wall. The Eighteen Provinces formed the national polity during the period of Manchu rule, until A.D. 1907; all of them still exist. They may be conveniently grouped in relation to the three main river systems, as follows:

1. *Yellow River (Huang Ho)*: Kansu, Shensi, Shansi, Honan, Hopei (Chihli), Shantung.
2. *Yangtze*: Szechwan, Hupeh, Anhwei, Kiangsu, Hunan, Kiangsi, Chekiang.
3. *West River (Hsi Chiang)*: Yunnan, Kwangsi, Kwangtung, Fukien, Kweichow.

Another obsolete polity, that of the first Republic, was the Twenty-four Provinces, *Êrh shih ssŭ shêng*. It comprised the eighteen named above and added Ningsia, Suiyuan, and Chahar of what was formerly Inner Mongolia; Jehol, which was included either in Inner Mongolia or Manchuria; and Sikang and Chinghai of Tibet. The administrative area known as the Twenty-eight Provinces, *Êrh shih pa shêng*, added to these Sinkiang (Chinese Turkestan), and Liaoning, Kirin, and Heilungkiang (the Three Eastern Provinces of Manchuria).

Such regroupings were made from time to time as Chinese control strengthened or weakened in the outlying minority areas, which have had varying political status *vis-à-vis* China. To-day the People's Republic of China (map 1) comprises, as well as the above-named eighteen provinces, the autonomous area of Tibet (Sikang, Chinghai, and Tibet); the autonomous area of Chinese Turkestan (Sinkiang); the Inner Mongolia Autonomous Region (including the former provinces of Suiyuan and Chahar); the four Manchurian provinces of Jehol, Liaoning, Kirin, and Heilungkiang; and, prospectively, the island province of Taiwan (Formosa). The province of Ningsia has been done away with, and its territory incorporated with that of Kansu. Other outlying territories – for instance, Outer Mongolia (the Mongolian People's Republic), Korea (the Korean Democratic People's Republic), and parts of Indo-China – have also at one time or another been under Chinese control, but to-day lie outside the national frontiers.

The Eighteen Provinces of China Proper constitute a roughly circular land mass with a million and a half square miles of territory and a population of some 500 millions. They lie between longitude 100° and 120° E., and latitude 20° and 40° N. It comes as rather a shock to realize that Peking, with a mean January temperature of 16 degrees below freezing, lies in the same latitude as Gibraltar; and that Canton, on the tropic of Cancer, has occasional falls of snow. China, in fact, has a colder winter climate than any country in the world of corresponding latitude.

Climate

China's weather results from a regular alternation of continental and oceanic air movements. In summer, hot air in the interior of Asia rises and flows out towards the ocean, creating an area of semi-permanent low pressure in Mongolia and Siberia. Warm, moist air now flows in a north-westerly direction across China from areas of high pressure in the Pacific; and there is a high seasonal rainfall, tapering off towards the north-west. In winter, conditions are reversed. Cold, dry air now flows from the north-west across the sub-continent to stabilize the low-pressure area over the relatively warmer ocean, bringing dry and cold winters. Other factors such as cyclonic storms complicate the picture; but on the whole we may say that the prevailing winds in south China are damp and south-easterly, and in north China, dry and north-westerly. These north-west winds have been a factor of some importance in the life of the Chinese, as we shall see from time to time (cf. pp. 34-5).

Regional Divisions of the Eighteen Provinces

The fact that China is roughly circular in shape may be of some help in simplifying our notions of its physiography. Taking Pakhoi and Taku Bar as extreme south-west and north-east points on the coastline, a circle drawn through them, and passing through Shanghai, faithfully follows the coastline for some 160 degrees. It then cuts across Hopei, passes just south of the Great Wall near Peking, skirts the northern boundary of Shansi, follows the northern section of the great bend in the Yellow River (the Ordos Bend), bisects Kansu, skirts the western boundary of Szechwan, passes through Kunming in Yunnan, and then follows the frontier of Kwangsi and Indo-China back to its starting point. It thus encloses an area of some 1,400,000 square miles,

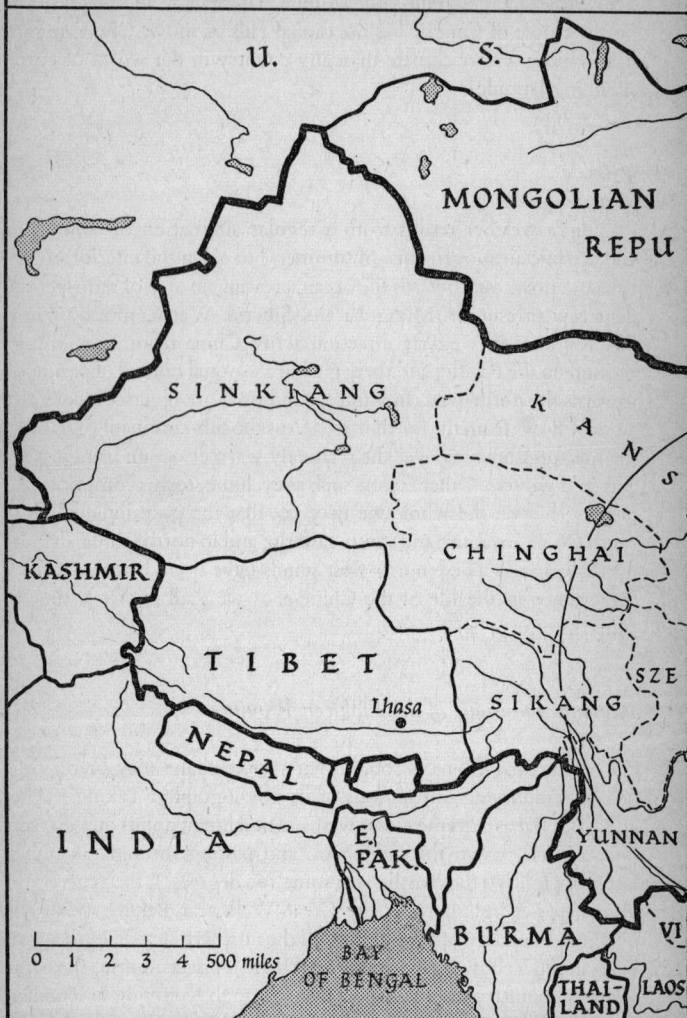

The People's Republic of China

U. S.

MONGOLIAN
REPU

SINKIANG

KANS

KASHMIR

CHINGHAI

S

TIBET

Lhasa

SIKANG

SZE

NEPAL

INDIA

E.
PAK.

YUNNAN

0 1 2 3 4 500 miles

BURMA

VI

BAY
OF BENGAL

THAI-
LAND

LAOS

Map I.

or almost all of China Proper, and has its centre near I-chang on the Yangtze (map 1).

If we now divide this circle into a northern and a southern half, we split China into two sharply defined regions, North and South. Marked physical differences, especially in climate, have brought into being two separate Chinas with distinct racial, linguistic, and other traits, while the natural barriers between them have cut them off from each other during long periods in their history. Indeed, not until the Han period (205 B.C. to A.D. 220), when the South was for the first time largely brought under control, was its influence on the North more than marginal. It is as near the truth as makes no matter to say that the formative elements in Chinese civilization – its material culture, its written language and literature, its *mores* – all began in the North; and almost everything dealt with in the first two chapters of this book concerns the North alone. The Yellow River valley, its principal feature, has with good reason been called the cradle of the Chinese race. The actual geographical change, we should hasten to add, lies somewhat north of our diameter, around the 34th parallel, and follows the watershed made by a succession of mountain ranges which run from west to east – the eastern extension of the Kun-lun, the Tsin-ling, and the Huai-yang which curves away somewhat to the south-east (map 2). In order to show just how deep this North–South difference lies, we have drawn up a table which shows some of its ingredients. It is based largely on material collected by G. B. Cressey in the thirties, so that the picture it gives would not be true in certain respects of China to-day.[1]

We must make clear that these differences are not absolute. The gap between North and South has, of course, been bridged from time to time by powerful unifying forces, of which the present government is the one that comes first to mind. The written language, in a land of diverse dialects, is another; Buddhism was another, and the tendency of the Chinese Court to seek refuge in the South when threatened by rebellion or invasion from the third century A.D. onwards was another. Nor was the early development of Chinese civilization entirely a one-sided affair; well before Han times the State of Ch'u, which lay largely in the South, was making its contribution to the culture of metropolitan China, and by Han times the whole area of the Yangtze

1. G. B. Cressey, *China's Geographic Foundations. A Survey of the Land and its People*, New York 1934.

NORTH	SOUTH

1. CLIMATE

NORTH	SOUTH
Cold winters; hot, dry summers.	Cool winters; hot, moist summers.
Dust storms.	Typhoons.
Rainfall often inadequate.	Rainfall usually abundant.
Prevailing winds north-westerly from Inner Asia.	Prevailing winds south-easterly from the Pacific.

2. RACE

NORTH	SOUTH
Average height 169 cm.	Average height 161 cm.
Almond eye percentage 11–21.	Almond eye percentage 36.
Uniform hybrid race.	Racial varieties, including many aboriginal pockets.

3. LIVELIHOOD

NORTH	SOUTH
4–6 months growing season.	9–12 months growing season.
1–2 crops annually.	2–3 crops annually.
Dry terrace cultivation.	Irrigated terrace cultivation.
Kaoliang, millet, wheat, beans.	Rice.
Frequent famines recorded.	Fewer famines, offset by overcrowding of population.
Smooth coastlines, poor harbours, little fishing.	Irregular coastline, good harbours, much fishing.

4. VEGETATION

NORTH	SOUTH
Grassless and treeless, brown landscape in winter.	Abundant forests, green all year round.
Typical tree: pine.	Typical tree: bamboo.
Parts afforested until c. A.D. 800.	Almost whole area afforested until c. A.D. 1300.

5. TRANSPORT

NORTH	SOUTH
Roads, two-wheeled carts.	Flagstone trails, coolie transport.
Draught animals: donkey, mule, camel.	Draught animal: water buffalo.

6. SOCIETY

NORTH	SOUTH
Classical and conservative, scholars.	Radical and restless, merchants.
Mandarin dialect spoken.	Diversity of dialects.
Emigration to Manchuria.	Emigration to south-east Asia.
Foreign intercourse by land.	Foreign intercourse by sea.

Table 1. North and South compared and contrasted

basin had been incorporated absolutely into China as a nation. But local tradition, in the absence of first-class communication from one area to another, is a strongly-enduring quantity. The persistence in the South, and especially in the far South, of regional pockets with variations in race, custom, and dialect, and of aboriginal minorities who have never become Chinese, suggests with what difficulty, and how late, south China succumbed to the process of 'sinification' from the North.

The vertical diameter of our circle divides an eastern from a western half, and here also significant differences are to be found. Most of China is hilly – indeed, only some 30 per cent of the land surface is available for agriculture – but generally speaking the mountains lie in the west; while the eastern half includes a vast area of alluvial plain made up of the drainage plains of the Yangtze, Huai, and Yellow Rivers, as well as that of the West River (Hsi Chiang) in the south. The average elevation in the western half lies between 5,000 and 3,000 feet, while that of east China ranges from 3,000 feet to sea-level – representing two steps down from the plateau of Tibet. The western half, with the exception of the rather anomalous Red basin of Szechwan, is naturally rather thinly populated, while eastern China is one of the most densely inhabited regions in the world, with an average of something like 400 persons per square mile, rising in the Yangtze plain to as high as 2,000. Western China, and especially the south-west, where there is a concentration of non-Chinese tribes, is in many respects under-developed compared with eastern China. Yet there has never been between east and west China the same cultural rift as separates North from South. Relative ease of communication along the line of the great mountain and river systems has helped to bring about this west–east uniformity.

A final contrast must be drawn. It is between the north-west and the north-east – that is, between the left and right upper quadrants of our circle. Here China gained her first political and cultural identity, one which may be thought of as the adjustment of forces operating between two highly contrasting natural habitats, Plateau and Plain. The former lies mainly in the north-west, comprising the highlands of Kansu, Shensi, and Shansi, and the latter lies in the north-east and includes the alluvial plains of eastern Honan, Shantung, and Hopei.

Apart from obvious topographical differences – the Plateau overlaid with a deep cover of the famous 'yellow earth' or loess (map 3

18

and pp. 33-5) - the two regions are not of equal economic value. Loess is by constitution a very fertile soil, but it is easily eroded by wind and water. So, in the north-west, deforestation and faulty methods of cultivation on the loess slopes, result in heavy run-offs from rain, washing away the soil, silting up the streams, and inundating crop-lands in the valleys with mud. To make matters worse, rainfall in the north-west is the lowest of all China. The Plateau, by comparison with the Plain, is infertile.

We have evidence that in prehistoric times this contrast in productivity was not so marked. Nevertheless, I think there can be no doubt that the natural advantages of the Plain are enough to account for the general drift of peoples from west to east in China, both in prehistoric and early dynastic times. Professor Li Chi conceives of a prehistoric 'We' people of the Plain, and a 'You' of the Plateau. The former had highly developed ceramic techniques. They had that curious emblem of Chinese culture, the *li* tripod (p. 136 and figure 18). They practised scapulomancy (pp. 108-9). And they built defensive walls of stamped earth round their settlements. On and near the Plateau were the 'You' peoples. They were almost certainly not racially foreigners, but they may have been 'poor relations' of the 'We' group; and if we go on the evidence of their Painted Pottery Culture (pp. 42-6), they at one time spread out eastwards as far as south Manchuria. In China itself they do not seem to have got much further east than northern Honan. Then they receded, and the latest phase of the Painted Pottery Culture is found high up in Kansu. Li Chi's conception of the 'We' and the 'You' is thus supported, and indeed largely inspired, by the findings of archaeology.

The theory of ebb and flow between Plateau and Plain has been further elaborated by Fu Ssŭ-nien. He points out that traditions concerning the alleged first Chinese dynasty, the Hsia, seem to indicate that it originated in the Plateau region. Its successor, the Shang-Yin, is associated with the Plain. The third dynasty, the Chou, had its origin in the west. Half-way through its life the royal house moved east, and from 771 B.C. onwards took up residence in central Honan. The next rulers of north China, the Ch'in, also came from the west. The successful rebellion that overturned the Ch'in Empire began in the east, in Anhwei and Kiangsu. The Han dynasty had its first capital in the west, and then, half-way through, shifted east as the Chou had done. It can scarcely be a coincidence that the two great military conquests

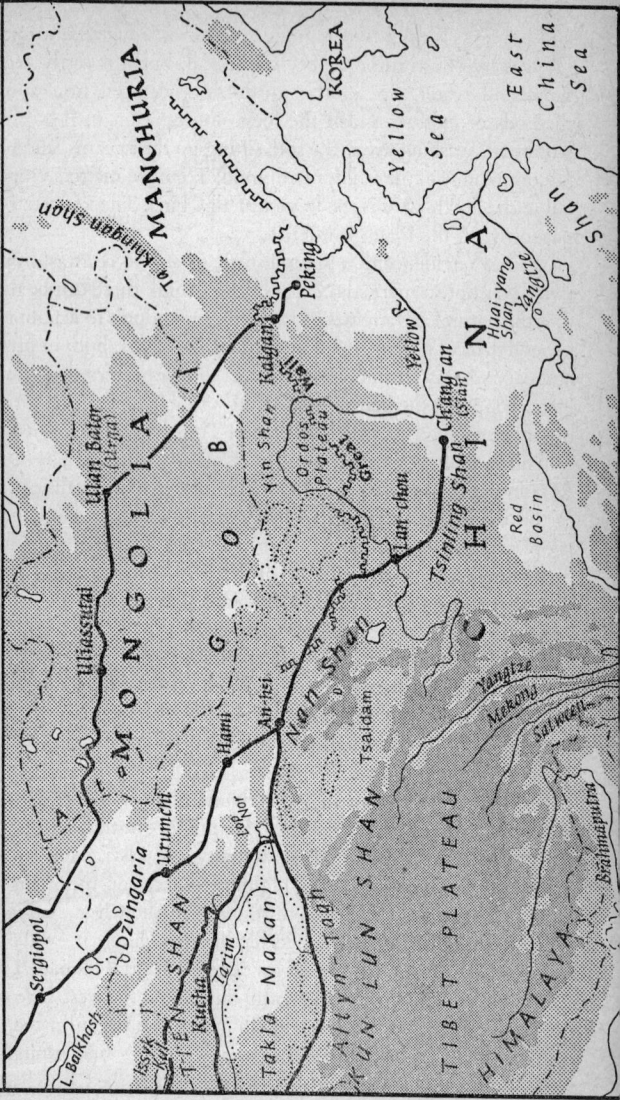

China: Physical Isolation

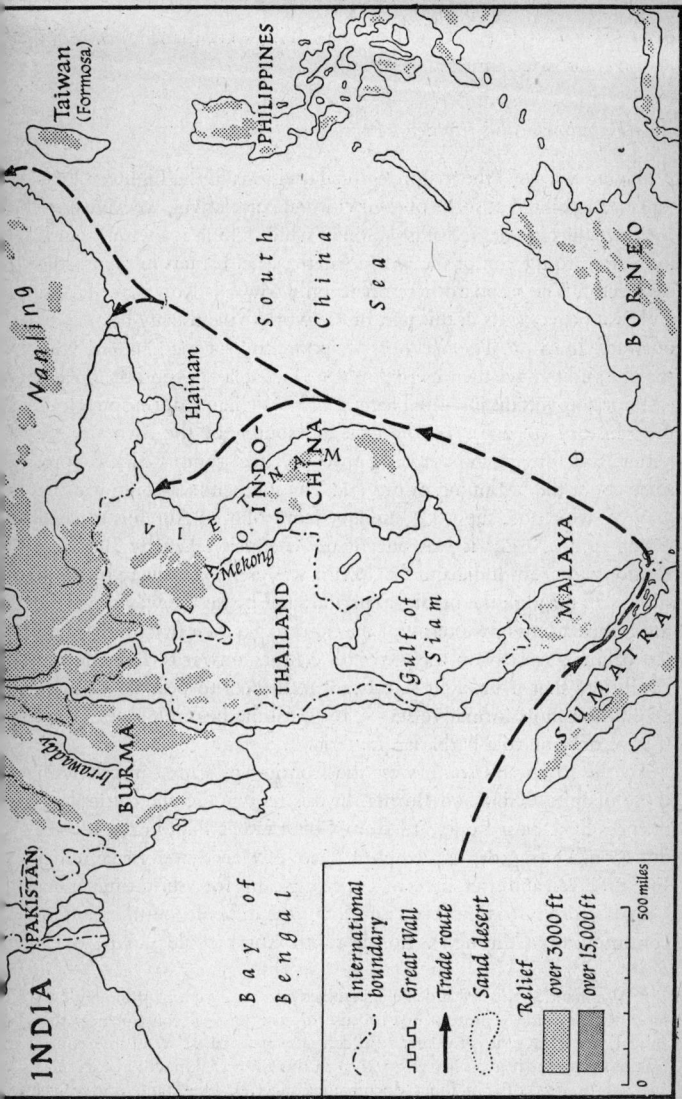

Map 2.

INDIA

PAKISTAN

BURMA

Irrawaddy

Nanling

Taiwan
(Formosa)

PHILIPPINES

Hainan

South
China
Sea

BORNEO

VIET
NAM

LAOS

INDO-
CHINA

M

THAILAND

Mekong

Gulf
of
Siam

MALAYA

SUMATRA

B a y   o f
B e n g a l

International
boundary

Great Wall

Trade route

Sand desert

Relief

over 3000 ft

over 15,000 ft

0   500 miles

21

of pre-Han China, the Chou and the Ch'in, were made by western peoples, and were directed eastwards.

The Isolation of the Eighteen Provinces

Having discussed the major regional divisions of the Eighteen Provinces, and hinted at some of their cultural correlatives, we have now to notice the high degree of isolation in which China as a whole stands in relation to the rest of the world (map 2). Let us start in the north-east sector. The seaboard here opens only towards Korea and Japan. Cultural movements in this part of the world have usually been in an outward direction. The harbours are poor; and for the Chinese, who may be said to have their backs to the sea, what lay beyond the north-east horizon was insubstantial legend or poetic fancy during much of their history (p. 290). To the east and south-east the harbours are better, and foreign shipping has probably used south Chinese ports since about the beginning of our era. The southern sea-route was the way by which the supposed embassy from Marcus Aurelius reached China in A.D. 166;[1] it was one of the channels taken by Buddhist missionaries from India and Ceylon; it was used extensively by Arab traders all through the medieval period; and it was the way the great maritime nations of western Europe came to get their first foothold on the Chinese coast from the sixteenth century onwards. But one can hardly say that it brought significant influences to bear on Chinese civilization in its formative stages, for until the beginning of our era it gave only on to a barbarian hinterland.

To the south and south-west the frontiers of China march with those of Indo-China and Burma. In this region also the cultural influences have passed outward from China rather than in the reverse direction. During the expansionist phase of Han dynasty rule under Emperor Wu and later, parts of Tongking came for a short time under Chinese administration (pp. 184–5), but the difficulty of maintaining communication through a hostile south China could not be over-

1. We mention this isolated alleged embassy – actually it was presumably no more than a trade venture – not because of any political consequences that ensued, but because it is the first recorded occasion of East–West intercourse by the sea route. It is briefly referred to in the Chinese dynastic history *Hou han shu* (p. 174). For a fuller documentation cf. J. Needham, *Science and Civilisation in China*, vol. i, Cambridge 1954, pp. 197–8.

come. Emperor Wu, who attempted to establish a trade-route to India and the Near East by way of the south-west, was held up again and again by the barbarian K'un-ming tribes, and the attempt failed. Further, the Burma route presented terrible physical obstacles. Much of it lay through wild, fever-infested jungle; and the parallel deep defiles of four huge rivers – the Yangtze, Mekong, Salween, and Irrawaddy, all running close together in a north–south direction – had also to be negotiated. To the west, China's natural isolation is almost complete, since it is bounded there by the loftiest plateau in the world, giving only on to Tibet.

But to the north-west a definitive route is found. It passes up the long arm of Kansu north of Nan Shan (the so-called Kansu Corridor) and runs by way of a series of oasis-towns across Chinese Turkestan to the Pamirs.[1] Hence it goes by way of the Karakoram Pass into Afghānistān and India; or, after crossing the Pamirs, into Ferghana, Transoxiana, and the Middle East. It is perhaps the most famous road in world history. Along it travelled the silk trade between China and the Roman Orient. It was the main route by which Buddhism reached China. It was the channel of fertile intercourse between China and the Middle East in T'ang times. It is in fact by far the most important link connecting China with the outside world during most of her history. And the cultural influences that affected China in prehistoric times because of its existence may have been scarcely less profound; indeed, it is not long ago that scholars like James Legge and Terrien de Lacouperie quite firmly believed that the entire Chinese race had reached China from western Asia by way of it. Even so, we must not rate the Silk Road too highly as a channel of communication between East and West. If travellers' reports are to be believed, it is one of the most appalling journeys a man can make. The Pamirs, the Taklamakan Desert, the Lop Desert, and the Gobi are formidable obstacles, and even in the days when the road carried regular traffic, courage and imagination of a high order must have been needed to travel it.

To the north lies the open country of Mongolia and Manchuria, the one weak point in China's *cordon sanitaire*. It leads directly to the steppe belt, the home of pastoral nomadic tribes which have from

1. At An-hsi, in north-west Kansu, the road gives off a northern branch which passes north of T'ien Shan, via Hami, to Urumchi and then crosses Dzungaria in a north-westerly direction to Semipalatinsk; thence, north of the Aral Sea and the Caspian, to the Caucasus and Black Sea.

time immemorial threatened the lands south of the Great Wall. Pastoral nomads and agriculturists are never on the best of terms. To the Chinese the nomad was always something of a barbarian; the latter, in his turn, regarded the great wealth of the fertile north China plain as his for the taking and for long periods of Chinese history plundered there more or less as he chose. In the course of time much nomad stock has been added to the hybrid north China race, no doubt with invigorating physical effect. But culturally China has benefited scarcely at all from the presence on her northern frontiers of these unpredictable people – the complex of Mongol, Turkic, and Tungusic tribes, whose movements have so enlivened the history of Eurasia.

True, in their role of culture-agents between East and West the nomads did from time to time, willy-nilly, introduce new elements into Chinese life. But this contribution was always marginal, the involuntary outcome of contact between peoples for whom there could be no real community of outlook. To seal off this vulnerable frontier, and to complete the natural isolation of their country, the Chinese built, stage by stage, the Great Wall. It is, as Dr Sirén has said, the ultimate expression of their faith in walls as defensive projects. But judging by the evident ease with which the nomads crossed it, one wonders whether it had much more than psychological value as a security measure.[1]

To sum up at this stage, China, by virtue of her position in the extreme south-east of Eurasia, and because of the systems of rivers, mountains, and deserts that shut her off along nearly all her land frontiers, has achieved a high degree of cultural quarantine during much of her history. When we consider with what difficulty China was able to get into communication with her great neighbour India, let alone with the civilizations of Western Asia and the Mediterranean, we shall not wonder at the extreme individuality of her culture, and of those she nurtured in the Far East. It is only what we should expect.

1. The point is debatable. Genghiz Khan, after all, was held at the Wall for two years before his final march on Peking (p. 528). J. Needham (see footnote p. 22), p. 101, argues that large bodies of enemy horsemen would take some time to capture and pass through gates in the Wall, or to build ramps, thus allowing the Chinese a breathing-space to send out reinforcements. But taking into account the steady onslaught of nomad invasion in north China in the second century B.C., in the fourth to sixth centuries A.D., in the late T'ang and entire Five Dynasties periods, and again at the end of the Sung, it is difficult to believe that the Wall really justified itself as a defence measure.

Greater China

Cultural exchanges between China and countries surrounding her have been mainly outwards. These countries include Indo-China, Burma, Assam, Chinese Turkestan, Mongolia, Manchuria, Korea, and Japan. China is thus the centre of a natural geographical and cultural unit – what we have in mind when we speak of 'the Far East'. Yet she has never had political authority in Japan, and only for short periods in Indo-China, Burma, and Assam. In Korea her suzerainty began in 108 B.C. and has been exercised there at various times ever since. Her influence in Tibet has been very strong since the beginning of the eighteenth century, her suzerainty there being recognized by Great Britain and Russia at the Peking Convention of 1906. Chinese Turkestan, Mongolia, and Manchuria have from time to time been even more closely linked to the parent country.

This last great arc of territories – Turkestan, Mongolia, and Manchuria – formed in the Neolithic period a sort of placenta from which China took much nourishment; her early history cannot be properly understood unless they are taken into account (pp. 37–42).

They are themselves shut in by a complicated massif of mountains that starts with the Pamirs in the south-west, and stems north-east in an enormous crescent containing T'ien Shan, Altai Shan, the Khangai, Tannu, and Sayan Mountains fanning out from the southern end of Lake Baikal, and the Yablonoi and Stanhovoi chains which cut off Manchuria to the south and carry through to New Siberia (map 4). This great mountain belt, separating Chinese Turkestan, Mongolia and Manchuria from Russian Turkestan and Siberia, forms the ultimate limit of our survey. At various places, especially near Krasnoyarsk on the Yenesei River and Irkutsk on Lake Baikal, prehistoric sites with bone, ivory, and flaked-stone industries have been located. The glaciations of this mountain belt have not been properly mapped (but cf. p. 34), nor has their chronology yet been brought into line with the European series, so that it is impossible to say how old the sites are, or whether they are contemporary with the Upper Paleolithic cultures that stretched across the Eurasian steppe belt towards the end of the last glaciation in Europe. Zeuner dates them provisionally between 72,000 and 25,000 years ago,[1] while typologically, the tools

1. F. E. Zeuner, *Dating the Past*, London 1946, p. 166.

have been compared to those of the Aurignacian, Solutrean, late Magdalenian, and Azilian industries of Europe.

In the later Siberian sites microliths of a distinctive type begin to appear; and a connexion undoubtedly exists between these and those found at Mesolithic sites in northern Manchuria to the south-east. These in turn link up with Neolithic sites in central and southern Manchuria, and eventually, I believe, with those of the north China plain. Another series may stem across the Gobi in the direction of the Ordos Desert of Suiyuan (p. 36).

China as the Centre of a 'Pacific Culture'

We have strayed somewhat into the province of archaeology. That is because the further we extend our geographical horizon, the further back in time do we have to go in search of cultural influences that may have acted on China. It is hardly relevant to the theme of this book to discuss the possibility that China itself – or we should rather say some centre of high culture on the north-west littoral of the Pacific – may have been distributing influences as far afield as the Arctic coasts of north America, central and southern America, and the south Pacific in late prehistoric times. The theory is still in its infancy, but its implications are evidently highly rewarding – namely, that Far Eastern civilization is an extensive and largely autochthonous growth, whose connexion with the other great river-valley civilizations of Eurasia may be very much slighter than was formerly supposed. It is based on observed similarities in physical appearance, language, social organization, material culture, and so forth, between existing peoples of north-eastern Asia and those of other parts of the Pacific area, as well as upon the findings of archaeology, and is discussed at greater length than can be done here by H. G. Creel.[1]

EARLY MAN IN CHINA

We have no evidence of hominids in China or the surrounding areas before the beginning of the Pleistocene period; that is, before about

1. Cf. H. G. Creel, *The Birth of China. A Survey of the Formative Period of Chinese Civilization*, London 1936, pp. 46–7.

a million years ago. On the other hand, a group of fossils believed to date from early in that period, some half a million years ago, has now come to light. Remains of Lower or Middle Pleistocene hominids in Java, of Peking Man in north China, and of what may be an even more ancestral hominid in Kwangsi, all go to show that one of the main centres of early human evolution lay in eastern Asia.

Theories on a possible 'cradle of the human race' are from the biological point of view somewhat suspect. But thought-patterns are conservative, and the notion that hominids had their origin in one particular part of the land-mass still tends to be uppermost in our minds. It is worth mentioning, therefore, that whereas twenty years or so ago the theory was that mankind evolved on the edge of the glacial–pluvial, steppe–jungle belt, of which central Asia was thought the most likely sector, contemporary fashion inclines to south and central Africa as the probable points of origin.[1] This assessment is based on discovery of a rich fauna of fossil apes of Miocene and Lower Pliocene age in that part of the world, and on a revaluation of what should be considered 'primitive' human features and what not. We must therefore add that not a single proved human fossil of Lower or even Middle Pleistocene age has yet been recovered in Africa.

Giant Man?

Early Pleistocene hominids of the Far East, on the other hand, are undeniable realities. In 1935 a molar tooth of enormous size came to light in a Hong Kong chemist's shop followed shortly afterwards by two others; and Dr von Koenigswald, the leading authority on Java Man, concluded after examining them that they belonged to an anthropoid which he called *Gigantopithecus*. A Peking anthropologist, the late Professor Weidenreich, later claimed that they were truly hominid. The cave-deposits in Kwangsi, whence the teeth are believed to have come, date from the Lower Pleistocene according to the evidence of the fossil remains of their animal population. *Gigantopithecus*, as his name suggests, was a huge creature about twice the size of a

1. Cf. L. S. B. Leakey, 'The early history of man', in *S.N.* no. 17 (1950), pp. 36–7: 'To-day there are probably few left who would seriously give Central Asia pride of place as the region most likely to be the "cradle of the human race", for recent discoveries in South and Central Africa have consistently altered the whole picture.'

gorilla, and gigantism may therefore be a 'primitive' feature of humans. It is still too early to say much about this creature and his relationship to other Far Eastern hominids, if human he was, but Dr Weidenreich thinks he may be regarded as one of their ancestors. According to this notion, the species or sub-species represented by the Java giant, *Meganthropus*, and by the three types of Java Man, would be successive descendants of *Gigantopithecus*, who may have appeared in south China with the Himalayan uplift of the Late Tertiary. Peking Man would be a northern offshoot.

Peking Man

The Pleistocene cave-site near the village of Chou-k'ou-tien, some 35 miles south-west of Peking, was first visited by Dr J. G. Andersson in 1918. Three years later Dr O. Zdansky discovered there a molar and a premolar tooth of human type, and in 1929 Dr W. C. Pei found at the same site remains of crania and parts of jaws. Since that time the whole *gisement* has been systematically excavated, with the result that skeletal remains of some dozens of individuals – men, women, and children – have been brought to light. They comprise by far the biggest assembly of early Pleistocene human fossils known.

One of its first investigators, Dr Davidson Black, proposed the name *Sinanthropus pekinensis* for the new hominid, thus giving it the phylogenetic status of two other archaic human or 'sub-human' supposed genera – namely, *Pithecanthropus* of Java, and *Eoanthropus* of Piltdown, England – each of which seemed in some respects morphologically intermediate between modern man and modern apes, and so nearer than either to the parent stock from which they emerged.

These generic distinctions are gradually being abandoned. Piltdown Man is to-day an altogether discredited being; but Peking Man and Java Man have gone, so to speak, from strength to strength. Early discoveries have been repeatedly corroborated by subsequent finds. Fossilized animal remains prove beyond doubt that both belonged to the early part of the Pleistocene period. Peking Man, by general consent, lived during the warm temperate period between the First (Günz) and the Second (Mindel) Glaciations of Europe; perhaps four hundred thousand years ago. Furthermore, ever since the finding of *Sinanthropus* crania, a relationship between this hominid and Java Man had been hinted. From the study of forty *Sinanthropus* and six *Pithecanthropus* individuals, Professor Weidenreich was led to conclude that they were simply different races of the same species.[1]

Not only do generic and specific distinctions vanish, but certain other characteristics of both hominids, particularly the erect posture which can be deduced from the shape of the leg-bones, suggest that they belonged to the same genus as Neanderthal Man (*Homo neanderthalensis*) and modern man (*Homo sapiens*). Both, according to the International Rules of Zoological Nomenclature, belong to the species *Homo erectus*, Peking Man being comprised in the sub-species *Homo erectus pekinensis* and Java Man the sub-species *Homo erectus erectus*.[2]

While his erect posture may be said to have elevated Peking Man to the same generic level as ourselves, another feature which he shares with Java Man, namely a massive bony ridge across the eyebrows previously though to be primitive – that is, of a sort likely to be found in ancestral ape–human stock – now seems to be nothing of the sort. It is not a feature of primitive apes. We have to go further back in time, in other words, to find the common ancestor; the critical juncture is not located at the anthropological level of either Peking Man or Java Man. Hence the possible significance of *Gigantopithecus*. But Peking Man cannot have marched far along the branch line of strictly human evolution; his brain capacity is only some 1,040 cubic centimetres. This is higher than that of Java Man (average 870 c.c.); but it is a good deal lower than that of Neanderthal Man (average 1,400 c.c.) and of modern man (average 1,300 c.c.). Now cranial capacity must have increased fairly rapidly after man had learnt to walk upright and had his hands free for holding things, so we can assume that Peking Man had not long learnt to do so. In this respect he is truly primitive.

---

1. Cf. F. Weidenreich, 'The Sinanthropus population of Choukoutien (Locality I), with a preliminary report on new discoveries', in *B.G.S.C.*, vol. xiv, no. 4 (1935), p. 246: 'The degree of divergence may correspond to one such as exists between the living races of mankind to-day….' It is perhaps worth recalling that as long ago as 1936 Weidenreich, admittedly never a fervent admirer of Piltdown Man, had this to say of him: 'The sooner the chimera of "Eoanthropus" is erased from the list of human fossils, the better for science.'

2. Cf. F. E. Zeuner (see footnote p. 25), p. 43.

THE ARTEFACTS OF PEKING MAN

Peking Man is especially interesting because of the presence of associated implements at the site (figure 1). This combination of tools and fossilized remains of early man is rare. The anthropologist is usually faced with a stone industry – for example, the Clactonian – unsupported by skeletal remains; or with human remains – such as

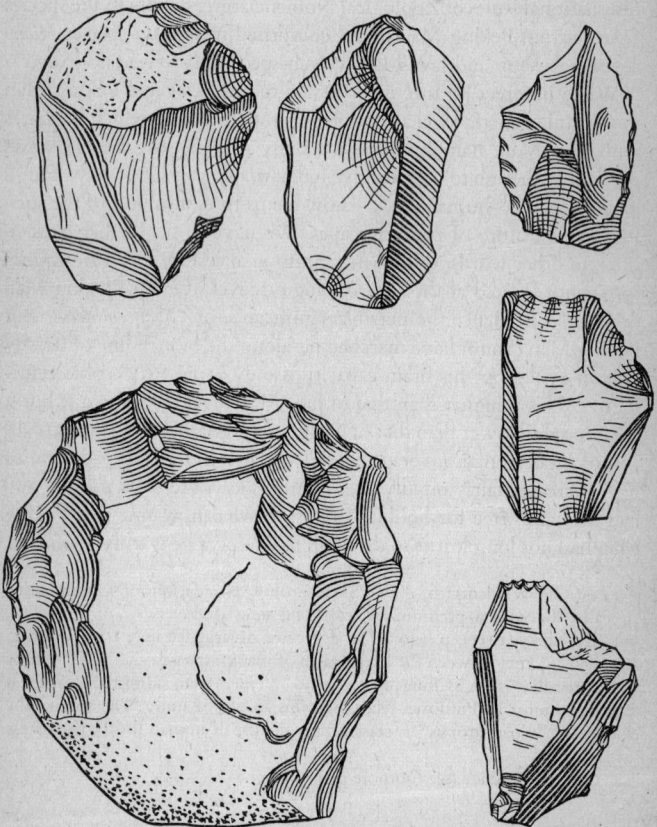

Figure 1. Stone implements of Peking Man. (Redrawn from Oakley.)

those of the Heidelberg Man – about whose material culture nothing definite is known. The value of a deposit containing both, and dating from the earliest period in which man is known to have left his traces, must, I think, be obvious.

Perhaps the most significant thing about the stone industry of Peking Man is that there are no true hand-axes among it. Hand-axes are made by the 'core' technique, whereby the implement is fashioned out of a block of stone by chipping or flaking until the required shape is reached. It contrasts with the 'flake' technique, by which flakes detached from a parent core themselves become the tools. The stone industries of Paleolithic Man can be broadly divided into these two types. Core-tools have been found in various parts of western Europe; in north, east, and south Africa; in Palestine; and in southern India; and the impression one gets is that the hand-axe culture is a southern, forest one. On the other hand, the flake industries are spread over most of northern Eurasia, including Scandinavia, England, Germany, France, Switzerland, the northern Mediterranean, southern Russia, Siberia, Mongolia, and the Gobi. They seem to be associated with a northern, steppe culture. If we include among them a tool technique producing thick, heavy flakes and rough parent cores called 'chopping tools', then we can extend the distribution of the flake industries through north-west India to Burma, Malaya, and Java. The stone industry of Peking Man seems to belong to this northern Eurasian and eastern Asiatic group.

Now a distinction is also made between *Homo sapiens* and his forbears (Neoanthropic Man) and Neanderthal Man and his relatives (Paleoanthropic Man); and the former, as far as we can tell, used hand-axes, while the latter made flake-tools. We thus have reason to suppose that both Peking Man and Java Man may have been very early representatives of the Paleoanthropic stock, perhaps ancestral to Neanderthal Man. So Zeuner says that if Heidelberg Man can be regarded as the oldest known representative of the Neanderthal stock, then 'the earliest Neanderthal Man could well be the descendant of the Pithecanthropus group'.[1]

PEKING MAN THE ANCESTOR OF THE MODERN CHINESE?

The skull of Swanscombe Man has been used as evidence for the existence of Neoanthropic Man as early as the Second Interglacial, which

1. F. E. Zeuner (see footnote p. 25), p. 298.

Zeuner dates between about 430,000 and 230,000 years ago. In that case the separation of Paleoanthropic and Neoanthropic Man must have occurred at an even remoter period. As long as we accept Peking Man as a member of the former stock, it is difficult to see how any of his distinctive characteristics could have been inherited by the modern races of mankind. But Professor Weidenreich believes that 'nothing contradicts the assumption that Sinanthropus is a direct ancestor of recent man', and goes so far as to say that we have evidence of a 'direct genetic relation between Sinanthropus and the Mongolian group of recent mankind'.[1] This evidence, which only a qualified anthropologist could evaluate, is based on a distinctive thickening of the lower jaw-bone, and so-called 'shovel-shaped' upper incisor teeth common to both.

Weidenreich points out that the division between the classic Neanderthal group and recent man is not nearly so watertight as was at one time believed – that types like the Mount Carmel population of Palestine represent a stage intermediate between the two. He further suggests that the eastern Asiatic sub-families that we have been discussing, including Peking Man, belong to an earlier stage of human evolution than either the Paleoanthropic or the Neoanthropic, to which he gives the name Archanthropinae, or 'Primary Man'. The question is whether a representative of this stock could have handed down some of its distinctive characteristics, by direct genetic transmission over something like half a million years, to 'at least certain groups among the Mongolian population', and in particular to the modern Chinese.[2]

I do not think we can expect an answer to this question until archaeology provides us with skeletal material serving to link the Upper and Lower Paleolithic cultures of China. Perhaps it should be remarked that a tendency to claim the highest possible antiquity for the Chinese race, what La Barre calls an 'appetite for ancestral time depth', is no less characteristic of modern Chinese anthropologists than it is of our own. They find their champions among those Westerners who have themselves reacted against the prevailing Occidocentrism of Western anthropology. But that the Chinese can claim exclusive rights of descent from the oldest known tool-using hominid must, for the time being, remain a doubtful possibility.

1. F. Weidenreich (see footnote p. 29), pp. 436–40.
2. Cf. F. Weidenreich, *Apes Giants and Man*, Chicago 1947, p. 84.

Middle and Upper Paleolithic Man in China; Loess

Although in Europe skeletal remains of early Pleistocene Man are rare, the Late Middle and Upper levels, corresponding to the Middle and Upper Paleolithic stages of stone industry, are full of them. Precisely the reverse is the case in China. Skeletal remains disappear almost completely between the period of Peking Man and a date usually estimated as about 25,000 years ago; that is, over a period of several hundred thousand years. This huge gap, the first of two in the prehistoric record, is partly bridged by discovery of artefacts, but no skeletal material, at a few isolated stations in the Ordos Desert and one at Chou-k'ou-tien. The last is apparently the earliest of these. Several hundred flake-tools were recovered, including side-scrapers, chisels, and points similar in many ways to those of Peking Man, but made of better materials and more frequently re-touched. The industry has been assigned by Pei to the Late Lower or Early Middle Paleolithic,[1] and the associated fauna includes species that evidently belong to the Middle Pleistocene. But neither industry nor fauna has been studied in detail.

From this period, presumably something like 300,000 years ago, we traverse a great space of time during which the Second (Mindel–Riss) Interglacial, the Third (Riss–Würm) Interglacial, and the first phase of the Last Glaciation (Würm I) were occurring in Europe, until we reach a period represented by sites discovered in the Ordos region in 1923 by the Catholic Fathers Licent and Chardin. Again no skeletal remains were found. But artefacts and fossil remains of a rich fauna were scattered at various depths in the loess deposits, and the region seems to have been occupied by humans during much, if not all, of the period of loess formation.

LOESS

Loess, better known to us by the name 'yellow earth' (*huang t'u*), is a fine-grained rock or soil which covers most of north-west China like a blanket, filling up the depressions and lying deepest in the valley bottoms (map 3). Estimates of its depth vary; but in parts of Kansu

1. W. C. Pei, *An Attempted Correlation of Quaternary Geology, Palaeontology and Prehistory in Europe and China.* University of London Institute of Archaeology Occasional Papers, no. 2, London 1937, p. 9.

and Shensi south of the Ordos Plateau it is at least 300 feet thick, becoming progressively shallower to the south-east. In central Honan its depth is 50 feet or less. When consolidated it is a friable rock easily eroded by wind or water, showing no horizontal stratification, but with a tendency to vertical cleavage. For this reason the topography of loess country is highly unusual. Vertical walls 100 or more feet deep are formed by water erosion, roads cut their way through to a depth of 40 feet or more, and the rock-face is in many places honeycombed with elaborately constructed cave-dwellings, so that much of the life is lived well below the surface of the land.

We have already remarked (p. 25) that the glaciations of eastern Asia have not been properly mapped. On the other hand, we can trace four cycles of erosional activity followed by sedimentation during the Pleistocene period in China, and it is tempting to equate these chronologically with the four main glaciations of Europe. Whether that can be done has yet to be proved, although evidence of fossil animal remains suggests that the cycles were, in fact, roughly contemporary. At any rate, the bulk of China's loess – the Ma-lan deposit – seems to have been put down during and after the erosional cycle preceding that now in operation, and covering a period from the Late Middle through the Upper Pleistocene, corresponding to the Third (Riss–Würm) Interglacial and the Last (Würm) Glaciation in Europe. The period of loess formation, on the basis of that chronology, may have begun about 100,000 years ago, and have reached completion within about 20,000 years of to-day.

We now believe that the Ma-lan loess was deposited by wind action. North-westerly winds blowing from the high-pressure belt of inner Asia were then much stronger than they are to-day. These winds picked up disintegrated materials from the poorly consolidated Mesozoic and Tertiary rocks in the region of glaciation and carried them towards the south-east, depositing the coarser fraction in the form of dunes, and blowing the finer further afield. Winds continued to work on the newly-formed dunes, a fact that explains why erosion of dunes in a north-westerly direction is a marked feature of the topography in parts of Mongolia and Manchuria; and why, when dunes were used as dwelling-sites, the material remains should have been eroded out and deposited in the dune bottoms, with a consequent absence of stratification. The element carried from the dunes was re-deposited, over and over again, in increasingly finer form. So we find that the loess of the

34

south-east, which is fine, gives place to coarser soils towards the north-west until sandy dune and desert conditions are reached in the Ordos region of to-day; and also that the loess lies deepest towards the direction from which it was blown; that is, towards the north-west.

Loess frequently lies above, or is woven into, water-laid deposits of an earlier age. Among these are the San-men clays which were eroded out of yet earlier formations and deposited as lake- and river-sediments early in the Pleistocene period. Again, fresh erosion after the Ma-lan cycle has in recent times led to the formation of what Andersson calls 're-deposited' loess;[1] and this process, accompanied by sedimentation of alluvia, is still going on to-day in the great plains of north-east China. Dust-storms are typical of the winter weather around Peking. The eolian dust is sometimes carried as far as 500 miles out to sea.

The Ordos sites are at Yu-fang-t'ou south of Yu-ling in Shensi, at Shui-tung-k'ou near Ning-hsia, and near Sjarra-osso-gol, a river flowing along the southern border of the Ordos Plateau in Suiyuan (map 3). At the beginning of the Ma-lan phase the Ordos was evidently well-watered and the resort of large game animals; for under the loess are layers of sand and gravel containing shells of fresh-water molluscs, and the fauna within the loess is exceptionally varied. It includes a number of species now extinct. Some are typical of the Lower Pleistocene, such as an elephant, *Elephas cf. namadicus*, and the woolly rhinoceros, *Rhinoceros tichorinus*. Others belong to Upper Pleistocene levels, such as the aurochs, *Bos primigenius*, and the giant Asiatic loess ostrich, *Struthio anderssoni*. And yet others have survived through to to-day – although not in the same region – such as the red deer, *Cervus elaphus*, and the big-horned sheep, *Ovis ammon*. The flake industries also show progressive development from crude scrapers, borers, and gravers at Yu-fang-t'ou to finely worked microliths at Sjarra-osso-gol.

On the evidence of the fauna, this Ordos industry can be dated to the Upper Pleistocene period, the equivalent European fauna being that associated with Neanderthal Man. Some of the stone tools show similarity to Mousterian and Aurignacian flakes; whereas the microliths could not, if they had been found in Europe, be assigned to an earlier period than the Magdalenian. Taking all factors into account, therefore, the date 50,000 B.C. would seem to be well within the period

1. A rather misleading term considering the fact that all loess has been deposited more than once.

of the Ordos industry. How far back into the loessic phase it goes, or how far into the Upper Pleistocene, is still anybody's guess. As to its possible relationship with other Upper Paleolithic cultures in Asia, a link may well exist between it and the flake industries found by N. C. Nelson around Orok-nor in Outer Mongolia; and hence, ultimately, with the Siberian Paleolithic.[1]

We next come upon human skeletal remains at the Upper Cave of Chou-k'ou-tien.[2] The fauna is rich, including a number of Upper Pleistocene forms such as the cave bear and cave hyena, but far more numerous are recent species such as were quite familiar members of Upper Paleolithic stations in Europe, and which still inhabit the region to-day. On the other hand, certain species found in the Upper Cave are now restricted to south China, and Pei thinks, because of this, that the deposit must be pre-Neolithic. The skeletal remains are those of modern man; and curiously enough they seem to belong to more than one race; three skulls examined by Weidenreich show proto-Mongoloid, Melanesoid, and Eskimoid features respectively.

The stone industry is poor. There are a few bi-polar core-tools showing no trace of secondary chipping, and some flint or quartz scrapers which, as Pei observes, 'are hardly superior to those of the *Sinanthropus* deposit'.[3] On the other hand, bone and shell industries were well developed, many of their products being known also in the Neolithic cultures of China and Europe. These include bone needles and pendants, and perforated beads made of pebbles, teeth, fish-bones, and marine shells, often polished and painted red with haematite. Presence of marine shells must mean that these people, whoever they were, had contacts with the coast well over a hundred miles to the south-east; and the haematite came, apparently, from a place almost as far distant to the north. The Upper Cave at Chou-k'ou-tien has been dated about 25,000 B.C. It is the latest Paleolithic site known in China, but whether its inhabitants were in any way related to the Ordos–Mongolia group is as yet unproved.

1. Chêng Tê-k'un remarks that the implements from these two regions are identical in type and that 'the paleolithic inhabitants in Mongolia was [*sic*] closely related to the Ordos Man'. Cf. Chêng Tê-k'un, 'An introduction to Chinese civilisation. 1. Early inhabitants', in *O.*, vol. i, no. 1 (Aug. 1950), p. 33.

2. Located by W. C. Pei in 1930 and fully explored by him in 1933–4.

3. W. C. Pei (see footnote p. 33), p. 10.

Mesolithic and Neolithic Cultures in the peri-Gobi Region

The second great gap in the archaeological record is what Andersson calls the 'Neolithic hiatus'. His words are worth repeating. He says: 'This period, which may correspond approximately to the Mesolithic and Early Neolithic, was a time of abundant rainfall, which in that part of the world must mean a genial climate. In other words the region certainly abounded in game and must have formed a pleasant habitat for primitive Man. However, as far as I know … no indisputable Mesolithic or early Neolithic site has so far been found in northern China.'[1]

Nothing, it seems, is known of the conditions of human life in north China from about 25,000 to about 4,500 years ago. The reason is not necessarily insufficient excavation, for literally hundreds of Late Neolithic sites have come to light; which must, I think, argue a huge increase in population in China Proper around the latter date. Just why this occurred when it did has never been satisfactorily explained. Andersson's statement, nevertheless, needs some qualification.

To begin with, Mesolithic cultures are quite common in south China. The sites are located in Szechwan, Yunnan, Kweichow, and Kwangsi, and the industries relate to the Bacsonian and Hoabinhian series of Indo-China. They have been dated about 10,000 years ago. Implements include finely-worked axes, knives, scrapers, and hammers; but the characteristic tool is a shouldered axe, which must have been used for forest-clearing or hollowing out canoes. A few worked antler and bone implements have survived. We do not know what sort of economy these peoples practised, but their camp-sites are mostly located on the foreshores of rivers, and one presumes that they were fishers, hunters, and fowlers. They do not seem to link up with the Late Neolithic cultures of the north.

But the Mesolithic and Early and Middle Neolithic cultures of the peri-Gobi regions did apparently point directly towards north China, and contributed to the earliest Neolithic cultures in China we know of. In other words, there is no real 'Neolithic hiatus'. The development simply took place outside the China of to-day.

The term 'Mesolithic' scarcely stands for a distinct typological phase, since Mesolithic communities inherit flake-tool traditions from

1. J. G. Andersson, *Researches into the Prehistory of the Chinese*, being *B.M.F.E.A.*, no. 15 (1943), p. 296.

the Upper Paleolithic. But with this qualification the material cultures of all Mesolithic communities are surprisingly alike. A small, often minute, flake-tool – the microlith – is typical. There is much horn and bone, often worked into spearheads, fish-hooks, and harpoons. We may assume, therefore, that Mesolithic peoples subsisted mainly on hunting, fishing, and plant food-gathering. But traces of agriculture are also sometimes found. Axes and adzes may have been used as primitive hoes, as is suggested by a characteristic lustre on the surfaces of some. And there is a curious composite tool, consisting of a bone haft along one side of which was set a series of small flint flakes, edge to edge. This was evidently a sort of sickle, though whether it was used for cutting wild or cultivated grasses we cannot safely say.

The peri-Gobi Mesolithic communities seem to have been an integral part of this Old World complex. Looking over items in their material culture, as we shall do in a moment, we cannot fail to be struck by the apparent resemblance they bear to the Mesolithic cultures of Europe and Africa (represented by the Capsian industry), Palestine (the Natufian), and southern India.

Movement of Mesolithic Populations of Eastern Asia

At the beginning of the Mesolithic period, perhaps 10,000 years ago, typical microlithic industries flourished round the shores of Lake Baikal in Siberia. For some reason, probably the onset of a cold period at the end of the Pleistocene, the communities that possessed them began to migrate south-east, and occupied parts of Mongolia and Manchuria. Increasing severity of winters and gradual encroachment of the Gobi towards the south-east kept them on the move.[1] Throughout Mongolia and Manchuria their dwelling-sites, once located on the shores of lakes, are to-day dunes; the black-earth strata which contain the cultural remains are overlaid by partly-consolidated yellow sand and have loess beneath them. Movement of populations throughout the Mesolithic and Early and Middle Neolithic terminated, I surmise, when some of them at last reached the north China plain, late in the Neolithic period. Let us see how the movement went on in the Manchurian sector of the culture (map 3 and table 2).

1. The general theory of this movement has been advanced by Chêng Tê-k'un, 'An introduction to Chinese civilisation. 2. The beginnings of culture', in O., vol. i, no. 2 (Sept. 1940), pp. 28–9.

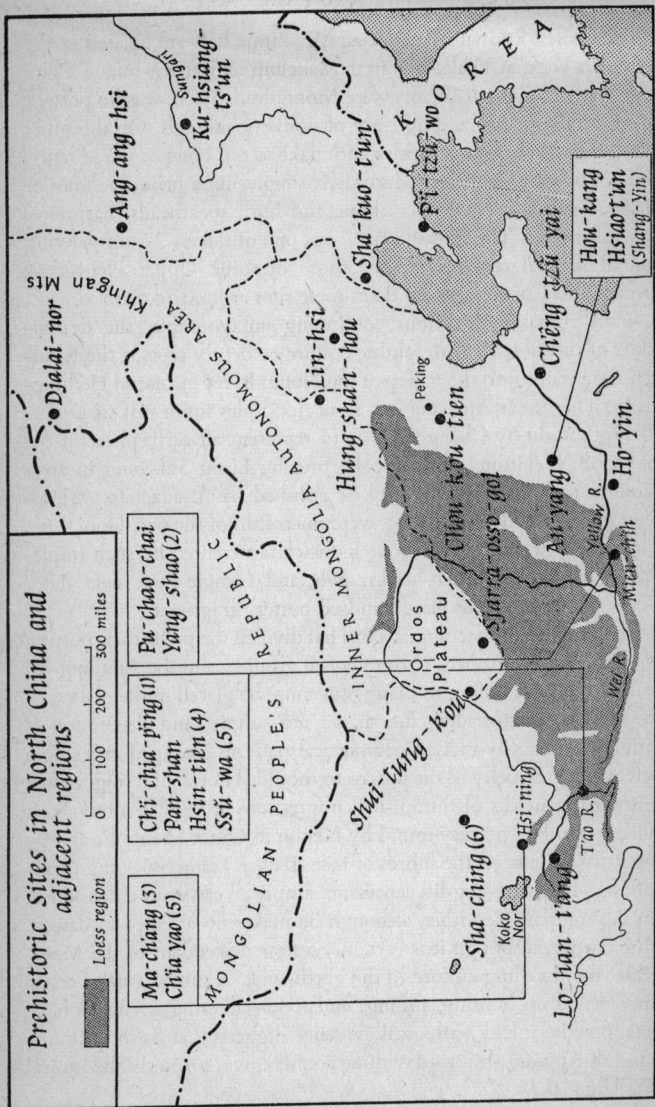

Map 3.

Prehistoric Sites in North China and adjacent regions

Loess region

Ma-chiang (3)	Chi-chia-p'ing (1)	Pu-chao-chai
Chia yao (5)	Pan-shan	Yang-shao (2)
	Hsin-tien (4)	
	Ssŭ-wa (5)	

0 100 200 300 miles

MONGOLIAN PEOPLE'S REPUBLIC

INNER MONGOLIA AUTONOMOUS AREA

Khingan Mts

KOREA

Sungari

• Ku-hsiang-ts'un

• Ang-ang-hsi

• Djalai-nor

• Lin-hsi

Hung-shan-hou

• Sha-kuo-t'un

• Pi-tzŭ-wo

Hou-kang
Hsiao-t'un
(Shang-Yin)

• Chêng-tzŭ-yai

Peking

Chou-kou-tien

• An-yang

• Ho-yin

Sjara-osso-gol

Ordos Plateau

Yellow R.

Mien-ch'ih

Shui-tung-kou

Wei R.

• Hsi-ning

Koko Nor

Tao R.

• Sha-ching (6)

• Lo-han-t'ang

39

The earliest known Manchurian Mesolithic sites are located in the far north-west, at Djalai-nor near Manchuli and at Ku-hsiang Ts'un near Harbin. The inhabitants were Mongoloid. There was no pottery among the remains, and no trace of domestic animals. On the other hand, there were typical sickles with flakes set in bone or wood hafts; and a few adzes with lustred surfaces, suggesting a primitive hoe- or *Hackbau*-culture. There were bone and horn spearheads, harpoons, and fish-hooks. The flint industry was one of flakes. Accompanying animal skeletal remains include those of some Upper Pleistocene species, and Chêng Tê-k'un dates these sites around 10,000 B.C.

With climatic conditions continuing unfavourable, the descendants of this northern Mesolithic culture evidently crossed the Khingan mountains into the valley of the Nonni River in central Heilungkiang. The site at Ang-ang-hsi, some 300 miles south-east of Djalai-nor, is thought by Chêng Tê-k'un to represent an early phase of the peri-Gobi Neolithic. Surface collecting by Liang Ssŭ-yung in 1931 brought to light a small group of polished basalt adzes (p. 74), although most of the stone tools were microliths of the peri-Gobi type. There was a characteristic bone industry represented by such implements as fish-spears, fish-hooks, awls, and a single bone sickle-haft. There were also some three hundred pottery fragments.

The Japanese archaeologist Torii has divided the prehistoric pottery of Manchuria into three chronological groups; and the Ang-ang-hsi ware should, according to Liang Ssŭ-yung, be placed in the earliest of these. It is hand-made; the shapes are simple, and decoration is limited to roughly-incised geometrical patterns arranged in a single belt around the belly of the pot, or to moulded horizontal ridges often bearing the marks of thumb-nail impressions at regular intervals. It much resembles pottery found by Nelson in Outer Mongolia and by the Russian Petri on the shores of Lake Baikal. Liang Ssŭ-yung therefore says that Ang-ang-hsi represents simply an eastward extension of the Mongolian Neolithic, although he makes no attempt to date it. Nor can we, although it is certainly a near descendant of the Mesolithic lake-dwelling culture to the north-west. A similar sort of economy, based on hunting, fishing, and food-gathering, seems to have been practised; and geological evidence suggests that the neighbourhood of Ang-ang-hsi, to-day dune country, was formerly the littoral of a large lake.

Still later, and still further south, is Lin-hsi in northern Jehol, nearly

500 miles south-west of Ang-ang-hsi. This site was also investigated by Liang Ssŭ-yung, who found several elements not present in the earlier Manchurian cultures. Of these by far the most outstanding were abundant remains of upper and lower parts of mills for grinding grain very much like the *metates* and *manos* still used in Mexico by the Hopi Indians; testifying, of course, to a well-established agricultural economy. The pottery is also much more varied and abundant than at Ang-ang-hsi. It is a fine-bodied grey ware decorated in many different ways, but most frequently with rows of stamped oblong or triangular forms (*Kamm-Keramik*). Some of the ware is burnished. But the most noteworthy technical advance shown by the pottery is that it is wheel-turned. On the other hand the stone industry was backward, the vast majority of implements being detached flakes and cores; only a single polished axe was reported.

Lin-hsi, clearly, is a site of intermediate character – advanced ceramic techniques and an agricultural economy on the one hand; on the other, a stone industry still microlithic in character. We are, of course, faced with the question of whether some contemporary Neolithic culture in the north China plain, if such a thing existed, contributed the advanced elements we find at Lin-hsi. But on the whole this stage is probably best regarded as a straightforward development from cultural conditions such as that represented by Ang-ang-hsi. The earliest known Neolithic culture of north China, as we shall see, is characterized by painted pottery and it is significant that not a trace of any such ware was to be found at Lin-hsi. No attempt has been made to date Lin-hsi, as far as I know; but it seems to me beyond doubt that this site lies, in point of date, between Ang-ang-hsi and the one next to be described. It is a type-site for the Early Manchurian Neolithic.

For present purposes only one more Manchurian site need be mentioned. This is at Hung-shan-hou near Ch'ih-fêng in Jehol, a further 100 miles south-east of Lin-hsi. It was investigated by the Japanese, Hamada, in 1937; and two stages were discovered. Hung-shan-hou II does not concern us, since it is contemporary with the historical Han period in China. Hung-shan-hou I, on the other hand, may represent the critical phase of cultural intercourse between Manchuria and the north China plain during the earliest known Neolithic phase in the latter region. It has features that Chêng Tê-k'un calls 'dualistic', some being typical of the peri-Gobi Neolithic and others evidently coming in from south of the Wall. On the one hand, there are peri-Gobi microliths showing an advanced re-touching technique; on the other, many red potsherds with remains of painting. At this stage, it is clear, there was some communication between the Neolithic culture of Manchuria and that of north China. On the evidence of the painted pottery, I believe that Hung-shan-hou I may be dated not much later than the earliest Painted Pottery site in north China, or about 2500 B.C.

Now there are no stratigraphical fixed points for the peri-Gobi Culture, and any attempt to assign dates to the stages represented by Djalai-nor, Ang-ang-hsi, Lin-hsi, and Hung-shan-hou, on internal evidence, is really rather futile. We can never be certain that parts of the peri-Gobi area were not at various times cultural backwaters.[1] A technique may well have persisted in one region long after the inhabitants of another had discarded it; and it is, of course, bad methodology to use technological criteria in order to build up a chronological sequence of sites. Nevertheless, assuming that these four sites do in fact stand for consecutive stages in the evolution of the peri-Gobi Neolithic, I think the dates 8000–2500 B.C. probably enclose them. This period is earlier than that to which the oldest known Neolithic sites of north China belong. And the peri-Gobi Neolithic was a flourishing and protracted culture. Reviewing these facts in the light of Andersson's remark that 'no indisputable Mesolithic or Early Neolithic site has so far been found in North China' we can draw but one conclusion. It is that material cultures of the peri-Gobi Neolithic are to a large extent ancestral to those south of the Wall, if indeed the latter were not themselves simply the outcome of a natural extension of a southerly flow of population from the Gobi and Manchurian lowlands into the fertile river valleys of north China, some time in the third millennium B.C. In chapter one we hope to discuss some of the cultural elements that may have been introduced into north China as a result.

Neolithic Cultures of North China

Until 1921 no Neolithic site had been located in China, and it was generally supposed – for example by Laufer, a man thoroughly familiar with the field of Chinese antiquities in his day – that there had

1. Late Manchurian sites such as P'i-tz'ŭ-wo, Hung-shan-hou II, etc., represent a Neolithic culture that persisted while the Bronze Age was flourishing in north China.

been no prehistoric period corresponding to the Neolithic stage in China, or, for that matter, to the Paleolithic.[1] But in that year J. G. Andersson discovered Neolithic remains at the village-site of Yang-shao Ts'un in western Honan, and in the course of the next year or so located dozens of others over a huge area extending from Kansu to south Manchuria; a very few of these sites are indicated on map 3. All were characterized by the presence of pottery fragments of a fine red ware evidently not made on the wheel, but built up by hand, probably by ringing, and finished with the belt-mould. Much of this

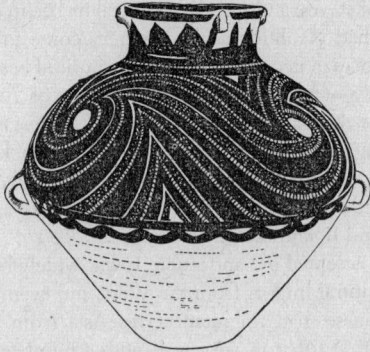

Figure 2. A mortuary urn from the Neolithic
cemetery in the Pan Shan hills, Kansu.

ware was undecorated, but many fragments bore traces of painting. Then, in 1923, hundreds of exquisitely painted vessels were recovered intact from burial-grounds in the Pan Shan hills of southern Kansu. These are, by general consent, among the finest of the world's Neolithic pottery (figure 2). Apart from the technical skill they manifest, they are deeply satisfying as pots. Form and decoration are perfectly married, the full curve of the *galbe* being repeated in the bold sweep of the spiral- or circle-design that encloses the upper part of the body. Colours are quiet and harmoniously blended.

1. Cf. B. Laufer, *Jade: A study in Chinese Archaeology and Religion*, Chicago 1912, p. 55: 'It is therefore ... not justifiable to speak of a stone age of China, and still less, as we shall see from a consideration of native records, of a stone age of the Chinese.'

The pottery was outstanding. But other remains shed much light on the racial and social characteristics of the Painted Pottery peoples. Skeletal material proves that the population belonged to a uniform stock which has been called 'proto-Chinese' and which, according to Professor Hamada, eventually infiltrated into much of the Far East. The proto-Chinese lived at the same cultural level as other Late Neolithic Man over the whole temperate belt. Millet was the staple crop, and dogs and pigs were kept. There is evidence of the manufacture of silk (p. 219) and of basket-weaving. Recent excavation at Pan-po near Ch'ang-an in Shensi shows that the people lived in huts with circular floors, made of staves, and probably conical or beehive-shaped.

No sooner had Neolithic painted pottery come to light in China than resemblances in décor and shape were noticed between it and the painted pottery of western Asia; in particular of Anau in western Turkestan, but also of sites in Baluchistan, Afghānistān, Iran, and the lands bordering on the Black Sea, the so-called 'Black Earth region'. So close were these resemblances that Arne took the view that the Chinese Painted Pottery Culture (*ts'ai t'ao wên hua*) was contemporary with Anau I and II, and estimated its age as 3000 B.C., a date that was for some time accepted by Andersson. It was widely believed that the ware was a cultural import from the West, and even that its makers, the proto-Chinese, had migrated across Asia from the Near East. This latter notion fitted in very well with a number of vague ideas about the likelihood of the Chinese having originated in the West, and having reached China by migration *en masse* at some time in the prehistoric period. To-day, with the leading exception of Bachofer, authorities are reluctant to believe that any such movement took place. Some painted pottery has been found in central Asia, but note has been taken of the weakness of this link, and of the greater technical and artistic perfection of the Chinese wares. In his latest chronology of Chinese Painted Pottery stages, Andersson has thought it wiser to ignore Western parallels, and to take as his starting-point the few available dates offered by Chinese history. Bachofer, on the other hand, supposes that a *Herrenvolk* with painted pottery made its way from the Black Earth region – represented by such sites as Schipenitz in Poland – to the river valleys of north China by way of the central Asiatic steppes. This theory,[1] which as far as China goes is based solely on

1. For a detailed criticism cf. J. G. Andersson (see footnote p. 37), pp. 280–91.

similarities between its painted pottery and that of the West, is drastic
in its implications, but seems to me to lack a sense of historical proportion. All we can say with any assurance is that a connexion does undoubtedly exist between the painted pottery of the two sides of Asia.
But how the influence was transmitted, or in which direction, is a
question that cannot be answered until all the links in the chain are
made available.

I have already said that painted pottery was an attribute of the 'You'
peoples as opposed to the 'We' (p. 19). In 1928 a Neolithic site
of quite different nature from those of the Painted Pottery Culture
was discovered at a place called Ch'êng-tz'ŭ-yai in Shantung, by the
Chinese archaeologist Wu Gin-ding.[1] Ch'êng-tz'ŭ-yai has become the
type-site for what is now known as the Black Pottery Culture (*hei
t'ao wên hua*). The ware is altogether different from the red painted
pottery. It is black and unornamented. It is wheel-turned; and the
extreme thinness of the wall – down to as little as a millimetre – as
well as its brilliant burnished finish, seems to point to a long-estab-
lished ceramic technique. The shapes of Ch'êng-tz'ŭ-yai vessels
strongly suggest that they, or others like them, were models for the
first bronze ritual vessels – *li*, *ting*, and *tou* being especially prominent
(pp. 136–8, 141).

Marked contrast between these two types of ware has helped to
amplify the concept of the 'You' and 'We' peoples, and to crystallize
in the minds of some writers the idea of an eastward cultural invasion
inside China on the part of the Painted Pottery peoples, followed by a
withdrawal. Various suggestive facts were noticed: that the painted
pottery arrived latest and stayed for the shortest time in eastern sites
such as those of South Manchuria, and had its greatest lease of life in
the western sites in Kansu; that the pottery shapes taken over by
bronze art are *not* those of the painted ware, but are those characteristic
of black pottery; and finally, that the *li* tripod, which has survived as
a permanent and distinctive vessel-type – a 'symbol of Chinese art
from prehistoric stages up to modern times', to use Andersson's
words – is not found in the north-west until very late in the Neolithic
period there. It is confined to the fifth and sixth of the stages into
which Andersson divides the Painted Pottery Culture (p. 49), dating
from 1000 to 500 B.C. In the region of the Plain, on the other hand, it
is found everywhere from western Honan to Shantung and south

1. Cf. G. D. Wu, *Prehistoric Pottery in China*, London 1938.

Manchuria, and from the second, Yang-shao, stage (2200–1700 B.C.) onwards.

All these facts suggested that the two cultures were fundamentally distinct, that the eastern one was more 'Chinese' than the western one, and that a line of demarcation could be drawn between them indicating the ultimate eastward extension of the Painted Pottery Culture. On the whole, I believe this is a true picture. There is definite evidence of a Neolithic stronghold of quintessential 'Chinese' life in the east, on the Plain; rather than in the west, on the Plateau. On the other hand, it must be admitted that the distribution of Far Eastern painted pottery is very much broader than was believed, say, fifteen years ago, when Creel wrote his *Birth of China*.[1] The ware is now known from as far afield as Szechwan, northern Anhwei, northern Kiangsu, Hopei, Formosa, Lamma Island, and, of course, south Manchuria. Similarly we must modify the notion that black pottery is altogether confined to the Plain, for it has been found not only at Yang-shao Ts'un, but also at several sites further west; and a relationship between it and the black pottery of Tepe Hissar in Iran, even, has been proposed; this last ware may antedate that of Shantung by a thousand or so years.[2]

The original theory of a single invasion eastwards on the part of Painted Pottery peoples into a stronghold of people using black pottery – this being a ware exclusive to the Plain – will clearly have to be modified. But in general terms I feel sure it is true. The evidence is that there were two distinct and opposed Neolithic cultures in prehistoric north China, and that painted red pottery is typical of one, black pottery of the other.

Problems of Dating

The earliest historical dates for western Asia lie around 2800 B.C., corresponding to the Early Dynasty of Sumer; and a fairly reliable chronology, based on king-lists and confirmed by archaeology, can be

1. Cf. H. G. Creel (see footnote p. 26), pp. 44–8.
2. Cf. S. Kaplan, 'Early pottery from the Liang Chu site, Chekiang province', in *A.C.A.S.A.*, vol. iii (1948–9), pp. 13–42. Kaplan suggests that a group of Black Pottery peoples, with Iranian antecedents, may have penetrated to the north China plain by way of Manchuria, some time in the third millennium B.C. The comparison he makes between Iranian and Far Eastern black pottery certainly tends to support his theory; but as far as I am aware, no Manchurian Black Pottery site has yet been discovered.

built up from this period onwards. Furthermore, the *tells* and *tepes* of Mesopotamia and Iran, with their continuous occupational histories represented by dozens of strata, allow us to establish a relative archaeological sequence, beginning with undated material immediately beneath that to which an historical date can be assigned, and going down to the lowest stratum of a particular site. Such a sequence of archaeological material below the date-line may be found repeated at other sites containing even earlier levels; and this overlap can be used – rather like the tree-ring method of building up an absolute chronology for American Indian prehistory – to give a *relative* date to any stratum at any site over a large area.

But in China the case is quite different. Historical texts provide lists of kings going back to the beginning of the legendary Hsia dynasty – about 2000 B.C. – but archaeology cannot corroborate anything said to have happened before about 1300 B.C. At a famous site near An-yang in northern Honan (pp. 108–9) oracle bones have been found inscribed with the names of the rulers of the Shang-Yin dynasty and confirming the succession as recorded in the historical king-lists. The Shang-Yin dynasty is traditionally said to have begun in 1766 B.C. and to have ended in 1122 B.C.; another less-favoured tradition gives its dates as 1558–1051 B.C. But Professor Karlgren has shown that neither is reliable, the former being based on Han dynasty computations, and the latter on a text compiled after the tenth century A.D. The first date on which both traditions agree is the year 841 B.C.

Karlgren, making use of a genuine historical document of the third century B.C. quoted in later literature, as well as other pre-Han texts and inscriptions on bronzes, has uncovered various lines of evidence all pointing to the year 1027 B.C. for the end of the Shang-Yin dynasty, and this date has recently been corroborated by Professor Dubs, following Tung Tso-pin, whose calculations are based on eclipses recorded on the oracle bones. Allowing 500 years as its duration, Karlgren places its beginning not later than about 1500 B.C. The An-yang site was a late Shang-Yin capital first occupied in the year 1300 B.C., or thereabouts, according to this dating.[1]

So much for the earliest historical dates. A relative sequence extending back from the date-line depends, as we have seen, on stratified

1. Cf. B. Karlgren, 'Some weapons and tools of the Yin dynasty', in *B.M.F.E.A.* no. 17 (1945), pp. 101–44. Cf. also H. Dubs, 'The date of the Shang period', in *T.P.* vol. xl (1951), pp. 332–5.

material, and in this respect Chinese archaeology is very badly served. There are no such things as *tells* or *tepes*. Few sites betray evidence of long, continuous habitation. The 15 feet or so maximum depth of Ch'i-chia-p'ing, one of the richest of the Kansu sites, compares poorly with the 100 feet or more of many Mesopotamian *tells*. All sorts of unfavourable factors intervene. In the dune country wind erosion has generally destroyed all trace of stratification, the heavier cultural element sinking gradually down to the dune bottom as the sand is blown away. In other cases earthquakes are believed to have destroyed stratigraphical evidence.[1] In others, climatic conditions have made digging impossible.[2] Local prejudice against digging for archaeological ends and the activities of professional grave-robbers and bandits are yet other accidental hindrances to field archaeology in China.[3] Lastly, it has to be said that until quite recently archaeological excavation has not always been carried out by men qualified to make the best use of their opportunities. All this means that dates assigned to phases before 1300 B.C., when the An-yang capital was founded, must be treated with the utmost reserve.

The most useful stratigraphical sequence so far unearthed is one from a site near An-yang. At Hou-kang, some 2 miles to the north of the Shang-Yin site, Chinese archaeologists of the Academia Sinica found red pottery in the lowest layer (Hou-kang I), black pottery in the middle layer (Hou-kang II), and white pottery in the upper layer (Hou-kang III). This is a most interesting juxtaposition. The red ware, most of which is unpainted, is regarded both by Andersson and Wu Gin-ding as of Yang-shao age, or even earlier. The black pottery, according to Wu, is somewhat earlier than that of Ch'êng-tz'ŭ-yai, the type-site for this ware. The white pottery is thought to be contemporary with, or perhaps a little earlier than, a white ware found in the historical section of the site. At Hou-kang, at least, the makers of the red pottery lived before those who made the black. And those who made the black lived before the opening of the historical phase at An-yang in 1300 B.C.

1. For instance at Chu-chia-chai, excavated by Andersson in 1923.

2. At Ang-ang-hsi, in 1931, Liang Ssŭ-yung was unable to excavate in order to establish stratigraphy because the ground was frozen solid.

3. Members of the Academia Sinica, excavating in 1935 at An-yang, worked at all times under the protection of an armed guard. For a photograph cf. H. G. Creel (see footnote p. 26), pl. 2.

The upper level at Ch'êng-tz'ŭ-yai (Ch'êng-tz'ŭ-yai II) contains bronze, and since the capital of the Chou State of Tan (c. 1000–684 B.C.) lay in the immediate vicinity, Dr Li Chi has surmised that this was the place. The lower level (Ch'êng-tz'ŭ-yai I) cannot be dated from internal evidence. But there is perhaps reason to believe that it may have been an early Shang-Yin settlement. Several Shang-Yin capitals are supposed to have been sited in this region, and the remains at Ch'êng-tz'ŭ-yai do include many elements of what seems to have been a Shang-Yin culture. Among these are pounded earth walls, and a white ware like that at Hou-kang III. But more significant were sixteen ox scapulae which, although uninscribed, had certainly been used for divination by the technique described in chapter three (p. 109), which was apparently a distinctive Shang-Yin practice. If Ch'êng-tz'ŭ-yai is indeed an early Shang-Yin site, then its date may be not very far from 1500 B.C. when the dynasty opened.

Let us finally examine the dating of the Painted Pottery Culture, for upon it the dating of all known prehistoric cultures in China depends. Andersson, who was perhaps more familiar with the material than anyone else, has arranged it in a site-sequence based on a stylistic evolution which he thinks is chronological. He has thus formulated six stages covering the whole culture in Kansu and Honan, as follows:

1. Ch'i-chia-p'ing	2500–2200 B.C.	
2. Yang-shao [1]	2200–1700 B.C.	
3. Ma-chang	1700–1300 B.C.	
4. Hsin-tien	1300–1000 B.C.	
5. Ssŭ-wa, Ch'ia-yao	1000–700 B.C.	
6. Sha-ching	700–500 B.C.	

The latest stage represented in this table is of course well on into the historical period. The most prominent remains at Sha-ching are hut ruins dating from the Han dynasty (205 B.C. to A.D. 220) with contemporary coins and pieces of iron in abundance. In the adjacent grave-fields, where was the painted pottery, bronze objects were found, but no iron. It therefore looks rather as if this cemetery dates from not long before the beginning of the Iron Age in China. The first historical reference to the use of iron in China is to the year 513

1. The Yang-shao stage is itself divided into Early, Middle, and Late phases, the first represented by the site of Lo-han-t'ang, the second by Ma-chia-yao and Pan Shan, and the third by Chu-chia-chai.

Table 2. An Attempted Chronology of the Mesolithic,

DATE	Traditional History	Painted Pottery
10,000		
	Mythological culture-heroes (Pan Ku, Fu Hsi, Shên Nung)	?
2500	Legendary Emperors (Huang Ti, Shao Hao, Chuan Hsü, Ti Ku, Ti Chih, Yao, Shun)	Ch'i-chia-p'ing (1), 2500–2200
	? Hsia Dynasty, c. 2000–1500	Hou-kang I Yang-shao Ts'un (2), c. 2200–1700
1500		Ma-chang (3), c. 1700–1300
	Shang-Yin Dynasty, c. 1500–1000	
1000		Hsin-tien (4), c. 1300–1000 Ssŭ-wa (5), Ch'ia-yao (5), c. 1000–700
	Chou Dynasty, c. 1000–255	
		Sha-ching (6), c. 700–500
250	Ch'in Dynasty, 221–205	
	Han Dynasty, 205 B.C.–A.D. 220	

All dates based on Andersson and Karlgren. Unless otherwise indicated, all dates are B.C. Numbers in brackets refer

Neolithic, and Bronze Ages in North China and Manchuria

CHINA		MANCHURIA
Black Pottery	Bronze	
		Djalai-nor
?		Ang-ang-hsi
		Lin-hsi
		Hung-shan-hou I
	?	Sha-kuo-t'un
Hou-kang II, *c.* 1700–1500		
Ch'êng-tz'ŭ-yai I		
T'ai-p'ing-ch'ang I	Hsiao-t'un	
	Hsin-tien, c. 1300–1000	P'i-tz'u-wo I
	Ssŭ-wa	
	Ch'ia-yao	
Ch'êng-tz'ŭ-yai II	Ch'êng-tz'ŭ-yai II	
	T'ai-p'ing-ch'ang II	
	Hsin Ts'un	
	Hsin-chêng	
	Li-yü	
	Chin Ts'un	
	Shou Chou	
	Ch'ang-sha	P'i-tz'u-wo II
		Hung-shan-hou II

to Andersson's Painted Pottery stages and names in italics
to pottery sites where traces of bronze have been found.

B.C., and Andersson accordingly assigns the Sha-ching site to the period of 200 years before the opening of the fifth century B.C.

The only other fixed point claimed by Andersson is 1700 B.C. for the end of the Yang-shao stage. This is arrived at by taking the date 1500 B.C. for the opening of the white pottery stage at Hou-kang III and allowing 200 years for the preceding black pottery stage represented by Hou-kang II. In that case Hou-kang I, contemporary with the Yang-shao stage, would have terminated in 1700 B.C. The dates given for Hou-kang II, 1700–1500 B.C., accord very well with the idea that its black pottery is somewhat earlier than that of Ch'êng-tz'ŭ-yai I, which may have opened about 1500 B.C.

All Andersson's other dates are arrived at by estimating the length of time likely to have elapsed while each stage was working itself out; he himself admits that much of it is guesswork.[1] But a relative chronology of this type is the best we can hope for under present conditions. Perhaps one day the history of China will be taken a few hundred years further back into the past. We may discover earlier Shang-Yin sites with inscribed materials, and may even be able to prove the historical existence of the Hsia. If this happens, we shall undoubtedly know much more about the relative datings of the Painted and Black Pottery Cultures, and hence about their filiations with similar cultures outside China proper.

1. For instance, there is some uncertainty whether Ch'i-chia-p'ing is or is not pre-Yang-shao in age. It should also be said that the site contains only small quantities of painted pottery.

Chapter Two

JADE

An Element in Neolithic Chinese Culture

In *Yüeh chüeh shu*,[1] a book attributed to the first-century A.D. Han dynasty writer Yüan K'ang, is reported a conversation supposed to have taken place in the fifth century B.C. between the king of the southern State of Ch'u and his minister, Fêng Hu-tzǔ. Naming some of the legendary culture-heroes of antiquity, the minister says: 'In the time of Hsien Yüan, Shên Nung, and Ho Hsü, weapons were made of stone … later, at the time of Huang Ti, of jade … in Yü's time of bronze. … To-day they are made of iron.'

This proposition, we must agree, shows remarkable speculative insight. It holds its own with the scientific theory of Lucretius (98–55 B.C.) on successive use of stone, bronze, and iron weapons by ancient man (*De rerum natura*, bk. 5, 1283–8), and interpolates a material of which Lucretius knew nothing; namely, jade. It also forecasts the concept of the Three Ages of human material culture first expressed by C. J. Thomsen in 1836. It may even be said to foreshadow Lord Avebury's subsequent division of stone implements into two morphological and technological groups, the paleolithic and the neolithic, the former comprising tools made by flaking, the latter tools with smooth, polished surfaces worked or finished by other methods than flaking. For this may be the meaning behind Yüan K'ang's contrasted use of the terms 'stone' (*shih*) and 'jade' (*yü*).

It was not, of course, a scientific theory in the modern sense. And Hirth, basing his notion on the passage, makes a bad methodological blunder in speaking of a 'Nephrite Age' sandwiched between those of stone and bronze, and covering the second half of the third millennium B.C.[2] Such a notion has neither sociological, technological, nor

---

1. Yüan K'ang, *Yüeh chüeh shu*, 'History of the secession of Yüeh', *S.P.T.K.*, vol. lxii (1920–2), p. 93b.

2. F. Hirth, *Chinesische Ansichten über Bronzetrommeln*, Leipzig 1904, p. 18. The word 'nephrite' means true jade as opposed to jadeite and other hard stones with similar properties (p. 56).

chronological meaning. It might for instance make sense if we could show that use of jade for making implements was widespread throughout society at that time, instead of other sorts of stone. But that was obviously not so. All evidence suggests that this beautiful but obstinate material was very rare in prehistoric China – rarer possibly than at any time since – and that only the wealthiest could afford to use it. And while the prehistoric Chinese undoubtedly *did* know jade, and held it in particular esteem, its introduction led to no social consequences of the sort, say, that marked the coming of bronze and iron.

Again, to speak without further qualification of a 'Nephrite Age' following one of stone is ambiguous, for jade *is* stone, although stone of a very special kind. The terms 'paleolithic' and 'neolithic', as we have said, stand primarily for two observed distinct types of stone craftsmanship; yet for practical purposes the 'Stone Age' can be divided into an earlier Paleolithic and a later Neolithic period, in China no less than in other parts of the world. Now it is true that jade was introduced into China in Neolithic times. It is also true that jade-carving is one branch of Neolithic stone craftsmanship – indeed its highest achievement. But we cannot equate the Neolithic period with a 'Nephrite Age' merely because jade was then being used. Still less justified would we be in taking jade-carving as a standard for Neolithic tool technology in general; the vast bulk of Neolithic implements were made by far less specialized methods. Hence the term 'Nephrite Age' has no technological significance. Finally it must be pointed out that jade has gone on being used in China ever since its first introduction. The term 'Nephrite Age' cannot therefore be used to name a particular period in Chinese history.

Why, then, do we suppose that Yüan K'ang may have had in mind the vague notion of a Neolithic period and culture when he spoke of an age of jade? Simply because the word *yü* could have had no exact mineralogical significance for him, but would have been used to name almost any hard stone with a smooth and highly polished appearance, such as objects of true jade known to him must always have presented. In postulating a phase during which rough-looking stone implements were replaced by superior ones with smooth polished surfaces, he would in all probability naturally turn to the words *shih* and *yü* as the quickest way of specifying the difference he had in mind.

Since Yüan K'ang mentions personages for whom traditional Chinese history provides dates, a rough chronology of his four periods can be drawn up which it would be unwise to reject out of hand. Thus Yü the Great, in whose time weapons were made of bronze, is said to have begun his reign in 2205 B.C. – or about 2000 B.C. according to revised dating; and although we cannot as yet push back the beginnings of the Bronze Age to much before 1300 B.C., it may well have had an earlier history, so far uncovered, of several hundred years (p. 113). The legendary Huang Ti, during whose time weapons were made of jade according to Yüan K'ang, is supposed to have begun his reign about the twenty-fifth century B.C. Here, then, is what we may perhaps regard as an early Chinese estimate of the onset of the Neolithic Age in China; and we see immediately how close it is to that given by modern archaeology (p. 49).

Very few peoples have used jade at all freely, and most of them – Chinese, North-west Coast American Indians, Aztecs, Mayas, and Maoris – come within the hypothetical Pacific culture-area of which China may be regarded as the centre (p. 26). Yet the fact that jade is not native to China, and the likelihood that central Asia was the main source of supply in prehistoric times, give grounds for supposing that jade-carving may have been acquired by the Neolithic Chinese from a non-Chinese people. Leaving this aside for the moment, the plain fact is that the craft reached its highest pitch of perfection only in China, of whose material culture jade has been an outstanding element during some 4,000 years. Awareness of this tradition led Andersson to say: 'Upon now turning to the use of jade in prehistoric China I feel it my duty to call attention to the fact that the penchant for, not to say the worship of jade, the substance itself, seems to have formed a bond that links prehistoric and dynastic China together, differentiating the Chinese race from the rest of mankind.'[1]

Jade-carving might be called the Neolithic craft *par excellence*, for of all stones that can be worked to suit the needs of man it is the most intractable; yet jade-carvings from Neolithic contexts in China are matched in technical and artistic accomplishment only by some of the contemporary pottery. Even more significant from the technological point of view is the fact that fresh jade is so hard that it can be cut only by one or other of the few stones harder than itself. Steel makes no impression on it, provided it is in fresh condition. In spite of the fact, therefore, that metal tools were probably being used early in the Bronze Age as means by which pastes containing the abrasive stone

1. J. G. Andersson (see footnote p. 37), p. 261.

were brought into frictional contact with the jade, and that rotary tools of iron may have come into use as early as the sixth or fifth century B.C.,[1] the ultimate contact is still between stone and stone. In this sense jade-carving is, and always has been, a lithic industry. Jade techniques and, I believe, many traditional jade shapes emerged from a Neolithic background; and it is in association with the Neolithic period in Chinese history that I propose to discuss the craft.

The Material

What, then, is 'jade'? Unfortunately this word, like the Chinese *yü*, came into being long before the time of mineralogical analysis, with the result that stones of widely differing physical structure and chemical composition have been called jade.[2] Even among mineralogists to-day there is no exact agreement as to how it should be defined. The word used above, nephrite, names a calcium–magnesium silicate having a structure of minute crystals in the form of a felted mass of short fibres. This is quintessential jade – what Chinese to-day call *chên yü*, 'true jade', as opposed to *fu yü* or 'false jade', which would include serpentines, pyrophyllite, and other hard stones. On the other hand, the substance best known to the West as jade – the translucent emerald- or dark-green stone commonly worked into articles of jewellery – is *not* nephrite, but jadeite. Although superficially this mineral closely resembles true jade, and although the working of it is in the hands of the same Chinese lapidaries, jadeite differs from jade both in composition and microscopic appearance, being a sodium–aluminium silicate with a crystalline structure of small granules. There is no evidence that it was worked in China before the eighteenth century A.D., and we shall not be dealing with it in this account. On the other hand, we can by no means be sure that all objects chosen for illustration here are indubitably nephrite. Very few

1. There is historical record of the use of iron in the year 513 B.C. Cf. also Yüan K'ang's reference to use of iron in the fifth century B.C., above.

2. Our word 'jade' seems to be derived from the Spanish *piedra de ijada*, 'stone of the loin', so called because the Spaniards came across jade, or rather jadeite, being worn in America in the form of amulets giving protection against kidney diseases. Our word 'nephrite', for true jade, incorporates this belief in jade as a cure for nephritic disorders.

jades, whether in museums or private collections, have been submitted to the delicate tests needed to prove their true nature.[1] But for present purposes that does not greatly matter, since we are primarily concerned with the sorts of object normally made out of jade rather than with the material itself or the methods by which it was worked. A recent account of the origin and development of Chinese jade-carving by Professor Hansford deals fully with these related topics.[2]

About A.D. 100 a certain Hsü Shên compiled a book destined to become one of the most influential ever written in Chinese, *Shuo wên chieh tzŭ*, or 'An Explanation of [Ancient] Figures and an Analysis of [Compound] Characters'. *Shuo wên* is an attempt to account for the structure of Chinese written characters in terms of the constructional principles upon which its author believed they were composed, and it is therefore rather a 'scriptionary' than a dictionary in our sense (p. 565). Yet it does define words, or at least describes the things they stand for. Such, for example, as the entry under the character *yü*, for jade: '*Yü* is the fairest of stones. It is endowed with five virtues. Charity is typified by its lustre, bright yet warm; rectitude by its translucency, revealing the colour and markings within; wisdom by the purity and penetrating quality of its note, when the stone is struck; courage in that it can be broken but cannot be bent; equity in that it has sharp edges which yet injure none.'[3]

Now, as we have remarked, any stone matching such a description would probably have been called *yü*. But Hsü Shên and others who spoke about jade must have been familiar enough with the sensible properties of real nephrite to reserve for it a separate category in their minds, even if, like us, they were not always able to tell it apart in practice. In other cases writers referring to *yü* could scarcely have deceived themselves or their readers into supposing that nephrite was meant. For the word soon took on a eulogistic meaning, so greatly was jade itself valued. It came to denote substances that were not precious stones, or necessarily minerals at all. The *yü* which, when

1. Empirical tests based on appearance are unreliable. Even the well-known belief that a steel point will not scratch jade is not always justified (cf. footnote 2, p. 58). The Becke test for refractive index is conclusive so long as the nephrite has not undergone chemical change – as it may do, for instance, as a result of prolonged burial. Diffraction X-ray examination seems to be the only infallible means of identifying nephrite.

2. Cf. S. H. Hansford, *Chinese Jade Carving*, London 1950.

3. Translated by S. H. Hansford (see footnote above), p. 31.

eaten in powdered form, was said to confer ceremonial purity on rulers, and the *yü* of various sorts used as medicines, whatever they may have been, could not possibly have been mistaken for true jade.

Again, the word has always been associated with ceremonial and decorative objects such as are shown in plates 1–8, and the character used to write it enters as an element conveying meaning into the composition of many other characters designating such objects (figure 14c). They were not always made of nephrite, but nephrite was especially reserved for their manufacture. They were *conceived of* as made of jade. Thus association between the mineral and objects made of it became fixed in people's minds, and the rôle of jade – the substance – permanently cast. The word *yü* is therefore sometimes used equivocally to designate objects made of jade and not the substance itself.[1]

The qualities of true jade are partly described in the paragraph from *Shuo wên* quoted above. In less fanciful language, jade is ice-cold to the touch; it is translucent when cut thin; it is so hard that it cannot be scratched by steel;[2] it emits a musical note when struck; it takes a high, oily polish. Ideally, and in its most prized form, it is white. But presence of chemical elements and compounds, especially of iron, chromium, and manganese, serves to give it a characteristic range of neutral colours; among these, various shades of green are perhaps most common.

Techniques of Working Jade

The difficulty in working jade is due to its extreme hardness (6½ on Mohs' scale). It can be cut only with stone harder than itself, such as quartz sand (7), crushed garnets (7½), and corundum (9). Corundum, or the artificial product carborundum, in the form of a sand thoroughly moistened with water, is generally used to-day. This semi-liquid

1. For example, the term *Han yü* is often used by modern Chinese dealers to denote small decorative objects made of yellowish-brown jade of a type supposed to have been worked during the Han period, and therefore sold as genuine 'Han jades'.

2. So long as it is in fresh condition, that is. Naturally, a piece of nephrite that has become partly decomposed after long burial can be scratched with steel on the affected surfaces. Desmond Gure, 'Notes on the identification of jade', in *O.A.*, vol. iii, no. 3 (1951), pp. 115–20, goes so far as to say of some alleged burial jades that even those parts not visibly decomposed can sometimes be scratched with a knife.

abrasive is applied to the edge of the 'cutting' tool while at work, so
that the material is very slowly ground through in the required direction. The movement of the tool is rotary, except in the case of saws
used for trimming blocks of raw material, which are operated by
either one or two men with a back-and-forth motion. Rotary tools
made of steel, iron, wood, or leather, and operated by treadle lathes,
include a large cutting disc, smaller cutting discs, drills, gouges, and
grinding and polishing or 'buffing' tools. Despite this extensive equipment and despite recent introduction of improved abrasives, the process is still laborious in the extreme. Hansford, who made a first-hand
study of the traditional craft as practised to this day in Peking, says
that a single cut through a foot-cube block, using the four-handed saw
and carborundum as an abrasive, would take several weeks' work.

Obviously the Neolithic worker was far less well equipped. The
Maoris of New Zealand, who until recently were living at a neolithic
level of material culture, seem to have used wet sand as an abrasive
and a variety of 'cutting' tools such as sandstone slabs, quartzose slate,
jade itself, wood, and even leather. The results are simpler, but the
operation seems to have been no more and no less laborious. So one
observer, Major Heaphy, estimated that to work a slab the size of an
octavo book and about $1\frac{1}{2}$ inches thick into a roughly triangular shape
to make a *mere*, or war-club, would also require the constant labour
of about a month. The only other essential instrument in use among
the Maoris was the drill. This consisted of a spindle to which was
attached some sort of fly-wheel, such as a disc of whale cartilage, or
two stones of roughly equal size. The drilling point was made by
fixing sharp pieces of flint into the end of the spindle, or was simply
the pointed head of the spindle itself. Hansford believes that tubular
drills, perhaps of hollow bone, were sometimes used.[1]

We may assume therefore that the tools of Neolithic Chinese jade
craftsmen included saws of various sizes and some form of drill. As
for the saws, almost any sort of lamina would have served; Hansford
suggests that one may have been a well-known type of stone knife
which crops up time and again at Neolithic sites inside and outside
the Great Wall (p. 77). This often has two or more small perforations
at the back of the blade, and Andersson believes that these were means
whereby the knife was 'dressed' with leather to make it more com-
fortable to hold (figure 5).

1. Cf. S. H. Hansford (see footnote p. 57), p. 90.

We have just mentioned perforations. These are quite common features of early Chinese jades, and range from a few millimetres to an inch or more in diameter. A drill was, of course, used for making them. Marks of rotary action are to be seen on many, as well as evidence of drilling from both sides; for the borings do not always meet flush, and the holes are often bi-conical in section due to gradual wearing away of the soft drill head; where the perforation has been made from one side only, the hole is usually conical. Objects showing partly drilled and discarded borings have been found among prehistoric material; and in one of these, discovered by Andersson, a circular core still remains – proof that the drill was tubular. Andersson says it was a hollow bone. Hansford, on the other hand, believes that a bamboo tube was used. He has shown that drilling jade by this means is perfectly feasible, by doing so himself using ordinary builders' sand as an abrasive.

Sources of Chinese Jade

Jade, as far as we know, is not native to China proper. Hansford has painstakingly examined all the literary evidence on which rests the claim that it is, or once was; but he concludes that there is no foundation for such a belief. It has arisen through faulty identification of other stones as nephrite, and through habitual use of vague terminology. The actual source of jade used in China is in the mountains and river-valleys of Khotan and Yarkand in Chinese Turkestan, 2,000 miles or so distant from the centres of early Chinese culture (map 4).

In his report in chapter 123 of the first great Chinese history, *Shih chi* (p. 174), the explorer Chang Ch'ien notes much jade-stone in Khotan, which he visited about 125 B.C. He adds that Khotanese jade was collected and transported to the Emperor, and implies that the trade was of long standing. The late Professor Haloun has given evidence to show that a traffic in jade existed between the Chinese and their neighbours to the north-west, the Yüeh-chih (p. 179), as early as the fourth century B.C.[1]

Chinese Turkestan has certainly supplied the bulk of nephrite for China during the last 2,000 years, and we are bound to agree with Hansford that it probably always did. The only other source of jade

1. G. Haloun, 'Zur Üe-Tsi Frage', in *Z.D.M.G.* vol. xci (1937), pp. 306 ff.

(A) Axe, Neolithic period; from Chinese Turkestan. L 6 ins (p. 72)

(B) Axe, Neolithic period; from Hsin Hsien, Honan. L 5 ins (p. 72)

(C) Celt-like implement, Chou dynasty (c. 800 B.C.). L 7$\frac{13}{16}$ ins (pp. 72-3)

(A) Adze, so-called *chên kuei*, Chou dynasty or
earlier. L 9⅜ ins (p. 76)

(B) Chisel, Neolithic period; from the Pan Shan hills, Kansu. L 3⅞ ins (p. 75)

(c) Chisel, Neolithic period; from the Pan Shan hills,
Kansu. Present L 2½ ins (p. 75)

(A) Dagger-axe, *ko*, Shang-Yin
dynasty. L 17 13/16 ins (p. 87)

(B) Knife, so-called *hu*, probably
Shang-Yin dynasty. L 11 5/8 ins (p. 80)

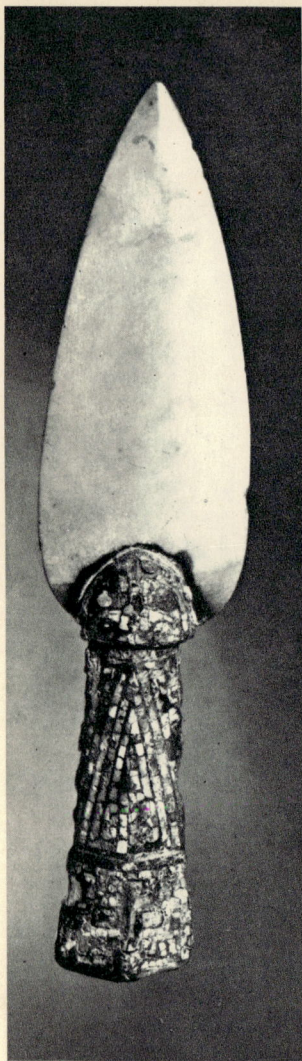

(A) Spearhead, Shang-Yin dynasty. L 7¾ ins (p. 83)

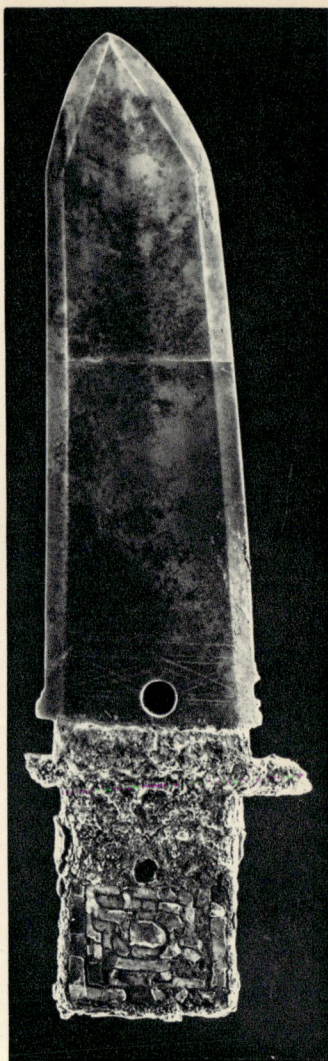

(B) Dagger-axe, *ko*, Shang-Yin dynasty. L 11⅝ ins (p. 87)

(A) Neolithic period; from the Pan Shan hills, Kansu. D 5⅞ ins (p. 89)

(B) Han dynasty; from Lo-lang, Korea. D 8⅝ ins (p. 89)

(C) Probably Chou dynasty. D 8¾ ins (p. 89)

Perforated discs, *pi*-forms

(A) H 19⅝ ins (p. 98)   (B) H 8⅛ ins (p. 98)

(C) H 2⅝ ins (p. 98)

Perforated tubes, *ts'ung*, all probably Chou dynasty

6

(A) Bird, perhaps Neolithic period; said to have been found near
T'ai-yüan, Shansi. L 5½ ins (p. 106)

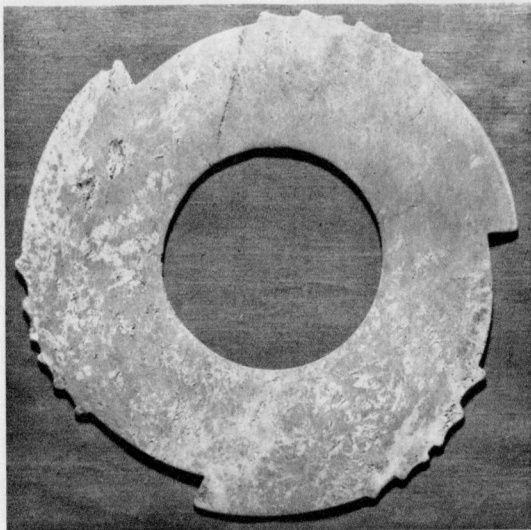

(B) Perforated disc, *hsüan chi*, Shang-Yin dynasty.
D 7¾ ins (p. 94)

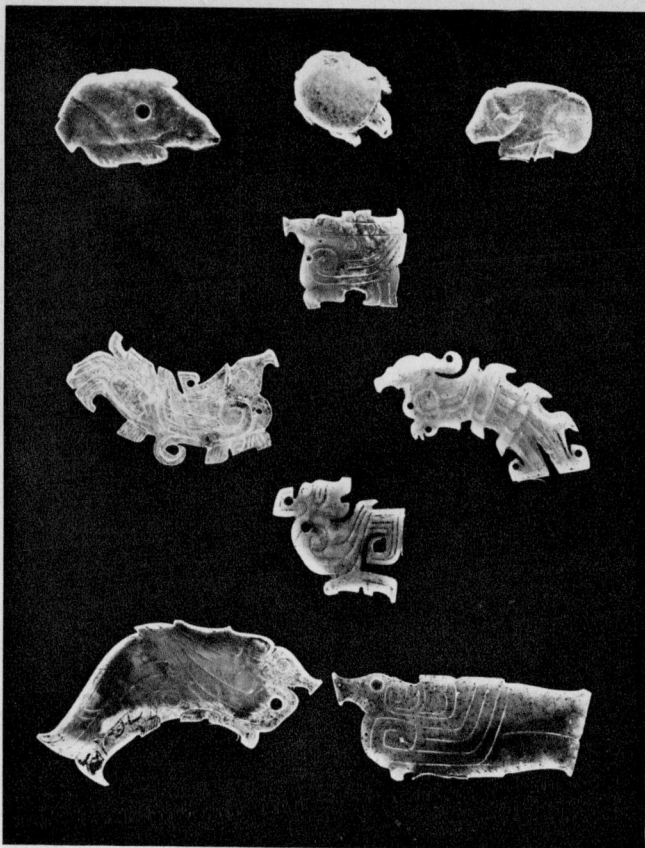

(A) Tortoise   (B) Turtle   (c) Water buffalo pendant

(D) Bird pendant

(E) Bird pendant   (F) Bird pendant

(G) Dragon-bird finial

(H) Bird pendant   (I) Bird pendant

Pendants and amulets, all probably early Chou dynasty, about half natural size
(pp. 62, 106)

8

that might have been known to the prehistoric Chinese is the area round Lake Baikal. Siberian jade has a rather distinctive appearance owing to the presence of small particles of black graphite embedded in the stone, which leads the Chinese to call it 'spinach jade'. Prehistoric implements made of this material have been found in Siberia near Tobolsk, Barnaul, and Yakutsk,[1] but there is no record of its importation into China until quite recently. On the other hand, among the jades illustrated in colour by Andersson in his *Researches into the Prehistory of the Chinese* (footnote p. 37) are a flat tablet and an annular disc reproduced here on plates 2b and 5a, which look as if they might conceivably be made of Siberian jade. We must also admit the possibility that some Siberian jade may not be of the 'spinach' variety.

The Beginnings of Chinese Jade-carving

If now jade came thousands of miles across central Asia to reach China during prehistoric times, the question arises who brought it, and when? We have given reasons for supposing that at least some of the Neolithic cultures outside the Great Wall are earlier than those of China Proper (pp. 38-42). The Chinese Turkestan branch of the peri-Gobi Neolithic has been examined by Bergman, who regards it as typical of the whole complex.[2] Among finds from this region he records a few polished jade axes – one or two picked up on the Lop Nor desert floor by Stein and Hedin, and others purchased by Pelliot at Kucha (plate 1a). If these tools are contemporary with other Neolithic remains in Chinese Turkestan, as there seems no reason to doubt, then they may well represent the earliest jade-craft of the East.

Jade, the material, may thus be a local central Asiatic ingredient in the peri-Gobi culture, which, like some tool-types from the north, filtered into China late in prehistoric times. The reader will perhaps be wondering whether there may not be some historical connexion between the introduction of jade from central Asia into China, and the possible

1. Ch. E. de Ujfalvy, *Expédition scientifique française en Russie, en Sibérie et dans le Turkestan*, etc., 6 vols., Paris 1878–80, vol. iii, p. 146.
2. Cf. F. Bergman, 'Archaeological researches in Sinkiang: especially the Lop-nor region', being publication vii of *Reports from the Scientific Expedition to the North-western Provinces of China under the leadership of Dr Sven Hedin*, Stockholm 1939, pp. 13–37.

Western origin of the Painted Pottery Culture. We have one suggestive piece of evidence. The finest group of Chinese jades reasonably
considered to be Neolithic – and one of the very few whose provenance
can be safely asserted – is that obtained by Andersson by purchase
and excavation at burial-sites in the T'ao River valley of southern
Kansu in 1923 (plates 2*b*, *c*, 5*a*). The T'ao River, as we see from map
3, was a key area for the Painted Pottery Culture. The sites there are
contemporary with no less than five of Andersson's stages (p. 49), of
which the earliest is dated by him as beginning about 2200 B.C. If
the date of his jade collection is at all close to this, as seems likely, then
the Chinese tradition that jade was introduced during the reign of
Yü the Great some time in the twenty-fifth century B.C., as stated by
Yüeh chüeh shu, begins to appear quite plausible. Put together, these
vague pointers seem to show that the earliest Chinese jades to which
even a provisional date can be given are, in fact, associated with the
Painted Pottery Culture; and that jade-carving may well have been
brought to China from as far west as Chinese Turkestan halfway
through the third millennium B.C.

The Symbolism of Early Chinese Jades

With very few exceptions the early jades of China are worked from
flat slabs not more than a few millimetres thick, themselves cut either
from pebbles and small boulders, or else – and this was almost certainly a later development – from quarried blocks. They fall into two
main groups, the first comprising small decorative amulets in the
form of beads, buttons, pendants, and plaques to be worn with or
sewn on to clothing (plate 8); and the second a variety of objects
whose use, as is generally believed, had to do with ritual and ceremonial. Most common in this group are the tablets traditionally called
kuei. They are of many shapes, and native tradition attributes various
functions to them, but generally seems to have regarded them as
tokens of sovereign power and feudal rank.

The shapes of *kuei* and other ritual jades are of a sort that we would
call 'abstract' were we to encounter them in contemporary art. Miss
Ramsden, comparing them with the work of sculptors such as Bar-
bara Hepworth and Brancusi, says: 'There is, at least, in all of them
the same sensuous enjoyment of the material for its own sake, the

same interest in its expressive possibilities as a medium, the same exquisite workmanship and austere simplicity.'[1] But we must not because of this resemblance assume that the aims of their creators were at all similar, or that their shapes should be interpreted simply as essays in 'pure form'. How, then, *are* they to be interpreted?

Before we turn to the obvious explanation, let us glance at traditional Chinese and European views on the purpose and meaning of these early jades. Towards the end of the Chou period was written the substance of a book long since known as *Chou li*, or 'Chou Rituals'.[2] This work, which is attributed by tradition to that model administrator of early Chou times, the Duke of Chou (p. 117), purports to give an account of ceremonial practices as carried out during his day, and defines the duties of officials responsible for their upkeep. It is in fact an imaginary reconstruction, as its bias towards formal numerical categories suggests. That such books appeared late in the dynasty is simply because some of China's noblest political aspirants were then making a last despairing attempt to institute law and order at a time of anarchy and force. They therefore invoked tradition. But tradition had been broken, and the history of the early Chou period become mere hearsay. Its social and political conditions were a dim and confused memory; and pretty well the whole of its material culture, as well as that of the Shang-Yin dynasty, had been replaced. State ritual had become so corrupted and vulgarized by usurpers not entitled to practise it, that nobody knew what it was supposed to mean.

Under such conditions any systematic inquiry into the part played by traditional jade-forms in early Chou ritual, or any reasonable explanation of their shapes, was out of the question. It was not even required. All that was necessary was that they should be fitted into a formal scheme, allotted functions, and given names. When the author of *Chou li* spoke of the *ya chang*, for example, he evidently meant merely a tablet (*chang*) whose form suggested a tooth (*ya*). If what he called *ya chang* is the jade we now know by that name (figure 3*a*), there is some reason why he should have failed to recognize it as the descendant of a Shang-Yin bronze weapon, the 'dagger-axe' (figure 8). For the *ya chang* exemplified the gradual but inevitable debasement of form that overtakes any object that is reproduced times without number, for a purpose and in a material not its own; especially when

1. E. H. Ramsden, *An Introduction to Modern Art*, Oxford 1940, p. 21.
2. É. Biot (trans.), *Le Tcheou-li, ou Rites des Tcheou*, 2 vols., Paris 1851.

the material is one like jade, which by its intransigence forces on the craftsman a more summary treatment of the original theme. And to make correct identification even more difficult, bronze prototypes had by this time disappeared.

The author goes on to say that, in the hands of an appropriate authority, the *ya chang* served to mobilize and control soldiery and frontier guards. That may have been its function in his day; it *may* even have been so at the beginning of the Chou period, although there is nothing to show that this was so. But that it was so in Shang-Yin times, to which such specimens as that illustrated on plate 3a can reasonably be dated, seems most improbable. All we can safely say is that there remained a shadowy association in the mind of the author between the form of this jade and war.

But observe what happens when arbitrary label and allotted function themselves become hallowed by tradition, and when even the late Chou copies begin to disappear. The commentator Chêng Ssŭ-nung, of the first century A.D., blandly observes: 'The *ya chang* is carved into the shape of a tooth; teeth symbolize warfare, and hence troops are [were] levied by means of this instrument, for which purpose bronze tallies in the shape of a tiger are used at present.'[1] And so the idea connecting this object with a tooth – or teeth, for commentators speak of more than one tooth – begins to take hold. By the second century A.D. Chêng Hsüan is reported as saying that the *ya chang* has teeth like those of a hoe along the side of its pointed end. Chêng's comments on the three classics concerned with Chou rituals, as well as those of other Han scholars, got incorporated in the Sung dynasty compilation *San li t'u*, or 'Illustrations to the Three Rituals Classics', first published in A.D. 962. With nothing to go upon but these random jottings and his own imagination, its author Nieh Ch'ung-i undertook to depict for posterity the true likenesses of the objects of Chou ritual. His version of the *ya chang* is shown in figure 3b.[2]

In 1889 the antiquarian Wu Ta-ch'êng published his *Ku yü t'u k'ao*, 'An Illustrated Study of Ancient Jades', using as a starting-point pieces in his own collection, and combing the classics for hints by

1. B. Laufer (see footnote p. 43), pp. 101–2.
2. Nieh Ch'ung-i, *Chê ch'êng chêng shih chia shu chung chiao san li t'u* (illustrations of objects referred to in the Three Rituals, with a collection of comments compiled by Nieh Ch'ung-i (A.D. 962), and further notes by Chêng Chê-ch'êng), *S.P.T.K.*, 4 pts. in 1 vol., Shanghai 1936, ch. 10, p. 3b.

which to identify them. Wu tried his best to see these objects with fresh eyes, and to some extent he succeeded. He rejected as patently absurd many of the identifications made by earlier authors; such, for instance, as those who compiled *Ku yü t'u p'u* – a book written in the eighteenth century A.D. but purporting to be Sung – who unblushingly present drawings of a pair of *kuei* tablets which they say belonged to Yü the Great himself (p. 55). But even Wu could make no real

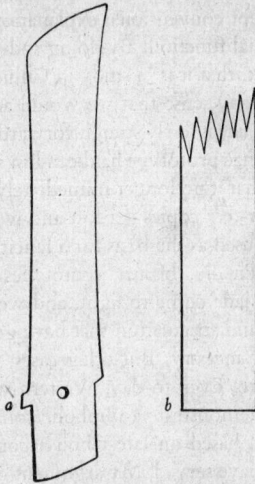

Figure 3. *a*, jade object identified by Wu Ta-ch'êng as the *ya chang*; *b*, the *ya chang* as imagined by the author of *San li t'u*.

break with the archaizing habit that had for so long impeded antiquarian studies in China. He identifies as a *ya chang* an object in his collection based quite obviously on a 'dagger-axe'. But he clings to the *Chou li* account of its ceremonial function and says that the form was 'chosen from among military weapons' as being particularly suitable for that purpose.

Yet *Ku yü t'u k'ao* represents a considerable advance; and Wu's Western successor, Laufer, relied almost entirely upon it in writing his own account of jade. As he says of the specimen now under discussion, it is, as illustrated in *Ku yü t'u k'ao*, 'a palpable and living reality', whereas the drawing in *San li t'u* is 'a fantasy corresponding to no real or possible object'.[1] But the step that both Wu and Laufer failed to take was to emancipate themselves, as a *prima facie* condition for proper study, from the unreal world of political wish-fulfilment represented by *Chou li* and other pre-Han texts, and to a lesser degree from the web of cosmological speculation woven by later commentators. Time and again Laufer draws attention to a resemblance between the shapes of jades and those of actual implements or weapons; but he continues unhesitatingly to accept conventional explanations of their symbolic content and ceremonial function. By doing so he weakens the claim he makes for his book, that it is 'a study in Chinese archaeology and religion' – at least in any sense that we would accept to-day.

The case of the *ya chang* is fairly straightforward. It receives its name at a time when its bronze prototype has been lost sight of and its shape become so distorted that it no longer immediately suggests a weapon. Then even these latter-day copies get lost and we are left with a bare name. This in turn is used as the basis for a fanciful reconstruction of the original object. Finally, bronze prototypes and contemporary imitations of these in jade come to light, and we can clear away the successive layers of blind speculation that have gradually blotted out the jade's true line of ancestry. But other cases, presently to be discussed, are still obscure. Even to-day, Western writers will go to almost any lengths to demonstrate a symbolic content in the shapes of ancient Chinese jades, based on late Chou accounts of the purposes they are supposed to have served. My argument is that before we uncritically accept this principle of formal symbolism underlying jade shapes, we should first try to discover whether some of them cannot be simply explained as imitations of authentic craft tools or weapons; and whether others may not themselves originally have been designed for actual practical use.

Jade Used in Imitation of Tools and Weapons

In his Frazer lecture given at Liverpool University in 1949, Professor Gordon Childe several times spoke of the manner in which craft tools 'made by the application of science and employed for perfectly rational ends' acquire, in primitive societies, magical properties of their own. Proof of this, he said, is that amulets in the form of

1. B. Laufer (see footnote p. 43), p. 102.

miniature models of such tools – for example, the polished axe – are widely distributed in Neolithic contexts throughout the Mediterranean area from Egypt to France. The copies, by sympathetic magic, partake of the virtue of the originals.[1]

Many of the ritual jades of China, I believe, are objects of this type. That is, they were first conceived of and made in imitation of functional prototypes, whose efficacy they shared. Already at Ang-ang-hsi, presumably dating from the earliest phase of the peri-Gobi Neolithic (p. 40), we find stone implements, specially selected for their fine quality, buried in fixed relation to the corpse.[2] Substitutes made of jade, the most beautiful mineral known in the pre-metal era, and whose value was heightened by rarity and by costs of transport and manufacture, would, I believe, have been thought specially efficacious for ritual and burial purposes. On this assumption the bulk of early Chinese jades, though not necessarily all, may never have been intended for actual use, however strongly their shapes may plead. It is true that jade is very durable and keeps a keen edge. It is also true that a jade object used as a craft tool would be no less efficacious, because it had been so used, when it eventually came to be consigned to the grave. But bearing in mind the intractability and rarity of jade, I find difficulty in believing that it was habitually used for making actual tools; the extreme fragility of many specimens – for instance, the 'dagger-axe' of plate 3a – definitely argues to the contrary.

1. V. Gordon Childe, *Magic, Craftsmanship, and Science*, Liverpool 1950, pp. 14–15. We have some evidence of the making of miniature copies of craft tools in China. Chang Hua (A.D. 232–300) says in his *Po wu chi*: 'Fine stones in the shape of small axes are frequently seen among the people. They are styled axes of the crash of thunder (*p'i-li fu*) or wedges (adzes, chisels?) of the crash of thunder (*p'i-li hieh [hsieh]*)'. Cf. Laufer (see footnote p. 43), p. 64. At Momien in western Yunnan the explorer Anderson, in the 60s of the last century, bought many jade miniatures of authentic craft tools which he supposed had been worn as personal amulets. He took them to be relatively modern, but this need not necessarily have been so. Cf. B. Laufer (see footnote p. 43), p. 31. Bushell describes a similar miniature axe which he says is pre-Han, 'perforated for use as an amulet with rounded corners and bevelled rim, one face being perfectly flat, the other having a bevelled cutting edge; in Burma as well as in south-western China, such amulets are supposed to make the wearer invulnerable'. Quoted by B. Laufer (see footnote p. 43), p. 34.

2. Liang Ssŭ-yung says that of nineteen stone implements with fine chipping over the entire surface, found at Ang-ang-hsi, seventeen came from the two burials.

The contention is, then, that the shapes of a great many ritual jades known to us by the Chou dynasty names of ritual and ceremonial objects with which they have at one time or another been equated, imitate functional precursors that were tools or weapons, and that we need look no further for the explanation of their forms.

Again, I take the view that these jades were not originally meant for any other use than as burial objects. It would probably be going too far to assert that such lovely jades as those illustrated on plates 2b and c, and 3a and b, obviously modelled on tool- and weapon-types, were made *exclusively* for burial purposes. In historical times objects made specifically for burial have generally been cheap imitations of those made for use by the living, and nothing made of jade could ever have been considered cheap. Ritual and ceremonial use by the living is the traditional role assigned to early Chinese jades; and perhaps an analogy can be found in the dual purpose served by the bronze sacral vessels to be discussed in chapter three. Like the jades, they were modelled in the shapes of actual utensils – in this case domestic pots made of clay; during the lifetimes of their owners they were used ritually, and were buried with them when they died. But allowing the ritual and ceremonial part that jade may have played in prehistoric Chinese society – and that no doubt grew in importance as time went by – the notion that its main role was then to serve the dead still seems to me a right one. By far the finest pots recovered from the Kansu cemeteries were, as is generally admitted, mortuary urns never intended for domestic use by the living – a striking instance of the care with which the prehistoric Chinese attended to the well-being of their dead. Bestowal of jade, I argue, was another.

We have said nothing so far about means of dating early Chinese ritual jades. Generally speaking, no such means exist. Specimens are rarely if ever inscribed, so that epigraphic clues for assigning a date are lacking. Again, there is the tricky question as to how far stylistic comparisons with bronze art can be used to date pre-Han decorated jades, since designs suited to one medium were rarely practicable in the other (p. 87). Finally, very few jades indeed have been recovered under supervision from sites where association with datable objects might provide a key; early exceptions are those excavated or bought by Andersson from the Neolithic cemetery in the Pan Shan hills of southern Kansu, and others recently recovered from An-yang. In other cases, whether a particular jade is Neolithic, Shang-Yin, Chou, or even Han, may be anybody's guess.

Fortunately, uncertainty of dating does not greatly affect the value of a typological study. For while it is perfectly true that such a complex shape as that of the bronze 'dagger-axe' will undergo modification and gradual distortion when translated into jade, the forms of many Neolithic implements, such as provided models for ritual jades, are simple enough to have passed into the new material unchanged, and do not seem to have undergone much subsequent modification. For example the *pi* illustrated on plate 5*b*, dating from about the beginning of our era, has a decorative design cut into its surface. But it is recognizably the same type of object as the Neolithic *pi* shown above it, made perhaps 2,000 years earlier. For our purpose it is less important to know the date of a given piece than to find for it a convincing prototype among the mass of Neolithic material only recently become available for comparative study.

Classes of Chinese Ritual Jades

The uses to which jades of the classes listed below were put may very well have changed during the long period during which they were made; especially, perhaps, during the course of the Chou dynasty. If, as we hold, the earliest of them were simply mortuary objects, it is also probable that many of their descendants were taken over for ritual functions of the sort described by *Chou li*. In the account that follows we therefore follow the convention of calling them all 'ritual' jades. But this is a mere label. Some whole classes of objects may never have been involved in ritual; for example, the *hsüan chi* and *ts'ung*, which, according to one theory, were extremely practical astronomical instruments and nothing more.

Again, we are putting forward the view that ritual jades were generally speaking based on implement prototypes. But jades belonging to the last three classes do not readily reveal this ancestry, and in fact may well be *sui generis* and without forebears, made expressly to fulfil some highly specialized function. We shall discuss the case of each in turn below.

Wu Ta-ch'êng's drawings of jade objects in his collection, which feature as text-figures in Laufer's book, form the starting point of this

ADE

inquiry. But Wu made no systematic classification of jades based on similarities in shape. It is quite impossible to say, from a perusal of his drawings, what he himself would have regarded as the typical shape of, say, a *chên kuei*, for objects of vastly dissimilar appearance are called such; and, *mutatis mutandis*, objects that seem to me to be of the same fundamental type, he calls by a variety of names. This explains why some classes include several different names of objects, and why the same name crops up in more than one class. Finally, the table is not meant to be comprehensive; although taken together with the accompanying plates it does, I believe, include most types of ritual jades the reader is likely to meet with in public or private collections.

CHINESE RITUAL JADES

CLASS	PROTOTYPE	JADE DESCENDANT NOMINATED BY WU TA-CH'ÊNG
1	Polished stone axe or celt (plate 1*a, b, c*)	*yüan kuei* *chên kuei* *ta kuei* *ch'ing kuei* *yen kuei*
2	Imperforate hand adze or chisel (plate 2*b, c*)	*yüan kuei*
3	Shaft-hole adze (plate 2*a*)	*chên kuei*
4	Rectangular knife (plate 3*b*)	*hu* *ta kuei*
5	Bronze dagger-axe (plate 3*a*, 4*b*).	*ku kuei* *yen kuei* *ta kuei* *ya chang*
6	Bronze socketed spearhead (plate 4*a*)	?
7	? (plate 5*a, b, c*)	*pi* *huan* *yüan*
8	? (plate 7*b*)	*hsüan chi*
9	? (plate 6*a, b, c*)	*ts'ung*

Table 3. Chinese ritual jades and their tool or weapon prototypes.

70

The ungrooved polished stone axe is of all craft tools the one most representative of Neolithic culture. Dozens of finely-polished specimens have come from Late Neolithic sites in north China, and Andersson has made some attempt to divide them into morphological groups. I scarcely think it worth while bothering here with the slight variations in shape thereby disclosed. For our purpose only one need be mentioned, the 'northern rounded' type. This axe is typically long and slender, with an average length of some 15 cm. Looked at in side view it is a somewhat flattened and very regular ellipse; while the contours, seen in surface view, are all gently rounded. Some examples have a small perforation towards the butt, no doubt a means whereby a socketed handle was lashed to the blade. In this, and in all other groups of axes discriminated by Andersson, with the exception of the 'square-cut' type, contours are always gently rounded; and to that extent they tally with the classical description of jades called *yüan kuei* (p. 73).

Whatever variations in shape these axes display, all have one feature in common. Seen in side view, their contours are absolutely symmetrical about the long axis. In other words, they are true axes; as opposed to adzes, in which the plane of the front face turns abruptly in to make the cutting edge, so that the contours are *not* symmetrical about the long axis when seen in side view. Further, in the true axe the cutting edge lies in the same plane as the cutting stroke. Whereas in the adze, whether hafted or not, the cutting edge is always at right angles to the plane of the blow.

When in 1912 Laufer was reviewing the evidence which led him to conclude that the claim for a Stone Age in China was unfounded (p. 43), he could point to very few examples of polished axes. And since these came from outlying areas such as Yunnan and northern Shantung, he was content to think that they were not made by Chinese peoples. They belonged, he said, 'not to the archaeology of the Chinese, but of China in a geographical sense'.[1] Since Laufer's day, evidence has accumulated showing that the polished stone axe was in general use throughout eastern Asia during the Neolithic period. Jade examples from Chinese Turkestan and Siberia have already been mentioned. In Manchuria a single specimen, not of jade,

1. B. Laufer (see footnote p. 43), p. 32.

JADE

was found in the Middle Neolithic site of Lin-hsi, but axes are every-day features of later sites further south.

In a summary of Far Eastern prehistory written in 1932,[1] Professor Hamada discusses a widely-held migration theory which states that Shantung was populated by Tungusic, non-Chinese tribes in early historical times; and particularly by the Su-shên – considered to be an-cestors of the modern Manchus – who had reached China by way of northern Mongolia, bringing with them, among other tools, the per-forated stone axe. On the contrary, says Hamada, the Shantung per-forated stone axe is indistinguishable from that found in Shensi and is thus no evidence in favour of the migration theory. He concludes that the perforated stone axe was an entirely native Chinese tool-type; the natural ancestor, he says, of *kuei* in use during the Chou period.

The implications of a theory of population migration in historical times are altogether too vast to be taken up here. But it is, of course, a fact that no Neolithic site yet discovered in China proper can be dated earlier than about 2500 B.C.; whereas to the north, running through Manchuria, is a chain of sites that seem to lead us back by easy stages through the Neolithic period to a Mesolithic phase, and covering a time-span of perhaps 6,000 years (pp. 38–42). Since perforated stone axes have been found in Manchuria, I see no reason for supposing that this type originated on Chinese soil. Far more likely, it found its way to China from the peri-Gobi culture area, although not necessarily as the result of mass migration.

Of the three objects illustrated on plate 1, two are Neolithic and the third is undoubtedly a Chou piece. The first (plate 1*a*) is one of those bought by Pelliot at Kucha. This region is not very far from the source of jade supply in Khotan, and the axe, it seems to me, may well have been used as an actual tool. On the other hand, the second Neo-lithic piece (plate 1*b*), bought by Andersson at a place near Hsin Hsien in Honan, was presumably manufactured some 1,500 miles away from the known source of jade, and I think we may assume that this was a mortuary jade; its form is typical of the 'northern rounded' axe. The Chou piece (plate 1*c*) is presumably derived from the perforated 'northern rounded' axe. It is a most distinguished piece of jade-carv-ing, the material being white nephrite with brown-and-yellow mottling. If we want a clue to the fluid arabesque pattern that covers

1. K. Hamada, 'T'ung ya wên ming chih li ming', in *F.J.H.C.*, vol. ii, no. 2 (1932), pp. 27–53.

its upper surface, we have to seek it among the decorative motives of Second Phase bronze art (pp. 167–70); they are not of the sort that would naturally occur to the jade-carver, who is clearly happiest when disposing of purely rectilinear patterns such as those shown on plate 3a. Indeed, only complete ascendancy of bronze styles during this phase (ninth to sixth century B.C.) could have induced him to break a stylistic rule in order to undertake so formidable a task.

We can only guess what ceremonial use the Chou piece may have served. Objects resembling it in general shape were identified by Wu Ta-ch'êng as the *yüan kuei* spoken of in *Chou li*. As depicted in Laufer's book [1] they have the same slim and rounded form as our jade, and two of them are perforated towards the butt end. According to *Chou li*, *yüan kuei*, or 'rounded *kuei*', carried a silk cord – presumably passing through the perforation – and served to 'regulate virtue'. We may perhaps remark that our specimen is 7·8 inches long, a near approximation to the canonical length of 9 Chou inches (= 7·6 English inches) specified by *Chou li*.

Later commentators elaborate the story of *yüan kuei*. Chêng Hsüan says that the jade was conferred by the ruler on those of his feudatories who gave consistently loyal and virtuous service; and Chêng Ssŭnung says that it was rounded so that it might serve to arouse virtue and bring good feelings to maturity; the theory being, apparently, that a rounded object symbolized virtue and a pointed one depravity.

We have seen that a rounded form is characteristic of most types of Chinese polished stone axe. Whether such a tool was really the original model of the *yüan kuei* is uncertain. For who can say definitely what the latter looked like? What *is* apparent is that several of the jades identified by Wu as *yüan kuei* are derived from a stone-axe prototype. And here we may get the clue to their real purpose. Among the very few Neolithic burials scientifically excavated in the north China area, three had single specimens of fine stone axes placed near the head of the corpse. These were at Wa-kuan-tsui in southern Kansu (Middle Yang-shao, *c.* 2000 B.C.); Pien-chia-kou, in the same locality and of the same period; and Tan-t'o-tzŭ (P'i-tzŭ-wo), in the Liaotung Peninsula (Late Manchurian Neolithic). The tools, though not of jade, were evidently *objets de luxe*, and among the deceased's most valued possessions. Substituting for such objects replicas of them made of jade, the most valuable mineral of all, seems a natural step forward.

1. B. Laufer (see footnote p. 43), figs. 25–7.

Burial with the dead was, I conclude, the original role of jade tablets in the shape we associate with *yüan kuei*.

Other flat objects with small perforations towards the butt end, called *chên kuei, ta kuei, yen kuei*, and so on by Wu Ta-ch'êng, may be derived either from the polished stone axe or the bronze dagger-axe (class 6). In spite of certain resemblances they bear to long chisels, presence of perforations at the butt ends of these jades is, I think, conclusive evidence that the implement from which they descend was hafted by means of a socket in the handle, to which it was secured by lashing through the hole. In that case the blade lay in the same plane as the cutting stroke, and the implement must have been an axe.[1]

CLASS 2: OBJECTS DERIVED FROM THE HAND ADZE

The asymmetrical imperforate hand-adze or chisel is, in one form or another, a thoroughly familiar ingredient in Neolithic cultures from all parts of the peri-Gobi area and north China. Among the earliest examples are a number of black basalt adzes from Ang-ang-hsi (p. 40); but the type is also found at Middle and Late Neolithic sites in south Manchuria, for example at P'i-tz'ŭ-wo I and Sha-kuo-t'un. In China itself, the tool has been found at sites ranging from Kansu to Hopei. Its shape is usually trapezoid, the cutting edge being wider than the butt, so that the sides slope outwards. The butt is usually a straight edge, but in one series it is slightly rounded; and on the whole these tools are small, averaging less than 4 inches in length. All are markedly asymmetrical when seen in side view; the front or upper surface turns abruptly inwards a few millimetres above the cutting edge, whereas the back face is almost flat, or has a gently rounded curve. Some examples may have been hafted, no doubt to the flat upper surface of the shorter arm of a bent wooden or bone handle. If hafted, the cutting edge was of course at right-angles to the long axis of the handle.

These tools may be regarded as forerunners of the splendid jade chisels acquired by Andersson in north China. A group of seven come from burial-sites in the T'ao River valley of southern Kansu. Only

1. On this criterion the following jade objects illustrated by Laufer after Wu Ta-ch'êng might all be derived from either type of axe: figs. 21–3 (*chên kuei*), 24 (*ta kuei*), 28 (*ch'ing kuei*), 29 (*yen kuei*), and 32–3 (*kuei*). Cf. B. Laufer (see footnote p. 43), pp. 90–8.

one of these was excavated by Andersson personally, but the remainder were bought at the site, and there is no reason to suppose that all of them are not genuine Neolithic pieces, contemporary with the magnificent funerary urns recovered from the same place (figure 2) and dating from the Middle Yang-shao stage (c. 2000 B.C.). Another jade chisel was excavated at Lo-han-t'ang, a site about 100 miles northwest of the T'ao River, thought by Andersson to belong to the Early Yang-shao stage (c. 2200 B.C.). And another group of five comes from the vicinity of Yang-shao Ts'un itself, in Honan.

All are of one or other of two types. The more common is a flat chisel with relatively broad cutting edge (plate 2b); but another type, to which belongs the superb object illustrated on plate 2c, is proportionally much thicker and narrower, and has a high, solid shoulder sloping rapidly in towards the cutting edge. I think it very unlikely that these jades were ever used as tools. Everything points, rather, to their being imitations in precious stone, and for burial purposes, of an authentic and valued craft tool.

Various types of *kuei* illustrated by Wu Ta-ch'êng might be claimed as descendants of this tool, but nearly all have a small perforation towards the butt end, which, as we have seen, points to an axe rather than an adze prototype. In fact none of the jades shown in Wu's drawings seems to me to resemble Neolithic hand adzes sufficiently closely to make worth while opening up the question of their possible connexion with objects mentioned in *Chou li*.

CLASS 3: OBJECTS DERIVED FROM THE SHAFT-HOLE ADZE

This implement, which might have served equally as a flat hammer, mace, or hoe, is characterized by a large central perforation through which the handle passed, so that the plane of the striking edge was at right angles to that of the blow. The implement is not very common in Neolithic contexts in the Far East, and seems to have made its appearance rather late. Bergman illustrates a single specimen from Lop Nor;[1] and Hamada found several at P'i-tz'ŭ-wo I, including a handsome porphyry example buried at the head of the corpse in one of the two graves belonging to the site. This specimen he compares with another found under similar conditions at Hamacho near Dairen, on the Liaotung Peninsula, and he points out their formal resemblance to

1. F. Bergman (see footnote p. 61), pl. 4 : 21.

kuei. Andersson reproduces a single implement sufficiently close to the type to be included, acquired in Hsin-an Hsien, Honan.

Certain types of ritual *kuei* are quite obviously derived from this craft tool. Plate 2*a* shows a famous example in dark-brown nephrite mottled with green, formerly in the Eumorfopoulos Collection, and now in the British Museum. What is apparently the very same piece is illustrated by Laufer, who describes it as a 'jade hammer-shaped symbol of Imperial Power'; [1] Laufer's text-figure reproduces one of Wu's drawings, so that there seems no doubt that the specimen now in the British Museum was in fact owned by Wu Ta-ch'êng himself. Wu identified it with the *chên kuei* described in *Chou li* as a tablet 12 (Chou) inches high,[2] held by the sovereign in his hands when, with the *ta kuei* in his girdle, he offered sacrifice to the morning sun in the spring. Leaving aside the question whether any such ceremonial was ever carried out in this way, it seems scarcely possible that all jade examples of this type are properly identified as *chên kuei*, in view of the fact that these, like *yüan kuei*, were supposed to have been the personal property of the Chou sovereign. It is an argument that Laufer uses elsewhere, but which he seems to have dropped in this case. Accordingly he accepts Wu's identification of the type as *chên kuei*, and says nothing about any other function such objects might have served.

Wu Ta-ch'êng's argument, it seems to me, rests on shaky foundations. Let us see what they are. *Chou li* says that the *chên kuei* has a *pi* in the centre; and the character used to denote *pi* in this instance is one that meant nothing more than 'must' in late Chou times. Evidently, then, it stands in place of some other character similarly pronounced, or else has lost a determinative element that would give some clue to its meaning (p. 563). But which? Herein lies the evil genius of Chinese exegetics; for in such a situation the commentator has generally felt free to use any one out of the entire range of available homophones to justify his particular interpretation of the original meaning. So Chêng Hsüan says that the character *pi* meaning 'a cord, ribbon' should be read; and Biot, in his translation of *Chou li*, follows the footsteps of this commentator in saying that the tablet had a cord called *pi* attached to its centre, by which it was suspended. Wu Ta-ch'êng rejects this explanation. In *Shuo wên* (p. 57) he finds a character *pi*, written as in

1. B. Laufer (see footnote p. 43), fig. 20 and p. 87.
2. Twelve Chou inches were approximately equal to 10 English inches. The present specimen is 9½ inches high.

Chou li but with the determinative for 'wood' or 'tree' added. The scriptionary defines this word as meaning firstly a palisade, and secondly a socket in such a thing as a spearhead, into which a handle might be inserted. *That*, says Wu, is the character and meaning intended by *Chou li*. The reference, he says, is to a tablet with a hole bored in it of sufficient diameter to take a handle. The jade in his collection has a hole meeting this requirement. It must accordingly be the *chên kuei* of which *Chou li* speaks.

I do not think there is any need to stress how faulty is this reasoning, which Laufer described as 'sober and judicious'. But what is strangely ingenuous is that Wu goes on to illustrate two more jades which he names *chên kuei*, yet which are quite unlike the previous example, both being long and narrow and with perforations that are neither central nor anything like wide enough to take a handle. Indeed, these specimens seem to derive much more directly from an axe of some sort than from the shaft-hole adze. As for jades in the form of the latter tool, the question still remains unanswered what was their function in Chou and earlier Chinese society, if not to serve as objects buried with the dead, whose virtue sprang from the efficacy of the shaft-hole adze? That they had any such role as that attributed to *chên kuei* by *Chou li* seems to me a quite unwarrantable assumption.

CLASS 4: OBJECTS DERIVED FROM KNIVES

A series of knives variously describable as 'rectangular', 'trapezoid', or 'semi-lunar' crops up over the whole Far Eastern area. In Asia itself, varieties of these knives are to be found to-day in use among the Chukchee Eskimo and the Kuriaks of New Siberia. They have also been found in prehistoric sites in the Aleutian Islands and Japan, as well as at several places in Manchuria, of which the earliest is Ang-ang-hsi and the latest Tan-tʻo-tzŭ (Pʻi-tzʻŭ-wo) on the Liaotung Peninsula. In China they have been found over the whole Neolithic area in the north, as well as at An-yang.

These knives are just as widespread through America. They are especially common in the North-western Eskimo area, where they occur as the 'woman's knife' or *ulu*, mounted in wood or ivory handles. The most advanced American form – in which the back edge or handle is quite straight, but the front or cutting edge is a continuous arc – is reached in the Second Laurentian culture of Ontario, Quebec, New England, and New York (*c.* A.D. 500–900).

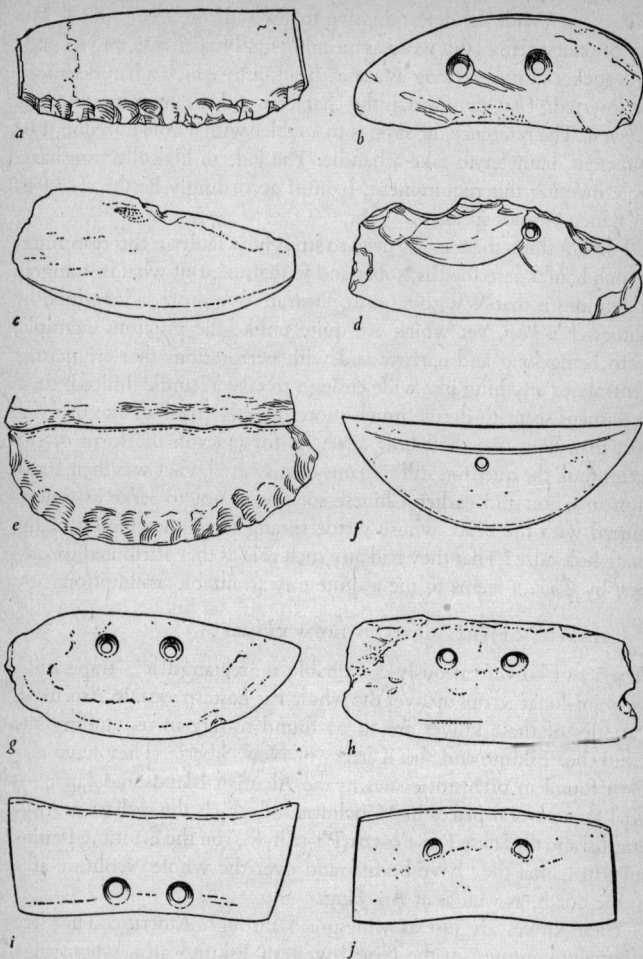

Figure 4. The rectangular or semi-lunar knife in the prehistoric and primitive cultures of north-east Asia and Amerindia: *a, b*, Ang-ang-hsi and Ch'ih-fêng (Manchuria); *c, d*, Chukchee Eskimo and Aleut (Siberia); *e, f*, North-west Coast American Indian and Laurentian II (Amerindia); *g, h*, prehistoric Japanese and Yamato (Japan); *i, j*, Lo-han-t'ang and modern iron knife (north China).

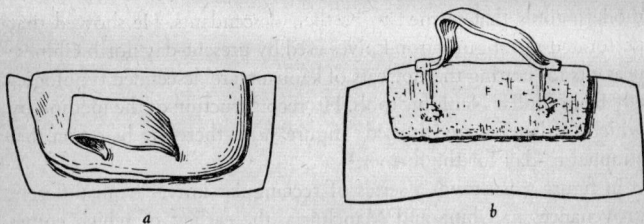

Figure 5. *a*, prehistoric Chinese stone knife; *b*, modern Chinese iron knife. The former dressed by Andersson on the model of the latter. (Redrawn from Andersson.)

Despite its wide geographical range, the type is really unmistakable. Figure 4 shows some variants in its form, which is that of a flat slab usually about twice as long as broad, the cutting edge being rather longer than the handle and always bevelled. The cutting edge is normally somewhat convex, but it may well be almost straight with slightly rounded corners. One well-defined Chinese group, from the Early Yang-shao site of Lo-han-t'ang, has a characteristic concave and strongly-winged handle. One, two, and even three perforations, arranged in line along an axis usually near to the back edge or handle, are customary features.

Minor variations aside, these knives clearly all stand in generic relationship and represent a typical tool of the eastern Asiatic culture area and of Amerindia; an ingredient, it may well be, in the hypothetical 'Pacific culture area' of which we have several times spoken (cf. p. 55).

Many of the archaeologists who have unearthed rectangular and semi-lunar knives at Neolithic sites in China and Manchuria have noted their resemblance to modern iron knives in use in the Far East to-day. Liang Ssŭ-yung, commenting on a specimen from the Early Neolithic site at Ang-ang-hsi (figure 4*a*), says that he is reminded of the Eskimo 'woman's knife' or *ulu* (figure 4*e*). And speaking of a similar knife from Lin-hsi (figure 6*b*), he says that it is rather like that used by itinerant tanners of Peking, the curved blade being half-moon shaped. Chêng Tê-k'un observes a resemblance between the rectangular variety and the 'broad kitchen knife of the cook'. And in 1935 Andersson devoted a chapter of his *Children of the Yellow Earth* to likenesses between Neolithic implements recovered by him and modern tools that seemed to be their descendants. He showed that perforated rectangular iron knives used by present-day north Chinese peasants for cutting the ripe ears of kaoliang are descended typologically from similar Neolithic tools. His reconstruction of the method by which the latter were 'dressed' (figure 5a) is therefore based on that adopted to-day for the former.[1]

In figure 6 is shown a series of rectangular knives from different provenances in China and Manchuria, the earliest of which comes from Ang-ang-hsi and the latest is a modern iron knife from north China. These specimens are not arranged to demonstrate an evolution in shape, but they *are* arranged chronologically. Here, then, we are again confronted with a tool of peri-Gobi type, one which must presumably have entered China late in the Neolithic period. It seems to have bequeathed its essential form to a type of ritual jade commonly found in Western collections, where it is usually labelled *kuei*; a specimen is shown on plate 3b. These jades are usually slimmer than are Neolithic examples made of other materials, and they often have an extra perforation at one end. But their resemblance to the Neolithic knife is otherwise striking, especially in respect of the perforations and the long bevelled cutting edge.

Figure 6h reproduces a drawing made by Wu Ta-ch'êng of a jade object in his collection.[2] Wu believed it to be a jade writing-tablet once used by the Chou sovereign; and this identification Laufer accepts, although he correctly notes the general similarity of the jade to a knife. Quite what Wu's identification is based on is by no means clear. We are told by *Chou li* that there was a sort of flat, rectangular tablet called *hu*, used for keeping the records of Imperial audiences. But this, it seems, was made of wood. According to the fourth-century B.C. *Li chi*, or 'Record of Rites', use of jade for writing-tablets was a prerogative of the ruler and such tablets were known as *t'ing*. So in

1. J. G. Andersson, *Children of the Yellow Earth*, London 1935, pp. 200–23 and figs. 90–105. Cf. also J. G. Andersson (see footnote p. 37), figs. 121–2.
2. The drawing is that featured by B. Laufer (see footnote p. 43), fig. 40.

Figure 6 (opp.). The conservation of a tool type. Prehistoric stone knives from Manchuria and north China, compared with two dynastic jades and a modern iron knife: *a*, Ang-ang-hsi; *b*, Lin-hsi; *c*, Lo-han-t'ang; *d*, Lo-han-t'ang; *e*, Ma-chia-yao (Painted Pottery sherd); *f*, Chu-chia-chai; *g*, modern iron knife; *h*, jade object identified by Wu Ta-ch'êng as the *hu*; *i*, jade knife of plate 3a.

a

b

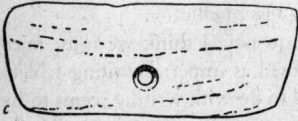

c

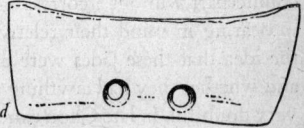

d

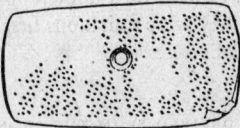

e

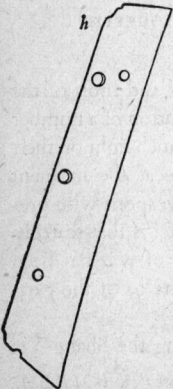

h

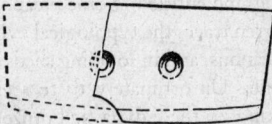

f

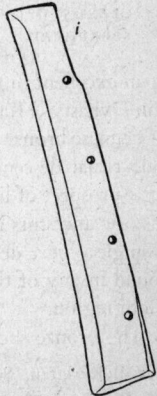

i

g

81

the *Tso chuan* commentary (fourth century B.C.) on *Ch'un ch'iu*, 'Spring and Autumn Annals (of Lu State),' we find: 'a *t'ing* is a writing-tablet (*hu*) made of jade.'

We therefore have the testimony of classical texts and their commentaries that a jade tablet called *t'ing* was used by the sovereign as a writing-tablet (*hu*) in Chou times. But the description given in *Chou li* scarcely seems to support Wu Ta-ch'êng's identification of it with the jade of figure 6*h*. How could the three perforations, so laboriously drilled, have served to increase such an object's utility as a writing-tablet? Laufer suggests that a band was passed between them so that the tablet could be fastened in a horizontal position at the girdle. Perhaps so; but that the holes were drilled at all is surely much more probably because they were distinctive and essential features of a prototype, the Neolithic knife, and could not therefore be omitted from its jade counterpart without a corresponding loss of efficacy.

Bearing in mind their relative frequency, I think we must reject the idea that these jades were ever used as imperial writing-tablets; and whether they had anything at all to do with writing seems to me very doubtful. In late Chou times, assuming they were then still being made, they no doubt served as ceremonial objects symbolic of some sort of feudal authority. But in view of their obvious derivation from knives, I suggest that they were imitations first made in jade only to be buried with the dead.

CLASS 5: OBJECTS DERIVED FROM THE BRONZE SOCKETED SPEARHEAD

In an excellent monograph entitled 'Some weapons and tools of the Yin Dynasty',[1] Karlgren traces the typological evolution of a number of Chinese bronze weapons, and in so doing sheds much light on their jade ritual descendants. Unfortunately there seems at the moment little prospect of linking up these dynastic bronze weapons with prehistoric ancestors in north China. For the strange fact is that scarcely a single object definitely identifiable as a weapon of war has been found in any of the prehistoric sites, either of China or of the peri-Gobi region.

The bronze socketed spearhead was in use during the Shang-Yin

1. B. Karlgren, 'Some weapons and tools of the Yin dynasty', in *B.M.F.E.A.*, no. 17 (1945), pp. 101-44.

period, as finds at the An-yang site attest. Sometimes the hollow socket continues down to the point of the blade – no doubt a casting device – and sometimes this socket extension seems to be represented in vestigial form by a pair of incised lines forming a broad triangle at the base of the blade (figure 7a, b). Examples, the blades of which are of jade and the sockets bronze with turquoise or malachite inlay, are fairly common in Western collections. That illustrated on plate 4a, formerly in the Raphael Collection and now in the British Museum,

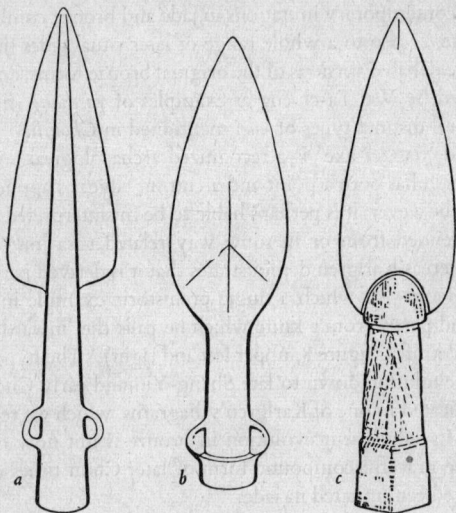

Figure 7. Three Shang-Yin spearheads: a, b, bronze;
c, jade, with bronze handle inlaid with turquoise.

is typical. This was not of course an actual weapon. The question is whether it was made solely for burial, for ceremonial display, or for both. In appearance (figure 7c) it resembles the second type of socketed bronze spearhead, the broad, triangular gripping-end of the bronze socket corresponding to the vestige of the socket extension in the bronze piece.

None of the jades illustrated by Wu Ta-ch'êng remotely resembles this composite type of weapon, and the question of its identification with ritual jades mentioned in Chou li does not arise. Indeed it seems to be associated exclusively with the Shang-Yin period; I do not know of any example which, on stylistic grounds, could be definitely assigned to that of the Chou.

CLASS 6: OBJECTS DERIVED FROM THE BRONZE DAGGER-AXE

The weapon called *ko* by the Chinese, on the other hand, has a long and complicated history. Its own evolution in metal, beginning in Shang-Yin times, is tortuous enough. But it also gives rise to close and apparently contemporary imitations in jade and bronze combined, or in jade alone, as also to a whole range of later ritual jades the shapes of which are debased versions of the original bronze forms, and which are identified by Wu Ta-ch'êng as examples of *ya chang* (figure 3*a*) and of several distinct types of *kuei* mentioned in *Chou li*.

The word 'dagger-axe' is a recognized archaeological term for a weapon which has both a point and a cutting edge; as applied to the Chinese *ko*, however, it is perhaps liable to be misinterpreted to mean an axe descended from or in some way related to a long-handled dagger. Whereas Karlgren demonstrates that it is derived partly from a slot-hafted axe – of which a single prehistoric example in stone is known – and partly from a knife which he calls the 'inward curving animal-head knife' (figure 8, upper left and right).[1] The hypothetical stages in its evolution down to late Shang-Yin and early Chou times are well indicated in one of Karlgren's diagrams, which we reproduce as figure 8. Its subsequent evolution in bronze is not now our concern, for the graceful compound form of later Chou times does not seem to have been imitated in jade.

In some bronze *ko* of Shang-Yin date the tang was cast with an upright shaft-hole into which the wooden handle fitted (figure 9*c*). But the great majority were hafted by means of a slot in the handle through which the tang of the weapon passed. Firm articulation was secured by a variety of means. In most cases a pair of lugs, projecting at the junction of blade and tang, no doubt fitted into grooves in the handle alongside the main socket, and were lashed into place by means of cords. In other examples we find a single median perforation, sometimes on the tang, sometimes on the blade, and this, too, must have

1. The fact that this evolution was already completed in Shang-Yin times is taken by Karlgren as evidence for the antiquity of the inward-curving animal-head knife in China, which in turn bears on the vexed question of the priority of Siberian bronze cultures in which it features (cf. pp. 111–12).

been intended to serve as an attaching device, used either with or
without the lugs. Karlgren supposes that the type with lugs or attachment holes is earlier than that with upright shaft-hole, which quickly
superseded it.

A number of jade specimens show unmistakable signs of descent,
however remote, from the bronze dagger-axe. Some have been recently recovered from An-yang, and are beyond doubt contemporary
with the bronze weapons on which they were modelled. Others are
known to us because they have been given places of honour in the
great Chinese collections of the last century, such as that of the Imperial viceroy Tuan Fang, and through the writings of such as Wu

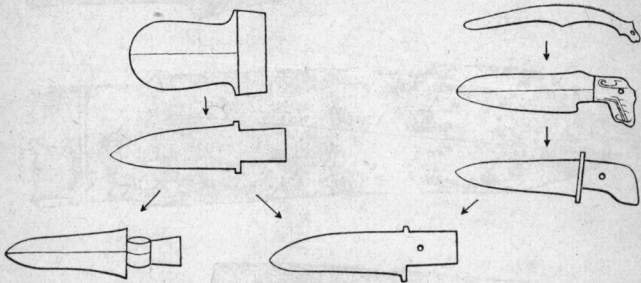

Figure 8. The evolution of the bronze dagger-axe
according to Karlgren.

Ta-ch'êng. As a rule we cannot tell what was the original provenance
of these, and it would be a safe guess that some are archaistic products
of the Sung period. Among them are some, like the *ya chang* of figure
3*a*, which are provided with lugs. Yet their general appearance is unconvincing. They may be late Chou, Han, or even Sung, but they
never give the impression of having been made by craftsmen working
direct from original models.

From the point of view of the jade craftsman the lug is an unnecessary inconvenience, and in a piece intended only for burial or ceremonial display it may be dispensed with, being replaced by a much
more easily-made perforation. The jade version of a *ko* shown in
figure 9*a* comes from An-yang. It has no lugs, but at the back edge of
the tang is a semicircular notch; and this, I think, must have been an
attaching device. Another jade *ko* from An-yang is shown in figure 9*b*,

and here the tang has a number of indentations at the edge. Attempts have been made to explain such notches, found on Neolithic objects of pottery, bone, stone, and jade, as remnants of some system of numeral magic.[1] But even if that were so in the case of a jade such as this, I think the primary purpose of the notches was still to serve

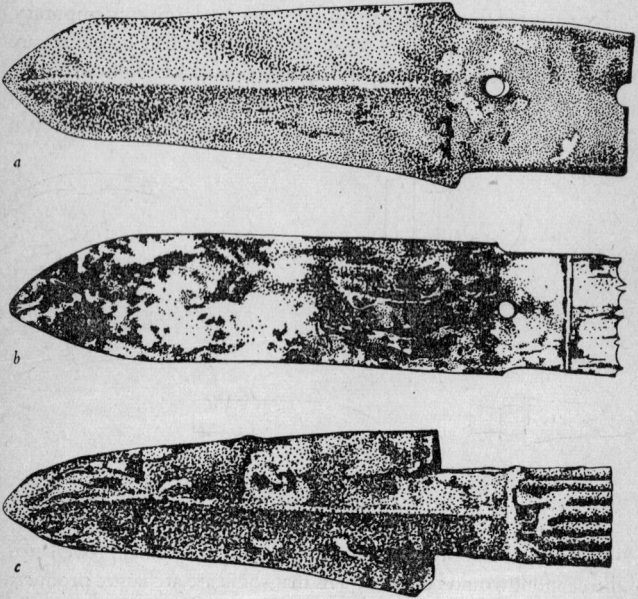

Figure 9. Three Shang-Yin dagger-axes: *a*, *b*, jade; *c*, bronze.

as a means of lashing. They may have been elaborated from the semi-circular single notch of the previous example, or copied more directly from the striped and indented tangs of bronze *ko* with shaft-holes such as that shown in figure 9*c*.

We are now in a position to explain the general shape and significance of the splendid jade *ko* illustrated on plate 3*a*, attributed to the

1. Cf. J. G. Andersson (see footnote p. 37), pp. 252–5, who compares incisions on a Neolithic ceremonial stone axe with indentations on a jade axe of the Chou period.

Shang-Yin period and quite clearly an *objet de luxe*. The somewhat curved blade proclaims, according to Karlgren's theory, the inward-curving animal-head knife from which it partly descends. The hole on the tang is for articulation with a slotted handle, while the indentations and stripes are the formalized descendants of those on the *ko* of figure 9*b* and *c*. This is superb jade technique. The rectilinear carved patterns, especially the band of lozenges and triangles at the base of the blade, are the jade-carver's natural response to difficulties of working his material. Hansford has drawn attention to the characteristic differences that usually exist between styles of decoration suitable for bronzes and those suitable for jades. He nevertheless believes that a number of well-known bronze motives may have been borrowed, perhaps quite late in the history of Chinese bronze-casting, from the repertory of the jade-carver. Among these he puts the squared spiral, the lozenge, and the segmented flanges of bronzes (p. 160). Two of these devices, as we see, appear on the present specimen.

Plate 4*b* shows a composite *ko*, its blade of jade and its tang of bronze inlaid with turquoise. The jade portion of this type of weapon seems to have bequeathed its shape to the tablet traditionally known as *ku kuei*, '*kuei* ornamented with grain pattern', which *Chou li* says was 7 inches long and was given by the Emperor to his bride-elect. An example appears on a bas-relief of the Han period reproduced in *Chin shih so*, twelve volumes of researches into inscriptions upon bronze (*chin*) and stone (*shih*) objects of antiquity first published in 1822. The cut (figure 10*a*) shows a flat oblong plaque about two and a half times as long as broad, with one end carved away symmetrically to a sharp point, covered with a typically Han diaper pattern of lozenges with a nodule at the centre of each.[1]

With this piece in mind, Laufer says of the *ku kuei* that its shape is 'presumably derived from that of a spear', but I have set alongside it in figure 10 the jade portion of a jade and bronze *ko* in the William Rockhill Nelson Gallery of Art, Kansas City, in order to show what I take to be its true affinities. A piece identified by Wu Ta-ch'êng as a *ku kuei* is very similar in shape and also has one side ornamented with diapered lozenges, while the other is decorated with rows of raised knobs. This is the so-called 'grain pattern' (p. 256 and plate 5*b*).

1. Fêng Yün-p'êng and Fêng Yün-yüan, *Chin shih so*, 'Reproductions of Inscriptions on Metal and Stone', 24 fasc., Shanghai 1906, fasc. 20, p. 17b.

Following their usual practice, commentators managed to read an elaborate symbolism into the shapes of *ku kuei*. The first-century A.D. historian Pan Ku, to whom is attributed a compilation entitled *Po hu*

Figure 10. *a*, jade object of the type called *ku kuei*, re-drawn from *Chin shih so* and compared with *b*, the jade portion of a Shang-Yin jade and bronze dagger-axe.

t'ung, says there that the pointed upper part of the tablet means the male principle *yang*, and the lower squared section the female *yin* (p. 270). No explanation of this symbolism is offered by Pan Ku. But Laufer accepts it, and goes on to say: 'This may hint at a possible original phallic significance of this emblem. ...'[1] In view of its probable descent from the blade of a dagger-axe, there seems no good reason to believe any such thing of this jade's shape.

1. B. Laufer (see footnote p. 43), p. 99.

CLASS 7: ANNULAR DISCS

We come now to a group of jade objects whose use in ancient China has long been the subject of much discussion and little agreement among Chinese and Western scholars. Outstanding among them are the annular discs which Hansford calls, generically, 'pi-forms'. The pi itself has a central perforation (hao) which Êrh ya, a glossary written in the second or third century B.C., says is only half the width of the jade substance encircling it – that is, its diameter is a fifth that of the whole ring; whereas the yüan has a perforation twice the width of the body substance, so that its diameter is half that of the whole ring. And in the ring called huan, body substance and perforation are of equal width, so that the diameter of the latter is a third of the whole. But these exact proportions are rarely if ever to be found, and may have been laid down retrospectively not earlier than the Han period. Many of the objects known to us as pi – indeed, perhaps most – have perforations occupying considerably more than a fifth of the total diameter, and some more than a third. But it would be splitting hairs to insist that they are therefore huan. For practical purposes they are pi, the form that has gained such prestige as a cult object during the last 3,000 years that it might serve as a distinctive emblem of Chinese material culture, in much the same way as the li tripod is felt to do. In what follows I intend to make no typological distinction between pi and huan. On the other hand the ring called yüan, in which the perforation is very large, does seem to belong to a different typological group. From many Neolithic sites in Manchuria and north China, as from the Shang-Yin site at An-yang, have been recovered ring-like objects made of marble, shell, or jade, the shapes of which suggest that they were used as bracelets. Jade rings approximating to the dimensions laid down for yüan, therefore, while probably not actually suited for use as bracelets, are perhaps correctly regarded as imitations of these.

PI-FORMS

To begin with, it is apparent, and I believe needs no proof, that the pi spoken of in pre-Han texts is in fact an object like those illustrated on plate 5. In the second place, it is now generally believed both by Chinese and Western scholars that the pi was used from time immemorial for worship of Heaven (T'ien) and that its shape symbolized, directly or indirectly, the dimensions of that cosmic principle. Laufer, for instance, illustrates three *pi* in colour, the first labelled: 'Jade disk representing image of the deity Heaven', and the second and third: 'Jade disks symbolic of the deity Heaven'. He does not explain wherein the imagery lies, but merely observes that 'the shapes of these images were found by geometric construction, a jade disk round and perforated representing Heaven. ...'[1] But Schindler, followed by Karlgren, says that the *pi* is identical in form with the ancient graph for 'sun' (figure 11*a*, now written as 11*b*), and that both depict the sun disc. Hansford suggests that both graph and *pi* may portray the sun shining in the surrounding vault of heaven. Hentze,

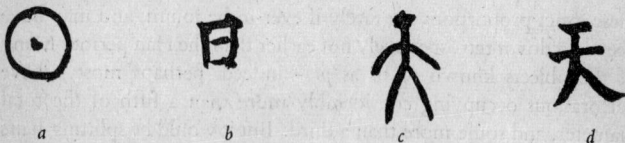

a   *b*   *c*   *d*

Figure 11. *a*, oracle bone graph, equated with *b*, modern *jih*, 'sun';
c, bronze graph, equated with *d*, modern *t'ien*, 'heaven'.

while agreeing that the *pi*-form and the graph can be equated, holds that both represent a wheel, which he believes was the symbol by which the ancient Chinese represented the sun.

We have several times seen how Han and later Chinese scholars went to inordinate lengths to explain the shapes of traditional jades, reading into them a symbolism that is usually forced and sometimes downright absurd. As regards the *pi*, we must ask what literary evidence connects it with worship of Heaven? How early does this notion make its appearance? How old is the idea that the shape of the disc actually symbolized Heaven? And how can the answers to these questions be brought into line with archaeological fact and with what we know of ancient Chinese religious practice?

None of the texts judged to be earlier than *Chou li* (fourth century B.C.) connects *pi* discs with the worship of Heaven. The most they say is that *pi* were auspicious jades appropriate for sacrifices. They also say that *pi* were offered by the sovereign to feudal princes on occasions

1. B. Laufer (see footnote p. 43), pls. 21–2 and p. 21.

of ceremonial visits, and that they were feudatories' symbols of authority. In *Chou li*, chapter 18, occurs the famous entry: 'He [the Master of Religious Ceremonies] pays homage to Heaven with the *ch'ing pi* [a *pi* of greenish or bluish jade].' But *Chou li* also gives several other uses for *pi* of one sort or another. A *pi* was used, together with other jade tablets, in burials of members of the ruling family; a *pi* was offered to the ruler by feudal princes who visited Court, and another served in the investiture of lords of the fourth and fifth ranks. Evidently in Chou times *pi* were by no means exclusively used in worship of Heaven, if we take *Chou li* as guide. Indeed, the persistent belief of Han and later scholars that they were so used seems to rest entirely on the isolated passage quoted above.

But even assuming that at least one of the functions – perhaps the most important – of *pi* in pre-Han China was for worship of Heaven, does it follow that the jade actually represented the cosmic deity by virtue of its shape? That view is not expressed until the second century A.D., when the commentator Chêng Hsüan cryptically remarks in allusion to the *Chou li* passage: 'The *pi* is round and symbolizes Heaven'. It is this view that has been adopted by all later Chinese scholars, and that has been passed on to the West.

It might be argued that the multiplicity of uses to which *pi* were put in late Chou times, according to *Chou li*, is simply a case of corruption of ritual practice at that time; and that in the early part of the dynasty and prior to it the disc *was* used exclusively for the worship of Heaven. What evidence can we bring forward to test this surmise? *Pi*-forms have been found in at least one prehistoric context in China. Seven specimens, three of them beautifully carved in jade, came from the Neolithic burial-site in the Pan Shan hills, and were among objects bought there by Andersson in 1924 (plate 5a). And, significantly, one of them was said to have been found lying on the chest of a skeleton. This find, as we have seen, is probably contemporary with the site, which dates from the Yang-shao period (*c.* 2200–1700 B.C.).

If jade discs of the type recovered by Andersson in the Pan Shan hills were *not* used in worship of Heaven, then that role must have been assumed in later times, presumably in the dynastic period. What evidence have we that Heaven was being worshipped in China during prehistoric times, or even as late as the Shang-Yin period? As far as I know, none at all. Apart from the fact that they went in for elaborate burials, we know nothing concrete about the religious beliefs of the peoples of the Painted and Black Pottery Cultures in north China. So we certainly have no *a priori* grounds for assuming that objects of the sort illustrated on plate 5*a* were used in worship of Heaven or that their original shapes were symbolic of that principle.

As far as concerns the Shang-Yin people, it is fairly well agreed that they did *not* worship Heaven. They addressed oracular questions to a variety of nature-powers and deceased ancestors. But Heaven does not appear among these oracles. Their chief deity, if that is the right word, was a being or beings called Ti or Shang Ti – an expression in which the character for *shang* means 'above', 'superior', or perhaps 'ultimate', and that for *ti*, later used to mean 'Emperor', was an appellation given to their kings. So that by Shang Ti may have been meant something like the first ancestral Shang-Yin sovereign, or even the whole galaxy of royal ancestors. The character used by the Chou to mean Heaven, T'ien, does appear in the oracular sentences; but nowhere, according to Creel, with the signification of a god or spirit.[1]

After the Chou displaced the Shang-Yin, they apparently came to equate the old Shang Ti with their own chief deity T'ien, for we find both terms being used interchangeably in early Chou texts and bronze inscriptions. Now, if T'ien was then conceived of as an abstract cosmic principle appropriately symbolized by an annular disc, we have to explain a curious fact. The early Chou graph of the character now written as figure 11*d*, *t'ien*, takes the form shown in figure 11*c*; and this is quite plainly an anthropomorphic symbol. We are forced to conclude that the idea behind T'ien was not, originally, that of an abstract cosmic force. Creel's theory is that 'the idea of Heaven as a vague symbol of the vast power of the great spirits and the place where they dwell' is secondary; and that the primary idea of T'ien is simply 'a great man', and so a king, a dead king, and then a 'Great Spirit'.[2] The name given by the Chou to their reigning sovereign – T'ien Tzŭ, or Son of Heaven – would be entirely appropriate if, as Creel supposes, Heaven were regarded as a deified royal ancestor.

We cannot, in the nature of things, say whether this was so during the early part of the historical Chou period; for the secondary concept of T'ien as a cosmic force may have matured before the Chou gained control of north China. Equally, of course, it may not. As long as T'ien was still being thought of in its primary sense, for which the

1. Cf. H. G. Creel (see footnote p. 26), p. 342.
2. H. G. Creel (see footnote p. 26), pp. 342-3.

picture of a human figure was a proper symbol, such a notion would surely rule out any alternative symbolism, such as the *pi* is said to manifest.

We hesitate to accept the *pi*-form as a representational symbol of Heaven (T'ien), therefore, for the following reasons:

1. *Pi*-forms have been found in Neolithic contexts in China, and there is no reason to suppose that Heaven was worshipped during the Neolithic period.
2. *Pi*-forms have been found in Shang-Yin material, and Heaven was *not* worshipped by the Shang-Yin people, as far as we know.
3. We do not know when the concept of Heaven as a deified ancestor gave place to one by virtue of which it could be appropriately symbolized in the form of an annular disc.
4. If the *pi*-form represents Heaven, we should hardly expect to find such discs used for the variety of purposes attributed to them by *Chou li*.
5. The oldest claim for the *pi* that it symbolizes Heaven is not made until the second century A.D., probably 2,000 years or more after the first of such objects were made in China.

But if we reject the idea that the *pi*-form was originally an image of Heaven, what was it? One recent view is that it was a lithophone – a suspended sonorous stone of the sort spoken of in classical texts as used for making ritual music.[1] But if *pi* discs were so used, why do not the texts specify that important fact? Moreover, the author of this theory considers that *pi* came into existence only during the early Chou period. If by this he means *pi* approximating in their proportions to the strict diameter ratio of 5:1 laid down by *Êrh ya*, he may very well be right. But in fact he includes in his survey of annular jades perhaps used as musical instruments all discs down to a diameter ratio of 2:1 – that is, down to the canonical proportions of *yüan* – and there are several Neolithic annular discs (plate 5*a*) in which the ratio is considerably higher; he would, in other words, have to contemplate the possibility that such jades were being used for making music a thousand years or more before he believes they actually were. Nor does he claim to explain how its essential form fitted the jade for its supposed

1. F. A. Kuttner, 'The musical significance of archaic Chinese jades of the *pi*-disk type', in *A.A.*, vol. xvi, nos. 1/2 (1953), pp. 25–50.

musical purpose. We do not mean to suggest that *pi* discs were *never* used for musical purposes – very possibly they were – but merely that this was not their original function or significance.

Our general contention that the forms of ritual jades are derived from those of authentic craft tools would obviously apply in the case of the *pi*, were such a tool prototype to suggest itself. Hentze believes that the tool was a mace, or shaft-hole adze. This, I think, is a real possibility; but the typically trapezoid shape of the Neolithic adze seems to have been transmitted to such ritual jades as those of plate 2*a*, and one wonders why, if Hentze's theory is correct, the form should ever have been modified into the strictly circular shape of the *pi*. My own suggestion that the *pi*-form may be derived from the fly-wheel of a drill is of course no more than a guess, made in obedience to the unwritten law decreeing that all Western students of jade shall find something new to say about *pi*. But the drill was undoubtedly in use as a standard tool in Neolithic China, and a heavy fly-wheel of similar pattern to the *pi* disc may well have been employed to give it momentum. Wedged against a nodule of the bamboo shaft of such a drill, a disc shaped like a *pi* would, I should say, convert into a thoroughly efficient tool.

CLASS 8: ANNULAR DISC WITH SERRATED EDGE

It was Wu Ta-ch'êng who proposed to identify discs of the sort shown on plate 7*b* with the astronomical instrument *hsüan chi* spoken of in pre-Han texts. Neither he nor Laufer, who accepts his identification, make any attempt to explain how such discs might have been used for taking celestial observations. A remarkably ingenious explanation has recently been put forward by Henri Michel, and I propose to summarize it here.[1]

That the *hsüan chi* was some sort of astronomical instrument has always found acceptance among Chinese scholars. In the second chapter of the *Shu ching* or 'Book of History', we read that the legendary Emperor Shun employed the *hsüan chi yü hêng* to regulate the Seven Governors. What the latter were, nobody seemed quite to know. One common belief is that they were the sun, moon, and five planets. And Laufer, observing that on each of the three main divisions of the peri-

1. H. Michel, 'Astronomical jades', in *O.A.*, vol. ii, no. 4 (spring 1950), pp. 156–9.

meter of this jade there are six teeth separating five notches and a longer and shorter sector, says: 'I should like to regard the longest line as the symbol of the sun and the line opposite this one, on the other side of the section, being half the length of the sun-line, as emblematic of the moon, while the five indentations between might denote the five planets.'[1] Such a speculation does little more than show Laufer's aptitude for finding what he called 'a well-meditated symbolism' in jade shapes; it does not incline us to accept with greater readiness this particular identification of the Seven Governors. In *Shih chi* (p. 174), the historian Ssŭ-ma Ch'ien says that by the latter the seven stars of the Great Bear are meant; and it is worth noting that the Chinese still call the stars α, β, γ, and δ Ursae Majoris by the name *hsüan chi*. Ssŭ-ma Ch'ien, as we shall see, may not have been very wide of the mark.

Chinese expositors of the phrase *hsüan chi yü hêng* have expressed their views as to its meaning with some unanimity, as can be gathered from the following quotations:

1. The *hsüan chi yü hêng* is 'an instrument for observing constellations. It can be rotated. ...'
2. 'The *ki* [*chi*] is suspended to represent the sky, and one observes through the *hêng*. Turn the *ki* [*chi*] and look through the *hêng* to know the planets and the celestial houses. ...'
3. 'The part of the instrument which was turned was the *ki* [*chi*]; the part which was held in the hand was the *hêng*; both were made of jade. The degrees of motions were measured with them. ...'[2]

For reasons into which we need not go here, Hansford proposes as a literal translation for *hsüan chi* 'an observational or rotating contrivance made of jade', and for *yü hêng* 'a jade transverse'. The 'jade transverse' was clearly some sort of sighting tube, and the *hsüan chi* a rotatable object mounted upon it in some way. Michel's theory involves the equation of discs such as that of plate 7b with the *hsüan chi*,

---

1. B. Laufer (see footnote p. 43), p. 106.
2. Quoted by H. Michel (see footnote p. 94), p. 156 from H. Maspero, 'Les instruments astronomiques des chinois aux temps des Han', in *M.C.B.*, vol. 6 (1939), pp. 183–370. The first quotation is from the *Shu ching*, the second and third from the commentaries by Ts'ai Yung (A.D. 133–92) and Chêng Hsüan (A.D. 127–200) respectively.

as proposed by Wu Ta-ch'êng; and the *yü hêng*, with a well-known class of ritual jade called *ts'ung* (plate 6*a*, *b*, *c*). The question of this latter identification we will shelve for the moment, since it does not greatly affect the case of the *hsüan chi*. Any tube of suitable dimensions would do equally well as a *yü hêng*.

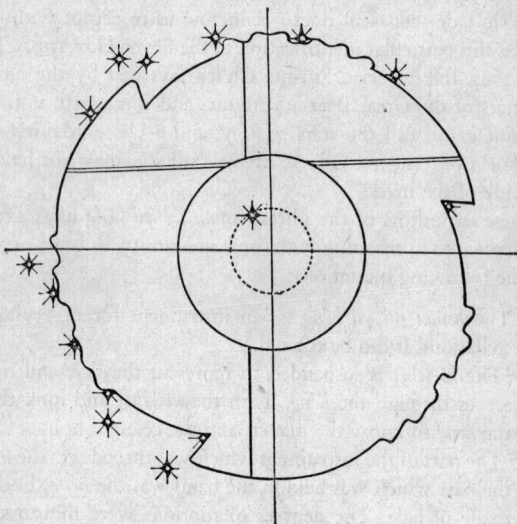

Figure 12. Jade object of the type identified as the astronomical instrument *hsüan chi*, showing its possible use as a stellar template. Stars in Ursa Major, Ursa Minor, Cepheus, and Draco are shown on its outer perimeter, while β Ursa Minor lies on the inner perimeter of the sighting tube (dotted circle). (Redrawn from Michel.)

According to Michel, then, the disc was mounted upon the collar of the sighting tube in such a way that it could easily be rotated. The instrument thus made was now directed towards the celestial pole. Michel explains that during a period including the latter part of the Shang-Yin dynasty and the whole of the Chou, the pole was not marked by a bright star. Owing to the precession of the equinoxes it lay, in 1000 B.C., some 16° from its present position close to α Ursae Minoris. The nearest bright star was then β Ursae Minoris, but even

96

this was never nearer than about 7°, or about fourteen times the moon's diameter. Yet it was vitally important for Chinese astronomers to determine the position of the pole; and from it that of the colure, an imaginary great circle passing through the pole and through the solstitial points on the ecliptic; these are the most northerly and southerly apparent positions reached by the sun in its annual motion, and all calendar-making requires the exact determination of their date.

Michel shows that if certain proportions between *hsüan chi* and *yü hêng* were maintained, the former could be rotated as a sort of template upon the latter, until certain stars near the pole fitted more or less exactly into the notches on the outer edge. These stars, as his diagram shows (figure 12), were d, g, ε, ζ, and η Ursae Majoris, ζ and φ Draconis; χ Cephei; and α Ursae Minoris, the present Pole Star. Upon looking through the tube, the pole would now be in the centre of the field of vision; and, if the inner diameter was of proper size, β Ursae Minoris was just visible at the edge of the field. Since this star revolved round the pole, it would appear to travel round the inner perimeter of the tube once in twenty-four hours.

Some *hsüan chi*, but by no means all, have a double line and a single line more or less at right-angles to it engraved on one surface. Laufer supposed that these were marks accidentally left by the saw, but Michel points out that the straight single line gives the positions of the solstitial points when the instrument is directed at the pole in the manner described.

Michel adds some plausible evidence taken from Chinese sources to build up his case that *hsüan chi* really were used in this way. Further, he points out that the engraved line indicating the solstitial colure is not always in the same relative position on the faces of different *hsüan chi*, and this he suggests is because the colure itself varied slightly over the long period of about a thousand years during which he assumes *hsüan chi* to have been in use in China. Therefore it is possible, he says, to calculate the approximate age of a given disc. From this unexpected quarter, then, might arrive help for the dating of early Chinese jades.

I cannot presume to make detailed criticism of this most exciting theory. But one or two objections, it seems to me, have to be met before it can be accepted in its entirety. The first concerns a possible historical relationship between the forms of *hsüan chi* and *pi*. Are they both originally of the same typological group? If so, which came first, and which is the derived form? According to Michel they are so related, and the prototype was the *hsüan chi*, its descendant the *pi*. But I scarcely think that could have been the case. As regards *hsüan chi*, I know of no specimen that can be confidently dated before about 1000 B.C. on the strength of excavation data; whereas *pi*-forms, as we have seen, go back to the Middle Yang-shao stage, about a thousand years earlier. In my view, therefore, the *pi*-form came first. But this, of course, in no way invalidates Michel's theory as to the practical use to which *hsüan chi* were put.

A second question concerns the minor serrations. Only two positions on the circumference of a given disc need to be established for its centre to coincide with a given third point. Why, then, the multiplication of serrations? Furthermore, their number and position vary quite noticeably; very few, if indeed any, *hsüan chi* have identical profiles.[1] If uniformity was not insisted on, is this not an indication that the serrations had some earlier, undisclosed function? In fact, serrations of this type are a frequent feature of ritual jades attributed to the Shang-Yin and Chou dynasties. They are especially common on perforated axes; and Andersson, who found notches cut in the sides of several stone implements from the Kansu sites, believes that both sorts of indentation served to operate some principle, so far undiscovered, of what he calls 'cryptic magic'. This might have been so also in the case of *hsüan chi*; but again, it would not necessarily affect the contention that the jade was, in historical times, an astronomical instrument.

CLASS 9: TUBE WITH SQUARE OUTER AND ROUND
INNER PERIMETER

The object thus described is the last ritual jade to be surveyed here. It is the one known to every jade collector since the days of Wu Ta-ch'êng as *ts'ung*, several sorts of which are mentioned in *Chou li*. Three typical examples appear in plate 6, and it will be seen that although the dimensions and proportions of *ts'ung* vary considerably,

1. One in the Buffalo Museum of Science, assigned by Salmony to the Shang-Yin period, has three groups of eight teeth instead of the usual six. Again, discs with the typical three main notches, but without the smaller serrations, have been recovered from pre-metal sites in Manchuria. No doubt these date from well on into the historic period in China, and perhaps have to be seen as degenerate descendants of more typical *hsüan chi*.

the essential form does not. It is that of a rectangular block, square in section. Along one axis, usually the longer, a wide perforation is drilled whereby the block is converted into a tube with circular bore, open at both ends. Upper and lower ends are normally cut away so that a low collar projects; this collar is usually round but is sometimes squarish – or what Andersson calls 'rounded quadratic' – in section. The proportions of *ts'ung* vary from those of a tall column (plate 6*a*) to a squat form that is little more than a ring (plate 6*c*). Many are unornamented, but probably more are engraved with geometrical designs, a pattern of horizontal grooves or strapping, with or without 'eyes', being especially favoured. *Ts'ung* seem to have been conceived of as made of nephrite, and many apparently were. But perhaps even more are of other hard stones used as substitutes for true jade.

Scholars have not always agreed that these jade tubes should be called *ts'ung*. For example, the authors of *Ku yü t'u p'u* (p. 65) depict several objects which we would call *ts'ung*, and label them *kang t'ou* or 'wheel-naves'; apparently on the strength of references in the classics to a 'jade chariot'; that is, one ornamented with jade fittings, used exclusively by the ruler. But if the 'jade chariot' was the prerogative of the ruler, how are we to account for the dozens upon dozens of known *ts'ung*? And are any two known *ts'ung* alike in their dimensions? Furthermore, literary evidence in support of this identification is hardly conclusive; for apparently the crucial passage on which it rests comes from a book that existed only in the imaginations of the authors of *Ku yü t'u p'u*. The interesting point is that they were led to make it, according to Laufer, through a chance remark in *Shuo wên*, under the *ts'ung* character entry, to the effect that *ts'ung* resembled wheel-naves. What led the seventeenth-century authors to that entry, if not the fact that the tradition connecting name and object, as in the case of the *pi*, was never entirely broken in China?

Presumably it was the existence of this tradition that enabled Wu Ta-ch'êng to identify his jade tubes as *ts'ung*. Certainly there does not seem to be any explicit description of them, either in *Chou li* or the commentaries. At any rate, the identification has been generally accepted; for instance, by Laufer, Pope-Hennessy, Erkes, Gieseler, Karlgren, and Michel. Of these, the last three part company with the others, since they believe that the *ts'ung* had a functional use before it became a ritual jade, although they differ as to what that function was.

Let us now see what *Chou li* and its commentaries have to say about this jade. The first reference is also the most famous. In *Chou li*, chapter 18, we read that the Master of Ceremonies makes six objects of jade with which to do homage to Heaven, Earth, and the Four Quarters. It adds: 'With the round tablet *pi* of greenish jade he pays homage to Heaven; with the yellow *ts'ung* he pays homage to Earth', on which Chêng Hsüan comments: 'The *pi* is round and symbolizes Heaven; the *ts'ung* is eight-cornered and symbolizes Earth.' Upon this single passage with its commentary rests the idea, held by Laufer, Pope-Hennessy, Erkes, Gieseler, and others, that the *ts'ung* is primarily a symbol of Earth.

A second passage in *Chou li* gives the names of six objects supposedly buried with the dead. Of these, the *ts'ung* was one. The passage is cryptic enough, but Chêng Hsüan sees fit to add that the *ts'ung* was placed on the abdomen of the corpse, the *pi* under the back, and that 'the *pi* and the *ts'ung* are, by their separation, symbolic of Heaven and Earth'. Here is a second, belated reference to a connexion between *ts'ung* and the deity Earth. The other references in *Chou li* are to *ts'ung* used as symbols of some sort of authority in princely households. The 'great *ts'ung*' was the symbol of authority of the queen, and corresponded to the *chên kuei* held by the sovereign (p. 76). A *ts'ung* 9 (Chou) inches long was presented by princes to the king, and one 8 inches long was used on embassies, apparently as a diplomatic credential. A 'toothed *ts'ung*' was used by the sovereign, and another by his consort, as a weight-stone. And a 'decorated *ts'ung*' was given by princes to the consorts of other princes on occasions of ceremonial visits. That is all we are told by *Chou li*.

On the strength of the meagre references to Earth cited above, a literary foundation that Karlgren has called 'poor not to say flimsy', Laufer built up his theory that the *ts'ung* is first and foremost 'a real image of the deity Earth'. The iconography, it must be admitted, is somewhat obscure. All we are told about the shape of the *ts'ung* – and that not until the second century A.D. – is that it is eight-cornered. This, says Laufer, means that there are four corners at each end, symbolic of the 'squareness' mentioned by commentators as a property of Earth. How, then, does he explain the multiplicity of uses for *ts'ung*, as mentioned in *Chou li*, if each is a 'real image' of Earth? Some he omits altogether. But he points out that the 'great *ts'ung*', the 'toothed *ts'ung*', and the 'decorated *ts'ung*' all have to do with women.

Earth, he says, was a feminine Principle. Therefore its symbol was appropriately adopted by women. From this outpost of feminism, Erkes takes us a step further into what is literally a no-man's-land of speculation; the form of the *ts'ung*, he says, represents the vagina, the concrete symbol of the feminine deity, Earth.

The question of the alleged sex of Earth, the great cosmic principle out of whose commingling with Heaven was produced mankind, is so controversial that I do not feel we can enter upon it here. On the other hand, the local tutelary God of the Soil, Shê, was certainly regarded as male. This deity has fathered an entirely different view as to the meaning of the *ts'ung*. Gieseler has come upon a passage in *Li chi*, 'Record of Rites', which says that sacrifice in the household was made to the God of the Smokehole, called Chung Liu, and in the State to the Soil God, Shê. He therefore supposes that the household god was a sort of lesser Soil God. He says that the *ts'ung* may originally have been a clay tube mounted in the smoke-hole, and used successively to symbolize the household god, Chung Liu, and the God of the Soil, Shê. The latter he apparently equates with the cosmic deity Earth, and hence arrives at the symbolic connexion between Earth and the *ts'ung*. This reasoning seems to me tortuous, and to rest on too many unlikely assumptions. In particular, the connexion between the tutelary deity Shê and the cosmic deity Ti is not easy to accept.

These speculations, based on the idea that the primary force of the *ts'ung* was that of a symbol of Earth, entirely fail to convince. There remain the functional explanations put forward by Karlgren and Michel, which may be viewed in the light of what little archaeological evidence is available. I have already mentioned that many *ts'ung*, as far as can be told from *Chou li*, were symbols of authority in princely houses. *That*, says Karlgren, is the significant fact. Association with Earth is secondary. How did *ts'ung* come to be regarded as symbols of the authority of the feudal overlord? Because they, or their precursors, were containers or protective envelopes for the all-important ancestral tablets of the ruling families. Karlgren supposes that the prototype of the *ts'ung* was a tall, hollow cylinder. To prevent this cylinder from rolling, or for convenience while being stored, four stone slabs or corner prisms were bound together with it to give its square outer section. The *ts'ung* we know are derived from these composite objects, and the grooves commonly incised at the corners

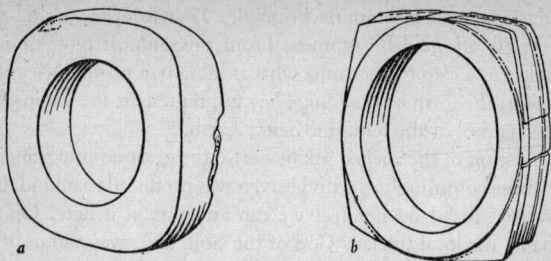

Figure 13. *a*, jade ring recovered from the Neolithic cemetery in the Pan Shan hills, Kansu, compared with *b*, jade object of the type called *ts'ung*. (Redrawn from Andersson.)

are simply vestiges of notches cut in the original slabs to hold the binding more firmly in place. If this really was the original role of the *ts'ung*, the fact that it became a symbol of princely authority in its own right easily follows.

What evidence does Karlgren put forward in support of his theory? We have already noticed that there are two main varieties of *ts'ung*: a tall type and a squat one. Some of the squat *ts'ung* may have been cut down from taller specimens, but I see no reason to suppose that all of them were. What would be the point? The question is, then, which type came first? For if the squat *ts'ung* is early and the tall variety late, Karlgren's theory would seem to fall to the ground; a squat *ts'ung* would be no use as a container of the tall ancestral tablet. Karlgren says that it can be shown on stylistic grounds that the tall variety is early, whereas Andersson believes that the squat variety came first. Among the jades bought by him from the T'ao River burial-sites in Kansu was a thick ring with a 'rounded quadratic' outer wall which he takes to be a primitive *ts'ung*, such as 'would have been shaped like this at a time when the artisans had not yet developed the skill of exact and complicated carving'.[1] And it is worth observing that the *ts'ung* shape and surface treatment are indeed complicated in comparison with the general run of ritual jades as we know them. I append Andersson's drawing of this piece put beside a 'dynastic' *ts'ung* formerly in the Eumorfopoulos Collection, so that the reader may form his own opinion as to the likelihood of their being typologically related (figure 13). Hansford's verdict is that the Neo-

1. J. G. Andersson (see footnote p. 37), p. 265.

lithic specimen does not resemble a squat *tsᶜung* sufficiently closely to be regarded as its prototype. In view of this conflict of opinion among experts, it would, I believe, be unwise to say categorically which type came first.

Other evidence to support Karlgren's theory is drawn from linguistic and epigraphic sources. It is difficult for a non-expert to evaluate this evidence, but briefly, it depends on the fact that in Chou times a single written graph often represented a number of words, differently pronounced, but of cognate meaning. Under the Han, determinative elements were added to these characters in order to separate out their meanings. So in Chou times the character for *tsᶜung* now written with the 'jade' radical on the left, appeared without this added element, as in figure 14*a*, and this was also the graph for *tsᶜung*, 'ancestral temple' – of which it is a pictogram. Hence Karlgren establishes a connexion between the jade and worship of ancestors.

Mention was made on p. 100 of an object called 'toothed *tsᶜung*', *tsŭ tsᶜung*, now written as in figure 14*c*; the character for *tsŭ* is interesting. Its right-hand element has been variously written since Han times with the 'horse', 'silk', or – as here – the 'jade' element on the left; and the translation of *tsŭ tsᶜung* may depend on which of these versions one accepts. But according to Karlgren, disagreement among Han commentators as to how the first character in the expression *tsŭ tsᶜung* should be written, simply means that in Chou times the graph had no

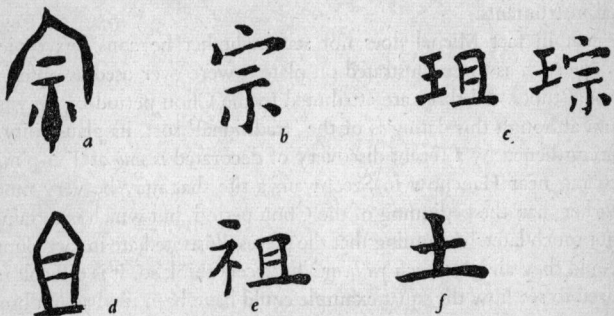

Figure 14. *a*, bronze graph, equated with *b*, modern *tsᶜung*, 'ancestral temple'; *c*, modern *tsŭ tsᶜung*, 'toothed *tsᶜung*'; *d*, bronze graph, equated with *e*, modern *tsŭ*, 'ancestor', and cognate in Chou times with *f*, modern *tᶜu* or *tᶜi*, 'Earth God'.

left-hand element at all. It was in fact written as in figure 14d, and was cognate with *tsŭ*, 'ancestor', (figure 14e). Here again is a semantic connexion with the idea of ancestors.

How, according to this theory, did the *ts'ung* become a symbol of Earth? From being the container of the royal ancestral tablet, it came to symbolize the ancestors themselves. Now the graph for 'ancestor' is, as we have seen, written as in figure 14d in Chou inscriptions. According to Karlgren it is a picture of a phallus. Again, the cosmic deity Ti was also known by another name, T'u, the character for which is to-day written as in figure 14f; but, says Karlgren, its Chou form was also the phallus pictogram. The royal ancestor and the cosmic deity Earth were thus cognate ideas, since the same graph stood for both. Hence the symbol of the royal ancestor, the *ts'ung*, served also as the symbol of Earth – although Karlgren does not say at what time it acquired this secondary role; but, partly because of its primary association with the family of the feudal overlord, it remained also a symbol of aristocratic authority.

Michel's theory is that the *ts'ung* derives its form from the sighting-tube, *yü hêng*. He believes that it owes its connexion with Earth to its use as an astronomical instrument, since the *yü hêng* was presumably adjusted to the terrestrial horizon. He says that its original function had been lost sight of 'after the terrible wars of the last centuries B.C. and the systematic destruction of books under Shih Huang-ti'.[1] The implication seems to be that all pre-Han *ts'ung* were actual astronomical instruments.

But in fact Michel does not state whether he considers typical *ts'ung* such as those illustrated on plate 6 were ever used as observational tubes. All three are attributed to the Chou period by Jenyns,[2] and although this dating is of the 'traditional' sort, its plausibility is strengthened by a recent discovery of decorated *ts'ung* at T'ai-p'ing-ch'ang near Hanchow in Szechwan, a site that may be very much earlier than the beginning of the Chou period, but which is certainly not much later.[3] Assuming that the pieces illustrated are in fact Chou, could they all have been *yü hêng*? I scarcely think so. It is difficult indeed to see how the squat example could have been used as an obser-

1. H. Michel (see footnote p. 94), p. 156.
2. S. Jenyns, *Chinese Archaic Jades in the British Museum*, London 1951, p. xxxi.
3. For this find cf. D. C. Graham, 'A preliminary report of the Hanchow excavation', in *J.W.C.B.R.S.*, vol. vi (1933–4), pp. 114–31.

vational tube. As for the tall one, this is nearly 20 inches high; whereas Michel speaks of the *ts'ung* as 'a square prism, generally 4–10 inches long and 3–4 inches wide'. Again, the diameters of *hsüan chi* known to me range from about 4–6 inches. Michel calculates that for a *hsüan chi* with its outer diameter $5\frac{1}{4}$ inches, being used in the year 600 B.C., a *yü hêng* 4 inches long would have been needed. What are we to make of an object nearly five times that length? Quite evidently *some* pre-Han *ts'ung*, at least, were not functional *yü hêng*. They must have already acquired other functions. Michel shows well enough how the symbolic connexion between the astronomical instrument and the deity Earth might have arisen; but he says nothing to explain the other roles accorded to *ts'ung* by *Chou li*.

If, finally, we agree with Andersson that the prototype of the *ts'ung* was an object like the Neolithic ring shown in figure 13, what becomes of the theory that the *ts'ung* was itself originally a sighting tube? Michel illustrates an example which he calls a 'primitive *ts'ung* (or *hêng*)', and which he assigns to the Chou period. This object could no doubt have been used in combination with the *hsüan chi*, but it is nevertheless a descendant of the squat type, if Andersson is right. Since the latter would be of no use as a sighting tube, such a function on the part of its descendants would be secondary, not primary.

In this respect Michel's theory suffers from the same drawback as Karlgren's. For neither Michel nor Karlgren can demonstrate that types of *ts'ung* suited to the functions attributed to them by either theory are primary, not derived versions of the *ts'ung*. Under these circumstances I should like to suggest, very tentatively, the the squat variety of *ts'ung* may have preceded the tall type, and that the authors of *Ku yü t'u p'u* may not have been altogether wide of the mark when they identified these jades as wheel-naves. It is surely at least possible that they descend from a wooden Neolithic prototype which was a bearing inserted into the hub of the wheel, and inside which the axle rotated. That would account satisfactorily for their square outer perimeter, a characteristic that Laufer found irreconcilable with the idea that they were used as wheel-naves. That idea, one might add, dies hard. A squat jade *ts'ung* found at the T'ai-p'ing-ch'ang site is so described by D. S. Dye, who dates it to within three hundred years either way of 1000 B.C.[1]

1. D. S. Dye, 'Some ancient circles, squares, angles and curves in earth and stone in Szechwan, China', in *J.W.C.B.R.S.*, vol. iv (1930–31), pp. 97–105.

Decorative Objects in Jade

Most of these take the form of small carved plaques cut from slabs a few millimetres thick. In Hansford's opinion they were usually, if not invariably, cut with metal tools. Those found with Shang-Yin material, and those reasonably assigned to that dynasty, or to the early Chou period, form a well-defined class. A good many pieces are perforated, and we can assume that they were sewn on to clothing as amulets or articles of jewellery; or fixed, as by nails, to other objects perhaps made of wood.

A brief study of Neolithic material from Chinese sites, or from those in surrounding areas, will show us immediately that scarcely any representational art was attempted in prehistoric China. One of the greatest mysteries of Chinese archaeology, it seems to me, is the sudden and spontaneous outburst of animal representation that apparently coincided with the first historical dynasty and the Bronze Age as represented by the An-yang finds (p. 112). Animal designs are everywhere; and one can truly say that some of these figures, in sheer verve and vitality, have never been equalled anywhere else. The forms are usually stylized; but, if it is sometimes difficult to tell precisely what species of animal is portrayed, the impression created of a type – of what the late E. H. Minns called 'the pure idea' of a feline, bovine, fish, and so on – is instantaneous and unmistakable. Strict attention to diagnostic detail was evidently not uppermost in the designer's mind. He sought rather to interpret the essential, private *élan* of a whole class. More will be said in the next chapter about the problem of animal representation in archaic Chinese art. We reproduce on plate 8 a group of these small decorative objects without further comment here.

Until the excavations made by the Academia Sinica in 1934-5, sculpture in the round was hardly supposed to have existed in China before the Han dynasty. The extraordinary jade piece reproduced on plate 7a is, to the best of my knowledge, unique. It is supposed to have come from a Neolithic site south of T'ai-yüan in Shansi, and the Museum authorities at the William Rockhill Nelson Gallery of Art, Kansas City, to which it belongs, assign it to the second or third millennium B.C. It is 5½ inches long, and made of green nephrite.

This is sculpture in the round, and if it could be confidently assigned to the prehistoric period it would represent an astonishing *tour de force*;

for it would probably have been carved without metal tools. Even allowing that its date is more likely to be late in the second millennium, and that this piece is probably contemporary with the Shang-Yin dynasty, it is still a superb imaginative essay; a condensation of the essential features of the bird – perhaps a pigeon – made without the least trace of effort in its execution or loss of vitality in the result. Anyone familiar with the work of Henry Moore or Brancusi, in which directness of expression is achieved by rigid elimination of non-essentials, must surely be impressed by the same quality manifest in this carving. Cutting away of the lower surface into a sort of lug suggests that it was at one time socketed into some other object, although it would be difficult to say exactly what.

Chapter Three

BRONZE

The Beginnings of the Bronze Age in China

IN 1898 or thereabouts occurred an event that was to prove outstanding in the annals of Chinese archaeology. At the hamlet of Hsiao-t'un some 2 miles north-west of the city of An-yang, which lies on the Peking–Hankow Railway in northern Honan (map 3), were discovered thousands of inscribed bones and tortoise-shells. We are not sure how the attention of scholars was drawn to the find; but the story goes that some of the bones were sold by Peking druggists as that standard item of the old Chinese pharmacopoeia, 'dragon bones', and that the Grand Secretary Wang I-jung came across some of them being pounded up in his kitchen. It may have been he who recognized for the first time the archaic written characters we now know to be those of the Shang-Yin dynasty. Various scholars joined in the search for more bones, and for the place of origin. Despite a smoke-screen put up by dealers and other interested persons, the site was finally located some ten years later.[1]

Well over a hundred thousand inscribed fragments are now known, and as excavation at the site continues, still more of the writings are being found. Most are incised with some sort of stylus, but a very few are brushed; and they are generally rather short, rarely comprising more than a dozen or so characters. Thanks to the fact that the forms of these show likenesses to graphs inscribed on the bronzes of the following dynasty, the Chou, and thanks to a tradition of epigraphical studies that extends back in China for at least 2,000 years, most of the characters can be equated with modern forms and the contents of the inscriptions read.

Recent discoveries suggest that writing in Shang-Yin times may have been more widespread through society than was at first believed, for an inscription of sixteen characters on an ox scapula was

1. For an account of circumstances connected with the An-yang finds, and a summary of evidence linking the Hsiao-t'un site with a late Shang-Yin capital, cf. W. P. Yetts (see footnote p. 10).

found a few years ago on the site of a house thought to have been occupied by a commoner. But the vast majority of the inscriptions can properly be called part of the royal archives of the dynasty. They consist of questions put to the ancestors who acted as oracles for the ruling house, addressed through the agency of scribes–priests–diviners. The favourite bone was an ox scapula. Questions – and occasionally answers – were written on one surface; the diviner applied the point of a red-hot tool to a specially prepared lentoid cut on the other, and the verdict was read from the conformation of cracks that appeared on the front face. This was the distinctive technique of scapulomancy to which we have already referred (p. 19).

The An-yang finds proved what scarcely a Westerner had believed up to that time: that this dynasty, which is the second in traditional Chinese history-books (p. 10), really did exist. In 1929 the Academia Sinica began systematic excavation at An-yang. Not only did the dynasty exist, but it existed – or at least its aristocracy did – in conditions of almost unbelievable splendour. Foremost among the treasures recovered from An-yang are hundreds upon hundreds of finely-cast bronze vessels. We have already seen (p. 47) that orthodox history gives 1766–1122 B.C. as the period occupied by the Shang-Yin dynasty, and how there are reasons for supposing that it actually began about 200 years, and ended about 100 years, later. There is a well-established tradition that the site at An-yang was occupied by the nineteenth or twentieth Shang-Yin sovereign, P'an Kêng, 273 years before the end of the dynasty; or about 1300 B.C. on the basis of the revised chronology. Accordingly, we can safely say that the art of bronze-casting was fully fledged in China at least as early as 1300 B.C.

Now arises a most curious point. We cannot find the least trace of any antecedent to this bronze art of the late Shang-Yin period. The curtain rises on a climax. Among all the archaeological sites which from every point of view are considered earlier than that at An-yang, not a single piece of bronze has been found. At Hou-kang near An-yang, the stratification of red pottery of Yang-shao age or earlier at the bottom, black pottery above, and Shang-Yin ware at the top seems to prove that typical Black Pottery and Yang-shao Painted Pottery sites are earlier than An-yang (p. 48). It is at such sites that the search for traces of bronze intensifies. But nothing at all has come to light.

Absence of bronze from sites believed to date from before about

1300 B.C. has led many Western writers, probably the majority, to assume that the art of bronze-casting was not evolved independently in China, but was received in more or less mature form from some quarter between west and north. I have referred more than once to theories put forward by Western writers on the Western origins of the Chinese (p. 23 and pp. 44–5). Biblical and Classical traditions of scholarship did not always make for unbiased judgements; and still to-day one need be no blind believer in the autochthonous origins of Chinese civilization to detect a disingenuous occidentalism on the part of some writers who profess to find 'Western' ingredients therein, against the run of evidence, or in its absence. Let us glance at a few Western opinions on the Bronze Age in China.

Max Loehr, writing in 1949, said: 'Metallurgy seems to have been brought to China from outside. Whence, is an open question; but whatever the sources were, the way led via Siberia and possibly, Eastern Turkestan.'[1] Eberhard, in his *History of China*,[2] has a number of conflicting things to say about the Chinese Bronze Age. So, on page 11, he says of the 'Yang Shao culture' – by which he must mean either the Yang-shao stage of the Painted Pottery Culture or the Painted Pottery Culture itself – that 'metal was as yet unknown'. Then on page 14 comes the surprising statement: 'We first find an important element of advance, bronze, in China in traces in the middle layers of the Yang Shao, about 1800 B.C.' It must be pointed out that the term 'Yang-shao', as used by Andersson, designates only a *stage* in the Painted Pottery Culture of north China, one dated by him about 2200–1700 B.C. (p. 49); and that there is no evidence of bronze at any site of Yang-shao age yet discovered. Andersson states that the earliest Painted Pottery site containing metal known to him is that of Hsin-tien, dated roughly 1300–1000 B.C. – that is, contemporary with An-yang. Referring to Shang-Yin weapons recovered from An-yang, Eberhard continues: 'The forms of the weapons and their ornamentation show similarities with weapons from Siberia; and both mythology and other indications suggest that the bronze came into China from the north and was not produced in China itself.' Earlier opinions along the same lines were expressed by Bishop when he said: 'It seems certain that the Bronze Age civilization, as an integrated complex,

1. M. Loehr, 'Weapons and tools from Anyang, and Siberian analogies', n *A.J.A.*, vol. liii (1949), pp. 126–44.
2. W. Eberhard, *A History of China*, London 1950.

reached China by way of the Central Asiatic steppe belt'[1]; and by Creel, who said that 'the basic technique of manufacturing and casting bronze was probably imported to China from the West'.[2]

With the exception of Creel's, these opinions all centre on the idea that certain features of the bronze art of An-yang, especially a group of curved knives with ring-headed handles, originated in Siberia; and more particularly that part of south-west Siberia containing the head-waters of the Yenesei and Ob rivers. In this area scores of burial-mounds (kurgan) have been excavated in the last fifty or so years, and a relative chronology has been built up. Nobody doubts that there is some connexion between Bronze Age cultures of southern Siberia and that of China as represented by the An-yang finds. But disagreement arises over two points – the absolute dating of the Siberian cultures; and, more important, which way the cultural influence worked.

There are, as far as I am aware, no present means of assigning absolute dates to the Neolithic and early Bronze Age cultures of Siberia. Jettmar, in a recent survey,[3] says that the first, the Afanasievo, belongs in part to the third millennium B.C. and that the subsequent Andronovo culture came several centuries later. This is vague enough; but even assuming a date in the first half of the second millennium for the beginning of Andronovo, we are still no further forward in settling the problem of filiations between Siberia and China at that time. Use of metal in the Andronovo culture, according to Jettmar, is still very limited; so that 'we can scarcely believe that China got its knowledge of metallurgy from the Andronovo Culture'. Nor, I believe, has anyone suggested that this was the influential stage.

Third is Karasuk, a name given by the Russians to several cultures believed to be contemporary, all of which are related to that of Shang-Yin China, according to Jettmar. But the dating of Karasuk is uncertain. Indeed, some attempts to place it before 1300 B.C., or thereabouts, seem to depend only on the assumption that it must be older than An-yang, an assumption that has yet to be proved. A bare chronology of the Russian Neolithic and Bronze Ages by V. A. Gorodzov,

1. C. W. Bishop, 'The beginnings of North and South in China', in *P.A.*, vol. vii (1934), p. 307.

2. H. G. Creel (see footnote p. 26), p. 49.

3. K. Jettmar, 'The Altái before the Turks', in *B.M.F.E.A.*, no. 23 (1951), pp. 135–223.

published in the *American Anthropologist* in 1933, listed five cultures within the stage 1500–1000 B.C. Karasuk was named as the fourth of these, but no indication was given as to whether it was regarded as coeval with the others, or as last but one in a series. This unfortunate list has become the occasion of a stand-up fight between two notable contestants, Loehr and Karlgren; but the upshot seems to be that neither it nor any other of the many estimates offered for the date of Karasuk can be regarded as reliable, or as constituting evidence regarding the direction of cultural exchanges between metropolitan China and the steppes. We should note in this connexion that Loehr himself, the champion of Siberia, admits: 'As to the absolute date of the Karasuk knives, we have no means of fixing it more exactly than typology and comparisons permit to do …'[1] – and observe that one such comparison is presumably that of the An-yang knives with their fairly firm historical dates, 1300–1000 B.C.

I have dwelt at some length on this topic in order to show how, on the strength of the wretchedest evidence, far-reaching conclusions are being reached about the origins of the Chinese Bronze Age. The only view warranted by present evidence is the one put forward by Jettmar when he says : 'I do not believe we should decide which is the older and which the younger, before we can survey these cultures to their whole extent.'

It is in any case hardly conceivable that bronze-casting as it existed in the thirteenth century B.C. should have been a recent innovation in Shang-Yin China. The 'integrated complex' of which Bishop speaks contains not only metallurgy but also 'animal style' art – with its seemingly endless array of naturalistic and stylized animal-forms as portrayed on the bronzes – and a written language. The last is already a polished tool when we meet it at An-yang. Creel says of it: *Every important principle of the formation of modern Chinese characters was already in use, to a greater or less degree, in the China of the oracle bones, more than three thousand years ago.*[2] Through how many generations did the Chinese language mature before it reached the peak of perfection

1. M. Loehr, 'Ordos daggers and knives. New Material, classification and chronology. Second part: knives (with author's drawings)'. in *A.A.*, vol. xiv, pts. 1/2 (1951), p. 132. The reader who wishes to get to the bottom of the Sino-Siberian Bronze Age controversy might well begin his excavations with this monograph, in which most of the participants are named, and their contributions cited.

2. H. G. Creel (see footnote p. 26), p. 160.

represented by the oracle-bones? And if this development took place outside China, where? But assuming that it did not, and that its earlier traces are yet to be found in China, and nowhere else, is it not likely that a more primitive phase of bronze-casting will be found in association with it?

The fact that neither element is present in the pre-An-yang Painted Pottery sites of the Plateau is not surprising. These represent outlying communities, which probably continued to flourish at a Neolithic level, without either metal or a written language, until long after the historical period had opened in eastern China; just as did other Neolithic communities in Manchuria and elsewhere. What *is* significant, perhaps, is that these are precisely the areas where we should expect to find traces of bronze and of a written language, had they been introduced into China from abroad.

Briefly, then, here are two inventions brought to a high degree of technical perfection and beauty, occurring together on the eastern side of China. They contain, it is true, elements for which outside parallels can be found; yet on the whole they are both utterly distinct from anything of their sort known in any other part of the world. And the only reason we have for supposing that earlier phases of the history of writing and of bronze art did not occur in China, as far as I can see, is that they are as yet undiscovered. Field archaeology in that country is still much too backward for us to be able to make reasonable inferences based on what it has *not* brought to light, and the origins of the Chinese Bronze Age, I conclude, are as likely to be found there as anywhere else.

The Society of the Bronze Age in China

The period now under survey opens about 1300 B.C., and ends with the fall of the Chou dynasty in 256 B.C. Apart from the fact that much of what has been written on the early history and social and economic life of these times is conjectural, we cannot in any case do more here than indicate the general pattern of life in Bronze Age China. The period falls into three natural historical phases. First, that of Shang-Yin overlordship, lasting from 1300 to 1000 B.C. or thereabouts; second, that of Chou overlordship, lasting for the succeeding two and a half centuries; third, a phase of political struggle and active warfare between independent States paying only nominal allegiance to Chou rule, lasting about five centuries from the middle eighth to middle third centuries B.C.

The social and political conditions in China during the first of these periods can only be inferred. Probably the right picture is that of a number of isolated 'islands' of higher material culture and greater wealth, rising out of a background society practising a mixed economy based on hunting, food-gathering, and primitive agriculture. These wealthier communities had an advanced agricultural economy and the use of metal, yet the territory actually under their control may have been quite restricted. They lived in walled towns. Bronze was, of course, the material hall-mark of their society.

It is perhaps significant that the oldest Chinese bronze implements known are not tools, but weapons. Military superiority enabled the bronze-using city-dwellers to bring into subjection more and more of the surrounding stone-using peasantry, and thus the introduction of bronze, as Lattimore makes clear,[1] was not so much economic in its effects as social; it served to confirm the ascendancy of a city-dwelling, military aristocracy. Reserves of the metal were conveniently stored in the form of sacrificial bronze vessels which could be readily melted down to make weapons as need arose. Thus the ritual bronzes with which we mainly deal in this chapter were far more than the material concomitants of a distinctive system of ancestor and family worship; they were also a formidable reserve stock of war material. And bronze continued to fight for the feudal nobility throughout the entire Bronze Age. While agricultural craft-tools were still being made of stone right up to the coming of iron in the fifth century B.C., and beyond, bronze brought no benefits to the peasantry, whose only contact with the metal could have been in time of war. They must have feared and detested it.

The bearers of the 'higher' Chinese culture of the early Bronze Age – the peoples of the walled towns – were, of course, political and military rivals. They were not, naturally, all at the same stage of development; but all were passing along the same road, equipped with their specialized agriculture and their knowledge of metallurgy. It seems likely that the Chou peoples in the west were going through a phase of social and technological development when the Shang-Yin peoples in the east had already reached a constitutional society and passed over from aggressive warfare to defence. The Chinese historian Fu Ssŭ-nien

1. O. Lattimore (see footnote p. 11), pp. 267–74.

believes that the Shang-Yin peoples held northern Honan and Hopei, and that there was another political group in the east, the 'I barbarians', who were contemporary with the Shang-Yin and whose territory extended as far as the valley of the Huai River.[1] There is now, I believe, no question of any fundamental racial difference between these peoples.

We cannot, of course, build up an adequate picture of the Shang-Yin realm based on what we know of a single late site. Creel estimates its total extent at the time of An-yang as about forty thousand square miles. The reasons he gives for supposing that Shang-Yin control did not extend west of the T'ai-hang mountains of eastern Shansi, or south of the Yellow River, or east of the rivers that flow north-east across Hopei and Shantung into the Gulf of Chihli, seem to me entirely sound.[2] But one wonders whether it extended even as far as this. The An-yang site seems to have been chosen as a capital because of its natural defensive strength. The Huan River, on whose south bank it lies, encloses it on three sides. It is protected by a range of hills not more than 17 miles away to the west – and it was from the west that attack was most feared – whilst the stretch of level plain in which it lay was a guarantee against surprise attack. True, no trace of a Shang-Yin wall has yet been found; but the Black Pottery makers, who inhabited the nearby Hou-kang site at some earlier period, had a wall of stamped earth that was 12 feet thick at the base, and there is every reason to suppose that traces of the Shang-Yin wall will be found when excavation is extended to outlying parts of the site. Furthermore, this was the last or last but one Shang-Yin capital. And it seems reasonable to suppose that the overlordship was by this time waning in power. Its effective control may not have reached much further than to the agricultural plain in the immediate vicinity of what contemporary inscriptions call 'The Great City Shang'.

But even if we had detailed knowledge of the geographical frontiers of this Shang-Yin realm we would still be no wiser about those that must have preceded it. The Shang-Yin rulers moved their head-

1. Discoveries made between December 1951 and February 1952 in the Huai River valley included some pottery of Shang-Yin type. The cultural implications of this find have yet to be decided; in particular, whether the northern parts of Anhwei and Kiangsu were at one time part of the Shang-Yin realm, or whether this pottery was part of the material culture of the 'I barbarians'.

2. H. G. Creel (see footnote p. 26), pp. 136–7.

quarters many times. Because of this, some have thought that they were pastoral nomads; but that is quite out of keeping with what we know of their economy as we find it at An-yang. On the other hand, their traditions may have been migratory.[1] Indeed, Chêng Tê-k'un says, on what evidence I do not know, that their original home was probably in south Manchuria, and that they migrated thence to the north China plain as a result of unfavourable climatic conditions. In any case, I see no reason why the Shang-Yin comity should not have been fairly mobile, setting itself up and moving on again as circumstances dictated. If so, it seems impossible that the overlordship could have amounted to a permanent State.

We know next to nothing of the classes of society in Shang-Yin times. The existence of a hunting and warrior nobility, who were also landowners and slave-owners, has to be taken for granted; for such a group is not mentioned in contemporary inscriptions. But this was probably not a feudal aristocracy in the strict sense, since there was no decentralization of feudal power to speak of, and the nobility continued to live in the town. There was also an official class, among whom the scribes–priests–diviners were most important; and, as Creel says, 'there is some reason for believing that they may originally have been rather humble servants of the royal household, whose position gradually increased in power and dignity'.[2] A whole area at the An-yang site was evidently occupied by an industrial proletariat of builders, monumental masons, jade-carvers, bronze-casters, silk operatives, and so forth. Below the artisans was a fourth, indeterminate class of agricultural workers. Some of these were undoubtedly slaves, captured on military expeditions; others may have been serfs on the suburban estates of the landowning nobility, and local peasantry.

The second part of the Bronze Age opens with the Chou conquest of the Shang-Yin. Such an event is a natural starting-point for latterday myth-building and much of the Chou version of it shows signs of having been retrospectively concocted. But it seems safe to say that the Chou peoples came from the west, and followed the line of the Wei and Yellow River valleys in their march against the Shang-Yin;

1. There is, of course, a vital difference between pastoral nomadism and a migratory society 'practising', as Lattimore says, 'an agriculture that is permanent as a habit though temporary as to locality'. Cf. O. Lattimore (see footnote p. 11), p. 309.
2. H. G. Creel (see footnote p. 26), p. 129.

that they had known of the existence of the Shang-Yin for many generations; and that they recognized them to be the most advanced people living in the north China plain. They may have been their tributaries and keepers of their western marches.

We have already seen how a sense of cultural inferiority may have prompted the Chou to invent the genealogy that established their right to rule north China (p. 10). They claimed to be descended from the Hsia. But according to orthodox history the Shang-Yin genealogy also ran into the Hsia. Thus, however it came about, the Chou had managed to give themselves the air of being related to the Shang-Yin. Whether they were so in fact is open to question, although there are stories of Shang-Yin princesses being sent to the west as wives for their early rulers. In any case, there seems no doubt but that they valued Shang-Yin culture, and were anxious to preserve it. Indeed, within the bare limits of safety, they encouraged such potentially subversive practices as sacrificial rites to the Shang-Yin royal ancestors, which were carried out under their patronage.

Consider events that took place shortly after the Chou came into power. The first king of the new dynasty, Wu, enfeoffed the son of the last Shang-Yin king with the metropolitan part of the old Shang-Yin domain, the region then known as Mei. In taking over his fief the Shang-Yin vassal was assisted by two of King Wu's brothers. Wu died a few years later, and during the minority of his son a third brother, the famous Duke of Chou, acted as regent. The other two, probably in jealousy, incited the Shang-Yin vassal to revolt. With a great deal of trouble the Duke of Chou eventually crushed the rising, had the vassal put to death, and enfeoffed yet another of his own brothers with the old Shang-Yin territory, thereafter the State of Wei; and the inscription on the vessel illustrated on plate 14a refers to some of these events.[1] But it was evidently vitally important that the old Shang-Yin rites should be kept up. Within less than two years a half-brother of the last reigning Shang-Yin king had been found and given a small State in eastern Honan called Sung. And for nearly 700 years Sung State stayed a repository of Shang-Yin culture, a backwater shut off from the main current of political activity during the Chou period.

As far as concerns material culture, and particularly bronze-casting, there seems to have been no real break with tradition on the accession

1. For a translation cf. W. P. Yetts, 'An early Chou bronze', in *B.M.*, vol. lxx (1937), pp. 168–77.

of the Chou. Styles changed, but only gradually; the technique deteriorated, but only after some time. Faced with evidence of this sort, we can reach but one conclusion about the Chou people and their racial origins. They were not barbarians; nor were they invaders of different race. They were Chinese, whose social organization and material culture were simply provincial versions of Shang-Yin China. When the Chou came into power there was no period of acclimatization to be got through. Shang-Yin legal and penal codes, ceremonies, sacrifices, and so forth were readily understood, and quickly adopted, and the Chou settled down to administer the whole of China north of the Yangtze.

Taken all in all, it is perhaps remarkable that they held it together as long as they did. Their political conceptions, it is true, seem to have been much broader than those of their predecessors. But everything was against them. Their capital in the Wei River valley near modern Ch'ang-an was badly situated as a centre of government. It was ill-served with communications; and the country naturally broke up into cantons separated by formidable topographical barriers, each of which had the makings of an independent State. The policy of granting fiefs to its military aristocracy also held the seeds of an excessive decentralization of Chou rule. Each feudal overlord was the civil and military head of his fief, with every opportunity of making himself independent of the central authority. The year 771 B.C., when the Chou king moved his capital from the Wei River to Lo-yang in central Honan following attacks by the Jung barbarians, marks an end of effective Chou rule.

Throughout the third period – that of the so-called 'Spring and Autumn Annals' (722–481 B.C.) and 'Warring States' (481–221 B.C.) – the geographical field covered by 'Chinese' history was expanding. At the beginning of the Chou period fiefs were small, and there was a large number of them. Those on the periphery were 'warden' States – defensive outposts of the Chinese way of life set against the barbarian peoples who ringed it round. But the ultimate limits of possible Chinese advance had not been explored; and the first 300 years of Chou rule are marked by expansion and consolidation on the part of the border States, and by a series of barbarian wars. This encroachment, undertaken in the first place for purely defensive reasons, was carried on in four key areas – in the south, the north-west, the north, and the north-east; and it led to the rise of four great outlying powers: Ch'u in the south, Ch'in in the north-west, Chin in the north, and Ch'i in the north-east. So vast were the territories brought under the control of these four hegemonies that each individually probably came to control more effective power than the united efforts of the entire congeries of central States, the *chung kuo*, could command. The expansion of Ch'u throughout the Yangtze watershed, in particular, was a deliberate and successful piece of independent empire-building.

The political history of the period from 771 to 256 B.C. is complicated in detail, but its general pattern is easily grasped if we take into account the topographical position and consequent strategic requirements of each individual State. Each of the four big Powers made its bid for supremacy. Ch'in's final victory was due partly to a strong natural defence system, partly to ease of west–east communication along the Wei and Yellow River valleys into the north China plain, and partly to the uncompromising realism with which its rulers carried out their plan to bring all China under one rule (p. 176). The Ch'in Empire (221–206 B.C.) marks the end of feudal decentralization in China, and the beginning of bureaucratic administration and a central government; it also marks another stage in the age-old ebb and flow between Plateau and Plain.

When allowances for the special characteristics of each individual independent State have been made, the social organization of Chou times is seen to be roughly similar to that of the Shang-Yin overlordship. The basis of its economy remained an industrial and agricultural proletariat of artisans, peasants, and slaves. In a properly-run State, says Mencius, everybody should be able to eat meat and wear silk. Chou society, like that of the Shang-Yin, was all too clearly divided between a majority who ate millet, wore hemp clothes, and used stone implements and earthenware utensils, and a ruling minority of meat-eaters who wore silk and had bronze. The warrior nobility of Shang-Yin times has as its counterpart the five ranks of hereditary feudal aristocracy of the Chou. Merging into the lower reaches of the aristocracy on the one hand, and the upper ranks of the proletariat on the other, was a bureaucracy that served the political purposes of the feudal overlord, and later of the independent State. The most influential members of this class, the *shih*, were professional military and political advisers, scribes, and so forth; these were *literati*, and out of them emerged, towards the end of the Chou period, a distinctive group of scholar gentry of whom Confucius will serve as exemplar.

Among them, some closely identified themselves with the destinies of the States they served; but others managed to secure an independent, 'journeyman' status, and travelled from one State to another, selling policies the high-sounding moral tone of which all too often concealed only bare political expediency; yet others turned their backs on the whole sanguinary business and explored the domain of personal, private experience. By the fourth century B.C. every sort of philosophical doctrine, from the most outright totalitarianism to 'no-government' and the simple life, was being actively circulated. The range of late Chou philosophical speculation makes this the most brilliant period in the history of Chinese thought. Socially, the outcome was to create the nucleus of a scholar class destined to secure an unshakable hold on the administration of Imperial China.

Bronze Materials

The ritual bronze vessels of ancient China are among the most exquisite objects in metal ever made. We now know of over 12,000 of them, and about a third are inscribed. But not only do the bronzes form a *corpus inscriptionum* of surpassing interest to the historian; by their very existence they bring to life the whole character of the period in a way that no historical account could ever do. The secular bronze art has not the same stature, and we shall have less to say about it here. We propose, therefore, to discuss the materials and techniques of bronze casting; the functions of the ritual vessels; their classes; and the decorative styles they display. A study of inscriptions would take us too far into the fields of epigraphy and palaeography, and we shall do no more than mention their general nature.

In modern times nearly all copper and tin produced in China come from Yunnan and Kueichow in the south-west. Usable ores are not known to-day in the vicinity of An-yang, but there is a local tradition that both copper and tin were formerly mined in the mountains some 14 miles north-west of the site, as is suggested by the names of certain places in that region in which the word for 'copper', *t'ung*, occurs. The mountains themselves are called T'ung Shan.[1] Refining, smelt-

1. Cf. W. P. Yetts (see footnote p. 10), p. 25. He adds: 'Two other place-names, T'ung Shan Chên and Nan T'ung-yeh or Southern Copper Foundry, testify to the tradition.'

ing, and casting the metal were evidently carried on within the Shang-Yin city, for abundant remains of malachite and charcoal-slag, pottery moulds, and other foundry products have been found there. Copper and tin were used in the approximate proportions of 83 per cent copper and 17 per cent tin; but lead, which occurs in Mediterranean bronzes in proportions varying between 3 and 11 per cent, occurs only in traces, if at all, in Chinese alloys of the pre-Han period.[1]

Bronze-casting Techniques

Three main techniques seem to have been employed for casting bronze objects during the Shang-Yin and Chou periods. They can be set out as follows:

1. Direct casting by means of temporary moulds of sand.
2. Direct casting by means of piece-moulds taken from permanent positive matrices.
3. Casting by means of temporary moulds formed through the agency of a wax model; the *cire-perdue* process.

In the first of these three processes a model of the object to be cast was made, perhaps of wood. The front face of the model was then pressed into loamy sand contained in one half of a flat 'flask', and the reverse face into the other. The model was next removed, inlets or 'runners' and outlets or 'risers' for the molten metal were made in the sand, and the two halves of the flask bound together. Bronze was poured into the mould through the 'runners' until it overflowed from the 'risers'. When the casting was cool it was removed; the bronze that had solidified in the 'runners' and 'risers' was cut off, and the surfaces smoothed. This was a simple and effective method for casting flat objects such as weapons and decorative plaques, although the surfaces of casts tended to be somewhat coarse and granular. But under-cut relief or hollow objects could not be cast, and the ritual bronzes were not made by this method.

Direct casting of bronze vessels may have been possible by making

1. An analysis of one Shang-Yin bronze sample yielded the following percentages: copper 82·39; tin 15·42; lead 0·45; gold 0·38; iron 0·09; sulphur 0·115; residue 1·20. Cf. H. Fernald, 'A new Chinese bronze in the University Museum, Philadelphia', in *J.A.O.S.*, vol. li (1931), pp. 16–22.

use of piece-moulds. A number of fragments of composition-material have been recovered from the An-yang site, bearing negative patterns of typical bronze designs. Some of these fragments have smooth edges and are provided with keys by means of which they could be fitted together; in this way a complete mould could be built up around a clay or composition core, with a space left between representing the bronze vessel to be cast. Small particles of bronze have been found in some of this negative relief, according to Karlbeck,[1] so that direct casting from them may well have been attempted. The question is whether they could have been used more than once for this purpose. It is far more likely that they were used for impressing the design on a wax positive model or as beds on which the wax model could be built up, following the *cire-perdue* process. This will be explained below.

There is, in the Victoria and Albert Museum, a pottery object in the shape of a well-known type of bronze vessel, the *hu* (p. 146). This seems to have been used as a positive matrix from which negative clay mould-sections were taken off, for there are traces of shellac on its surface, and vertical scratches such as would be made by a knife separating the enveloping clay into sections.

The third method – the *cire-perdue* or 'lost-wax' technique – is undoubtedly that by which the majority of Shang-Yin and Chou ritual vessels were made. The first step in this process was to prepare a clay core in the shape of the interior of the vessel later to be cast. The outer layers of this core must have contained a refractory material, such as powdered fire-brick, capable of resisting the heat of the molten metal, and a finely-divided binding substance. Upon the core were brushed successive layers of wax, until a thickness had been built up equal to that of the wall of the projected vessel. This was the wax model.

The required design now had to be rendered upon the outer surface of the wax. This might have been done directly by tooling with a sharp instrument, or by pressing upon it, while soft, the above-mentioned piece-moulds.

The plasticity of the wax allowed the craftsman to achieve the finest imaginable detail, and amazing precision in carving its surface. Thus, the background design of very many early vessels is a sort of squared spiral which, on examination, is seen to be a strictly rectangular trough $\frac{1}{32}$ inch or less in width, and $\frac{3}{64}$ inch in depth. The side walls run down vertically to this depth, where there is a square corner, the

1. O. Karlbeck, 'Anyang moulds', in *B.M.F.E.A.*, no. 7 (1935), pp. 39-60.

width at the bottom being exactly that of the top.[1] The design having been completed, a surrounding clay mould had now to be built up. But first, wax leads had to be attached to the model at suitable points, whereby to form the hollow cavities of the 'runners' and 'risers' through which the molten bronze was to circulate when the wax had melted out. Upon the wax were now brushed successive layers of clay, mixed with the same refractory and binding elements used in building up the outer layers of the core. This was a crucial stage, for great care had to be taken to ensure that these first coats penetrated the finest details of the design; the outer layers could be more roughly brushed on, and coarser clay used. In this way a substantial outer mould was built up. Pins or dowels had now to be inserted through the whole contraption – outer mould, wax model, and core – in order to hold the latter in position when the wax had escaped; these pins were carefully placed so that their traces would not interrupt the design where it was intricate or important.

The mould was now placed in an oven and heated until all the wax had escaped through the channels provided. While the mould was still warm, molten bronze was poured down the 'runners' into the hollow space left by the escaped wax. As the level of molten metal rose in this space, so it rose also in the 'risers', until its appearance at the surface showed that the casting was complete. When cooled, the outer mould and the core were broken away, and all that remained was for the caster to remove the runners and risers and the ends of the bronze pins, and to tool the cut surfaces.

Of the *cire-perdue* process as used by the Shang-Yin Chinese, Creel says, 'We think of the work of Benvenuto Cellini as superlatively fine, but those who have examined his castings say that they are full of spots where, the metal having failed to fill out the mould, metal "plugs" have subsequently been inserted and finished off with tools. It is agreed that while a very few of the best living craftsmen in Europe or America, aided by all the resources of modern science and technology, may be able to equal the casting of the Shang bronze workers, they can do no better. Modern metal workers themselves candidly acknowledge this.'[2]

1. H. G. Creel (see footnote p. 26), p. 113.
2. H. G. Creel (see footnote p. 26), p. 112.

The Purpose of the Ritual Bronzes; Inscriptions

Ritual bronzes were made for actual use at ancestral sacrifices. Ancestors are, of all cosmic beings, those to whom the Chinese have traditionally given pride of place. They were to be consulted about every important matter of domestic concern; their memory and achievements were to be perpetuated by constant ritual observance. But the living, too, would one day become ancestors. They therefore looked to posterity fitly to honour their name in turn.

Judging from their inscriptions, Shang-Yin vessels were made in honour of particular individual ancestors. A few graphs serve to record the ancestor's name, and less frequently that of the person who had the vessel cast. But early in the Chou period the inscriptions underwent a change of character. They became fuller; and we can now see how vital was the role that they, and the vessels that carried them, played in feudal Chinese society and religion. Not only do they record the name of the ancestor in whose honour the vessel was cast; they almost invariably name the donor, and, since his wish was to make his name illustrious to posterity, the precise circumstances that led to the casting. A suitable occasion would be that upon which the ruler – or feudal overlord – conferred upon the vassal a fief, gifts of clothing, or some other reward in recognition of valued service. The inscription might then contain the following sorts of information:

1. The date and place of the audience.
2. The officials present.
3. The edict of investiture.
4. The vassal's thanks.
5. The vassal's resolve to cast a vessel, or vessels, to mark the occasion.
6. The names of the ancestors on whose behalf the vessel was cast.

The inscription would end with pious hopes – sometimes for long life on the part of the donor; almost always with the wish that the vessel should be used by posterity. The formula 'may sons and grandsons for a myriad years cherish and use (this precious sacral vessel)' crops up over and over again.

I append a typical example of one of these fuller inscriptions (figure 15). It is to be found on a vessel long known to Chinese scholars as the *Sung ting* because it was made to the order of a certain Sung, on

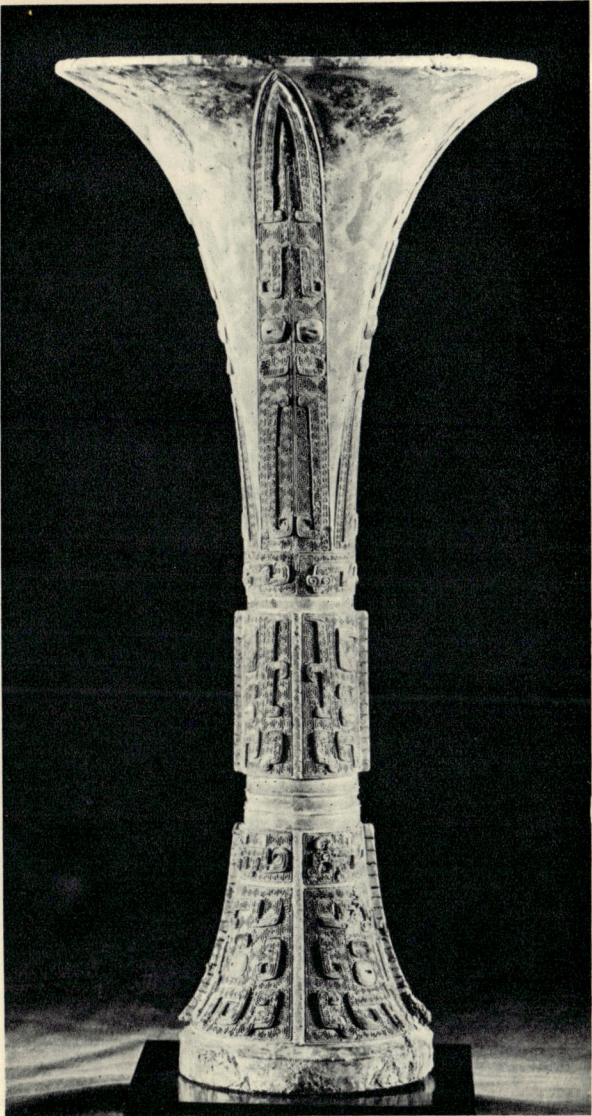

Ritual wine vessel, *ku*, First Phase (*c.* 1300–900 B.C.). H 13 ins (p. 148)

(A) Ritual food vessel, *ting*, First Phase (*c.* 1300–900 B.C.).
H 9¼ ins (p. 166)

(B) Ritual food vessel, *ting*, First Phase (*c.* 1300–900 B.C.).
H without handles 7 ins (p. 138)

(A) Ritual wine vessel, *yu*, First Phase (*c.* 1300–900 B.C.). H 10⅜ ins (p. 145)

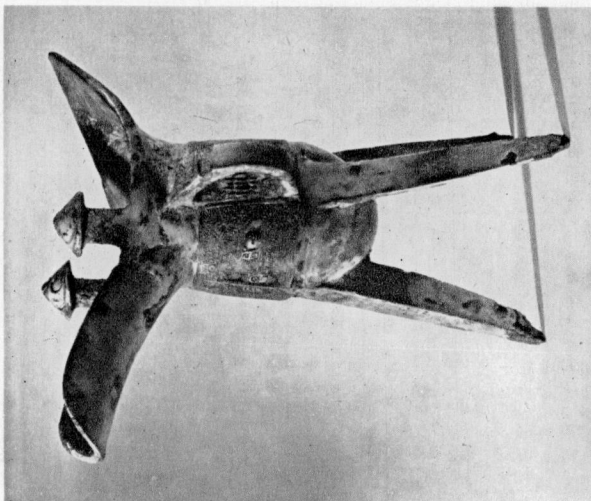

(B) Ritual wine vessel, *chüeh*, First Phase (*c.* 1300–900 B.C.). H 8 ins (p. 149)

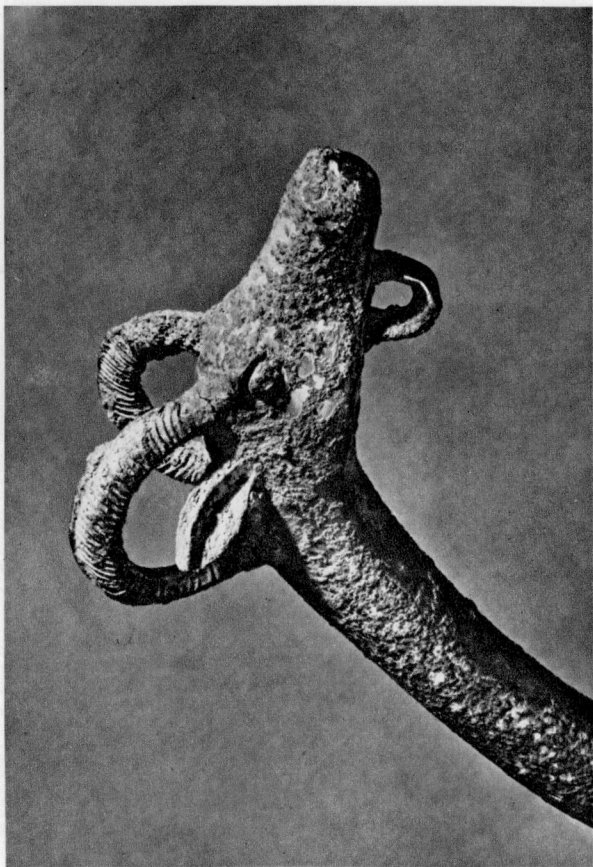

Cart-pole end in the form of an ibex head, early Chou dynasty (c. 1000 B.C.). L from muzzle to ear-tip 2⅝ ins (p. 155)

Ritual wine vessel, *tsun*, in the form of an elephant, First Phase (*c.* 1300–900 B.C.).
L 38 ins (p. 144)

13

(A) Ritual food vessel, *kuei*, First Phase (c. 1300–900 B.C.). H 9½ ins (p. 166)

(B) Ritual water vessel, *i*, Second Phase (c. 900–600 B.C.). L 15 ins (p. 152)

(A) Ritual water vessel, *p'an*, Second Phase (*c.* 900–600 B.C.). D 16½ ins. (p. 154)

(B) Ritual food vessel, *li*, Third Phase (*c.* 600–250 B.C.). H with lid 9¼ ins (p. 172)

15

Ritual wine vessel, *hu*, Third Phase (*c.* 600–250 B.C.). H 19 ins (p. 172)

an occasion when the Chou king sent him to govern Ch'êng Chou. This was a satellite town located some 10 miles east of the eastern Chou capital of Lo-i (770–255 B.C.), but the occasion celebrated in the inscription seems to have been before the move from the western capital of Tsung Chou – here simply called Chou – in 771 B.C.[1] It runs:

The 3rd year, 5th month, last quarter, *chia hsü* day; the King being at the Temple [of the former Kings] K'ang and Chao in the Chou capital. In the early morning the King arrived at the Great Room and took up his position. The Steward Hung assisted Sung in entering the Gate and taking his place in the middle of the Courtyard. The Lord of Yin received the King's Mandate. The King called upon the Recorder Kua Shêng to deliver the Decree in writing to Sung. The Royal Decree ran: 'Sung, we order you to [go and] govern Ch'êng Chou. We bestow on you [the income of] 20 families, and the supervision and charge of the newly-established [town of Ch'êng Chou]. We permit you to use the amenities of the Royal Palace, and bestow upon you a black garment, embroidered silk, a red skirt, a scarlet [jade half-ring] *huang*, a banner hung with bells and a horse-bridle, for use in your capacity as an official.' Sung prostrated himself, bowed his head, received the Decree Book, fastened it to his girdle, and so departed. In return he presented [a jade tablet] *chang* [and said]: 'I, Sung, dare in reply to proclaim the great glory and unfailing munificence of the Son of Heaven [the King], wherewith I shall make precious sacrificial wine and food vessels for my august father, my respected paternal uncle, my august mother, my respected paternal aunt, thereby to show my filial piety and to solicit tranquillity of heart, piety, pure blessing, a steady salary and long life. May I, Sung, enjoy a myriad years and the bushy eyebrows of old age. May I be a faithful servant, and may the Son of Heaven enjoy an auspicious end. May my sons and grandsons cherish and use [these precious sacrificial vessels].[2]

Classes of Ritual Vessels

Sacrifice to ancestors involved the offering of food and wine. Naturally, therefore, vessels for cooking, containing and serving

1. A reference to the temple of the deceased Chou king, Chao, indicates that the bronze was cast after his death. According to the revised chronology Chao was still reigning in 964 B.C. The *Sung ting* belongs stylistically to the Second Phase (pp. 167–70), and I myself would date it somewhere around the end of the ninth century B.C.

2. For help received in translating this inscription, I am indebted to Mr Wu Shih-ch'ang.

頌鼎釋文

隹三年五月既死霸甲戌
王在周康卲宮旦王格大
室即位宰弘佑頌入門立
中庭尹氏受王命書王呼
史虢生冊命頌王曰頌命
汝官𤔲成周貯廿家監𤔲
新造貯用宮御賜汝玄衣
黹純赤市朱黃䜌旂攸勒
用事頌拜䭬首受命冊佩
以出反入瑾璋頌敢對揚
天子丕顯魯休用作朕皇
考龔叔皇母龔姒寶尊鼎
用追孝祈匃康虔純祐通
祿永命頌其萬年眉壽
畯臣天子靈終子=孫=寶用

Figure 15. *Above*, inscription on the *Sung ting*; *below*, its decipherment into modern Chinese.

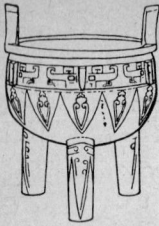
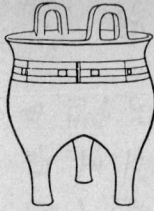

A

1　2　3
4　5

C

15
16
17

Figure 16. Bronze vessel types.

A. Food vessels: 1 *ting*, 2 *li*, 3 *hsien*, 4 *tou*, 5 *kuei*.

B. Wine vessels: 6 *ku*, 7 *yu*, 8 *hu*, 9 *ho*, 10 *chia*, 11 *chih*, 12 *tsun*, 13 *kuang*, 14 *chüeh*.

C. Water vessels: 15 *p'an*, 16 *chien*, 17 *i*.

128

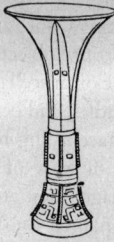
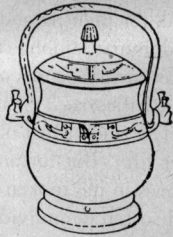

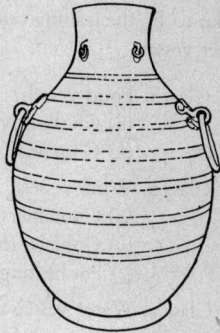

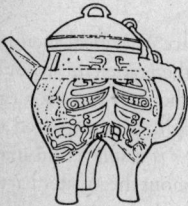
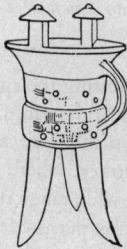

food, for pouring and drinking wine, and for mixing it with water, predominate among ritual bronze objects. There is also a small class of water utensils, and a number of miscellaneous objects associated with the sacrifice, such as tables, ladles, and bells. The total number of separately-named ritual objects, according to some classifications, is well over fifty. But fortunately, in view of the great number of homophones in the spoken language, they are all pronounced differently, and so can be individually named for Westerners by romanization, without reference having to be made to their written characters. For description here I have selected seventeen only. These classes, which I take to be the leading ones, are grouped below as food, wine, and water vessels.

Class 1. Food vessels:
    (*a*) Cooking vessels: *li, ting, hsien.*
    (*b*) Containers: *kuei, tou.*

Class 2. Wine vessels:
    (*a*) Containers: *tsun, yu, hu.*
    (*b*) Goblets: *chüeh, chih, ku, chia.*
    (*c*) For heating wine, or mixing it with water: *ho, kuang.*

Class 3. Water vessels:
    (*a*) Basins: *p'an, chien.*
    (*b*) Ewers: *i.*

The simplest way of indicating the appearance of typical members of these classes is by means of drawings. But the reader must not assume that the shapes shown in figure 16 are the only ones for each class of vessel. On the contrary, where we might have expected the most rigid conservatism, a wide range of shapes is displayed in many vessel classes; and where a class persisted throughout the greater part or the whole of the period, a distinct evolution of both shape and style can be discerned. Nor was shape necessarily uniform for any given type during a single phase. The typical early *ting* was a bowl-shaped vessel (plate 10*a*); but a rectangular version existed alongside it (plate 10*b*).

With the probable exceptions of the *chien* water-vessels, and perhaps of the *p'an*, all the classes of ritual bronzes listed above had been established by late Shang-Yin times, as represented by the An-yang site. One of the most powerful arguments, it seems to me, in favour of the idea that the Chinese Bronze Age must have had a long early history of which we as yet know nothing, is the fact that these bronze shapes – so unlike anything we can point to in western Asiatic or nomad art – should by then have reached so high a degree of individuality, a climax – not necessarily ultimate – in the evolution of their form. Consider, for example, the *chüeh* (plate 11*b*). Could formal elaboration be pushed further? In the extravagance of this weird shape, with its strange and at first sight meaningless excrescences, we surely have something analogous to what a biologist would call racial senility. And *à propos*, not only does the form of the *chüeh* show no evolution beyond this point, but the vessel itself seems to have died out after Shang-Yin times. Part of its ancestry, and indeed that of every ritual bronze vessel-type, was doubtless recorded in some other material – pottery, for example, or horn – but I am reluctant to believe that the final shape of the *chüeh* is anything other than a bronze one. When in fact we compare the shapes of these bronzes with pottery forms that have been cited as their ancestors, we find that in almost every case there comes a perceptible gap between the most highly-evolved pottery example and the simplest bronze version known. To this degree, at least, the bronze shapes are *sui generis*, and their history is written in bronze alone.

But, with that reservation, we must still look for the ultimate ancestors of bronze ritual vessels in the pre-metal sites of north China. Most seem to have had pottery prototypes. Furthermore, the number of these prototypes is fewer than that of the bronze classes they give rise to. Some bronzes, that is to say, seem to share common pottery ancestors (cf. figure 24). There is therefore a degree of organic unity between them, and we cannot expect to draw hard-and-fast lines between their shapes, any more than a biologist can between certain closely-related species of animals or plants. But not all the prototypes need have been of pottery. Perhaps some were made of horn or even of gourds. The archaeologist Kuo Pao-chün has claimed horn ancestors for both the *ku* and *chüeh*; his views will be described later, in the section devoted to these two vessels.

There remains to be mentioned the vexed question of the identification of the ritual vessels by name. Since no detailed contemporary descriptions exist, the only way we can be quite sure we are calling a vessel by its right name is when it is self-named in its inscription. It then establishes its own class. But less than two-thirds of all vessel classes can provide self-named examples. Of the seventeen surveyed here, nine can be so identified; they are the *li, ting, hsien, kuei, hu, ho, p'an, chien*, and *i*. Of the remaining eight, there is some doubt about the *chüeh* class, while the *tsun*, for reasons that will be explained presently, is a class rather apart; but the others – *tou, yu, kuang, ku, chih*, and *chia* – contain no specimens bearing their own names. The question is, then, how were names and identifications arrived at in these cases, and are they valid?

Very much the same circumstances applied as in the case of the ritual jades. Again the critical point seems to have been reached in Han times, after the upheavals of the third century B.C. Privately owned bronzes had by then been extensively confiscated by the heads of States and melted down for weapons, or else had been buried for safety's sake; so that sacrificial vessels had become rarities, and the occasional finding of one was greeted as an auspicious omen. When, in 112 B.C., a *ting* cauldron was retrieved from the Fên River in Shansi, such a stir was created that the reign-period beginning 116 B.C. was given an appropriate new name to commemorate the event. Some types of vessels, it is true, continued to be made in Han times, but only, apparently, for domestic use. A good many other classes had disappeared completely.

Han lexicographers and commentators on the classics thus faced a familiar situation – a large number of names of objects in pre-Han texts, for which no corresponding examples were now known. Accordingly, in describing the appearance of these vessels, they resorted to their imaginations. Those whose comments were later allegedly reproduced in *San li t'u* together with drawings of ritual objects ascribed to them, seem to have had not the remotest idea what the real vessels looked like. Their speculations in connexion with the class of vessel we now call *tsun* will be discussed below (p. 144).

But the Han scholars fell into more serious error. In Chou times names of ritual vessels often differed from State to State, and no doubt at different periods. These names found their way into pre-Han texts, and scholars often failed to recognize the synonyms. The result is that an unwarrantable number of classes got established.[1] The effect is not so noticeable among the classes with which we deal, for they include

1. A typical example of confusion resulting from multiplication of names on the one hand and loss of the originals on the other, is that of an alleged class called *mou*. Jung Kêng, in his *Han tai fu yü ch'i k'ao liieh*, 'A study of domestic utensils of the Han period', in *Y.J.C.S.*, no. 3 (June, 1928), says that only one

the most distinctive and oldest established; but in some of the less venerable classes, especially perhaps the *chien* and those called *yü* (not to be confused with *yu*), *an*, *hsi*, *hsüan*, and *p'ên*, shapes are so similar that one is bound to wonder whether some of them might not advantageously be eliminated.[1]

By Sung times a great revival in antiquarian studies was under way. It seems that the Sung Emperors wanted to surround themselves with examples of ancient high art, not only because of the intrinsic worth of the pieces, but also in order to build a material background against which Chou rites and ceremonies could be re-enacted. An imperial collection was begun as early as A.D. 1051. Fifty years later it contained over 500 pieces; and by the end of the reign of Emperor Hui Tsung (A.D. 1100–1125), on the eve of the destruction of K'ai-fêng by the Chin nomads (p. 527), it numbered over 10,000 pieces, many of them bronzes. Wealthy members of the official class were not slow to follow the imperial example. The first great illustrated catalogue of antiques, *K'ao ku t'u*,[2] lists objects – mostly bronzes – in the possession of thirty-seven private collectors as well as the Emperor. Vessels were assiduously sought; one official went so far as to pardon the crimes of criminals who succeeded in finding them for him. And we have direct evidence that by the end of the eleventh century A.D. the An-Yang site was yielding some of its store.

K'ao ku t'u and its fellow *Hsüan-ho po ku t'u lu*[3] set a new standard in Chinese antiquarian researches. Some of their explanations of decorative motives still have a moralizing flavour about them, and their identification of certain vessels as the personal property of well-known historical persons is certainly injudicious, but on the whole both

example of this class is known. His drawing of it, taken from another source, singularly fails to convince. Commenting on the name *mou* for a cooking vessel, Yen Shih-ku (A.D. 581–645) cites an unnamed authority who said: 'The *mou* is a small type of *fu*; what we nowadays call a *kuo*. It is also called a *tsŭ lo*.' Jung Kêng adds, reasonably, that Yen Shih-ku seems never to have seen a *mou*. Nor, perhaps, has anyone else.

1. In another paragraph Jung Kêng says that the only difference he can find between the vessels *hsi* and *hsüan* is that the inscriptions are not placed on the same parts of the body. This is scarcely a typological distinction.

2. *K'ao ku t'u*, by Lü Ta-lin. Preface dated A.D. 1092. Editions of A.D. 1600 and A.D. 1753 (revised).

3. *Hsüan-ho po ku t'u lu*, by Wang Fu and others. About A.D. 1123. Extant editions are of A.D. 1600 and A.D. 1752 (revised).

books are remarkably free from flights of fancy. The authors of *Hsüan ho po ku t'u lu* state that they personally examined most of the bronzes they illustrate; and indeed, despite having been re-cut many times since the original edition was prepared, these drawings and the wood-block imitations of ink-squeezes of inscriptions accompanying them have an air of verisimilitude altogether different from anything that had gone before. We reproduce as figure 17 a cut redrawn from the

Figure 17. *a, kuei* redrawn from *K'ao ku t'u*, compared with *b, kuei* in the William Rockhill Nelson Gallery of Art, Kansas City.

1753 edition of *K'ao ku t'u* put beside a drawing of an actual bronze vessel of the *kuei* class (p. 140). When allowances have been made for the linear conventions of the Chinese cut, it will be seen that the two are remarkably alike. The style much resembles that of bronze vessels excavated in 1923 in the town of Hsin-chêng, Honan, one closely similar to that of the *i* ewer of plate 14*b*. We need have no doubt that the Sung cataloguer had before him an actual Chou dynasty bronze of this style and period, the seventh–sixth century B.C. (pp. 167–70). Another example is given by Professor Yetts, whose drawing of a casket-shaped vessel recently excavated from An-yang is placed against a woodcut from the 1752 edition of *Hsüan-ho po ku t'u lu*. This shows a piece that the authors wrongly attribute to the Han period. But, as Yetts remarks: 'These two are so obviously alike, except as to minor details, that there can be no doubt that they belong to the same time and place' – that is, to the Shang-Yin period and the An-yang site.[1]

Revived interest in epigraphy, based on actual inscriptions, had started as far back as the fourth century A.D., and by Sung times a number of works on the subject had been written, of which seventeen still survive. Bronze graphs could now be deciphered and equated with current forms without much difficulty; so, in the case of self-named vessels, direct identification was possible. In other cases Sung cataloguers had to rely on inspired guesswork by which to identify the vessels themselves from brief descriptions of their functions in pre-Han texts, and from definitions offered by *Shuo wên* and other Han writings; in this manner they identified such vessel classes as *yu*, *ku*, *chüeh*, and *chih*, for which no self-named examples were known. Criticisms of their classification can, of course, be made; they have a tendency to use the generic name *tsun* as a sort of dumping-ground for vessels about whose precise status they were doubtful, and we thus find bronzes that to-day would certainly be called *hu*, *ku*, and *lei* capriciously assigned to that over-burdened class. Again, they make no distinction between *kuang* – vessels now believed to have been used for wine – and the water-ewers, *i*. And again, it is difficult to see why, having christened one square casket with the name *fang i*, 'rectangular sacrificial vessel', they should have chosen to identify two similar specimens of this early class as *Han lien* or 'Han toilet boxes' which they obviously are not. But these are minor exceptions. The Sung identifications have mostly stood the test of time.

1. Cf. W. P. Yetts (see footnote p. 10), p. 24 and figs. 5 and 6.

Arbitrary multiplication of bronze classes continued. The eighteenth-century Imperial catalogue *Hsi ch'ing ku chien* names no fewer than seventy-two. This number has in recent years been reduced by Jung Kêng to fifty-five; and Yetts, writing in 1929, proposed a list of twenty-five only, which he considered sufficiently distinctive to form valid classes.[1] It should be said that this list includes only ritual vessels and not other objects in bronze such as bells and drums whose purpose, too, was ceremonial.

We now propose to say a little in turn about each of the classes listed above. Our remarks will be confined to brief discussion of possible prototypes, general appearance, use, and main changes in form of each, as well as to broad generic relations between them. Their decorative treatment is dealt with separately; it does not vary very much from class to class.

1: LI (plate 15*b*)

This group takes its place at the head of the list both because of its antiquity and because of the distinctive shape of these vessels. Mention has already been made of *li* on p. 19, and on pp. 45–6 their distribution in north China during Neolithic times has been discussed at some length. We have seen that the pottery *li* is a regular inhabitant of the Honan–Shantung area, but only a haphazard and late visitor in Neolithic sites west of Honan. 'It is as though', says Creel, 'a magic circle has been drawn about the Honan–Shantung area, forbidding the *li* to leave it.' The pottery *li* is a substantially built vessel with a fairly wide range of shapes; but all are characterized by the fact that the lower part of the body runs smoothly into three hollow, bulbous legs, often with a striking resemblance to breasts (figure 18*a*). No doubt this resemblance is intentional, and sympathetic magic is intended. But, more practically, the cavity in the legs is a device by which cooking food is brought into closer contact with the heat of the fire. The form, as Creel says, is 'typically Chinese, unknown in other parts of the world'.[2]

The graph used for *li* (figure 18*b*–*d*), both on the oracle bones and

1. W. P. Yetts, *The George Eumorfopoulos Collection Catalogue of the Chinese and Corean Bronzes, Sculpture, Jades, Jewellery and Miscellaneous Objects. Vol. 1, Bronzes: Ritual and other Vessels, Weapons, etc.*, London 1929, pp. 42–51.
2. H. G. Creel (see footnote p. 26), pp. 48, 44.

in bronze inscriptions, shows what is evidently a picture of a pottery prototype such as that of figure 18a, a vessel of Yang-shao age, the salient features of which are three hollow legs, constricted neck, tall collar, and wide mouth. Some modification has taken place in the earliest

Figure 18. *a*, prehistoric pottery vessel excavated by Andersson; *b–d*, oracle bone graphs, apparently showing the same type of vessel and equated with the modern character for *li*, 'tripod'.

bronze versions we know. Instead of one or two handles placed at the side, bronze *li* normally have a pair of upright handles or 'ears' mounted on the mouth-rim, and the contours are less abrupt; but the derivation of the bronze form cannot be mistaken (figure 16A2). The class is self-named. It was made during the whole period under survey as well as during Han and later. The form is fairly constant, but there is a version with four legs instead of three, and a shallow type with flat spans between the legs and no handles that Karlgren says is distinctive of the Second Phase.[1] Some late bronze *li* have covers (plate 15*b*).

2: TING (plate 10*a, b*)

This class of cauldron is almost, if not quite, as ancient as the *li*; for pottery *ting* of Yang-shao age are known (figure 24*a*), and the question arises what, if any, is the relationship between them? The difference is that the legs of *ting* are solid and more or less cylindrical, and the body is more strictly hemispherical than in the case of *li*. The Han dictionary *Êrh ya* defines the *ting* as a *li* with solid legs; this is apt enough, but does not, of course, imply that the author considered the latter ancestral to the former. In fact, there is an intermediate pottery form, also rendered in bronze, that Karlgren calls *li-ting* (figure 24*c*). The legs of this vessel are hollow, but do not stand closely together, their junction with the body being 'sudden', like those of the *ting*. It would be tempting to regard this as the ancestral form from which both *li* and *ting* descend, yet its shape is more complex and subtle than either, and one is inclined to see it rather as their offspring, inheriting features from each. There, for lack of still earlier pottery forms, the problem remains. But I have no doubt at all that Andersson is right in supposing that the *li-ting* is not simply a dead-end ceramic form, but that it continued to evolve in the direction of the bronze *chia* and perhaps the *chüeh*. This aspect of the matter will be discussed below (p. 149).

Some bronze *ting* are self-named. The class was made throughout the whole known Bronze Age and on into Han times. Indeed, one doubts whether there was a time when *ting*, in one material or another, were *not* made in China. *Ting* of the First Phase are of two types. One has a round and rather deep, bowl-shaped body with 'ears' mounted on the mouth-rim, as in the case of *li* (plate 10*a*); the other is a rectangular form on four legs (plate 10*b*), and this variety is sometimes covered. Later *ting* show much modulation of form. In the Second Phase the body becomes shallower, and 'ears' no longer rise from the mouth-rim, but are mounted on the body, whence they curve out-

1. I anticipate here, by introducing a style period. Briefly, the First Phase of Chinese bronze art lasts until the ninth century B.C., the Second Phase from the ninth to the sixth century B.C., and the Third Phase from the sixth century to the end of the period (pp. 160–73).

ward and upward. Legs become thin and attenuated, and splay out at the junction with the body and at the foot so that they look rather like the legs of Chippendale chairs. An even greater variety of form is found in the Third Phase. The square type reappears, sometimes provided with a spout, opposite which is a single handle. As a rule, late *ting* are covered, and the cover has three equidistant projections – sometimes small animals modelled in the round (figure 29), sometimes ring handles – whereby the cover when turned over can be used as an accessory dish.

3: HSIEN

Vessels of this distinctive class may be described as 'steamers'. The form is composite, the lower portion of the vessel being shaped like a *li*, into the mouth of which fits a deep, bowl-shaped vessel. In bronze specimens the two portions may be cast separately or, more usually,

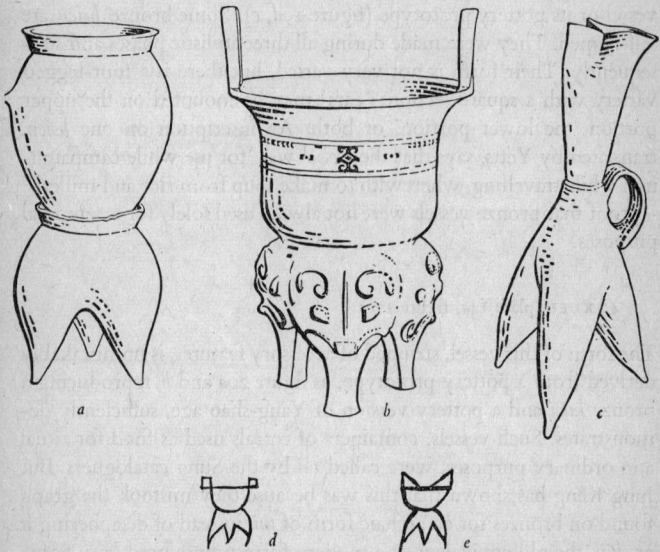

Figure 19. *a*, two prehistoric pottery vessels put together by Andersson to make a *hsien*; *b*, Shang-Yin bronze *hsien*; *c*, prehistoric pottery *hsien* from Manchuria; *d*, *e*, oracle bone graphs, apparently showing the same type of vessel and equated with the modern character for *hsien*, 'steamer'.

as one. The idea underlying the *hsien* is that food placed in the upper portion of the vessel is cooked by steam heat coming from the lower. Accordingly the bottom of the upper part of the vessel is perforated in pottery examples. In bronze specimens a grille is hinged on to the brim of the lower part, or to the base of the upper.

Andersson believes he has found prototypes of bronze *hsien* in pottery of Yang-shao age. At the site of Pu-chao-chai in Honan he found a vessel the inside bottom of which was perforated and coated with 'fur'; and in the same locality a *li* came to light which had a ridge running round the inside of the mouth, such as might have served to support an upper vessel. He accordingly reconstructed a prehistoric *hsien*, reproduced in figure 19*a*. I have added, for comparison, a pottery *hsien* from a south Manchurian site (figure 19*c*). But this latter is contemporary with the historical period in China, and should not be thought of as ancestral to dynastic bronze *hsien* (figure 19*b*).

The graph for *hsien*, as it appears on bronzes, shows a picture of the vessel or its pottery prototype (figure 19*d*, *e*). Some bronze *hsien* are self-named. They were made during all three stylistic phases and subsequently. Their form is not very varied, but there is a four-legged variety with a square section; 'ears' may be mounted on the upper portion, the lower portion, or both. An inscription on one *hsien*, translated by Yetts, says that the vessel was 'for use while campaigning, while travelling, wherewith to make soup from rice and millet' [1] – proof that bronze vessels were not always used solely for ceremonial purposes.

4: KUEI (plate 14*a*, figure 17*b*)

The form of this vessel, stripped of accessory features, is unmistakably derived from a pottery prototype, as figure 20*a* and *b*, reproducing a bronze *kuei* and a pottery version of Yang-shao age, sufficiently demonstrates. Such vessels, containers of cereals used as food for ritual and ordinary purposes, were called *tui* by the Sung cataloguers. But Jung Kêng has shown that this was because they mistook the graph found on bronzes for an archaic form of *tui*, instead of deciphering it as *chiu*, the old equivalent of a modern form pronounced *kuei*. Some *kuei* bear their names in their inscriptions; and the class continued to be made through into Han times.

1. W. P. Yetts (see footnote p. 136), p. 44.

Variant shapes are numerous. The starting-point is a round, rather shallow bowl mounted on a wide, shallow, and slightly spreading base (plate 14a). The bowl may have no handles at all, or two laterally-placed vertical handles, or four; or else the handles may be L-shaped ears, mounted below the mouth-rim, as in Second Phase *ting*. Special care was devoted to the design of the handle; the upper part is normally an animal mask, and from the underside of the lower part hangs a pendant that sometimes seems to simulate the tail, feet, or claws of a bird. Sometimes, on four-handled *kuei*, these downward projections

a   *b*

Figure 20. *a*, prehistoric pottery vessel excavated by Andersson; *b*, Shang-Yin bronze *kuei*. (Redrawn from Andersson.)

are continued so as to form legs by which the vessel is raised aloft. All known *kuei* seem to have had covers, and these could usually be reversed to act as extra dishes. Second Phase *kuei* are often mounted on a massive square stand cast together with the rest of the vessel; but *kuei* shapes are curiously unpredictable, and sometimes three rather puny-looking legs are found instead.[1]

5: TOU

Pottery ancestors of these food containers have been recovered in some numbers from the Black Pottery site of Ch'êng-tz'ǔ-yai, and also from Yang-shao and other sites in the Honan–Shantung area. The shape of the pottery version is like a cake-stand, and comprises a shallow dish mounted on a tall stem with a flared base (figure 21a); that of

1. An odd example in the Brundage Collection has a clapper-bell fixed on the inside of the hollow base.

the bronze *tou* is clearly derived from it. But there is a covered bronze variety wherein the bowl is a good deal deeper, so that when the cover is mounted the appearance is of a squat globe (figure 16*A*4). The lower portion of the vessel always rests on a tall flared stem; whereas the cover, which can be reversed to act as an independent vessel, is either provided with a single short flared projection to act as handle or foot, or with three equidistant ring-handles or small naturalistically modelled animals.

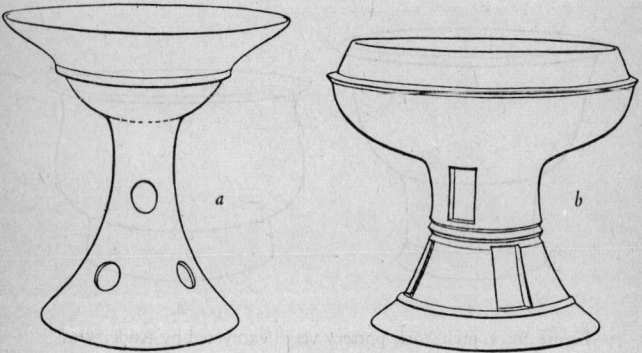

Figure 21. *a*, prehistoric pottery vessel excavated by Andersson; *b*, pottery *tou* from Korea, third–fifth centuries A.D.

No *tou*, as far as I am aware, is self-named. The class as we know it is a late one; in fact I can recollect no example in bronze earlier than the Third Phase. But the vessel was made well on into Han times in China, and in even later periods elsewhere. We reproduce for comparison (figure 21*b*) a pottery piece recently recovered from a grave in Korea, thought to date from the third–fifth centuries A.D. Likeness to its Neolithic Chinese ancestor is startling.

6: TSUN (plate 13)

This class, etymologically speaking, is not really a class at all. The oracle bone version of the modern character for *tsun* shows a narrow, bottle-shaped vessel with pointed base, tall neck, and somewhat flared mouth, held aloft by a pair of hands (figure 22*b*). Such vessels are familiar ingredients of Neolithic cultures outside China, not only in the Far East; and inside China they have been found at Yang-shao Ts'un and other sites of Yang-shao age. Andersson says that Chinese examples are of an advanced type, and that 'they certainly served very specific purposes and were placed in stands, the nature of which we can only conjecture'.[1] He also believes that the *li* tripod shape may have come about by fusing together three of these Neolithic '*tsun*' to make a single vessel. An outline drawing of a typical example of Yang-shao age is here placed alongside the oracle bone character for

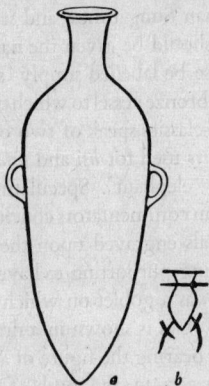

Figure 22. *a*, prehistoric pottery vessel excavated by Andersson, compared with *b*, oracle bone graph, apparently showing a pot of the same type, and equated with the modern character for *tsun*, 'sacrificial vessel'.

tsun (figure 22*a*, *b*). Neither vessel nor character bears any resemblance to the ritual vessels called *tsun* by Sung and later antiquarians.

The graph for *tsun*, often written with an additional element on the left, crops up time and again on ritual bronzes; very often either in the expression *pao tsun i* or *pao tsun ting*. An instance of the latter occurs in the inscription we have already translated, the three characters concerned being the eighth, ninth, and tenth of the twelfth column from the right. Both formulas have the meaning 'precious sacral vessels'; and it is quite evident that the word *tsun* in bronze inscriptions

1. J. G. Andersson (see footnote p. 37), p. 230.

has a general sense of 'sacrificial vessel' or possibly, more specifically, 'sacrificial wine vessel', but does *not* refer to any particular class of these.

We have already noted (p. 135) that the Sung cataloguers gave the name *tsun* to vessels that we would nowadays call *ku*, *hu*, and *lei*. Bit by bit the notion arose that vessels of a type resembling squat *ku*, but too large to have been used as goblets, were the original *tsun*; and the name is now fairly generally used by museum curators and collectors to label such vessels. This is undoubtedly a misnomer. Precedent for the usage is no older than Sung times, and it should be abandoned. In such cases the vessel should be given the name of the specific class it most resembles, or else be labelled simply 'sacrificial vessel'.

Is there, then, a class of bronze vessel to which the name *tsun* is correctly applied? Probably. The classics speak of two objects: the *hsi tsun* and the *hsiang tsun*. Characters used for *hsi* and *hsiang* mean, respectively, 'sacrificial animal' and 'elephant'. Speculating on the meaning of these expressions, the Han commentators concluded that vessels having representations of animals engraved upon them were meant. In the extant *San li t'u* a drawing purporting to have been made by Chêng Hsüan shows the *hsi tsun* as a goblet on which is an engraved outline of a phoenix. The *hsiang tsun* is shown in a drawing ascribed to Juan Ch'ên as a similar vessel bearing the figure of an elephant. Then, during the reign-period A.D. 307–13, the tomb of Duke Ching of the old Ch'i State at Ch'ing Chou was broken into, and two wine-vessels cast in the shape of oxen were taken from it. The secret was out. *Hsi tsun* were vessels modelled in the shape of sacrificial animals or birds; and *hsiang tsun* were modelled in the shape of elephants (plate 13).[1]

The Sung cataloguers proceeded to identify as *tsun* various animal-shaped vessels known to them; one such in the shape of an ox is labelled *Chou hsi tsun*, 'animal-shaped sacrificial wine-vessel of the Chou period', in *Hsüan-ho po ku t'u lu*. The authors quote Wang Su, a third-century A.D. commentator on *Li chi*, 'Record of Rites', who says that the *hsi* and *hsiang* vessels were fashioned in the forms of ox and elephant, and had their backs hollowed out. They add that the Han scholars had no examples in front of them, and so drew on their imaginations when they said that engraved outlines of certain animals were placed on vessels in the shape of goblets. This is all very scholarly

1. It is worth pointing out that elephants were native to northern Honan in Shang-Yin times, and possibly later.

and disinterested; but it is difficult to understand why, when the true explanation was available, the errors of *San li t'u* should have been perpetuated through several editions subsequent to the first of 962 A.D. It should be clear from the foregoing that if we are to use the word *tsun* at all as a designation for a bronze vessel class, we should restrict it to wine vessels in the shapes of animals, and qualify it by adding whichever of the words *hsi* or *hsiang* is appropriate; these being the forms sanctioned by classical usage.

7: YU (plate 11a)

These vessels may be described as covered buckets with swing-handles. No obvious pottery prototype is known, and Yetts has suggested that their ancestors may have been fashioned from gourds, possibly provided with handles made of plaited bamboo strips. The rhomboid pattern on the *yu* of plate 11a, he says, may be a memory of this type of handle.

No self-named example is known to exist, and the identification of these vessels as *yu* was made by the Sung cataloguers. Frequent references occur in classical texts – for example in *Shu ching*, or 'Book of History', and *Shih ching*, 'Book of Odes' – to gifts of 'a *yu* of black millet wine' made by feudal overlords to meritorious vassals. An inscription on a famous Second Phase bronze, the *Mao kung ting*, speaks of the gift of 'a *yu* of black millet wine' to a high official in grateful anticipation of loyal service to be rendered by him to the House of Chou; a passage in *Chou li* makes it evident that *yu* were also used to hold fragrant wine in the ancestral temple. These references all suggest that *yu* were wine-vessels and that they were suited for carrying wine from one place to another. A covered bucket is such a vessel, and we need have no doubt but that the Sung scholars gave the class its correct name. The inscription on a *yu* said to have come fairly recently from the An-yang site indicates that it is a 'sacral vessel made for travelling' – further evidence, perhaps, in support of the identification.

Specimens of *yu* known to us all belong to the First Phase, and we have no direct evidence that they were made subsequently;[1] so Karlgren cites the *yu* as one of his distinctive First Phase criteria (p. 160).

1. Jung Kêng (see footnote p. 132) illustrates as his fig. 9 a Han vessel with chain handle and stopper which he calls a *yu*. But to my mind it is far more like a *hu*. The vessel is not self-named.

This is odd, because there are textual references to *yu* of later times. The commentary *Tso chuan*, which is pre-Han, speaks of a '*yu* of black millet wine' in reference to an occasion in the year 632 B.C. And the above-mentioned *Mao kung ting* can certainly be assigned to the Second Phase on stylistic grounds; yet its inscription also speaks of a *yu*. The answer may be that these were not bronze *yu*.

The shapes of *yu* do not vary much. In most of them, the belly is low-slung and the shoulders slope; so that there is a shape-relationship with *hu* (below). The section may be round, but is more often ellipsoidal. Then the handle may be set in line with the long diameter, or at right-angles to it. The latter makes a more practical arrangement for carrying, and so may be earlier; with the handle in line with the long diameter, on the other hand, the important design on the two main faces of the vessel need not be interrupted.

8: HU (plate 16)

No pottery prototype has been claimed for this class as far as I know, but it is easy to see that there may well have been one; for the tall, graceful shape of many *hu* is of a sort that a potter would delight in

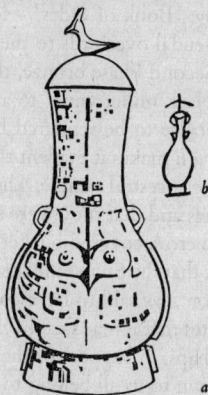

Figure 23. *a*, Shang-Yin bronze vessel, compared with *b*, oracle bone graph, apparently showing the same type of vessel and equated with the modern character for *hu*, 'flask' or 'bottle'.

throwing. *Hu* are among the largest bronze ritual vessels. Their forms show much diversity in proportions, but the basic features – low-slung belly, sloping shoulders, tall neck, and a slightly flared and rather narrow mouth – are almost invariable. All these are shown by the oracle-bone graph with which the modern character *hu* has been equated (figure 23*b*); it shows as well a pair of laterally mounted ring-handles, and a cover or stopper surmounted with a conical lid-knob.

Some *hu* are self-named. The class seems to have been made throughout the period under survey, and was still flourishing in Han times, when it gave rise to a range of fine glazed pottery imitations. On the whole it is best represented by late examples, such as the superb Third Phase specimen shown on plate 16, whereas First and Second Phase pieces are uncommon. *Hu* are normally provided with means of suspension. Sometimes these are tubular 'ears', mounted at the sides below the mouth-rim, sometimes there are free-hanging ring handles suspended from small loop handles cast with the vessel. Chains or cords were passed through the 'ears' or ring handles, and the *hu* could then be carried around like a *yu*. Indeed, a tall covered vessel of the First Phase, much resembling it, is often called *yu*. One so called is in the Pillsbury Collection in the Minneapolis Institute of Arts. Yet the outline drawing of this piece (figure 23*a*) might have served as a model for the oracle-bone graph equated with *hu*. Typologically, in fact, the tall so-called *yu* is not a bucket at all, but a flask or bottle; and its affinities, I believe, are more with the *hu* than with the squat, covered *yu* of the type shown on plate 11*a*.

9: CHIH

A vessel showing shape-relations with both *yu* and *hu* is the *chih*; again no pottery prototype has been claimed for it. The class is not self-named, and the Sung identification can only be regarded as tentative; it seems to be based only on the *Shuo wên chieh tzŭ* definition of *chih* as drinking-vessels. The class went out of fashion at the end of the First Phase, but was revived, under what seems to have been an archaizing impulse, during the Third Phase. *Chih* are like small *hu* lacking handles; sometimes covered, probably originally more often than not; sometimes round in section but typically oval; with a mouth rather wider and more flared, in proportion, than that of *hu*. At its best this is a most graceful, easy, sophisticated sort of vessel, strong yet feminine in the grace and sweetness of its line.

10: KU (plate 9)

According to Andersson this very lovely and distinctive class of
wine-beaker takes its shape from pottery vessels of the sort shown in
figure 21a, which I there proposed as forerunners of the bronze *tou*.
But Kuo Pao-chün says that the prototype of the *ku* is not a pottery
vessel, but one made of horn. His reconstruction shows two trumpet-
shaped pieces of animal horn interlocked at their narrower ends and
bound together at that point – the middle of the resulting vessel – by
a collar of similar material. Corresponding to these three horn sections
would be, if Kuo Pao-chün is right, the three main horizontal zones
of the bronze version (plate 9).

Ku are not self-named, and the Sung identification is speculative,
deriving from a *Shuo wên* definition of *ku* as drinking-vessels. The
character in question contains the elements for 'gourd', *kua*, and for
'horn', or 'angle', *chio*. It seems likely that *kua* is here a phonetic element, and *chio* a determinative or radical (p. 563). If so, does the presence of *chio* imply that the material of which *ku* are made is 'horn',
as Kuo Pao-chün supposes? Or is this a reference to the 'angles', or
vertical flanges, four of which run vertically down the middle and
lower sections of the *ku* of plate 9. In this connexion an enigmatic
utterance of Confucius (*Analects* 6:23) may perhaps give a clue. Speaking, seemingly, *à propos* of nothing in particular, he says: *ku pu ku;
tsai ku, tsai ku*, and this is usually translated as 'A *ku* without its flanges
[literally 'a *ku* not a *ku*']; what a *ku*, what a *ku*!' This may simply be
a pun on two different meanings of *ku*, but it is usually interpreted as
some sort of a stricture. On what? The idea that a single character
could stand for two entirely different things? Or that *ku* were no
longer being made in the proper way, with flanges? That is the meaning read by the nineteenth-century English sinologue James Legge,
among others.

Ku, as far as we know, were only made during the First Phase;
and for Karlgren they constitute one of its distinctive elements. But
Confucius lived at least 300 years after the end of the First Phase.
What *ku*, then, was he talking about? Either the Sung cataloguers
have identified as *ku* an altogether different class of vessel, or Confucius's *ku*, like the *yu* referred to on p. 146, was not a vessel of bronze
at all.

The forms of *ku* are almost invariable, although their proportions differ slightly. An interesting feature of many is a small cruciform perforation repeated four times, and appearing just below the middle zone. Various suggestions as to the meaning of these perforations have been made; perhaps best is that put forward by Yetts, who sees them as expedients to ensure correct apposition of four sectional moulds used in casting the vessel.

11 AND 12: CHIA and CHÜEH (plate 11b)

On p. 138 we put forward Andersson's view that the pottery *li-ting* is a forerunner of the bronze *chia*. Figure 24 has been assembled from various drawings made by Andersson in order to demonstrate how this evolution may have come about. A corresponding series of pottery shapes has been constructed by Li Chi to explain the form of the *chüeh*, and although this latter series starts from a handled jug with three rudimentary legs, one of his stages shows a vessel with constricted neck, wide mouth, side handle, and three legs that very much resembles the *li-ting* of our figure 24c. In other words, not only do the forms of bronze *chia* and *chüeh* testify to a common ancestor; that ancestor, we may provisionally conclude, was a pottery vessel of *li-ting* type.

If this view is correct, then the side handles of *chia* and *chüeh* may be typical survivals from a pottery ancestor. Other features – the three long, tapering, lance-shaped legs and the paired capped uprights – must be reckoned bronze innovations. But Kuo Pao-chün has another theory to account for these. He says that they are vestiges of three bamboo rods tied to the sides of a hollow horn which was the prototype of *chüeh* and *chia*; that the rods acted as legs, and that the capped pillars are the remains of their upper parts. I find it difficult to believe this. According to Yetts, the capped pillars were simply an expedient whereby the goblet could be removed from a fire in which it might have been placed to warm its contents. In most classes of bronze vessels, the side handles or lugs of their pottery ancestors are replaced by vertical 'ears' on the mouth-rim, through which a stick could be passed for lifting them into and out of the fire. But the side handles of *chia*, and especially the small side handles of *chüeh*, are not at all suited for this purpose. A pair of tongs, passing under the pillar caps, would serve much better.

As for the prominent, trough-like spout and 'tail' of the *chüeh* –

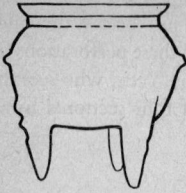
a

b

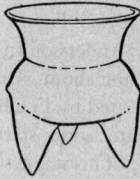
c

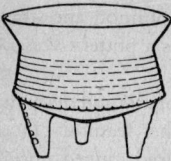
d

e

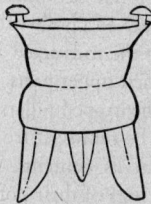
f

Figure 24. Shape relations between pottery and bronze *li*, *ting*, *li–ting*, and *chia*: *a*, prehistoric pottery *ting*; *b*, prehistoric pottery *li*; *c*, prehistoric pottery *li–ting*; *d*, prehistoric pottery *chia*; *e*, prehistoric pottery *chia*; *f*, Shang–Yin bronze *chia*.

features in which this goblet differs most noticeably from the *chia* – Li Chi can point to one Neolithic pottery vessel which shows the rudiments of a spout; but, as with the legs, its strange attenuation must certainly be a development in bronze alone. As I have previously remarked, the elaborate shape of the *chüeh*, and for that matter of the *chia*, could be taken as evidence of a long ancestry in bronze form.

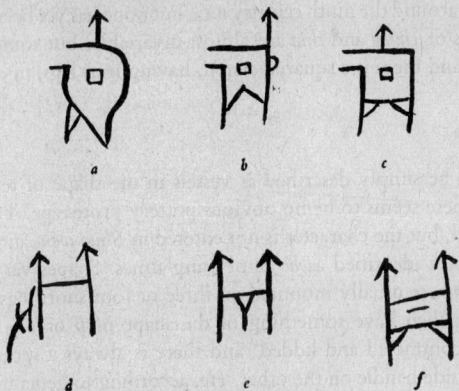

Figure 25. *a–c*, oracle bone graphs equated with the modern character for *chüeh*, 'goblet'; *d–f*, oracle bone graphs equated with the modern character for *chia*, 'goblet'.

Chia are not self-named; and there seems much doubt as to whether *chüeh* are, either. But archaic forms of the characters for each are known, and to me these are nothing more or less than pictograms; I append three examples for the *chia* and three for the *chüeh* (figure 25*a–f*). So distinctive is the shape of this latter vessel that the question has been raised whether it does not have some symbolic meaning. Starting with a definition given in *Shuo wên*, which says that the character denotes a bird and *chüeh* were made in the shape of birds, Lo Chên-yü has gone on to suggest that a bird's head with crest, eye, and beak can be discerned in the archaic graph looked at in side view. But, if so, an altogether novel principle seems to be at work here. We have seen that the shapes of some vessels – the *hsi tsun* and *hsiang tsun* – are modelled in the shapes of animals and birds; but these are instantly recognizable, naturalistic portrayals, having nothing in common with the cryptic and oblique reference to a bird – if that is what it is – concealed in the form of the *chüeh*.

Neither *chia* nor *chüeh* outlive the First Phase, as far as we know, and Karlgren regards them as distinctive of that period. It would be intriguing to discover the reason why these and one or two other bronze forms, with appearance so distinctive, should have passed out of fashion around the ninth century B.C., but none has yet been offered. The forms of *chüeh* and *chia* are almost invariable, but some *chia* are covered; and there is a square version, having four legs, in each class.

13: HO

These can be simply described as vessels in the shape of tea-pots or kettles. There seems to be no obvious pottery prototype. The class is self-named, but the character is not entered in *Shuo wên*, and the vessels were not identified as *ho* until Sung times. Shapes vary a good deal, but *ho* are usually mounted on three or four short legs, and the body may then have something of the shape of *li* or *ting*. But the mouth is contracted and lidded; and there is always a spout on one side and a side handle on the other. *Ho*, according to general opinion, were used for mixing wine with water. They persist throughout the entire period under survey.

14 AND 15: KUANG and I (plate 14b)

The general shape of both *kuang* and *i*, now reckoned to constitute separate classes, is that of a sauce-boat. No pottery or other prototype seems to suggest itself, and the whole history of the vessels is apparently written in bronze. Those we now call *kuang* were entered in the Sung catalogues as *i*, no distinction being made between the two classes. And whereas no vessel of the class *kuang* is self-named, a good many of those called *i* are so named. Where does the name *kuang* come from, and wherein lies the difference between these allegedly distinct classes? Wang Kuo-wei noticed that of the vessels inscribed *i*, none had covers, whereas the covered variety was never so inscribed. He concluded that the covered examples had a different function and were known by a different name. He proceeded to identify them with the *kuang* spoken of in pre-Han texts. In *Shih ching*, 'Book of Odes', mention is made of a lover drawing water from the *chin lei*, 'the bronze *lei*', and drinking it out of the *ssŭ kuang*. Wang Kuo-wei says that the sense of *ssŭ* here is 'bovine', and that a reference is intended to the ox, whose head, he claims, is displayed on the covers of these vessels. That is the evidence on which rests the opinion that these covered 'sauce-boats' are *kuang*, and to me it seems threadbare indeed.

In the first place, as Yetts observes, by no means all the covers are modelled in the shape of ox-heads. And secondly, since the reference in the Book of Odes is to the 'bronze *lei*', should we not expect that by parallelism the word *ssŭ*, qualifying *kuang* in the quotation, should also refer to the material of a vessel? One of the meanings of *ssŭ* is 'horn'.[1] Thirdly, the *kuang* we know scarcely seem to be the sort of vessels one would want to drink out of. Some have a vertical partition running across the shorter axis – which perhaps adds force to the idea that they were used for mixing wine with water, but surely detracts from their efficiency as goblets; and, if drinking-vessels, why the covers? And why the ladle, *shao*, so frequently found associated with them?

If we reject the view that these vessels are the *kuang* spoken of in pre-Han texts, the question arises, why not call them *i*? An interesting point now crops up. So-called *kuang* are not known to have been made after the First Phase, of which, according to Karlgren, they are distinctive. *I*, on the other hand, are perfectly familiar ingredients of the Second and Third Phases, but not a single specimen is known that can be assigned to the First Phase. Karlgren says that the *i* is a Second Phase innovation. Is it not natural to assume, in these circumstances, that so-called *kuang* and *i* are genealogically related; that is, that the *kuang* is simply an early version of the *i*? The use to which these vessels were put may or may not have altered. But this is not a case of two distinct sorts of vessel designed for different purposes. The form of the *i* evolved from that of the *kuang*. And we cannot be quite certain that the earlier version was not called *i*, for Yetts has drawn attention to a covered vessel the style of which accords with a Second Phase attribution; it is self-named *i*.

Until fresh evidence is brought to bear on this problem we may feel justified, therefore, in reaching the following conclusions; firstly, that reasons for naming the covered variety *kuang* are inadequate;

1. Cf. B. Karlgren, 'The Book of Odes. Ta Ya and Sung', in *B.M.F.E.A.*, no. 17 (1945), p. 93, who gives: 'the kuang vase of rhinoceros horn'.

secondly, that the covered variety is *not* distinctive of the First Phase; thirdly, that the covered variety may always have been known as *i*.

These vessels display much variation in shape. The covered ones have the cover and upper part of the body modelled in the shape of a zoomorph. In later examples – if I am correct in supposing that this is a case of formal evolution within a single vessel-class – the cover disappears, but the spout is still enclosed above by an animal mask, and the body is supported by four legs. At a still later stage the spout is open above, and the legs may then be replaced by a hollow, spreading base; from which, in still later examples, legs again begin to appear. Finally, versions are found having neither legs nor base; and in these, a free-hanging ring handle takes the place of the vertically hung fixed loop handle at the back.

16: P'AN (plate 15a)

These are shallow bowls or basins such as may evidently have descended from Neolithic pottery ancestors, although none such, as far as I am aware, has yet been claimed for them; the class provides self-named examples. It is not altogether certain that *p'an* date back as far as Shang-Yin times, although a single specimen found in one of the approaches to a Shang-Yin royal tomb at An-yang may very well belong to that period.[1] But we have early Chou examples, and *p'an* seem to have been made continuously thenceforward into Han times. They were water-vessels, designed for ablutions or for washing sacral vessels during the ancestral sacrifice, and the form they take is fairly constant. Most are circular, but there is a rare oval variety. Most have a shallow, wide, and slightly spreading base from which three puny legs, resembling those found on some Second Phase *kuei*, may arise. One late specimen has a single handle, opposite which is a spout by means of which the vessel can be more easily emptied. Handles are usually up-turned 'ears' mounted below the mouth-rim, but these

1. A well-known passage in *Ta hsüeh*, or 'Great Learning' (part of the compilation *Li chi*, 'Record of Rites'), may perhaps date from the fourth century B.C. It speaks of 'an inscription on the *p'an* of T'ang', the first ruler of the Shang-Yin dynasty, who, according to the revised chronology, began his reign about 1500 B.C. The 'inscription' has been shown by Kuo Mo-jo to be a mistaken reading of part of a genealogical tree which may or may not have been inscribed on a bronze *p'an*. Needless to say, the passage cannot be taken to prove that T'ang ever had such a vessel.

are sometimes replaced by ring handles freely-hanging from animal masks. The flat inner surface of *p'an* make them suitable for long inscriptions, among which is one having no less than 357 characters – a document comparable in size with, say, one of the chapters of the Book of History.

17: CHIEN

This class of bowls is cognate with others called by different names, such, for instance, as the wine vessel *yü* (p. 133). All may have had a pottery prototype, but no vessel identified as a *chien*, as far as I know, dates from earlier than the Second Phase. Thenceforth they were made until well into Han times.

The class provides self-named examples; and the graph shows a person bending over a bowl, apparently looking at his reflection in water. Whether written with or without the 'metal' determinative this character can mean 'to examine, inspect', but with the determinative it may also mean the vessel *chien* as well as a certain type of mirror. Perhaps this bowl served vicariously as a mirror; but references in pre-Han texts testify that it was normally filled with ice – either to preserve sacrificial food in hot weather, or a corpse against too rapid decay while awaiting burial. *Chien* scarcely vary in shape. They are normally deep bowls, circular in section, and provided with vertical loop-handles or free-hanging ring handles. They often reached considerable size. A specimen in the Cernuschi Museum, Paris, is no less than 40 inches across the mouth.

Secular Bronzes

The bronzes of the Shang-Yin and Chou periods include not only sacrificial vessels, but also a whole range of weapons, chariot- and harness-fittings and other impedimenta of war; and, during the Third Phase at least, mirrors. We do not propose to describe these classes of secular objects, but shall cite only a single example to point a contrast between their styles and the hieratic art represented by the ritual bronze vessels. The ibex head of the cart-pole end (plate 12) is of the type usually described as 'nomad' or 'Scythian'. To anyone familiar only with the décor of contemporary bronze vessels such an object might look un-Chinese; and the fact that this sort of fresh and natural-istic portrayal is not as a rule found on the ritual vessels might, as Karlgren says, tempt one to see it as a cultural importation from the nomads. But, as we have seen, there is no reason to award precedence to the Siberian materials with which this Chinese 'animal-style' art is habitually compared, and faced with cases such as the ibex head we may have to revise our notions as to what constitutes the 'Chinese' style in bronze décor. The museum authorities at the Honolulu Academy of Arts, whence the piece comes, date it about 1000 B.C. and call it 'pre-Scythian steppe style'. But close resemblances are met with in animal terminals of a group of knives from An-yang (figure 8, upper right), and this chariot-fitting may well therefore be a century or so earlier.

The Styles of the Ritual Bronzes

The ritual bronzes of ancient China do not by any means manifest a single decorative style. Style is an elusive quality – nowhere more so than in Chinese bronze art – and it is always easier, and generally sufficient, to sense the difference between two pieces rather than say precisely where it lies. Only when decorative elements are dissected out do we find that a prescriptive basis – what Karlgren calls a 'grammar' – really does exist for these general impressions of differ-ence. Motives found on some bronzes are altogether absent from others, or appear in stylized or degenerate form; on yet others, later in date, they may reappear in subtly different guise. Shapes, too, under-go the same apparent evolution.

Over the centuries during which bronzes have been seriously studied in China, vague indications have accumulated by which to assign an approximate date to any given specimen. External criteria, such as content of inscription, style of script, and occasionally proven-ance, yield clues by which a bronze can be given a relative chrono-logical position. But we must emphasize that only when the genuine-ness of a bronze – and of its inscription – is beyond dispute, and when the content of its inscription allows us to give it a definite date, is it of any real value as a key-piece by which others resembling it in style may be dated. Very few bronzes indeed meet these requirements. The work of Yetts, in identifying historically datable pieces that at the same time display characteristic differences in style, points the way by which we may hope eventually to date Chinese bronzes with margins of error measurable in years and not in centuries.

Various systems of marshalling the bronzes according to their styles are in use to-day. And the result is a confusion of names that must completely baffle the average museum visitor. A moment spent in considering one or two of them will not, I think, be wasted. Chinese experts who classified the great Chinese Government loan to the London exhibition of 1935–6 (p. 3) adopted the following divisions:[1]

1. Shang-Yin (?1766–?1122 B.C.).
2. Western Chou (?1122–c. 722 B.C.).
3. Period of the Spring and Autumn Annals (c. 722–481 B.C.).
4. Period of the Warring States (c. 481–221 B.C.).

Now we require of a stylistic scheme firstly that its chronological divisions shall correspond approximately – we cannot hope for more than that – with observable stylistic phases; secondly, that it shall avoid unfamiliar names. The above system failed on both counts. It used arbitrary historical divisions into which the stylistic phases simply would not fit; and terms which, although freely bandied about at the time, could have meant little or nothing to most people.

Professor Karlgren, after announcing a provisional classification in 1933 on the occasion of an exhibition of Chinese bronzes in Stockholm,[2] published four years later a modified version of this, in the second of his three great bronze studies[3]. It goes:

1. Archaic period (a) Yin [i.e. Shang-Yin]. Before 1122 B.C.
            (b) Yin-Chou. 1122–950 B.C.
2. Middle Chou. 950–650 B.C.
3. Huai. c. 650–200 B.C.

This scheme, too, is open to criticism. The term 'Huai' may be objected to for three reasons. Firstly, it is unfamiliar. Secondly, it is a geographical term used to denote a style of art – that style, as Karlgren says, 'flourishing in the latter part of the Chou and during the Ts'in

1. In presenting these systems I give the dates originally proposed by their initiators; the Shang-Yin period, as we have seen, probably lasted from 1500 to 1000 B.C.
2. B. Karlgren, 'The exhibition of early Chinese bronzes', in B.M.F.E.A., no. 6 (1934), pp. 87–95.
3. B. Karlgren, 'New studies on Chinese bronzes', in B.M.F.E.A., no. 9 (1937), pp. 1–117.

[Ch'in] dynasty, which, when first located with any certainty in any definite Chinese region, was attested in the Huai valley by Mr Karlbeck.'[1] Thirdly, as a geographical term it is incongruous in a scheme that otherwise employs dynastic names. One could perhaps argue that in archaeology it is often convenient to designate a culture by the name of its type-site. But bronzes in 'Huai' style have now been recovered from places as far apart as Shansi and Anhwei.[2] When the museum visitor encounters the label 'Huai' he is almost bound to associate it in his mind with a particular region; that is, if he associates it with anything at all. In other cases where a culture, called originally after a type-site, has been found over a much wider area, that name has been abandoned. We no longer speak of the 'Yang-shao Culture', because the painted pottery we once knew only from Yang-shao Ts'un has been discovered in nearly every province of north China. The term 'Huai' has now no better claim for survival.

Karlgren also manifests some confusion of thought in dividing his first period into two.[3] He claims that with the coming of the Chou dynasty new stylistic elements appeared, sufficient to produce a distinct style which lived on side by side with the pure Shang-Yin style, 'during the period of the Yin-Chou'. Surely this is an unnecessary complication? Karlgren adduces thirty-eight criteria which he says are distinctive of the Shang-Yin style; but of the Yin-Chou style he finds only four, and it seems likely that two of these will have to be discarded. To add to the confusion, he produces overwhelming evidence to show that during the whole of the Archaic Period there were also current a Primary and a Secondary style. And although the Secondary style is on the whole later than the Primary, it is not to be equated with the 'Yin-Chou' style. The reader must be wondering where all this is leading. To put the matter quite simply, most experts now agree that the bronze art of ancient China can be divided into three main stylistic phases. These phases were given approximate dates by Yetts, lecturing during the course of the International Exhibition of Chinese Art, in December 1935. His scheme is as follows:

1. B. Karlgren (see footnote p. 161), p. 90.
2. And as a result, when dividing the 'Huai' style into regional groups, Karlgren has to find another term for the Huai valley region itself.
3. Exception might also be taken to the use of the word 'Archaic', since it usually implies not only 'belonging to an early period', but also 'primitive'. The bronze art of Shang-Yin times is certainly not primitive.

1. First Phase, (Shang-Yin and Early Chou). Thirteenth to tenth century B.C.
2. Second Phase, (Chou). Tenth to sixth century B.C.
3. Third Phase, (Chou). Sixth century to end of Chou period.

This system seems the most acceptable. It does not introduce unfamiliar names; phases are not forced into arbitrary correspondence with historical periods; and dates are intentionally left vague. On the other hand, there can be no doubt about the reality of two distinct yet contemporary idioms during the First Phase, the Primary and Secondary styles adduced by Karlgren. I propose, therefore, to graft these on to Yetts's scheme while describing the characteristics of the First Phase.

*

Our first reaction to the art of the ritual bronzes may well be that we are coming into contact with something thoroughly unfamiliar, not to say hostile. The shapes of the vessels, and the strangely potent beings they advertise, convey the impression of a spirit that is almost barbaric, and we perhaps have to remind ourselves that they are, after all, highly civilized works of art. But the more prolonged our examination of structure and content, the less acute does this feeling of strangeness and hostility become. We find that we are acquiring a new and first-rate aesthetic experience.

The forms portrayed on the bronzes undoubtedly had some symbolic import, but of what nature we cannot say. All sorts of explanations of the better-known motives have been given by both Western and Chinese critics; but, as with the interpretation of early jades, these explanations rarely convince and are often entirely fanciful. The commonest motives are zoomorphs; animals are portrayed, but again it is not always easy to say just what sort of animals. They are usually very highly stylized.

But two sorts of stylization are possible. Animals portrayed in the steppe art of the Northern Nomads, for instance, are vividly alive no matter how contorted may be the attitudes in which, owing to technical limitations, they have been posed. It is an art characterized by what E. H. Minns called 'style instinct with life'. Even when basic forms are tampered with, so that deer antlers turn into heads of birds, fishes' tails unaccountably become rams' heads, small beasts parade on the limb joints, and so forth, the impression of actuality remains.

The animal forms of the bronzes are not stylized in this sense only; they have become, as it were, abstract or heraldic. This is especially true of the mysterious class known as 'dragons'. Just as much liberty is taken with their forms as we find in nomad art. Several heads share a single body, several bodies merge into a single head, composite animals appear, tails turn as inconsequently into birds' heads on Chinese bronzes as they do on Scythian plaques. But often it is from disintegrated or decomposed bodies that these secondary forms arise, bodies composed of nothing but a mass of meaningless spirals out of which peers only a pair of glaucous and protrusive eyes.

Animal forms, however stylized, are set against a background of geometrical shapes among which the spiral is ubiquitous. In bronzes of the First Phase, and to some extent of the Third, the artists seem to have been impelled by *horror vacui* to load every square inch of surface with this combination of zoomorphs and spirals. Forms that have been identified as plants, and even human portrayals, are not unknown on the bronzes (plate 15a). But these are interlopers. The obsession with animals is inescapable. We seem to be dealing with something in the nature of an iconography.

THE FIRST PHASE

Style criteria named by Karlgren for the period covered by the First Phase number thirty-eight. A Chinese bronze can confidently be dated between the thirteenth and tenth centuries B.C. or earlier, if it displays some of these elements and none of those introduced in later Phases. They may be divided into two groups, of which the first comprises vessel-types or part of vessels and the second decorative motives.

In describing the vessel-types we have already indicated those that Karlgren considers distinctive of the First Phase. Briefly, they are the rectangular *ting*, the *li-ting*, *yu*, *ku*, *chüeh*, *chia*, *kuang*, and the square casket called *fang i* (p. 135). According to this notion, therefore, the vessels shown on plates 9, 10b, and 11a and b must necessarily all belong to the First Phase. Parts of vessels include cylinder legs (plate 10a and b), legs of *ting* modelled in animal form, lid-knobs as opposed to discs (plate 11a), and vertical segmented flanges (plates 9, 10a and b, 11a and b).

The decorative motives divide into those portraying animals or parts of animals; and others that are purely geometrical. The animal forms are multitudinous, and one doubts whether any analysis of them can ever reach completion, although that is what Karlgren seems to be aiming at.[1] The most important will be discussed below.

T'ao-t'ieh. No motive in Chinese art has invited more speculation as to its meaning than this. It is a device in which two confronting zoomorphs in profile form the left and right sides of an animal mask seen in full face; the *t'ao-t'ieh* from the bronze of plate 10*a* has been isolated and redrawn as figure 26 to make apparent what is meant.

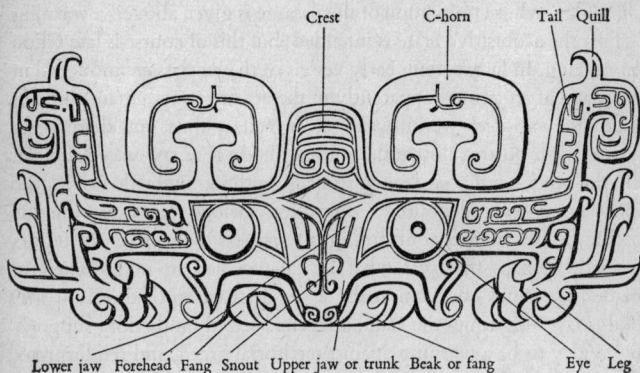

Figure 26. *T'ao-t'ieh* mask from the First Phase *ting* of plate 10*a*.

Not much would be gained by discussing theories as to its origin. Claims have been made that it arose in the West, and indeed merging of animal heads somewhat in this way is a feature of Mycenaean art; but the early history of the *t'ao-t'ieh* in China is quite obviously linked with that of bronze itself. And, as we have seen, no conclusion can yet be reached on the question of bronze origins. A similar device occurs in the art of Amerindia; yet this, too, may be a chance resemblance.

Chinese accounts as to the meaning of *t'ao-t'ieh* are conflicting. A passage in *Tso chuan* (p. 82) speaks of noxious spirits at large in the hills and wastes, and tells how these were depicted on the Nine

1. In addition to 'New studies on Chinese bronzes' (p. 157, footnote 3), his principal writings are: 'Yin and Chou in Chinese bronzes', in *B.M.F.E.A.*, no. 8 (1936), pp. 9–154; and 'Notes on the grammar of early bronze décor', in *B.M.F.E.A.*, no. 23 (1951), pp. 1–37.

Cauldrons of the legendary Yü the Great, to give people a fair idea of what they looked like. By the third century. A.D. the commentator Kuo P'o is identifying the t'ao-t'ieh with one of these. But a passage in Lü shih ch'un ch'iu, attributed to the third-century B.C. writer Lü Pu-wei, runs: 'On Chou vessels there was put a t'ao-t'ieh with a head, but no body. He is eating a man and (thinks he) is going to swallow him; but already his (the t'ao-t'ieh's) body is destroyed. The object of the design was to warn people that the hour of disaster was at hand.' One can easily see the allegorical possibilities of such a theme. According to Dr Waley, whose translation of the passage is given above,[1] a warning against the acquisitive State is intended; but this of course is late Chou moralizing. In fact, certain early vessels of the yu class are modelled in the shape of an animal apparently in the act of eating a man. But this is not the t'ao-t'ieh we know; and, as Yetts points out, there is no sign in such portrayals that the animal's body is in any way deficient. On the other hand, t'ao-t'ieh portrayals – although they do not indeed show a man being devoured – do exhibit various stages in reduction of the bodies of the confronting animals, as will presently be described. Perhaps that was what Lü Pu-wei had in mind when he made his curious observation about the destruction of the t'ao-t'ieh's body. By Sung times the cataloguers had seized on the idea supposed by Waley to be a warning against territorial greed, and reinterpreted it as an injunction against lust and gluttony.

Karlgren analyses the t'ao-t'ieh motive into six different types. But for our purpose only two need be mentioned. In the first of these, parts of the body, such as jaws, snout, horns, legs, and tails, however summarily treated and scattered, can yet be seen as distinct, accentuated elements raised above the spiral background. The mask of figure 26 is a good example of this class. In the second, the animal forms are indistinct, or what Karlgren calls 'dissolved'. They are there, but they need finding. Often only the eyes, as we said, betray their presence among the maze of spirals that form their bodies (plate 13).

The paired animals that compose t'ao-t'ieh masks are, generically, of the same nature as 'dragons' such as appear in other decorative zones of the body and in a variety of guises. We therefore proceed to a short description of these.

Dragons. The creature so equivocally called 'dragon' appears on bronzes in an abundance of forms and every degree of stylization

1. A. Waley, 'The T'ao-t'ieh', in *B.M.*, vol. xliii (1926), p. 104.

imaginable. We are led to suppose that all originate from representations of actual animals; for unmistakable tigers, elephants, rams, oxen, hares, snakes, and other beasts are often portrayed on First Phase pieces, and some reappear on bronzes of the Third Phase. Furthermore, the bare idea of felinity, bovinity, and so forth, is, as has been noted, nearly always present even when diagnostic detail is lacking. Indeed, it often creates its own disturbing sensation of actuality.

Within these ill-defined limits, the bronze designer, and especially the Shang-Yin designer, evidently felt free to vary the anatomy of the dragon as imagination prompted. From an artistic point of view, the result is that mechanical repetition is avoided; and in this feature of the design, subordination to a main plan goes hand in hand with what seems to be a delightfully easy and personal treatment of the theme.

The *t'ao-t'ieh* mask of figure 26 serves to illustrate points of anatomy of most dragons. As here, we can usually recognize a jaw, or jaws, armed with what Karlgren calls beak, but which might equally be thought of as tusk or fang; a snout; forehead; crest; horn; eye; body; tail; and leg. Many variations are to be found. In one, the head is lowered so that front jaw and snout have the appearance of a sort of trunk; in this variety both jaws are present and the mouth is open. When two such forms combine to make a *t'ao-t'ieh*, as they do in figure 26, the two foreheads in combination go to make a hooked shield. In a second type the head is erect (figure 27b) and beaked upper jaw and crest are very conspicuous. But what has happened to the lower jaw? It has apparently coalesced with the front leg.

Of horns, Karlgren distinguishes six varieties. Those he calls 'comma horns' and 'T horns' – the names describe the shapes – are properly attached to the body. But the others – those he calls 'bottle' (figure 27b), 'C' (figure 27a), 'S', and 'leaf' horns – are isolated from it. Although generalization is dangerous, we can safely say that 'C horns', variously orientated, predominate. Those of figure 26 and figure 27a are down-turned and up-turned respectively.

The body bears a variety of excrescences, as well as incised lines on its surface that sometimes suggest scales. The morphology here is utterly inconstant. Karlgren defines no less than thirteen varieties of 'quill' and 'curl' some of which I have labelled in figure 27a and b, following his definitions. As well as these, a tail usually rises erect from the dorsal surface. The body itself may be slit horizontally (figure 27a), in which case the upper section can also be thought of as a wing. One or two legs may be seen in profile representing, presumably, either a two-legged creature, or one with four legs. The former of these has since Sung times been identified as the *k'uei* dragon mentioned in pre-Han texts; but, according to Karlgren, wrongly so. Three pre-Han texts, *Kuo yü*, *Lü shih ch'un ch'iu*, and *Chuang tzŭ*,

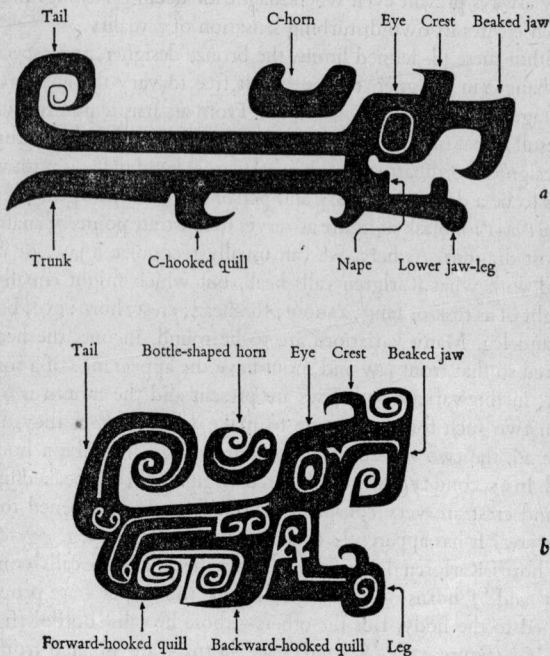

Figure 27. *K'uei* dragons: *a*, from a First Phase square *ting*; *b*, from the First Phase *yu* of plate 11*a*.

speak of the one-legged *k'uei* dragon, but they apparently mean literally a dragon with one single leg, not one having a single *pair* of legs.

I am aware how fragmentary this description of dragons on Chinese bronzes must seem; and some of the anatomical identifications may appear unlikely, and indeed absurd. I have tried only to draw attention to the more conspicuous and constant features exhibited by these creatures. Karlgren has gone to very much greater lengths in his analysis of their 'grammar'. The question is, how far 'grammatical' laws were actually obeyed, in the designing of dragons. To some considerable extent, no doubt; but, I am quite sure, *not* down to the finer points of detail. In these, it seems to me, the sensibility of the designer had full play. Mechanical adherence to a copybook pattern was not demanded, any more than it is expected in a spoken or written language. Hence it would be unwise to expect exact iconographic laws to emerge from analysis of every twist and turn the unpredictable bronze 'dragon' takes.

Blades. The upper part of the *ku* of plate 9 and the legs of the *ting* of plate 10 are ornamented with what Karlgren calls 'rising blades' and 'hanging blades'. Furthermore, the bodies of several First Phase vessel types, especially of *ting*, are decorated with rather similar triangular forms. Some of these quite obviously portray an insect – the cicada – in more or less stylized form; others, according to Karlgren, do not.[1] In others the cicada pattern is limited to the apex, the rest of the blade being occupied with an elongated *t'ao-t'ieh*.

We need mention only one other animal form distinctive of the First Phase. This is what Karlgren calls the 'free animal's head' (cf. plate 14a), which may be characterized as a decorative element that does not form part of a leg or handle, yet which *is* treated plastically. It may take the form of a *t'ao-t'ieh* or resemble more obviously the head of an ox, ram, hare, or other quadruped.

The remaining motives – those not deriving from animal forms – may be more briefly mentioned. The spiral appears in a variety of forms, and is the most important single motive after the *t'ao-t'ieh* and dragon. It is the device called by the Sung cataloguers *lei wên* or 'thunder pattern' – a designation evidently based on a chance resemblance it bears to the archaic form of the character *lei* for 'thunder'. Other geometrical devices are lozenges – often worked up into a large overall pattern – interlocked T's (figure 39a), vertical ribs, spiral bands, and what Karlgren calls 'T-scores' on the above-mentioned segmented flanges (plates 9 and 10a). Two elements found together on the *kuei* of plate 14a may perhaps originate ultimately from some plant form. One is the 'round eddy' or 'whorl circle', called by the Chinese *yüan wo*; and the other, called 'square with crescents' by Karlgren, is named *ling hua* or 'flower of the water-chestnut' by the Chinese.

1. Cf. B. Karlgren (see footnote 3 p. 157), p. 19.

It might now be helpful to submit two of the vessels here illustrated to brief description, citing in brackets those elements adduced by Karlgren as being distinctive of the First Phase.

Plate 10*a*. *Ting*. Of deep bowl-shape on three cylinder legs (K. 8) with vertical upright 'ears' rising from the mouth-rim. The body divided into six zones by vertical segmented flanges (K. 13) showing T-scores (K. 37). Each zone occupied by a dragon confronting its fellow in the next zone so as to form a single *t'ao-t'ieh* mask (K. 15). The dragons of the trunked variety (K. 19), the foreheads combining to form the upper part of the face, the trunks to form the lower part of the nose and nostrils. The horns C-shaped, the opening of the C facing downwards. The bodies decorated with spirals (K. 30). The background composed of squared spirals (K. 29). The legs of the vessel with hanging blades.

Plate 14*a*. *Kuei*. Of flattened bowl-shape, mounted on a wide and somewhat spreading hollow base. Two vertical flanged loop-handles at the sides, representing tusked animals with upright horns above, and with vestiges of parts of birds below. The body divided into three horizontal registers. The upper and lower decorated with *ling hua* (K. 38) and *yüan wo* (K. 35) with two free animals' heads (K. 14) on the upper register. The middle register with vertical ribs (K. 36).

It must be obvious from the foregoing descriptions that we have here two vessels in every way typical of the First Phase.

PRIMARY AND SECONDARY STYLES

In his 'New Studies on Chinese Bronzes', Karlgren divides bronzes of the First Phase into two groups, according as to whether they exhibit a 'primary' or a 'secondary' style of décor. The Secondary Style, he thinks, overlapped the Primary, yet was in general later, since elements present on Secondary Style bronzes are evidently stylized or vestigial versions of others found on Primary Style bronzes. Karlgren thinks that the two styles may have lived side by side for a century or so at An-yang and that the Secondary Style may have been the product of a rival school of casters, perhaps in service of some branch of the nobility more lately come into power.

Karlgren established the existence of Primary and Secondary Styles by dividing all First Phase decorative elements into three groups. Those in group A are associated with vessels in Primary Style, and are rarely if ever found on vessels in Secondary Style. Those in group B are similarly restricted to Secondary Style vessels. Those of group C may be distributed impartially among vessels of either type. I do not propose to deal with these elements in detail; the difference in feeling is fairly evident when one compares the two vessels described above. The *ting* is in the Primary Style, the *kuei* in Secondary.

But one important difference between most bronzes in these two styles needs to be emphasized. Karlgren has directed attention to the fact that what he calls a 'uni-décor' characterizes the Primary Style. No part of the vessel's surface is left empty of symbolic forms. As Karlgren puts it when speaking of the 'dragon', 'its accumulation was evidently meant to load the sacral vessel with a great dragon force, an enormous magical power'. But in bronzes of Secondary Style one is aware of a new feeling at work. It is seen in the tendency to dispose decoration in horizontal registers, thus making possible the sort of rhythmic contrast displayed by the *kuei* of plate 14*a*. Obviously a different effect is being sought. Something of the menace and potency of the *ting* (plate 10*a*) has evaporated by the time we reach the *kuei*. With the former it is the content that rivets our attention. With the latter this pressure is released, and one gets the feeling that the Secondary Style bronze caster, too, may have been less psychologically confined. The *kuei*, to use a loose phrase, is more of an essay in pure aesthetics; whereas the significance of the *ting* lies rather in its content than its style.

THE SECOND PHASE

The simplification, or what Karlgren calls 'attenuation', apparent in vessels of the Secondary Style, seems to have been taken a step further in the Second Phase (tenth to sixth century B.C.). The question is, how rapid was the onset of the new style. Karlgren speaks of the 'sudden appearance and equally sudden victory of a new bronze art', and indeed many elements of that of the First Phase were swept into oblivion at the coming of the Second. But others survived, among them the *t'ao-t'ieh* and the squared spiral, both occasionally found on Second Phase bronzes; certain types of dragons; animal heads on handles and legs of *ting*; vertical flanges; lobed handles; handles with rings through them; and the tendency to dispose the décor in a single horizontal zone, leaving the rest of the vessel undecorated – a scheme already foreshadowed by Secondary Style vessels of the First Phase. Many bronzes, in fact, and particularly some *kuei*, resist classification into either First or Second Phase. And this is only what we should expect. On general grounds we do not envisage one style utterly abandoned and replaced by another overnight; we look for a long overlap during which bronzes displaying transitional features were being made. We also expect that the earlier style will not disappear simultaneously over the whole area where bronzes were being made, but will survive for longer or shorter periods in isolated local pockets.

Whether, and to what extent, these two processes were at work during the tenth century B.C. we cannot safely say. It *is* true that the change-over produced some dramatic results. The disappearance of rectangular *ting*, *chüeh*, *ku*, and *yu* is difficult to account for. Stylistic innovations seem also to coincide with a marked deterioration in artistic and technical quality. But what brought about the stylistic revolution, if that is what it was? Karlgren suggests that it must have been connected with the policy of territorial expansion pursued by the fourth and fifth Chou sovereigns, but just how or why I cannot see.

Quite as surprising as the disappearance of well-known vessel types is an almost total eclipse of zoomorphs. Apart from handles modelled in animal form – often with a distinctive type of snail-shaped horn – they are scarcely to be found at all on Second Phase bronzes. True, the principal decorative element is often a zone of stylized figures in which vestiges of First Phase dragons may be traced; but they are remarkably self-effacing. Second Phase designers, in fact, seem to have been aiming at an even more purely decorative treatment of surface than did casters of First Phase Secondary Style bronzes; and at a more complete rejection of the bodeful monsters of the Primary Style, in favour of abstract motives which may have seemed in better taste.

Of these motives, three only need be mentioned. One is horizontal fluting, such as we see on the *i* of plate 14*b*. We may perhaps feel that this form of decoration belongs essentially to ceramics, and look for a pottery prototype. On the other hand, we have to admit that this may be an innovation from the Near East; for similar fluting is found on a gold jug and silver rhyton in the British Museum, from Achaemenid Persia and dating from the fifth century B.C. A second important decorative element is the scale pattern, whether arranged in a single band or hung vertically in a series of bands filling a considerable surface. The well-known *ting* which long formed the chief treasure of the Buddhist monastery on Silver Island in the Yangtze has a typical example of this imbricated pattern, part of which we reproduce as figure 28. The last device worth mentioning is the undulating meander, which may take the form of a simple line or of a broad band. Remnants of it are to be seen marking the upper edge of the top zone of decoration on the *hu* of plate 16. This is a Third Phase example, but it serves to give a rough idea what the motive, called by the Chinese *pan yün* or 'undulating cloud', looked like.

Figure 28. Imbricated ornament from the
Second Phase 'Silver Island' *ting*.

A word needs to be said on the chronology of the Second Phase. Its upper limit is fairly well defined. Discoveries of vessels such as the *kuei* of plate 14*a* at tombs near Hsin Ts'un, about 28 miles south-west of An-yang, indicate that the First Phase was still flourishing at the beginning of the Chou period; events referred to in the inscription on this *kuei* happened in the sixth year of King Ch'êng of that dynasty, so that on the basis of the revised chronology it can be dated about 1000 B.C. Yet a hundred years later the Second Phase was in full swing; for Karlgren has documented a group of bronzes bearing inscriptions assignable to the reign of King Kung (beginning about 900 B.C.), and displaying many Second Phase motives, but none that are typical of the First. We are therefore safe in saying that the Second Phase began to make its appearance early in the ninth century. But the lower limit is far less easily decided. Certainly the onset of the Third Phase was not marked by 'an instantaneous influx of new ideas', as Karlgren claims was that of the Second. Indeed, we are not absolutely certain that the Second Phase, wide as was the area of its appearance as compared with that of the First, ever penetrated at all into some of the eastern States. We know of no Second Phase examples from Sung

State in eastern Honan, for example. The possibility has to be admitted that Second and Third Phases were coeval for perhaps as long as two centuries, but in different parts of the country. In 1923 a hoard of more than a hundred Second Phase bronzes was discovered at Hsin-chêng in central Honan (p. 135). The site lay within the territory of Chêng State (eighth to fifth centuries B.C.) and there is some evidence that the vessels may have been made as late as the middle sixth century. No later date has been claimed for any Second Phase bronze, as far as I am aware.

THE THIRD PHASE

Vessels in the style of this Phase have been found over most of the area of the feudal States, from Li-yü in the north-west of Shansi to Shou Hsien in Anhwei. A famous set of bronzes, the Piao bells, was recovered in 1925 from one of several tombs outside the village of Chin Ts'un in central Honan, occupying part of the site of the late Chou capital of Ch'êng Chou, some 13 miles north-east of modern Lo-yang. They show typical Third Phase features, and if the date given by their inscriptions could be read with any confidence, we should have a valuable *terminus ante quem* for the beginning of the Third Phase. But many uncertainties attach to this inscription. The phrase 'the twenty-second year of the King', if by 'King' the rightful Chou king is meant, can only refer either to 550 or to 379 B.C.; and if the date is one or other of these, the wording of the inscriptions does seem to make the earlier one more likely.[1] But the earliest really reliable – and, as far as I know, generally accepted – date available is given by the inscriptions on a pair of *hu*, one of which is shown on plate 16. Yetts has shown that events there referred to must have happened in the year 482 B.C., shortly after which time the *hu* must have been cast.

The style of the Third Phase is hybrid. On the one hand, certain First Phase elements reappear in modified form. We say 'reappear', but the reader will have gathered from what has been said (p. 117 and above) that the continuity of Shang-Yin bronze art may never have

1. The curious fact that much of the Chin Ts'un find shows resemblances to late Third Phase and even Han dynasty material can be explained by supposing that the bells were already some three centuries old when they were deposited in the tomb. The suggestion has been made that the actual date of the burial was about 230 B.C.

been entirely broken, especially in eastern districts populated by Shang-Yin people after the Chou conquest, such as the State of Sung.[1] On the other hand, these elements are found associated with decorative elements and vessel-shapes quite typical of the Second Phase. And thirdly, to add to the confusion, other elements are evidently borrowed from the nomad art of the Ordos region. Lastly, a number of elements whose origins cannot be traced presumably occur for the first time.

The art of the Third Phase represents a new climax of bronze craftsmanship. Although the old and perhaps obsolete First Phase elements now restored – *t'ao-t'ieh*, free animal's head, *yüan wo*, hanging and rising blades, interlocked T's, and so forth – are all easily recognizable, their interpretation is much freer and more playful. The hieratic quality has been altogether banished, and increasing emphasis on purely decorative qualities, such as we found manifest in Second Phase bronzes, results in a richness of design which yet is controlled. Horizontal zoning is retained, but the pattern tends once more to fill the entire surface.

So complex are the problems of the inception of this apparent renaissance in bronze art towards the end of the Chou period that we propose to ignore them altogether here. The art historian has, however, several promising lines along which he may hope to proceed. Shou Hsien, whence some of the finest Third Phase examples come, was the site of a Ch'u capital from 241 to 222 B.C.[2] And Ch'u, as we have observed, was a southern, 'non-Chinese' comity in its origins. In the next chapter we shall see how solid are indications that many idioms in Chinese art during the last few centuries B.C. came from the south. Again, the question of reciprocal influences between the Third

1. The problem is perplexing. Karlgren advances four separate explanations for the reappearance of First Phase motives on bronzes of the Third Phase. The one he favours – that Third Phase art was in part a conscious renaissance and that Third Phase designers 'picked up a number of earlier elements ... suitable to be embodied ... in their new décor schemes', and consciously revived motives 'long since obsolete' – does not answer the question, where *were* the earlier elements that they could be picked up? Were actual Shang-Yin bronzes available as models in the sixth century B.C.?

2. One of the Shou Hsien bronzes is dated to the reign of Yu Wang (237–228 B.C.). As Karlgren points out, this object must have been deposited some time between the latter year and 222 B.C., when Ch'u was annihilated by Ch'in. Cf. B. Karlgren, 'Huai and Han', being *B.M.F.E.A.*, no. 13 (1941), p. 8.

Phase and nomad bronze art has not yet been settled. From some elements they have in common, such as the rope pattern of plate 15*b*, little can be learnt. But others, such as pear-shaped cells on the bodies of modelled animals like those of figure 29, are vestigial and meaningless in Chinese art, whereas this feature is found over the whole province of nomad art, translated into several different media; and evidence is that these cells were originally meant to be inlaid with turquoises and other stones. Another device, cited by Karlgren as distinctive of the Phase, is that of the 'turned animal head', such as is shown by the cattle that adorn the lid of the *ting* of figure 29; this also has been claimed as an original feature of nomad art.

Figure 29. Cow with turned head on
the cover of a Third Phase *ting*.

A fine *li* from the Brundage Collection at the Art Institute of Chicago (plate 15*b*) shows the Third Phase style at its simplest and most refined. Like vessels found at Li-yü in 1923, the body is divided into two horizontal registers, separated by a relief band or rib which in most examples simulates a rope. The registers are occupied with files of interlaced dragons, most of whose bodies are plain while others are filled with oblique striae. The spaces between the dragons are occupied with squared spirals. In general form and styled decoration this *li* much resembles a covered *ting* in the same Museum; the covers of both can be reversed to serve as auxiliary dishes.

Other motives of the synthetic Third Phase style are well shown on the fine *hu* of plate 16. The upper border of the topmost zone, rendered as a twisted cord pattern, simulates the Second Phase *pan yün* (p. 169). Borders of other zones are composed of a new element, the plaited cord pattern. The zones themselves are filled with forms, seemingly derived from the figured bands of the Second Phase (as shown on the *kuei* of figure 17). The tallest zone, at the belly of the *hu*, shows freely treated First Phase *t'ao-t'ieh*; and the climbing dragon handles are also reminiscent of First Phase types. Spiral-filling on the interlacing 'dragon' bodies of the main zones is yet another First Phase feature; but granulations, wavy striae, and comma-shaped hooks seem to be altogether new.[1]

1. Perhaps this is not entirely true of the comma pattern. According to Karlgren this independent element is an end-product of the breakdown of earlier *t'ao-t'ieh* and 'dragon' figures where physical features were progressively stylized during the Second Phase. Cf. B. Karlgren (see footnote 2 p. 171), pp. 31–4.

Chapter Four

LACQUER AND SILK

INTRODUCTION

Discovery of undoubted Chinese lacquers and silks of the Han period (205 B.C. to A.D. 220) at site after site from Korea to the Near East (map 4) alone might invite speculation about the Han Empire and its range of contacts. But thanks to the tradition of history-writing founded by Ssǔ-ma Ch'ien's *Shih chi*, 'Historical Records',[1] and to painstaking surveys of almost every aspect of social, economic, political, and military history in the first great dynastic chronicle, *Ch'ien han shu*, 'History of the Former Han Dynasty',[2] and its successor, *Hou han shu*, 'History of the Latter Han Dynasty',[3] we need ask of archaeology little more than corroboration of what we already know. In fact it does much more for us. The practice of burying with the dead not only their personal belongings, but also pottery models of every conceivable article of domestic use (*ming ch'i*), has provided us with a means of reconstructing Han daily life in fine detail. Material remains help to round out the picture of a fully documented phase of Chinese history.

That these various sources of information should be available is perhaps no accident. There is an air of urbanity about the period; an accent on corporeal values and worldly well-being that seems to go together with the bureaucratic belief in record-making for its own sake. In spite of its ups and downs, of internal rebellions, and a threat to its very existence from nomads in the north during its first hundred years or so, one can scarcely bring oneself to think of the Han period

1. Ssǔ-ma Ch'ien (*c.* 136–85 B.C.), *Shih chi*, translated in part by É. Chavannes, *Les Mémoires Historiques de Se-ma Ts'ien*, 5 vols, Paris 1895–1905.
2. Pan Ku (d. A.D. 92), *Ch'ien han shu*. The Imperial Annals, with which this work opens, have been translated in part by H. H. Dubs as *The History of the Former Han Dynasty*, 3 vols, London 1938–55.
3. Fan Yeh (A.D. 420–77), *Hou han shu*. This work is untranslated except for a few isolated chapters. For full bibliographical information on these, as for translations of isolated chapters of *Shih chi* and *Ch'ien han shu*, cf. J. Needham (see footnote p. 22), pp. 253–62 and 268–98.

in dramatic terms. The outlook on life of colonial officers and their women-folk in Korea, for instance, seems to have been no less self-contained and complacent than that of colonial administrators at all times, the world over. The inventory of chattels found in their graves reads like the catalogue of a departmental store: lacquered occasional tables with dishes, trays, bowls, spoons, and ladles; hats, leather shoes, fragments of silks and woollen clothes, and chests for clothes; seals of office and writing-brushes; belt-hooks, jewellery, combs, hair-pins, and mirrors; cosmetic outfits comprising nests of lacquered boxes holding pomades, face-powders, powder brushes, rouge, and mascara; even a divination set for fortune-telling. A civilized and self-conscious period, evidently. Yet, despite its grandeur, perhaps a trifle dull.

Lacquer and silk are, by general consent, luxury commodities. They are also highly suitable for export, being both light and strong; and each had reached a peak of technical and artistic excellence by Han times. Small wonder, then, that they quickly found their way on to foreign markets when, at the beginning of the first century B.C., China began for the first time to participate directly in world trade. Han lacquer and silk, in fact, serve to illustrate the theme of Chinese political expansion which we shall go on to discuss in a moment.

But in another and less obvious way lacquer and silk form a link by which we can connect material culture with the social and economic life of the times. For they served to satisfy a new demand from the home market. Both were costly, and both lent themselves to large-scale manufacture and standardization of quality. Precisely such ready-made symbols of wealth and class-solidarity are in demand whenever a large ruling class is found. Such a class now existed. The unification of China and the widening of her political frontiers had brought into being a vast new administration of civil and military officials. Furthermore, unstable economic conditions following the eclipse of the feudal nobility (p. 177) had caused a redistribution of wealth into the hands of industrialists, urban financiers and land-holders. These now became large-scale manufacturers. Consumer goods and raw materials produced under their direction – cereals, textiles, salt, iron and so forth – were marketed by a new merchant class who kept the whole *bourgeoisie* and Court nobility supplied with luxury articles while regulating the price of basic commodities to their own advantage. There were, as a matter of fact, Imperial lacquer and silk-weaving factories;

but production and sale were never Government monopolies, and it seems reasonable to suppose that by far the bulk of such wares was manufactured and sold privately (p. 193).

The Political and Military Background of the Han Empire

In order to discover how conditions arose favourable to the development of the Han silk and lacquer industries and the dissemination of their products over such a wide area of Asia, we must inquire into political circumstances at the end of the Chou period. Its last years were taken up with a life-and-death struggle, during which State after State was ruthlessly eliminated, to decide which should rule over all China. Ch'in, whose leaders were refreshingly free from any form of political idealism, emerged victorious and founded the first Chinese empire (221–206 B.C.). There seems no very obvious reason why it was so short-lived. Possibly because, although the policies advocated by its legalist advisers were very quickly put into practice, peace was a condition Ch'in had never had to face. She had been geared for total inter-State war, and for very little else. The disaffection now at large throughout north China – an oppressed peasantry led by feudal nobles who had lost their possessions and whose outlook was reactionary – this she seemed utterly incapable of dealing with. Ch'in had indeed united China, had embodied a political ideal from which there was to be no turning back, nor any going forward, during 2,000 years to come; but in so doing, she had created a national resistance movement directed against herself. The death of the First Ch'in Emperor was the signal for immediate and widespread revolt.

The onslaught was swift and decisive, and came from all sides. The Ch'in capital, Hsien-yang, lay more or less on the site of modern Ch'ang-an (p. 658); and the metropolitan province of Kuan-chung, 'the land within the Passes', approximated in extent to the natural fortress of southern Shensi. Here, for a short time, the Second Emperor was able to rule. But every other part of China was soon lost to him. A struggle for supremacy developed between the leading rebels. Hsiang Yü was an aristocrat, descendant of a famous Ch'u general, and Liu Chi, who had at one time served under him, no more than a petty village official by origin. But Liu marched west throughout the breadth of China, took an ill-frequented route through the passes into Kuan-chung, overcame a Ch'in army sent against him, and received the surrender of defenceless Hsien-yang in December 207 B.C. The Han dynasty officially began in the following year. In fact for four years to come Liu Chi and Hsiang Yü fought out their rivalry in an extended bout of marches, counter-marches, sieges, and so forth, until the latter finally capitulated in January 202 B.C.

The early Han rulers, one feels, had almost as little idea about what was needed to weld together the new Empire as had their Ch'in predecessors.[1] Their policy of granting fiefs to near relatives of the Throne, and to meritorious servants, threatened to restore the old feudal system in new guise. But thanks largely to the influence of moderate Confucianist advisers at Court, the dynasty maintained a precarious hold on China until 154 B.C. Then the balance swung heavily in favour of Government. In that year a rebellion involving seven vassal princes was decisively crushed, and the feudal nobility as a hereditary class in Chinese society ceased to exist. 154 B.C. was a turning-point in Chinese history.

During all this time China was becoming more and more aware of a disturbing force at work on her northern frontiers. The horse-riding nomads of the steppes had banded themselves together under the leadership of a Turkish people, the Hsiung-nu. These were the ancestors of the Huns who later appeared in Europe, and for simplicity's sake we shall henceforward call them by this more familiar name. The first Hun empire coincided, as we noticed (p. 11), with the Ch'in dynasty. We hear little of Hun maraudings in China until Han times, but from the early years of the new dynasty the Imperial Annals are full of such incidents. Bogged down with internal troubles, the early Han emperors had no effective answer to these raids; their policy was to placate the Huns wherever possible. This they did by sending Chinese princesses as wives to the Hun rulers, by making expensive gifts of manufactured articles,[2] and by opening annual border

1. When the Confucianist minister Lu Chia tried to impress Liu Chi with the weight of his Imperial responsibility by quoting precepts from the Classics the Emperor objected: 'I won my Empire on horseback. What need have I to bother with the Book of Songs and the Book of History?' Lu Chia replied, 'You won it on horseback, but can you rule it from there?'

2. So in 174 B.C. the Chinese Emperor sends to the Hun chieftain several embroidered silk gowns woven with many-coloured patterns; ten lengths of embroidered silk; thirty pieces of many-coloured woven silk; forty pieces of heavy red silk, etc., etc. In 51 B.C., seventy-seven sets of bed-covers are sent; in

fairs at which the nomads could obtain Chinese luxury goods by barter. The raids continued unabated.

The Reign of Emperor Wu (140–85 B.C.)

Emperor Wu was a Sun King; for his long reign saw China for the first time become a nation in her own right and a world power scarcely less mighty than Rome. This position she gained as the outcome of a planned campaign against the Huns, a campaign made possible by the successful resolution of her domestic affairs after the revolt of 154 B.C.

In 133 B.C. Emperor Wu made a start. A project to ambush the Hun chieftain, the *Shan Yü*, inside the borders of China misfired in that year; but four years later Chinese troops under General Wei Ch'ing fought for the first time in history outside the Chinese border, and other sorties were made through the northern commanderies in 128 and 127 B.C. In 124 B.C. came the first major victory. The *Shan Yü* again narrowly escaped capture at the hands of Wei Ch'ing's forces, who accounted for over 15,000 Huns killed or captured. Chinese troops now poured over the north and north-west frontiers, consolidating their hold on all territory inside the Wall, and beginning to probe up the Kansu Corridor towards the independent oasis kingdoms of Chinese Turkestan. In 123 B.C. a young cavalry colonel, Ho Ch'ü-ping, made a successful début, taking 2,000 heads or prisoners in an independent sortie. He was promoted to the rank of general. Two years later he made another brilliant raid through the Kansu Corridor, killing or capturing 30,000 of the enemy, and in the autumn of the same year received the surrender of the combined peoples of two petty kingdoms in north-west Kansu.

The main body of the Huns had by this time retreated to the northern edge of the Gobi Desert. The year 119 B.C. was an *annus mirabilis* for China. Wei Ch'ing and Ho Ch'ü-ping were ordered to make fresh attacks, each with 50,000 cavalry. Wei Ch'ing launched an expedition from the Yellow River Bend to a distance of more than 300 miles into

---

49 B.C., 110 suits of clothes; in 1 B.C., no less than 84,000 pieces of embroidered silk and 78,000 lb. of silk floss. But these later 'gifts' were almost certainly barter goods, the value of which was calculated, as a Han commentator says, 'on the value of what they offer us'.

the Gobi, located the *Shan Yü*, and was able to surround him and his men. For the third time the Hun chief escaped – at night, and in a sandstorm; the Chinese force nevertheless accounted for nearly 20,000 Huns. Meanwhile Ho, further east, penetrated to a depth of 700 miles into Hun territory, met with and fought the troops of one of the *Shan Yü*'s two delegates, and killed or captured 70,000 of them. On this expedition Chinese troops are supposed to have reached Lake Baikal.

Losses suffered by the Huns in ten years of campaigning – numbering between 80,000 and 90,000 dead alone – were enough to free China from the menace to her northern frontiers. Occasional raids still went on, and several major expeditions were launched by China, but from 119 B.C. or thereabouts the final issue was never in doubt. Between them, Wei Ch'ing and Ho Ch'ü-ping had broken the Hun military machine to pieces. Not for 300 years was China again seriously worried by nomad aggression, and when it then occurred (p. 304) it was of an altogether different nature. One result of Wu's military success was to free troops for fresh enterprises in the east and south (pp. 184–6); another was the opening up of central Asia. Chinese garrisons now stemmed far into Chinese Turkestan, paving the way for diplomatic and commercial intercourse with the West. China was expanding. 'Like silkworms', says *Hou han shu*, '[the Chinese] ate into the lands bordering the Huns, in a northerly direction.'

The Western Regions (cf. map 4, at end of volume)

Some fifty years earlier an event had taken place which indirectly helped to open up the greatest trade route of antiquity: that which carried Chinese silk across Asia to the Roman Orient and ultimately to Rome itself. A nomadic tribe, the Yüeh-chih, had been badly beaten by the Huns in western Kansu; and the main horde, the Ta Yüeh-chih, had fled to the west. That was in 165 B.C. For four years, between 164 and 160 B.C., they made their home in the Ili valley north of Lake Issyk-kul and the western end of T'ien Shan, until driven on again by another nomadic group, the Wu-sun. Then their fortunes changed. Continuing west, they came at last upon a settled agricultural people living in the middle basin of the Jaxartes River (Syr Darya). This was the independent kingdom of Sogdiana (Ch.

K'ang Chü), formerly a satrapy of Alexander's but long since separated from the main Seleucid Greek Empire by a powerful new neighbour, Parthia (Ch. An Hsi). The Sogdians, already weakened by wars against the Parthian Mithradates I, were no match for the Ta Yüeh-chih, who proceeded to occupy the whole region between the Jaxartes and Oxus Rivers by about 130 B.C.

South of the Oxus lay another kingdom with Greek traditions, its dynasty founded by a Macedonian; namely, Bactria (Ch. Ta Hsia). To Bactria the Ta Yüeh-chih now turned their attention; it was in their hands by 128 B.C. A hundred and fifty years later a certain Kujula Kadphises consolidated the five groups into which the Ta Yüeh-chih had split, and began the conquest of north-west India. Thus were laid the foundations of a great new empire, the Kushān, which at its zenith at the end of the first century A.D. was to reach westwards to within a few hundred miles of the Roman frontier on the Euphrates, and eastwards across the Punjāb to the United Provinces of Upper India. So it was that a nomad tribe from the other side of Asia – people who knew the Chinese and had traded with them as far back as the fourth century B.C. (p. 60) – came to lodge themselves solidly west of the Pamirs, on the borders of the civilized Western world.

The original defeat suffered by the Yüeh-chih at the hands of the Huns had been reported to the Han Emperor Wên, in a letter from the *Shan Yü*. Emperor Wu, who succeeded Wên, conceived the idea of forming an alliance with them against the Huns, without having any clear idea where they might be. He therefore sent a certain Chang Ch'ien, with a hundred attendants, to find them. This traveller was the first Chinese to write about western Asia as he himself had seen it; and his story proves him to have been one of the world's great explorers. No sooner did he leave China in 138 B.C. than he was captured by the Huns and held prisoner for ten years, during which time he married and had children. He then managed to escape, and continued his journey west, still bearing the Emperor's token of authority. Travelling north of T'ien Shan by way of the Dzungarian Gap and the Ili valley, he at last reached the headwaters of the Jaxartes, west of the Pamirs. Here was yet another independent kingdom, Ferghana (Ch. Ta Yüan). From Ferghana Chang Ch'ien crossed into Transoxiana (128 B.C.), where he found the Ta Yüeh-chih in secure possession, but far too occupied with their plans for the conquest of Bactria to contemplate so distant an alliance. Chang started back for China, was again captured by the Huns, again escaped, and finally reached home in 126 B.C., accompanied by his wife and one remaining attendant. He was given a marquisate.

The news brought by Chang Ch'ien of what came to be called the 'Western Regions' caused a certain stir, but its commercial implications were not properly understood. This was natural enough, since although Chang seems to have been a shrewd observer, his information about Parthia and places further west, which he had not visited, was extremely vague. There seems to have been no notion of the tremendous potential market represented by the Western world. Instead, what struck Emperor Wu most was his emissary's report of a hitherto unknown breed of horse, the so-called 'heavenly horse', t'ien ma, found in Ferghana and credited with supernatural powers. Wishing to procure some of the breed for use against the Huns, Emperor Wu sent a diplomatic mission to the Ferghana capital.[1] It was badly received and, on reaching the Ferghana frontier on their return journey, its members were callously murdered (106 B.C.). The following year the Emperor sent Li Kuang-li, brother of an Imperial concubine, with a riff-raff army of ex-prisoners and provincial recruits to besiege the Ferghana capital. But crops had failed throughout the north-west that year and the city-states of Chinese Turkestan were hostile. Only a few thousand men reached Ferghana, where they suffered an overwhelming defeat.

China's prestige along the road to the West was now at stake. Wu was committed to the conquest of Ferghana, and in 102 B.C. dispatched a vast expedition, including some 60,000 fighting men, to execute it. The capital was besieged for forty days, after which the inhabitants capitulated and obligingly beheaded their king; a few dozen 'heavenly horses' were obtained.

Here, in the valley of the Upper Jaxartes, west of the Pamir Divide, was the ultimate western limit of the Han Empire. In central Asia China was for the time being undisputed master, and embassies to countries further west now passed freely to and fro at a rate of ten or so a year. Inside a generation Chinese military genius had created a new imperialist power in Asia and thereby had shifted the whole

1. This place, known to the Chinese as Êrh-shih, is identified with Ura Tepe, 20 miles south of the great bend in the Jaxartes River.

balance of Asian politics. By crossing the Pamirs, Chinese armies had done what those of Alexander 200 years before had failed to do; and in the perspective of world history the result was immense. On the one hand, Chinese silk reached the markets of Rome, where it quickly became an important item in the Oriental trade which, according to Hudson, 'was one of the major factors in the economic decline of the Roman world'.[1] On the other, as will be recounted in the next chapter, Buddhism reached China – and from China, Japan – as a result of contact with India through the Kushān Empire.

After Emperor Wu's conquests, Chinese influence in central Asia wavered for a century or so, but was generally speaking dominant there. Then, during the interregnum of Wang Mang between the Former and Latter Han dynasties (A.D. 9–25), it lapsed; the Huns gained some influence in Chinese Turkestan, and the independent city-state of Yarkand (Ch. So-chü) was able to play off one Power against the other.[2] But in A.D. 73 General Pan Ch'ao, a brother of the author of 'History of the Former Han Dynasty' (p. 174), began once more to assert Chinese authority, in spite of isolationist opposition among the clique round the Throne. And Turkestan remained firmly Chinese until his death in A.D. 101. For some years afterwards it was again lost to China, and was then reconquered by Pan Ch'ao's son, Pan Yung, in A.D. 127.

In A.D. 97 Pan Ch'ao had sent an ambassador called Kan Ying, with instructions to proceed to a place in the west called Ta Ch'in. By this time China was aware that more was to be got from the West than impractical alliances and horses with supernatural powers. Ta Ch'in, we now believe, was the Roman Empire, or at least its eastern province of Syria. Chinese curiosity about Ta Ch'in probably meant that she was now roused to the idea of direct and large-scale trading with Rome through its Syrian outposts, thereby eliminating middleman

1. G. F. Hudson, *Europe and China: A Survey of their Relations from the Earliest Times to 1800*, London 1931, p. 99.
2. But this is the 'official' view of later Chinese historians. Sir Aurel Stein found a number of documents with Wang Mang reign-period dates at a fortified military post (*limes*) near Tun-huang, the gateway to Chinese Turkestan; and Chavannes concludes that Wang Mang maintained Chinese prestige there until the end of his reign, and that only at the beginning of the Latter Han period did it begin to weaken. Cf. É. Chavannes, *Les Documents chinois découverts par Aurel Stein dans les Sables du Turkestan oriental. Publiés et traduits par É. Chavannes*, Oxford 1913, p. vii.

profits. Speaking of Ta Ch'in in 'History of the Latter Han Dynasty', Fan Yeh says: 'They traffic by sea with An-hsi [Parthia] and T'ien-chu [India], the profit of which trade is ten-fold. They are honest in their transactions, and there are no double prices.'[1]

Parthia, as map 4 clearly shows, was a profit-taking intermediary in the now-expanding silk trade. China watched the silk as far as Parthia's frontiers, but of its subsequent fate they knew nothing; they understood only that there was a large consumer nation further west. The Parthians did nothing to enlighten them. Kan Ying was deliberately prevented from taking the direct overland route via Mesopotamia (Ch. T'iao Chih) to Syria. And when eventually he reached the Persian Gulf and was ready to set sail for Ta Ch'in – presumably a Syrian port was to be his destination – he was gently dissuaded from making the voyage. In *very* favourable circumstances, he was told, it could be done in two months; but mariners generally put three years' provisions on board. 'There is something in the sea', his informants added, 'which is apt to make man home-sick, and several have thus lost their lives.' Fan Yeh comments: 'When Kan Ying heard this, he stopped.'[2] Writing more than 300 hundred years after the event, Fan Yeh of course saw the situation far more clearly than did Kan Ying. Of Ta Ch'in he pertinently observes: 'Their kings always desired to send embassies to China, but the An-hsi [Parthians] wished to carry on trade with them in Chinese silks, and it is for this reason that they were cut off from communication.'[3]

Nevertheless, despite the unsolved whereabouts of Ta Ch'in, and Parthia's uncommunicativeness, trade in Chinese commodities was pushed relentlessly forward. Everyone stood to gain from it, of course. Map 4, which shows the distribution of Chinese silks and lacquers found in various parts of Asia, will serve as an index of its spread westward. Tun-huang in China; Edsin-gol in Mongolia; Lou-lan, Ying-p'an and Niya in Chinese Turkestan; Begram in Afghānistān; Dura-Europos and Halebie-Zenobia in Mesopotamia; and Palmyra in Syria, are all places on or near the direct trade-route to Rome.

1. F. Hirth, *China and the Roman Orient: researches into their ancient and mediaeval relations as represented in old Chinese records*, Leipzig, Munich, Shanghai and Hong Kong 1885, p. 42.

2. F. Hirth (see footnote above), p. 39.

3. F. Hirth (see footnote above), p. 42.

Chinese Expansion in the South and East

Our theme so far has centred round Chinese political expansion during the reign of Emperor Wu. This went on not only in the 'Western Regions' but also in the south and east. In the south-west attention was directed to finding a way through to Bactria and countries further west by way of India.[1] Several expeditions were launched, but all were halted in what is now the province of Yunnan by a hostile aboriginal tribe, the K'un-ming. In the neighbourhood of modern Kunming itself there was also a small independent principality called T'ien, founded by a general who had been sent from Ch'u State to conquer the region about 330 B.C. In 109 B.C. T'ien became incorporated in the Chinese Empire as the commandery of I-chou.

East of Yunnan, and south of the Yangtze, lie the present-day provinces of Kweichou, Kwangsi, Hunan, Kwangtung, Kiangsi, Fukien, and Chekiang. Scarcely any of this territory had been brought under Chinese control at the beginning of Wu's reign. Parts of Kweichou and Hunan formed the independent kingdom of Yeh Lang; Kwangsi and Kwangtung, with pretty well the whole of Tongking and northern Annam, composed the kingdom of Nan Yüeh, founded by a Ch'in general; to the north lay Min Yüeh, occupying Fukien; and further north, Yüeh Tung Hai occupied Chekiang. Between all these lay smaller independent groups.

In 138 B.C., following an attack by Min Yüeh, the king of Yüeh Tung Hai came with his people to live under Chinese protection north of the Yangtze, and Yüeh Tung Hai ceased to exist. Three years later Min Yüeh attacked Nan Yüeh, who called upon China to intervene. On the approach of Chinese troops the Min Yüeh army took fright, killed their king, and treated with the Chinese. Yeh Lang was already on more or less friendly terms with the Han peoples. Indeed, since 130 B.C. it had been given the status of a province called Chien-wei. The one obstacle to undisputed Chinese rule south of the Yangtze was therefore Nan Yüeh.

On the occasion of the Min Yüeh attack on Nan Yüeh in 135 B.C.,

1. An idea put forward by Chang Ch'ien, who, when he was in Bactria, noticed some bamboos and cloth that looked as if they came from Shu (Szechwan). On inquiry he learnt that these products were bought in India by Bactrian merchants.

Emperor Wu had sent a Chinese delegate with instructions to the latter. While in Pan-yü (modern Canton) this man, whose name was T'ang Mêng, apparently came across some preserves made from fruit which he suspected grew only in Szechwan; he was told that the fruit in question was sent down the West River, at the mouth of which Canton stands, from the kingdom of Yeh Lang. On his return to Ch'ang-an, T'ang Mêng discovered from Szechwan merchants trading there that what he had suspected was true. A road- and river-route led from Szechwan across Kweichow, and thence down to Canton. Nan Yüeh could be attacked from the rear.[1]

In 112 B.C., following allegations of scandalous incidents at the Nan Yüeh Court, Emperor Wu sent six generals, all leading armies of ex-convicts, to converge by various river-routes on Canton. A swift and easy victory was won against Nan Yüeh, and troops were immediately detached for mopping-up in various parts of Yunnan. The whole of China proper, as well as northern Indo-China, was now under Han rule. A rebellion in the latter region occurred in A.D. 40, but was put down by a brilliant campaign on the part of General Ma Yüan in A.D. 42-3, and Chinese settlers proceeded to move into Tongking and Annam, penetrating as far south as Thanh-hoa on the Chu River in northern Annam. In this area, brick tombs of Han settlers have recently been excavated and fragments of silk and lacquer, as well as many other remains of Chinese occupation, brought to light.

In the north-east an independent principality called Ch'ao Hsien had been founded in south Manchuria and north Korea by a Chinese adventurer, Wei Mên, at the beginning of the second century B.C. He had made his capital at a place called Wang-hsien on the Ta-t'ung River, a site now occupied by the town of Pyong-yang. Emperor Wu, intent on an alliance by which to outflank the Huns to the east, sent an envoy to the Court of Wei Mên's grandson in 109 B.C., but meeting with a cool reception, the envoy murdered a Ch'ao Hsien prince and returned to China claiming to have killed an enemy general. He was given a fief not far from Ch'ao Hsien.

The king of Ch'ao Hsien now revolted, and attacked and killed the former envoy. Emperor Wu thereupon sent a naval and military mission to annex Ch'ao Hsien. But liaison between the admiral and the

---

1. The reader will perhaps have noticed a curious similarity between this story and the one related of Chang Ch'ien (see footnote p. 184).

general was poor, and an inconclusive campaign ensued. After a year of fighting, during which the invaders were greatly helped by dissensions among the besieged of Wang-hsien, the entire principality capitulated to Chinese forces and four new commanderies were made out of its territory. Of these by far the most important seems to have been that centred on the capital, called by the Chinese Lo-lang; at its peak, Lo-lang commandery numbered some 315,000 people.

In 1909 Japanese archaeologists under Professor Sekino started to excavate the 1,300 odd Lo-lang tombs on the south bank of the Tat‘ung River, about 4 miles south-west of Pyong-yang. Some of the finest Han remains known to us have since been unearthed, including a few silks and an abundant collection of Han lacquers, all of superb quality. Further west, at Nan-shan-li and Ying-ch‘êng-tzŭ near Port Arthur on the Liao-tung Peninsula, at Pei-cha-ch‘êng near modern Kalgan in Inner Mongolia, and at Yang-kao near Ta-t‘ung in northern Shansi, more finds of Han lacquers have been made. These commanderies in the region of the Great Wall were outposts of the Chinese Empire set against the Huns, about whom a little more must now be said.

The Northern Regions

Meanwhile the nomads stretched in a great arc across the steppe belt. West of the Urals, lying north of the Black and Caspian Seas, were tribes known to Roman historians as Setae, Sarmatae, Alani, Roxolani, Aorsi, and so on. All were no doubt in contact with the Greek colonists settled on the Black Sea at places like Olbia, Chersonesus, Tanais, and Panticapaeum on the Kertch Peninsula of the Crimea. From these centres articles of Greek manufacture were freely sold to the nomads, a fact which accounts for the presence of objects bearing Hellenistic decoration in so many Scythian and Sarmatian tombs. Indeed, the nomads' cultural range was considerable. The Aorsi, we know, traded with Babylonia and even India through Armenian and Median intermediaries. And to the south-east, in Sogdiana and Bactria, the Ta Yüeh-chih were now in close contact with the Hellenistic culture of the Middle East, with its inheritance of Greek, Iranian, and eastern Mediterranean styles and decorative motives. Further east, the Huns, fleeing westward from the victorious

Chinese, were beginning to appear in Hither Asia; and beyond them, extending over the Altai region and Outer Mongolia, were more Huns.

In 1924-5 a Russian expedition led by P. K. Koslóv explored a group of tumuli in the mountains of Noin-ula near Lake Baikal, some 70 miles north of Urga and 7 miles east of the Urga–Kyakhta road. Excavation revealed that these were tombs of horse-riding nomads, very probably Huns. Objects found included some imported from China, others from the West, and others of local manufacture; but this last group was by far the smallest. A Chinese lacquer dish (cf. figure 46) bears a date corresponding to the year 2 B.C., and the strong likelihood is that the tombs belong to the first century of our era.[1]

Nomads are highly effective culture-agents. Noin-ula itself is something like 2,500 miles from the fringes of the Hellenistic world, yet textiles from these tombs are full of Western motives. We shall presently deal in some detail with Chinese silks found at Noin-ula; but discoveries such as this serve no less to demonstrate how extended was the reach of Greek culture over Asia at this time, and help to explain how it was that Hellenistic motives should have been able to find their way so freely into Chinese art. Let us therefore glance briefly at the list of Hellenistic subjects featured among the Noin-ula finds.

The art of the Hellenized Middle East from the end of the third century B.C. to the beginning of our era displays a rich variety of styles and decorative motives. Some are purely Greek in origin; others, inherited by Achaemenid Persia, are ultimately Sumerian, Babylonian, and Assyrian; yet others are Egyptian or Phoenician. And from the time the Romans established their protectorate over Asia Minor in 190 B.C. Roman art, with its mixed Greek and Etruscan parentage, was also being disseminated through the civilized world bordering the nomads.

Of the textile motives at Noin-ula, stylized plant-forms, such as tendrils ending in spirals, rosettes, and palmettes, can all be traced to Assyria and Egypt by way of Hellenistic art. A motive featuring a nude boy rising from a flower calyx, on two Noin-ula embroidered

1. Cf. C. Trever, *Excavations in Northern Mongolia (1924–5)*, Leningrad 1932. The best and most accessible short account of the Koslóv finds in English is W. P. Yetts, 'Discoveries of the Koslóv Expedition', in *B.M.*, vol. xlviii (1926), pp. 168–85. In describing decorative motives at Noin-ula I have drawn freely from this source.

woollen fragments, has as its counterpart a section of the frieze of the Forum of Trajan executed – by a Greek – in A.D. 114. An embroidered winged griffin on another woollen fabric must ultimately be Mesopotamian in origin, though the motive has been described as typically Greek and typically Persian; and it also appears on the above mentioned Greco-Roman frieze. A group of horsemen embroidered on another fragment ride horses of a type seen on Greek vases; and the decorative band beneath displays a characteristic motive of Greek vases, the anthemion, which can be traced ultimately to Egypt and Assyria. Assyrian also is the so-called Geneva Cross, which appears at Noin-ula in the form of an *appliqué* mosaic border to the centre-piece of a carpet; and this motive probably travelled East via Sarmatian art. Naturalistic animals – tortoises, carp, and eels – on a Noin-ula carpet are of a type similar to those found on the mosaic pavement of a villa excavated near the Farnese Palace, Rome, and they are disposed in much the same way. And that characteristic motive of nomad art, repeated several times at Noin-ula, where one animal is shown in the act of attacking another, may ultimately be Sumerian. It appears on the pillar of a harp found in the royal tombs at Ur (*c.* 3000 B.C.), where a lion attacks an ox; and on the sides of the platform of the Hall of Xerxes at Persepolis, the combatants being the same pair of animals.

*

Having tried to account in historical terms for the presence of Chinese lacquers and silks at sites in the Asiatic provinces shown on map 4 – namely, the Middle East, Siberia, Mongolia, Chinese Turkestan, Manchuria, China itself, Korea, and Tongking – we now propose to take up the separate stories of lacquer and silk in Han times. But decorative motives are common to both, and will therefore be treated in a short end-section on their own.

LACQUER

The Lac Tree in Han and pre-Han China

Rhus vernicifera, the lac tree (Ch. *ch'i shu*), grows to-day only in Annam, south China, Korea and Japan – whither it was introduced

Past and present distribution of the lac tree in China and locations of Han lacquer factories

Legend:

- ▨ Distribution according to Yü kung (4th century B.C.)
- ☐ Distribution according to Yen t'ieh lun (1st century B.C.)
- ◪ Distribution according to Shih chi, Ch.129 (1st century B.C.)
- ⊠ Distribution according to Pieh lu (1st century B.C.)
- ⊞ chü yüan (lac tree plantation)
- ○ Present distribution according to Mänchen-Helfen
- ● Han lacquer factory

Scale: 0 — 100 — 200 miles

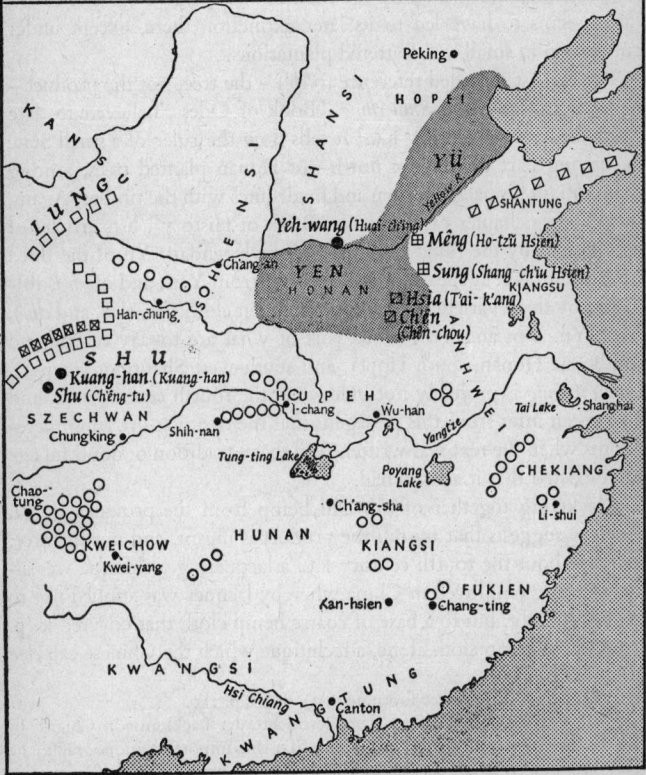

Map labels (as shown on map):

Peking

KANSU SHENSI SHANSI HOPEI

YÜ

Yellow R.   SHANTUNG

Ch'ang-an   Yeh-wang (Huai-ch'ing)   ⊞ Mêng (Ho-tzŭ Hsien)

LUNG   YEN   ⊞ Sung (Shang-ch'iu Hsien)

Han-chung   HONAN   ◪ Hsia (Tai-k'ang)   KIANGSU

SHU   ⊠ Ch'ên (Ch'ên-chou)   HWAI

Kuang-han (Kuang-han)   HUPEH   I-chang   Wu-han   Tai Lake   Shanghai

Shu (Ch'êng-tu)   Yangtze   CHEKIANG

SZECHWAN   Shih-nan   Tung-ting Lake   Poyang Lake

Chungking   Ch'ang-sha   Li-shui

Chao-tung   HUNAN   KIANGSI

KWEICHOW

Kwei-yang   Kan-hsien   FUKIEN   Chang-ting

KWANGSI

Hsi Chiang   Canton   KWANGTUNG

Map 5.

from the continent, according to J. J. Rein,[1] in the third century A.D. In China its northern limit is now the area between the Wei and Han Rivers in south Shensi. It grows at an elevation of between 3,000 and 4,000 feet.

Bearing in mind this southern distribution of the tree, can we assume that the original home of the lacquer industry was in south China? Not necessarily. In Han times, certainly, most lacquer products do seem to have come from southern parts; but there is literary evidence that the tree previously grew wild in north China, and not only on the uplands, but also in the plain. Gradual deforestation of north China, aggravated by too intensive tapping of the tree for its juice, seems to have led to its later extinction there, except under cultivation in small and scattered plantations.

The earliest recorded reference to *ch'i* – the tree, not the product – is in a song from the *Shih ching*, 'Book of Odes', believed to date from the seventh century B.C.[2] It tells how the ruler of a small State occupying part of modern north-east Honan planted trees, among them *ch'i*, in his palace garden and made lutes with the timber. Again, the *Yü kung* chapter of *Shu ching*, 'Book of History', lists articles of tribute sent by the Nine Provinces to the legendary Yü of the third millennium B.C. It speaks of *ch'i* and silk from Yen; and of *ch'i*, followed by three varieties of hemp or hempen cloth (*hsi*, *chih*, and *chu*), from Yü. Yen and Yü formed part of what are to-day central and south-east Honan, south Hopei, and south-west Shantung (map 5), but *Yü kung* is probably not older than the fourth century B.C., and all we can infer from this passage is that the tree was growing thereabouts when the text was written, and that a tradition of doubtful age then existed that it always had.

Bracketing together of *ch'i* and hemp from the province of Yü perhaps suggests that by *ch'i* the product is meant, and not the tree. For by about the fourth century B.C. a lacquering technique was already being employed in China whereby lacquer was applied not to wood directly, but to a base of coarse hemp cloth that covered it (p. 199), or to hemp cloth alone, a technique which the Chinese call *chia*

1. Cf. S. W. Bushell (see footnote p. 3), vol. i, p. 110.
2. Cf. O. Mänchen-Helfen, 'Zur Geschichte der Lackkunst in China', in *W.B.K.K.A.*, vol. xi (1937), pp. 32–64. To this important monograph, the only one in a Western language to deal with the early history of lacquer in China, I am indebted for much of the historical material that follows.

chu, 'lined with hemp cloth', and the Japanese *kanshitsu*, or 'dry lacquer'. Moreover, *ch'i* wood is poor-quality timber, and is hardly likely to have been mentioned in a list of tribute goods even if it had been done.

A Han treatise called *Yen t'ieh lun*, or 'Discourses on Salt and Iron', supposedly by the first-century B.C. writer Huan K'uan,[1] repeats the *Yü kung* story. In a chapter entitled 'Necessities of Life and Death'[2] the author speaks of *ch'i* coming from the regions traditionally called Yen and Yü, and it is perfectly apparent that here the tree itself cannot be meant. *Chou li* and *Li chi* also habitually refer to *ch'i* meaning 'lacquer', 'lacquered', and 'to lacquer'.

We have cited three texts mentioning *ch'i* from north-east China, and there are others (cf. map 5). But some late Chou and Han references seem to imply that the tree was already scarce in that part of the world. The expression *ch'i yüan*, 'lac-tree garden', meaning a plantation of cultivated trees, is occasionally met with as a place-name in such texts. The fourth-century B.C. philosopher who is supposed to have given his name to the book called *Chuang tzŭ* allegedly lived for many years at a Ch'i Yüan in the small State of Mêng, and as late as Han times a Ch'i Yüan existed inside the capital of Sung State.[3] We know that lacquer must have been scarce and valuable in Sung long before then; it was a general of Sung who, having lost a battle and much equipment against Chêng State in 606 B.C., was reproached by State artisans for wastage of armour. He replied that leather would always be available as long as there were cattle, and that there were still plenty of rhinoceros horns. But when asked where fresh supplies of cinnabar lacquer for proofing the armour were to come from, he had no answer to give.[4]

1. Huan K'uan, *Yen t'ieh lun*, revised with a commentary by Lin Chên-han, Shanghai 1936.
2. The significance of lacquer in this connexion will become evident when we deal with the outstanding role it played in funeral paraphernalia of the Han period and earlier (pp. 196, 200, 203).
3. Mêng is thought to be either modern Ho-tz'ŭ Hsien in south-west Shantung or T'ang-yin Hsien close by in northern Honan; the Sung capital lay in modern Shang-ch'iu Hsien in north-east Honan. For both cf. map 5.
4. Cf. Mänchen-Helfen (see footnote p. 190), p. 34; the source is the fourth-century B.C. *Tso chuan*.

Location of the Han Lacquer Industry

By Han times the main centres of production and manufacture had shifted to the west and south-west. *Yen t'ieh lun* speaks not only of lacquer from Yen and Yü, but also of cinnabar lacquer from Lung (western Shensi) and Shu (Szechwan); and Liu Hsiang mentions in his *Pieh lu* (first century B.C.) the lacquer of Han-chung in south-west Shensi. These references are to the raw material. But a commentary by the third-century A.D. scholar Li Ch'i on the *Ti li chih* chapter of 'History of the Former Han Dynasty' gives the names of ten State factories making various commodities in Former Han times; factory no. 7 was in Ho-nei Commandery, the region round modern Huai-ch'ing in northern Honan; factory no. 8, in Shu Commandery, was on or near the site of Ch'êng-tu, the modern provincial capital of Szechwan; and factory no. 9 lay in Kuang-han Commandery, identified with modern Kuang-han, some 30 miles north-east of Ch'êng-tu. These three factories, according to the commentator Ju Shun (*c.* A.D. 189–265), all produced lacquer goods.

We know from inscriptions on recently recovered lacquer-ware that factories 8 and 9 – those of Shu and Kuang-han – did indeed put out lacquer in Han times. Of twenty-six known vessels whose inscriptions record their place of manufacture, twenty-one come from Shu and five from Kuang-han. As for the Ho-nei factory, other literary evidence shows that it was located in Yeh-wang Hsien, corresponding to the above-mentioned Huai-ch'ing (map 5). In *Yen t'ieh lun*, chapter 29, the author is declaiming against the extravagant taste of his day and age, contrasting it with the simplicity of former times. *Then*, he says, people were content with vessels made of bamboo, willow, clay, and gourds for domestic use; 'whereas nowadays the wealthy go in for [lacquer vessels with] silver rims and gilt handles, gold *lei*, and bells of jade. The middle classes use Yeh-wang [lacquer] vessels [lined with] hemp cloth, and Shu gold-plated [lacquer] dishes (*pei*). Yet an ornamented [lacquer] dish costs ten times as much as one of bronze and still has no greater utility.'[1] On this evidence I see no grounds for dis-

1. Mänchen-Helfen perhaps fails to recognize the existence of the Yeh-wang factory because of copyists' mistakes appearing in the modern text of *Yen t'ieh lun*. The four characters which I have translated 'Yeh-wang [lacquer] vessels [lined with] hemp cloth' now read *shu yü chu ch'i*, which Mänchen-Helfen renders as 'far-sounding jade, and hemp vessels'. But as Lin Chên-han clearly shows in his commentary (see footnote p. 191), p. 110, *shu* and *yü* are

puting Ju Shun's statement that lacquer was made at factory 7, situated at Yeh-wang in Ho-nei.

No other factory is named in the inscriptions. Some inscriptions, however, give the names of workmen, and record date of manufacture, without specifying the place. Mänchen-Helfen supposes that these lacquers also came from Government factories, the names of workmen engaged in their manufacture being recorded so that defects could be traced to the individuals responsible. Certainly the bureaucratic mind seems to be at work here; but that does not mean, surely, that the factories were necessarily run by the State? In any case, most Han lacquers are uninscribed, and we can reasonably assume that these, at least, were manufactured under private enterprise.

There is no conclusive evidence to show that lacquer-ware was made anywhere outside China at this time. Mänchen-Helfen surmises that a basket of fine plaited grass and two wood sculptures found by Sir Aurel Stein at Lou-lan were lacquered locally, as also a birch-bark beaker from a tomb at Lo-lang in Korea. And Yetts supposes that the coffin-boards of a Han chieftain's tomb at Noin-ula – a fragment of one of which shows a goose flying through cloud-scrolls executed in red, yellow, green, and brown lacquer – were also lacquered locally; perhaps by a Chinese craftsman. But so specialized were techniques of manufacture, especially those involving lacquering over hemp cloth, painting, or inlaying, that production must certainly have been strictly localized – presumably in those regions where the lac tree itself grew. Mänchen-Helfen finds only one Han record of the tree growing outside China, and that is in Kashmir;[1] it can safely be said that by far the bulk of lacquers reported from colonial outposts were made in China, and by Chinese.

Composition and Mode of Preparation of Lacquer

We have spoken so far as if there were an agreed definition of what constitutes lacquer. That is not so. Indian, Burmese, and Sinhalese

---

mistakes for *yeh* and *wang*, characters that closely resemble them. With this correction *yeh wang chu ch'i* reads as a single phrase strictly parallel with the succeeding *chin ts'o shu pei*, 'Shu gold-plated [lacquer] dishes'.

1. The reference comes in the 'Western Regions' chapter of *Ch'ien han shu*, where Pan Ku speaks of the lac tree as native to Chi Pin, the region round Taxila. Cf. O. Mänchen-Helfen (see footnote p. 190), p. 57.

lacquer (Hind. *lakh*) derives from the gummy deposit on trees of an insect, *Tachardia lacca*, and is what we in the West call 'resin lac' or 'shellac'. When European craftsmen sought to imitate Far Eastern lacquer-ware in the sixteenth century and later, it was this substance that formed the base of their varnishes. But the properties of resin lac are quite different from, and generally speaking inferior to, those of true lacquer, which is the unadulterated natural juice of the lac tree. The discovery of this substance, and its exploitation as a protective and decorative envelope applied to articles made of wood and other materials, is something the world owes to China.

Trees, the average life of which is between fifteen and twenty years, are tapped in summer. They emit a grey, syrupy juice, the essential constituent of which, christened urushiol, after the Japanese *urushi*, 'lacquer', is a hydrocarbon with the chemical formula $C_{14}H_{18}O_2$; on exposure to oxygen, this substance spontaneously polymerizes – that is, it forms molecules of much higher molecular weight – and so behaves in a way as the earliest of all plastics known to man. Urushiol occupies 74 per cent of the volume of lacquer juice, the remainder being made up of 20 per cent water, 2 per cent albumen, and 4 per cent of a gum similar to gum arabic. After being strained several times through hemp cloth, lacquer juice is heated over a slow flame to remove excess moisture and is afterwards stored in air-tight vessels. It is then ready for use, with or without addition of colouring-agents.

Properties of Lacquer

Lacquer is almost unbelievably resistant to water. A lacquer object may lie buried in moist earth, or be flooded with water, for years and perhaps centuries; yet, provided no mechanical injury is sustained whereby the wood or fabric underneath is exposed to the action of moisture,[1] it will emerge as fresh and unimpaired as ever. Japanese archaeologists who excavated the Lo-lang tombs say that their solid wooden chambers, surrounded by hard clay soil, had acted as natural reservoirs, so that many of the tombs were heavily flooded. Yet they remark: 'lacquer objects have been wonderfully preserved in this constantly wet condition, though naturally they have changed their

1. If that happens, the wood swells on absorbing water, so that the lacquer flakes away when the objects are dried out.

original positions as a result of drifting about in the water.'[1] To this we may add that the Noin-ula *kurgan*, from which was recovered lacquer in superb condition (figure 46), were so water-logged that pumps had to be used throughout the excavation; and that the Ch'ang-sha tombs, where a great find of late Chou lacquers was made some fifteen years ago (plate 17*a* and *b*), were completely inundated by subsoil water.

By virtue of these and other qualities, such as high resistance to heat and acids, lacquer excels both as a protective envelope and as a vehicle for surface decoration. On their account it has always won the admiration of the West. As early as A.D. 1345 or thereabouts, the Arab Ibn Baṭuṭṭah visited Canton and particularly admired the brilliance and solidity of lacquers then being made for the markets of India and Persia. And lacquer was a leading export to western Europe during the seventeenth and eighteenth centuries. So the Jesuit missionary Le Comte, writing to the Duchesse de Bouillon from Peking in A.D. 1685, pays it this tribute:

'Besides the brightness and lustre which is the property of varnish [from Fr. *vernis*, 'lacquer'], it hath moreover a certain quality of preserving the wood upon which it is applied, especially as they do not mix any other matter with it. Worms do not easily breed in it, nay, and moisture scarce ever penetrates it, not so much as any Scent can fasten to it; if during meals there be any Grease or Portage spilt, if it be presently wiped with a wet Clout, one not only finds no remainders or signs of it, but does not so much as perceive the least smell.'

Uses of Lacquer

Its known preservative and water-resisting qualities led to use of lacquer as a protective dope on a whole range of materials and manufactured objects in Han and earlier times. In the manufacture of vessels such as those illustrated on plates 17–19 it was applied to wood alone, to wood covered with hemp cloth, and to hemp cloth alone. It was applied to the silk fabric of hats and the leather of shoes, in order to stiffen and waterproof these articles. The birch-bark beaker previously mentioned (p. 193) was presumably lacquered to make it waterproof, as was the grass-plaited basket from Lou-lan. Lacquered

1. A. Koizumi, *The Tomb of the Painted Basket of Lo Lang. Detailed Report of Archaeological Researches, Volume 1*, Keijo (Seoul) 1934, p. 4.

cushions of plaited bamboo were found at Lo-lang; and from the so-called 'Tomb of the Painted Basket', at the same site, a large collection of lacquered weapons of war and accessories, such as sword-sheaths and hafts, cross-bows, shields, and chariot-wheel spokes, came to light. As Mänchen-Helfen remarks, probably all war-gear was lacquered whenever possible, to protect it from rot and rust. Coffins at Noin-ula and Lo-lang were lacquered inside and out.

Further, lacquer was put to the same wide range of uses in pre-Han times. The find said to have been made at Ku-wei Ts'un, Hui Hsien, Honan, in 1929 belongs to the end of the Chou period; and here again lacquered coffin-beams were found. The date of the important find at Chin Ts'un has already been discussed (p. 170, footnote 1); it, too, seems to be late Chou. Lacquer played a very important part in the Chin Ts'un burial. All sorts of objects were coated with it, including bronze vessels, pottery vases, part of a cart, and some flat sheets of canvas which may have formed a table-top. The coffin was lacquered, and so were the walls of the burial-chamber. These last seem to have been lacquered after the burial objects were in position, for articles near them were splashed with drops of lacquer evidently fallen from the lacquerer's brush. And, perhaps by way of a *ming ch'i* (p. 174), the lacquerer left his entire equipment behind when he had finished the job.

Pre-Han lacquer was also used as an inlay on bronzes. A well-known group of First Phase bronze vessels, presumably Shang-Yin, has a characteristic inlay of dark material in the hollows of the casting; and it has generally been believed – although never, I think, verified – that this substance is lacquer.[1] The fashion for inlaying becomes noticeable again in Third Phase bronzes. Lacquer is used, as well as malachite, turquoise, gold, and silver.

1. The nearest to a definite statement seems to be that made by Dr H. T. Plenderleith, 'Technical notes on Chinese bronzes with special reference to patina and incrustations', in *T.O.C.S.*, vol. xvi (1938–9), pp. 33–55, who says (p. 38): '…. the black powdery inlays in Shang bronzes have proved to be mostly residues of carbon with some silica and phosphorus. … such black inlays in Shang bronzes may be the remains of some primitive form of lacquer of organic origin.' Use of lacquer in Shang-Yin times, both for inlay and for painting walls of death-chambers, is nevertheless reasonably certain. One of the 'royal' tombs excavated at An-yang in 1935 seems to have been decorated with motives copied from bronze design, in red, white, and black pigments whose base is thought to have been lacquer.

We have already seen how curiously hybrid is the Third Phase bronze style. Some of its motives – for instance, the twisted- and plaited-cord patterns that serve to divide horizontal zones on the vessels – show how ready were their makers to imitate in bronze the forms and textures of other materials. Månchen-Helfen thinks that metal inlays of the Third Phase represent the vestiges of an earlier art of lacquer-painting or -stencilling on bronze; for inlay not only fills the narrow channels of spirals, T-forms, and so forth, where it is perfectly appropriate, but also often occupies the broad, shallow areas forming the bodies of naturalistic birds, beasts, and humans in the hunting-scenes so typical of these inlaid bronzes. How were such spacious and freely-executed designs transferred to the bronze? Obviously by way of the wax model (p. 122). They may have been drawn by hand, stencilled, or stamped on wax by means of dies; but whatever method was used, Månchen-Helfen believes that the original design was painted with lacquer and a brush. Pre-Han texts speak of use of lacquer as a writing-material (p. 534). Why should it not have been used for painting also?

But if the bronze art of the Third Phase is a complex containing motives, styles, and techniques typical of art-forms other than bronze – such as painting in lacquer – it is no less the main channel through which all these features were later disseminated among the multi-tudinous art-forms of Han times. If therefore the inlaid bronzes of the Third Phase contain echoes of an earlier tradition of lacquer painting, we have equally to recognize that the styles and motives characteristic of these bronzes were in turn bequeathed to Han art generally, and made their appearance more or less indiscriminately in almost every medium – including lacquer – in which it found expression.

Painting in Lacquer the Ancestor of Later Chinese Pictorial Art?

That lacquer was used abundantly in pre-Han China is a comparatively recent *fait acquis* provided by the Chin Ts'un, Ku-wei Ts'un, and Ch'ang-sha finds. These no more than hint at what may have been a superb art of painting in lacquer during the late Chou period. Fragments of a lacquered frieze on the wall of the Chin Ts'un tomb chamber reveal tantalizing glimpses of what W. C. White supposes was a design, freely drawn in lacquer, of dragons and phoenixes. A

lacquered wood casket (*lien*) from Ch'ang-sha is decorated with figures
of men in long, graceful robes attending a banquet. Photographs of
this painting in a Chinese publication entirely fail to do it justice, but
the author may well be right when he says of it that 'no more important document in the early history of Chinese painting is known'.[1]

By Han times, painting in lacquer on lacquer displays such suavity,
such vitality and certitude, as to suggest that designers had long been
familiar with the graphic possibilities of the medium. We may well
ask whether pictorial conventions thus established may not have had
a profound effect on the subsequent course of Chinese painting. But
whether or no one feels inclined to give priority to lacquer as the
medium in which the pictorial genius of China first found expression,
Han lacquers are unquestionably outstanding documents in its early
development.

The Technique of Lacquering

PRIMING

Well before Han times it was known that the quality of lacquer-ware
could be improved by introducing an intermediate substance between
the lacquer and its wood base. I think we can assume that this was a
means of priming, not dissimilar to those employed in the practice of
European painting. The word *huan* is sometimes used in pre-Han texts
with the same sense as *ch'i*, 'lacquer'. But from Han citations it is clear
than *huan* was really a crude and early priming technique that perhaps
paved the way for *chia chu* (p. 199). *Shuo wên* defines it as 'lacquer
with ash [particularly bone-ash], mixed and applied'. Presumably this
mixture was spread like gesso on the wood support, allowed to dry,
and then ground smooth to form a surface suitable for the application
of lacquer alone. Corroboration seems to be afforded by a four-sided
wooden and lacquered *hu* (p. 146) found among the Chin Ts'un remains. For where the surface lacquer had flaked away, a hard composition was exposed lying over the wood base and forming a foundation for the outer layers. On a few Han lacquers the inscriptions state
that they are 'thrice *wan* (= *huan*)', and this presumably means that
articles were coated three times with lacquer and ash before the craftsman was satisfied that the priming was complete.

1. Chiang Yuen Yi (Chiang Yüan-i), *Changsha 'The Chu Tribe and its Art'*
Vol. 1. *Lacquer*, Shanghai 1949, Foreword (in Chinese) and pls. 11 and 12.

The Chin Ts'un finds also prove that genuine *chia chu* techniques were in use at least as early as the third century B.C. Hemp cloth or canvas formed a base on which lacquer was applied. W. C. White speaks of fragments of a vessel covered with brown lacquer painted with red designs and 'applied to a composition which was built up on a coarse fabric' and of 'large pieces of thick, substantially made lacquer on a canvas core' – these evidently being parts of a table-top.[1] How much earlier than the third century B.C. *chia chu* may be we cannot say for sure. But we have seen how close was the association of lacquer and hemp in the mind of the author of *Yü kung*, probably dating from the fourth century B.C. (p. 190).

By the Han period lacquer utensils can be graded into three qualities, depending on whether lacquer was applied to wood alone, to wood covered with a layer of cloth, or to an armature of cloth alone. The vast majority falls into the first category. Of eighty-four lacquer vessels found in the tomb of Wang Kuang, secretary to the Grand Governor of Lo-lang, only five show the *chia chu* technique, and these are lacquered over hemp cloth on a wooden base; the remaining seventy-nine are lacquered directly on to wood. Lacquer vessels from the Niya *limes* in Chinese Turkestan are also lacquered directly on to wood. And they contrast, suggests München-Helfen, with vessels from the more prosperous nearby Lou-lan, where a layer of hemp cloth is intercalated. In all Chinese Turkestan only a single vessel has so far been found in which lacquer was applied to an armature of hemp cloth alone; this process was evidently reserved for the finest and costliest wares, such as the cosmetic box of plate 19*b*, which was found in China, and which, according to the British Museum analyst Dr Plenderleith, has a base consisting of hemp cloth only. Lo-lang cannot provide a single example of this class, and we are forced to conclude that lacquers from colonial outposts – impressive as many of them are – do not by any means represent the whole *œuvre* of the period. The real masterpieces probably never left China.

Contemporary texts and actual inscriptions on lacquer vessels refer to the process variously as *chia chu*, 'lined with hemp cloth', or simply *chu*, 'on hemp cloth', but this does not necessarily mean that the wood foundation was in such cases dispensed with. Indeed, an inscription of A.D. 45 expressly names the vessel *mu chia pei*, 'a dish (*pei*) of wood lined [with hemp cloth and lacquered]'.

1. W. C. White, *Tombs of Old Lo-yang*, Shanghai 1934, pp. 89, 95.

Inscriptions, as I have remarked, often give names of workmen (*kung*) responsible for various stages of a vessel's manufacture. First comes the *su kung*. The original meaning of *su* is 'a plain cloth', but it quickly assumed the metaphorical sense of 'plain', 'white', or 'un-embroidered', and so came to mean the ground to which ornament is applied. With this range of meanings for *su* it is difficult to decide exactly what task was allotted to the *su kung*. He may have had to pre-pare the plain ground priming, *huan*; or he may have been responsible for glueing the hemp cloth on to its wood support; or for building up a hemp cloth armature if no wood support was used.

While on the subject of primings, let us note that the traditional Chinese painter used paper or silk to paint on, not hemp cloth or wood panel, as did the lacquerer. Nevertheless, these early Chinese lacquer-ing techniques seem to have developed in stages closely corresponding to those successively used by traditional European painters in oil or tempera. So the wood base, 'thrice *huan*', would correspond to the European primed wood panel; lacquering on a primed hemp cloth glued to a wood base seems to me practically identical with the Euro-pean technique of painting in oil or tempera on a primed canvas marouflayed to its wood support; and lacquering on hemp cloth alone would be the equivalent of painting in oil on canvas (cf. pp. 559–60).

LAYERING

The priming completed, the lacquerer, or *hsiu kung*, now took over. Several successive thin coats of lacquer were applied, each being allowed to dry out before putting on the next. In Ming and Ch'ing lacquers, multiplication of lacquer layers is carried to extreme lengths, for frequently thirty or more are applied. But the process is also of considerable antiquity. We read in *Li chi* – 'Record of Rites' – dating from Han times, that a coffin was prepared for the Chou feudal ruler as soon as he was enthroned. Each year throughout his life it was given a fresh coat of lacquer, after which it was allowed to dry and was then stored until the following year.[1] In this connexion a curious point must be noticed, one that perhaps links up with lacquer's most distinctive property: its resistance to water. To 'dry' effectively, lacquer needs a humid atmosphere, and a temperature of between 70° and 80° F. Accordingly, freshly-painted lacquer-ware was customarily

1. Cf. O. Mänchen-Helfen (see footnote p. 190), p. 37.

placed in a damp pit or trench dug in the earth and called the 'shadow-house'; under these conditions it attained its greatest pitch of hardness and durability. And here again we have an instance of the extraordinary conservatism of Chinese industrial techniques. In *Shih chi*, Ssŭ-ma Ch'ien tells how the Second Ch'in Emperor (p. 176) wished to lacquer the walls of his capital. His dwarf approved the idea, saying that no robber could ever hope to scale such smooth surfaces; he asked only how the walls were to be got into the 'shadow-house', and the project was abandoned.[1]

The outermost layer of lacquer was of crucial importance, for upon its smoothness of texture depended the brilliance and lustre of the finished article. The workman who applied it was a specialist called in the inscriptions *shang kung*, or 'workman [who lacquers] the topmost [layer]'.

Classes of Lacquer Decoration

CARVING AND RELIEF MOULDING

The article now passed into the hands of the *hua kung*, or painter, and others whose job was to decorate it; and here it will be convenient to examine briefly the main techniques of surface decoration displayed by Far Eastern lacquer-ware. It is traditionally divided into two main classes – painted lacquer (*hua ch'i*) and carved lacquer (*tiao ch'i*); but one might reserve a category for inlaid lacquer, both painted and carved, and for that in which relief decoration is worked up with a putty of lacquer, charcoal, lamp-black, and other substances. All these classes of decoration – and the lesser sorts into which both Chinese and Japanese connoisseurs customarily divide them – originated in China and have their roots in the range of technical processes available to Han lacquerers.

I do not know of any example of Han lacquer moulded in relief. But in the Low-Beer Collection there is an impressive pre-Han plaque that shows a form of *t'ao-t'ieh* (pp. 161–2 and 286–9) executed in this technique. The plaque evidently belongs to the late Third Phase, so that the technique may antedate by some seventeen centuries its supposed invention in Japan, where it is called *takamakiye*.

1. Cf. O. Mänchen-Helfen (see footnote p. 190), p. 37.

Lacquer when hard can be cut, carved, or engraved with as much precision as can ivory. This type of work reached its climax in the eighteenth century with the *tours de force* of the Imperial workshops of Peking, and there is little sign of it before Han times.[1] But we have examples of Han lacquer engraving in which the design is cut through to a more lightly-coloured priming (plate 18*b*), or else is filled in with white or sometimes red pigment; and the inscriptions themselves were cut in this way.

A character appearing in some Han lacquer inscriptions, naming the workman to whom lacquered articles were consigned after leaving the hands of the *hua kung*, has sometimes been read as *t'ung*, 'red' or 'to paint red'; whence the term *t'ung kung* is translated 'the decorator in red [lacquer]'. But it is now generally agreed that *t'ung* is really a variant of *tiao*, 'to engrave, to carve',[2] and that the *tiao kung* was he whose most important job was to engrave the inscription and to make it harmonize pleasingly with the rest of the decoration.

PAINTING AND INLAYING

Black and red seem to have been the earliest lacquer pigments used in China, the former probably derived from iron sulphate or lamp-black, the latter from cinnabar (sulphide of mercury) and – according to Chêng Shih-hsü – from saf-flower (*Carthamus tinctorius*) or saffron (*Crocus sativa*). Perhaps black is earlier than red.[3] The legendary Shun, *Han fei tzŭ* tells us, had sacrificial vessels lacquered black both within and without, whereas those commissioned by his successor Yü were black on the outside, red within. However that may be, use of black lacquer for the outside, red for inside, seems to have become conventional at least as early as the fourth century B.C., especially for decorating

1. The superb lacquer mounts of a late Third Phase sword and sheath in the Low-Beer Collection do not strictly qualify as carved lacquer since it is the wood foundation that is carved – in open-work convoluted animal forms – not the lacquer coatings.

2. It is written *tiao* in a decipherment of a Han lacquer inscription made by Chêng Shih-hsü in his *Ch'i ch'i kao*, 'A Study of Lacquer Utensils', Shanghai 1936, p. 17.

3. Thus, commentators on *Chou li* say that the *mo* carriage mentioned therein was unornamented; lacquered, that is, but only in a single colour. The character used for *mo* means 'black' (and later, 'Chinese ink'). Black lacquer, therefore, seems to have been considered the same as plain lacquer. It was also used as a writing material (p. 537).

coffins. Thus the outer shell of a coffin at Chin Ts'un was lacquered black outside, red inside; so were the coffins of Wang Hsü and his wife at Lo-lang. A lid belonging to Low-Beer, bearing the date 4 B.C., is lacquered black outside, red inside, as are almost all Han vessels from Chinese Turkestan, Lo-lang, Noin-ula, and elsewhere. Generally speaking, if the two colours are used together, red is applied on top of black, not *vice versa*. Perhaps there was a chemical component in the red that made it unsuitable for painting black lacquer over it. At any rate *Huai nan tzŭ* says, 'The dyer could dye blue over black, but not *vice versa*; the artisan could paint red over black, but not the other way round.'[1]

By late Chou times a white derived from white lead, a light blue-grey and another shade of red had been added to the lacquerer's palette, as we know from lacquers reported to have come from Ku-wei Ts'un. Green from a chromium compound, yellows from cadmium and ochre, and blue, are all found on Han lacquers and may not have been known previously. In chapter 93 of *Ch'ien han shu* (p. 174) we read that the Emperor's coffin was painted with vermilion inside, while the outer walls had representations of the green (*ch'ing*) dragon and white tiger, and of the sun and moon, painted in gold and silver respectively. These latter pigments were certainly in vogue by the second century A.D., for they are found on lacquerware from the 'Tomb of the Painted Basket' at Lo-lang, dating from that century.

Designs were not always painted with the brush. Mänchen-Helfen speaks of two lacquer bowls found by Stein at Tun-huang, on each of which a painted design of three concentric circles enclosing a central dot is so exactly repeated that it must have been applied with some mechanical aid. We have already noticed (p. 197) possible use of dies and stencils for lacquering on bronze vessels or their wax models in late Chou times.

Among the costliest and most beautiful painted lacquers of Han times were those ornamented with inlays of bronze, silver, gold, and tortoise-shell, with gilt-bronze handles, and feet and other accessories in metal. The workman named after the *shang kung* is the *t'ung êrh k'ou huang t'u kung*, an expression rendered by Mänchen-Helfen as 'the bronze-handle gilder'. But I think we may assume that the work of this craftsman included all embellishments of the sort mentioned

1. Cf. O. Mänchen-Helfen (see footnote p. 190), p. 36.

above. Some of these vessels must have been extravagant indeed. The cosmetic box of plate 19b has a quatrefoil device originally composed of silver plates inlaid on the lid, as well as inlaid silver figures of animals round the sides of both box and top of lid; and it is evidently an *objet de luxe*. Others may have been even more handsome.

Just as Pliny attacked the expensive tastes that were bankrupting contemporary Rome, so Huan K'uan and Kung Yü censured the Chinese fashion for luxury lacquerware. We have seen what Huan K'uan had to say (p. 192); in *Ch'ien han shu*, Kung Yü is reported as having stated that over five million cash were being wasted annually on the lacquers of Shu and Kuang-han, and tells how he followed the Emperor on one occasion into the Empress's Palace, and there saw richly-ornamented and painted lacquer dishes, and lacquer tables adorned with gold and silver. And as Roman historians approved the frugality of emperors who abstained from luxuries like Chinese silks, so, too, Fan Yeh in his *Hou han shu* praises Empress Têng, wife of Emperor Hsiao Ho (reigned A.D. 89–106), for renouncing the Szechwan lacquers with their gilt-bronze rims.

In later centuries Japanese lacquerers used gold and silver extensively. Previous to the discovery of Han lacquer, it was not thought that the Japanese *heidatsu* technique (Ch. *p'ing t'o*) – in which small strips of gold leaf were inlaid on lacquer – was any older than the T'ang period (A.D. 618–906). But we now know examples of Han *p'ing t'o*. According to Trever,[1] thirteen fragments of a black-and-red lacquer box found at Noin-ula are inlaid with thin strips of gold foil, depicting in three friezes, 'hunting scenes, beasts and birds, man's figure in long gown and bands of spirals'; and Sekino speaks of a vessel from Lo-lang in *p'ing t'o*, showing wild geese flying between painted cloud-scrolls.

But on the whole, as we have said, lacquers found at Lo-lang and other Chinese outposts, even if made in Szechwan, scarcely seem to be the luxury wares the texts make so much of. Very rarely are they inlaid with gold or silver. Perhaps they reflect the less gaudy tastes of a later period. More probably they are simply cheaper versions of the *objets de luxe*. So the silver-inlaid quatrefoil of the cosmetic box (plate 19b) has as its counterpart a quatrefoil painted in yellow and outlined in red lacquer on several Lo-lang boxes. Similarly, yellow lacquer used in the depiction of animals and birds – such as the duck

1. C. Trever (see footnote p. 187), p. 48 and pl. 31.

flying through cloud-scrolls on a Noin-ula fragment – was almost certainly intended as substitute for a gold inlay.

We have dealt with six workmen whose functions are known to us from contemporary inscriptions on lacquer. They are: the workman who prepared the priming; the lacquerer; the lacquerer of the outermost layer; the gilder; the painter; and the engraver. Two others are mentioned. One was the *ch'ing kung*, an expression usually translated as 'cleaner' (and perhaps 'polisher'); the other is the *tsao kung*, who may have been the foreman or the person responsible for checking the finished article off its long production line. An inscription of the year A.D. 3 on a vessel found at Lo-lang informs us that the workshop team of eight at the 'western factory' in Shu Commandery was then composed of Messrs Fêng, Kan, T'an, Ch'un, T'an, Jung, Chêng, and I respectively. A year later, as we learn from another inscription, Lü has displaced Fêng and Kan, and the remaining six craftsmen are given as Huo, Ku, Ch'in, Jung, P'ing, and Tsung; from which it will be seen that only Jung has kept his old job. These men must have been masters, since between them they were apparently responsible for the whole output of the factory. No doubt each had apprentices working under him by whose labour output could be kept up; but the mere fact that their names were recorded on the finished article, as a means of showing with whom responsibility lay for each stage of its manufacture, proves that supervision must have been personal and strict all along the line. To some extent the master-craftsmen changed their jobs around; we can, in fact, follow the movements of individuals as their names crop up in successive inscriptions.[1]

To round off this section on lacquer, I append an English version of the inscription in sixty-seven characters on the vessel shown on plate 19*a*, bearing a date corresponding to A.D. 4. It runs:

The fourth year of the *yüan shih* reign-period (A.D. 4). Made at the western factory in Shu Commandery. Imperial pattern (*tsao ch'êng yü*). A lacquered, carved, and painted wood cup (*pei*) with gilt-[bronze] 'ears'

1. Fêng, for example, was painting lacquer ornament in 4 B.C. Two years later he becomes engraver. In one inscription of A.D. 3 he is named as the layer of the priming; in another of the same year he is again painting the décor. By the following year he is named in three separate inscriptions as the engraver, and he is still engraving as late as A.D. 8. Over the period 4 B.C. to A.D. 8, the list of engravers on ten separate vessels runs as follows: Jung, Fêng, Jung, I, Jung, Jung, Fêng, Fêng, Fêng, Fêng.

(handles). Capacity one *shêng*, 16 *yüeh*. Priming by I; lacquering by Li; outer coat by Tang; gilding of the 'ears' by Ku; painting by Ting; [inscription] engraved by Fêng; cleaning [and polishing] by P'ing; passed by Tsung. Officer commanding the Factory Guard, Chang; Manager, Liang; Deputy, Fêng; Assistant, Lung; Chief clerk, Pao.

A few comments are, I think, called for. The phrase *hsi kung*, 'western workmanship', seems to indicate the existence of eastern and western lacquer factories in Shu analogous, no doubt, to the eastern and western silk workshops at the Capital spoken of by Kung Yü. The expression *ch'êng yü*, 'riding carriage', is, as Mänchen-Helfen says, merely a formula meaning the person of the Emperor, and the phrase *tsao ch'êng yü* cannot therefore be translated as Swann does in a similar context, 'made (in the same style of workmanship) as his majesty's personal cart'.[1] The *pei* is the commonest of Han lacquer vessels. It is an oval dish with crescent-shaped side-handles (plates 17*b*, 19*a*), said to have been used for wine, but more probably a food vessel; two *pei* are especially designated 'soup *pei*' in their inscriptions.[2] This most distinctive vessel may have originated from a half bottle-gourd, as Hamada thinks, or have had a wood or clay prototype. But wooden and clay *pei* found in Chinese Turkestan, Manchuria, and Korea, are simply cheap imitations of lacquer *pei*. *Pei* were also made in bronze – and, as the reader will remember, we are told that ten of these could be bought in Han times for the price of a single lacquer *pei* – in silver, and in jade. The unit of capacity *shêng* was the volumetric equivalent of 24,000 millet seeds, or about 7 fluid ounces (0·35 pint). There were 20 *yüeh* in a *shêng*. With the exception of *tiao*, which we discussed on p. 202, there is general agreement as to how the characters in this, and other similar inscriptions, should be read. The translations of the titles of offices given at the end of the inscription, however, are not definitive. The inscription contains one puzzling feature: after the three characters *tsao kung tsung*, which we translated as 'passed by Tsung', the word *tsao* recurs, apparently without purpose. I can only suppose that Mr Fêng, who had the job of engraving this inscription, started to repeat the previous phrase by mistake, and had written *tsao* before he noticed his error.

1. N. L. Swann, *Food and Money in Ancient China. A Translation of Han Shu 24*, Princeton 1950, p. xii.
2. O. Mänchen-Helfen (see footnote p. 190), p. 58.

Silk is perhaps China's greatest single contribution to world material culture. But whereas with other Chinese products – lacquer and porcelain, for example – the West was content to import as much as it could, and make up the balance with some sort of imitation, real silk was always a material strictly *hors concours*. A steady supply at fixed and reasonable rates could never be guaranteed; and as demand grew, it was soon realized that the quality of Chinese silk was such that no other known fibre could possibly serve as substitute. There was only one way out of the impasse. To get silk thread[1] in bulk, the West had to learn the whole art of Chinese sericulture: how to rear the domestic silkworm; how to reel off its continuous filament, several hundred yards long from the cocoon; and how to breed the moth in captivity so as to safeguard next season's supply. In A.D. 552, or thereabouts, eggs of the Domestic Silkmoth, *Bombyx mori*, were smuggled into the Byzantine Empire concealed in a hollow tube, according to the contemporary Procopius, by certain Indian monks who had lived for a long time in Serinda. The balance of opinion inclines to regard this country as the region of modern Chinese Turkestan; another view is that it was Cambodia or Champa.

Reeled silk provides the finest natural textile thread known to man. So, where intensive sericulture is practised, there one might expect to find advanced methods of loom construction, complex weaving techniques, and high-quality textiles. And correspondingly, in a society relying mainly on short-staple fibres, such as flax, cotton, and wool, which make relatively inferior yarns, textile processes are likely to be less forward. That this is true as a general principle is confirmed by a

---

1. The terms 'fibre', 'filament', 'thread', and 'yarn' are used somewhat haphazardly in Western writings on silk. I take them to have the following meanings: the single *filament* extruded by the silkworm is made up of two continuous *fibres* secreted by a pair of silk-glands and bound together by silk's natural gum, sericin. In reeling, several filaments are agglutinated and perhaps slightly twisted together, to make silk *thread*. *Yarn* is a term properly applied to the spun thread of short-staple fibres such as cotton, and cannot strictly be used to name reeled silk thread. While it is true that some Chinese silk was always produced from the short-staple fibres of damaged cocoons or waste silk, and also from the cocoons of 'wild' silkworms (p. 211), all of which had to be spun into yarn, the vast bulk of it was woven from continuous reeled silk thread.

remark made by the textile historian Vivi Sylwan, who says: 'I, like others, arrived at the conclusion that the technical development in textiles, from relatively primitive methods toward the somewhat mechanized forms which preceded the more modern machine production, has taken place mainly in the silk workshops.' [1] In order to assess the extent to which Western weaving practice may have been modified by the introduction of Chinese silk fabrics at the beginning of our era, we ought therefore to consider how far silk was known in the West before that time. Literary and archaeological evidence, as we shall see, suggests that sericulture was not sufficiently developed in the West to have left its mark on Western textile practice. Hence an *a priori* assumption that the art of weaving in general was more advanced in China at this time, and that if technological borrowing went on, the debtor was the West.

Support for this view comes from the textiles themselves. Chinese silk fabrics made an overwhelming impression when they first appeared in the Near East. In 'touch' – fineness, closeness, softness, and suppleness – in lustre and brilliance of colour, and in scale and complexity of design, the new weaves far outmatched the heavy tapestry woollens and linens then being made in Syria. As the monk Dionysius Periegetes, writing in the third century A.D., put it: 'The Seres [that is, the Chinese] make precious figured garments, resembling in colour the flowers of the field, and rivalling in fineness the work of spiders.' [2] That these fabrics awoke a spirit of emulation among Western weavers is, I think, demonstrable. Thus by the end of the third century A.D. the Han system of pattern-building begins to appear in certain Syrian weaves,[3] and a little later in early Sassanid Persian silks and Egypto-Roman figured woollens. Silk fabric was made in Byzantium soon after Constantine chose it as his capital in A.D. 324,

1. Vivi Sylwan, 'Investigation of Silk from Edsen-gol and Lop-nor', being publication xxxii of *Reports from the Scientific Expedition to the North-western Provinces of China under the Leadership of Dr Sven Hedin*, Stockholm 1949, Preface, p. 1.

2. Cf. S. W. Bushell (see footnote p. 3), vol. ii, p. 92.

3. Indeed so close is the superficial resemblance that it has not always proved easy to say quite definitely whether such third-century A.D. fabrics were woven in the West or in China. A patterned silk from Dura-Europos was taken to be a warp rep by Pfister in 1937, and was therefore assumed to have been woven in China. A later analysis made in 1945 showed it to be a weft rep, good indication that it was in fact woven in Syria. For the significance of these remarks cf. p. 228.

but the decorative influence most strongly at work was an Eastern one; few Hellenistic motives are to be found.

Nor is this all. The history of the loom itself during the first few centuries of our era is obscure; but examination of actual textiles suggests the sort of equipment that must have been employed to make them. Western weavers did not at the outset have means of making exact reproductions of Chinese patterned silks. To anticipate a little, the drawloom, by which a complicated pattern can be woven semi-automatically in repeats in either or both directions of the cloth, seems not to have been known to the West before the sixth century A.D., and not definitely even then; [1] whereas the Han patterned silks give clear evidence of having been woven by means of a pattern-making device coming within the general category of drawloom. Introduction of Chinese silks to the West may thus have been followed by that of technical inventions first developed in China. 'It is clear ...', says J. F. Flanagan, 'that the Chinese weavers were acquainted with a pattern-making contrivance at least a few centuries before the Egypto-Roman weavers produced their figured-wool materials.' [2]

These conclusions are nevertheless hotly disputed. The onus of disproving them lies, I feel, on those who believe with Mlle M.-Th. Schmitter that 'the invention of technical processes in the West [by which Mlle Schmitter means those connected with pattern-weaving] is earlier than the opening up of the Silk Road'; [3] and with Hans Rebel, that China was not the oldest user of silk for textile purposes, but that priority should be awarded to India.[4]

What Constitutes Sericulture?

Before asking whether the West was familiar with sericulture before the coming of silk from China, we had better try to decide what

1. Among those who believe that it appeared later than the seventh century A.D. are Sylwan and Hentschel, 'Eine chinesische Seide mit spätgriechischem Muster aus dem 5. bis 6. Jahrh.', in *O.Z.*, vol. xxi (1935), p. 22. Charleston, on the other hand, concludes it may have been known in the sixth century A.D. Cf. R. Charleston, 'Han damasks', in *O.A.*, vol. i (1948), pp. 63–81.

2. J. F. Flanagan, letter in *B.M.*, vol. xxxvii (1920), p. 215.

3. M.-Th. Schmitter, 'Chine ou Proche Orient?', in *Rev. A.*, vol. xiii (1939), p. 90.

4. H. Rebel, 'China als Ursprungsland der Edelseide', in *W.B.K.K.A.*, vol. ii (1927), pp. 47–64.

sericulture is. Silk-producing moths belong to two families, the Bombycidae and the Saturniidae. The former includes some sixty species, of which *Bombyx mori*, its food-plant the domestic mulberry, is best known. But at least six other Bombycidae produce silk in Bengal alone; and another, *Bombyx mandarinae Moore*, feeds on the wild mulberry in parts of central and south China and can be thought of as a primitive variety of *Bombyx mori*. Among the Saturniidae is *Antheraea pernyi* (=*Bombyx pernyi*, *Bombyx fantoni*), sometimes called the Chinese Tussore, feeding on several species of oak in north China; *Philosamia cynthia* (=*Attacus cynthia*, *Bombyx cynthia*), feeding on *Ailanthus glandulosa*, the Tree of Heaven, in China and India; *Philosamia ricini* (=*Attacus ricini*) feeding on the Castor Oil in Bengal and Assam; and *Antheraea mylitta* (=*Bombyx mylitta*), the Indian Tussore, whose food-plant is *Zizyphus jujuba*, the Sidra tree. The fibres and filaments produced by all these silkworms vary as to shape, microscopical appearance, and size. The *Bombyx mori* fibre is more homogeneous than are those of other silkworms, most of which show longitudinal striations corresponding to the fibrils of which they are composed. The *Bombyx mori* filament is more or less round in section, those of other silkworms are flattened. The filament of *Bombyx mori*, and in particular of *Bombyx mori* reared in China, is a good deal finer than those of the others, as the following table of *mu* diameters (*mu*= 0·001 mm.) makes clear: [1]

Bombyx mori

China (Han)	20–30
China (modern, Canton)	21·8
Japan	27·3
Syria	29
France	31·6
Broussa	31·7
Philosamia ricini	30
Philosamia cynthia	40
Antheraea pernyi	40–60
Antheraea mylitta	80–90

Silk reeled from cocoons of *Bombyx mori*, because of these structural differences, is of finer quality than that produced by any other

1. This table is based on figures given by R. Pfister, *Textiles de Palmyre*, 3 vols, Paris 1934, 1937, 1940, vol. i, pp. 39, 56.

known silkworm. It is silk *par excellence*, and it bears witness to longer and more intensive cultivation than does any other silk.

We customarily speak of *Bombyx mori* as 'domesticated', and of all other silkmoths as 'wild'. But just as there is no hard-and-fast line separating agriculture from food-gathering, so there is no absolute distinction between sericulture based on *Bombyx mori* and other types of silk production. For example, *Antheraea pernyi* – the chief 'wild' silkmoth of China – is wild only in the sense that the silkworms feed outdoors on oak shrubs where they spin their cocoons; while *Bombyx mori* is fed on selected picked mulberry leaves indoors, and spins its cocoon on specially prepared straw trusses. But in every other respect the cultivation of *Antheraea pernyi* is sericulture. The oak shrubs grow in plantations, and are carefully pruned. Moths are bred in captivity; and the cocoons of the autumn crop, in which the chrysalids lie dormant throughout the winter, are kept indoors for several months.[1]

As with agriculture, what matters is not the extent to which man intervenes in natural processes, but the degree of control he exercises over them. Success in sericulture depends on being able to rear large batches of silkworms under controlled and uniform conditions. The reason for this is simple. The chrysalis is only in the cocoon for a matter of eight to ten days. At the end of that time it secretes a liquid solution, with which to dissolve the gum (sericin) binding together the loops of the cocoon filament, and makes its escape as an imago moth. This fluid solvent leaves an indelible stain on the silk, and denatures the filament, so that a cocoon from which the moth has escaped is useless for reeling. All that can be done with it is to card the silk from it, as one would a short-staple fibre, and spin it into yarn on a distaff. But spun silk yarn lacks the qualities that give to reeled silk its uniqueness as a thread; it is less regular, is lustreless, and has a lower tensile strength and elasticity.

The silk farmer, it follows, must ensure that all his silkworms are at the same stage of development if he wishes to reel the silk. If he cannot predict to a day or so the stage a particular batch of cocoons has reached, he has no alternative but to kill the chrysalids inside their

1. Unlike *B. mori*, *Antheraea pernyi* is bivoltine, producing two crops a year. Moths from the winter cocoons emerge at the end of March and lay eggs that hatch a month later. After a life-cycle of about seventy days, the second generation of moths emerges and a second cycle ensues. The autumn crop is harvested during September and October.

cocoon by means of boiling water or by steam heat, with a consequent deterioration in the quality of the reeled silk. And, quite clearly, if he exercises no control at all over the life-cycle, but simply collects cocoons from the food-plant as he finds them, he cannot normally hope to be able to reel the silk at all. No doubt the oldest silk threads used for weaving were spun from empty cocoons damaged by the escaping moth. The discovery that the filament was continuous, and could be reeled off unbroken, may not have been made until long after man began to bring the insect under control.

True sericulture *must* have as its aim reeling silk from the cocoons, as opposed to spinning it. The insect must be reared in captivity, and all stages in its life-history subsequent to hatching must be closely supervised by the silk-farmer. With these conditions as criteria, what evidence have we from classical texts that sericulture was practised in the West before the coming of Chinese silks? Let us observe that when Greek or Roman authors speak of sericulture, their language is vague and prosy, and carries little conviction. They seem not to understand what they are talking about. Yet, had sericulture been practised at all extensively in the Western world during the first few centuries before and after Christ, can one doubt that they would have left us detailed information about it?

The Cos Silkworm

Aristotle (384–322 B.C.) is the first Westerner to mention a silkworm. In his *Historia Animalium* (bk. 5, para. 19) he speaks of a large grub (*bombyx*), 'as it were, horned',[1] that passes through several metamorphoses in the space of six months. Thereupon, 'a class of women unwind and reel off the cocoons of these creatures, and afterwards weave a fabric with the threads thus unwound; a Coan woman of the name of Pamphile, daughter of Plateus, being credited with the first invention of the fabric.'[2]

The island of Cos, in the eastern Aegean, was well known to antiquity for the production of a textile (*bombycina*) and of clothing (*Coae vestes*), that gained much notoriety because of the sheerness of its

1. Presumably a reference to the large upstanding process on the abdomen.
2. D'A. W. Thompson, *Works of Aristotle translated into English*, vol. iv, Cambridge 1910, p. 551b.

weave. The practice of wearing it spread, evidently, from the Roman *demi-monde* to the upper classes and led to much outraged or facetious comment. Varro (116–27 B.C.) talks about 'glass togas', and Pliny (A.D. 23–79) says that Pamphile 'has the undeniable distinction of having devised a plan to reduce women's clothing to nakedness'.[1] Sketchy as is Aristotle's report, and uncertain the exact meaning of the terms he uses, there can be no doubt but that the textile fibre used for Coan cloth was silk from a silkmoth. But which?

Pliny, in his *Natural History* (bk. 11, paras. 25–7), repeats Aristotle's words in a garbled version, and then goes on to embroider them with a rambling and almost meaningless description of the *bombyx* of Cos, and how its 'fleece' is 'thinned out into threads with a rush spindle' for the making of clothing for men and women alike. In this account Pliny mentions four trees, the cypress, terebinth, ash, and oak; and although he does not explicitly say that the silkworm (*vermiculus*) feeds on them, it is difficult to see why else they should have been mentioned. Demaison has suggested that the *bombyx* in question was *Lasiocampa otus*, one of the Bombycidae, the caterpillar of which feeds precisely on cypress, oak, and a terebinth, and cocoons of which have also been found on the ash.[2] This Mediterranean silkmoth is to-day both wild and rare. It need not always have been, and Aristotle's talk of 'unwinding and reeling off the cocoons', if we have got the hang of it, does seem to point to a variety brought firmly under human control. But if what Pliny says about 'thinning out into threads with a rush spindle' is to be taken seriously, then we are led away from the idea of a domesticated silkworm to that of a wild one; for it might be supposed that he is referring to the carding and spinning of silk from cocoons damaged by the escaped moths.

Neither author speaks of breeding the insect in captivity, although Pliny does make some mention of 'small moths' that, after surrounding their bodies with a 'coiled nest' of some sort of down, are 'taken away by a man, put in earthenware vessels, and reared with warmth and a diet of bran'. Whatever the state of sericulture on Cos in

1. H. Rackham (transl.), *Pliny Natural History with an English Translation in Ten Volumes*, vol. iii, London 1940, pp. 477–81.

2. L. Demaison, *Recherches sur les soies que les Anciens tiraient de l'île de Cos*, Rheims 1884, p. 13. Cited and discussed by R. Pfister (see footnote p. 210), vol. 1, p. 55. The filament of *L. otus* corresponds closely to that of *Bombyx mori*. It is round in section, unstriped, and with a *mu* diameter ranging from 24 to 26 (cf. p. 210).

Aristotle's day, Pliny was apparently quite unable to give a coherent account of it 400 years later, when the silk industry there was evidently a fast-fading memory. What seems to confirm this view is that Pliny's account of the Coan industry in no way tallies with the few observations he makes about sericulture in the far-off land of the Seres. Yet he knew that clothes woven from the Chinese thread were of essentially the same quality as those he believed came from Cos. His remark about Pamphile's iniquitous discovery should be compared with what he has to say about the Chinese thread, which 'enables the Roman matron to flaunt transparent raiment in public'; why then did he fail to trace each material to the same natural source? We are forced to conclude that what he tells us about silk production on Cos, when it does not simply repeat Aristotle, is pure invention.

Silkworms in Other Parts of Western Asia

Pliny mentions one other thing of interest. In *Natural History* (bk. XI, paras. 25–7) he speaks of a *bombyx* native to Assyria, but unfortunately in terms that give us no possible hint as to what sort of creature it was. Perhaps he refers to a wild silkworm. The Chinese firmly believed that wild silkworms were to be found in Syria (Ta Ch'in) and that their silk was used for mustered fabrics – that is, cloths woven from more than one sort of textile fibre. Speaking of Ta Ch'in, *Hou han shu* says: 'There is also a fine cloth which some say is made of the down of the water-sheep and the cocoons of wild silkworms.' And *Wei lüeh*, compiled before A.D. 429 and referring to events of the period A.D. 220–65, gives a fuller account of this enigmatic fabric: 'There is a fine woven cloth which is said to be made with the down of the water-sheep. It is called "cloth from the west of the sea"…. Some say that not only sheep's wool is used in weaving it, but also the bark of trees (bast fibres?) and silk thread from wild cocoons.'[1]

Now we know that mustered cloths *were* being woven in the Near East about this time, especially in Syria. Archaeological finds at

1. The 'water-sheep' was probably the marine mollusc, *Pinna*, and its 'down' the byssus used as a textile thread in Roman Syria. For later ramifications of the 'water-sheep' notion into European, Arabic and Chinese folklore cf. J. Needham, (see footnote p. 22), pp. 200–2.

Palmyra dating from between A.D. 83 and 273 show that silk-linen, silk-wool, and linen-wool musters were woven – the first-mentioned fibres in each case composing the warp of the material; and Dura-Europos provides examples of textiles with wool warp and cotton weft. But in all cases where silk was used, there are strong indications that is was reeled Chinese silk from *Bombyx mori*, imported in the form of raw silk thread,[1] and not spun silk from a western Asiatic wild species. So, in one example from Palmyra, the diameter of the fibres was between 10 and 12 *mu* – corresponding to 20–24 *mu* for the filaments – which is good evidence of a *Bombyx mori*, and hence Chinese, origin. In several instances the thread was dyed red with madder; and this, as we shall see, also suggests Chinese provenance.

Chinese historians, then, were probably misinformed about the use of silk from native wild silkworms in the mustered fabrics of Ta Ch'in. But from the Palmyra find comes proof that wild spun silk *was* used in Syria at this time, though not in musters. Several beige and pink taffetas from the site are woven with silk the filaments of which are too coarse to be those of *Bombyx mori*, and which are also flattened and striated. Is this evidence in favour of the Assyrian *bombyx* mentioned by Pliny? Not necessarily. One type of fibre with a *mu* diameter of 18 may very well have come from *Philosamia cynthia* (China); another, its *mu* diameter 30, is perhaps silk of *Antheraea pernyi* (China); and two others from Palmyra, and one from Dura-Europos, with *mu* diameters of 40, 45, and 42 respectively, must certainly be fibres of *Antheraea mylitta*, possibly from south China but more probably from India. Discovery of a skein of spun silk by Bergman in 1930 at Edsin-gol, not far from the Silk Road, goes some way to support the view that the West was importing Chinese silk yarns from wild silkworms in Han times.

There is thus no evidence from archaeology to prove that spun silk from a native wild silkworm was being used in western Asia at the beginning of our era; such wild silk yarns as have been found in Western Asiatic weaves could easily have been imported either from China or from India.

Yet not only did the Chinese believe that the West had a wild silkworm, they were also firmly convinced that sericulture based on a domestic species was practised there, and that fabrics were woven

1. By 'raw silk thread' is meant thread in which the filaments are still enclosed in, and stuck together with, their natural gum. Cf. p. 225.

from the reeled silk. Speaking of Ta Ch'in, *Hou han shu* (ch. 88) says: 'The people are much bent on agriculture, and practise the planting of trees and the rearing of silkworms.'[1] And again: 'The country contains much ... thin silk-cloth (*ling*) of various colours.'[2] *Wei lüeh* says: 'Their domestic animals are the horse, the donkey, the mule, the camel, and the mulberry silkworm.'[3] And *Wei shu*, written before A.D. 572 with reference to the period A.D. 386–556, seems to repeat *Hou han shu* when it says: 'The country produces all kinds of grain, the mulberry tree and hemp. The inhabitants busy themselves with silkworms and fields.'[4]

How did this idea get about? According to Hirth and others, because Syria was indeed producing a 'thin silk-cloth of various colours' at the beginning of our era; one woven from Chinese silk thread. The Chinese, to whom its existence was reported, mistakenly supposed that it came from a Western silkworm. The theory holds that these fabrics were in fact the *sericas vestes*[5] to which Seneca refers when he says in *De Beneficiis* (bk. 7, para. 9): 'I see silken clothes, if one can call them clothes at all, that in no degree afford protection either to the body or the modesty of the wearer, and clad in which no woman could honestly swear she is not naked.' Seneca's language shows that he had in mind a fabric no less open to censure than had been the *bombycina* of Cos. Hirth concluded that the *ling* of Ta Ch'in were made in Syria for the Roman market in deliberate imitation of, and as substitutes for, the infamous Coan cloths.

Apart from the traditional Chinese view that there was a domestic silkworm in western Asia from which fine silk-cloth was made, was another that first appears in *Wei lüeh*. It gives a clue to the mystery of this fabric, woven from thread that the Romans attributed to the Chinese (Seres), and the Chinese to the Roman Orient (Ta Ch'in). 'Furthermore,' it says, speaking of Ta Ch'in, 'they were at all times anxious to procure Chinese silk thread (*ssǔ*) for unloosening (*chieh*), so as to make foreign fine silk-cloth (*hu ling*).' Nothing in this conflicts with Hirth's explanation. But what did the Chinese author mean by

1. F. Hirth (see footnote p. 183), p. 40.
2. F. Hirth (see footnote p. 183), p. 41.
3. F. Hirth (see footnote p. 183), p. 69.
4. F. Hirth (see footnote p. 183), p. 50.
5. The Latin *sericum* derives from the Greek *ser*, probably from archaic Chinese *sieg* (modern *ssǔ*, 'silk thread'). Compare also Korean *sir*, Mongolian *sirkek*, Russian *seolc*, English *silk*, etc.

'unloosening'? Pliny, while speaking of Chinese silk processed in the West, uses the expression *redordiendi fila rursusque texendi*, which Hirth took to mean unravelling an already-woven Chinese fabric and then re-weaving its threads into a finer cloth. But the expression could equally well refer to degumming Chinese raw silk thread, thus separating out the individual filaments composing it, and then re-reeling these – presumably to make a lighter type of thread. Now Pliny uses a similar phrase, *redordiri fila rursusque texere*, when speaking of the Coan industry. Whatever this may mean, it surely cannot describe the re-processing of an already manufactured thread or woven fabric, for why should Coan weavers so radically alter what they themselves had produced? Colonel Yule took *redordiri fila rursusque texere* to be a fanciful reference to unwinding the silk filament from the 'woven' cocoon, and then 're-weaving' it.[1] If, of course, both expressions mean the same thing – namely, unreeling the silk filament from the cocoon – the first might be cited as evidence that Chinese silk was reaching the West in the form of cocoons. But the Chinese account makes it clear that cocoons were not in question, but thread.

My own view is that neither Chinese nor Roman author knew more than that Chinese silk was submitted to *some* industrial process on arrival in the West, and before being woven into the favoured loose-textured gauze. As for Hirth's explanation, try as one may one cannot imagine how a fabric containing as many as seventy warp threads and forty wefts *per centimetre* (p. 235) could ever have been unwoven and converted back into thread. Furthermore, the Chinese account specifically says 'silk thread', *ssŭ*, and not cloth.[2] In my opinion, therefore, Hirth was wrong in supposing that Western weavers unwove Chinese cloth. As for the second possibility, a lighter silk thread could conceivably be produced by separating out the component filaments and re-reeling them, but no particular advantage would be gained. Chinese silk thread was already as fine as was

1. Sir H. Yule, *Cathay and the Way Thither*, 2nd edition, 4 vols (London 1915–16), vol. 1, p. 199.

2. Hirth's translation of *ssŭ* as 'silk' is ambiguous. He backs up his theory by quoting the thirteenth-century A.D. Chinese author Ma Tuan-lin, who says: 'They were at all times anxious to procure Chinese close-textured white silk-cloth (*chien su*) for unloosening so as to make foreign fine silk-cloth'. But this passage uses exactly the same characters as *Wei lüeh*, except that it substitutes *chien su* for *ssŭ*. In view of its late date, I cannot see that it has any value as evidence.

allowable for normal weaving techniques; and the sheerness of a gauze would in any case depend more on the looseness of the weave than on the fineness of its threads.

I suggest that the process referred to by *Wei lüeh* as *chieh*, and by Pliny as *redordiendi fila rursusque texendi*, may have been degumming – removing the sericin in which the filaments lie when normally reeled – and then simply 'throwing' the loosened filament into a twisted thread. We shall later present evidence that Chinese silk thread, *ssŭ*, was thus treated in the West, and suggest a reason for it. In the meantime, let us observe that the expression *tsa sê ling*, translated by Hirth as 'thin silk-cloth of various colours' (p. 216), seems to mean more exactly 'thin silk-cloth containing threads of several different colours', i.e. polychrome silk. If this is so, we should note that in such a silk the threads must necessarily be dyed before weaving, and that threads cannot properly be dyed until they have been degummed. It would be possible to weave raw thread into self- or single-coloured cloth, but not into *tsa sê ling*. Since silk thread as opposed to cloth was exported from China to the West in a raw state, it follows that Western weavers would have had to degum the thread before dyeing it, if the intention was to weave polychrome silks.

Ling woven in the West, therefore, so far from indicating a Western source of raw domestic silk, as the Chinese at one time believed, serves rather to prove its utter dependence on China as a source of supply. Western evidence for the importation of Chinese skeined raw silk comes from the *Periplus of the Erythraean Sea*, an itinerary of shipping routes in the Red and Arabian Seas written by an unknown Greek-speaking merchant soon after the middle of the first century A.D. We learn that raw silk thread (νῆμα) was shipped to Red Sea ports from Barbaricum (at the mouth of the Indus near modern Karachi); from Barygaza (the modern Broach at the mouth of the Narbada River some 400 miles to the south-west); and from Limyrice at the mouth of the Ganges – presumably having come overland through Lhasa. The *Periplus* makes it quite clear that this silk came from China, known to its author as Thina, and that it reached Barygaza and Barbaricum by way of Bactria (map 4).

Our inquiry into the state of Western sericulture before the introduction of *Bombyx mori* from China in the sixth century A.D. leads therefore to the following conclusions:

1. There was no sericulture based on *Bombyx mori* before that time.
2. A primitive type of sericulture, perhaps based on *Lasiocampa otus*, was practised on the island of Cos perhaps for several centuries before the beginning of our era.
3. Sericulture was unknown in any other part of the West.
4. Some spun silk may have been produced from Western wild silkworms, but if so the quantity must have been very small; and there is no archaeological evidence that any was made at all.

In what follows we intend to give a brief account of the early history and traditional practice of sericulture in China, together with properties of fibre and thread, and then discuss the types of loom on which early Chinese silks may have been woven. Finally we shall examine the characteristic features of Han silk weaves, as far as they can be told from surviving examples.

Chinese Sericulture

Silk was allegedly given to China by a 'culture heroine', the legendary Empress Hsi Ling Shih, who about the middle of the third millennium B.C. taught 'how to treat the cocoon and the silk in order to give the people clothes which would protect them from head injury and cold'.[1] Silk may actually have been in use within a few centuries of that time. A single cocoon of an unidentified silkworm was found at the Neolithic site of Hsi-yin Ts'un in Shansi, thought to be contemporary with Yang-shao Ts'un (*c.* 2200–1700 B.C.). The cocoon had been cut, although whether by man or by the escaping moth one cannot say. It would of course be rash to base any conclusion on this single find; but we have ample evidence of silks from Shang-Yin times, thanks to brilliant pioneer studies by Dr Sylwan.[2] Textiles used for wrapping bronze objects buried with the dead sometimes get impregnated with corrosion products from the metal and become, as it were, fossilized, so that details of the weave can be made out under a

1. V. Sylwan (see footnote p. 208), p. 17.
2. V. Sylwan, 'Silk from the Yin Dynasty', in *B.M.F.E.A.*, no. 9 (1937), pp. 119–26.

microscope. Dr Sylwan has examined fragments of silks adhering to two bronze objects, an axe and a vessel of the *chih* class (p. 147), both of which can be assigned to the First Phase on stylistic grounds. We shall presently deal with details of these weaves; but Dr Sylwan's conclusion that the thread used for these textiles was reeled silk of *Bombyx mori* is of first-rate importance to textile historians, since it gives a provisional *terminus ante quem* for the introduction of true sericulture in China. The art goes back, that is to say, to at least 1000 B.C.; it may well have had a previous history of several centuries, so far uncovered.

Granted that the Shang-Yin people practised sericulture, one may safely assume that their techniques differed only slightly, if at all, from methods used in China down to recent days. Sericulture is a traditional art which, by the very nature of the materials it employs, admits of little change.[1] Every stage, from cultivation of the food-plant to conservation of eggs during the winter, is, in China, subject to exact precepts that have an air of ritual about them; and the following description, based on a report made in 1880,[2] would probably serve equally well for the industry as it was 2,000 and more years ago.

The Food Plant

Two varieties of the white mulberry, *Morus alba*, are commonly recognized in China. *Yeh sang* is the wild mulberry, a plant producing small and relatively few leaves, but with abundant fruit, and of a hardy stock. *Lu sang*, the domestic or cultivated mulberry, produces few berries but much foliage. Silkworms fed on the former yield silk that is coarse and of inferior quality, so that the general practice in starting a plantation is to sow fruit of the hardy wild stock, and graft cuttings of the domestic variety when the saplings have grown a foot or so high.

Berries are sown about mid-June, and saplings are ready for grafting by the following spring. The cuttings, which are about 3 inches

1. Readers living in England may find it possible to visit the silk-farm at Ayot St Lawrence, Hertfordshire, where they can inspect all stages in cultivation, from hatching to reeling. Apart from such modern introductions as thermostatic control of temperatures in hatching and feeding rooms, and power-driven filatures, the methods are essentially those of traditional Chinese sericulture.

2. Various authors, *Silk*, a series of reports on the state of the silk industry in China, published by order of the Inspector-General of Maritime Customs, Shanghai 1881.

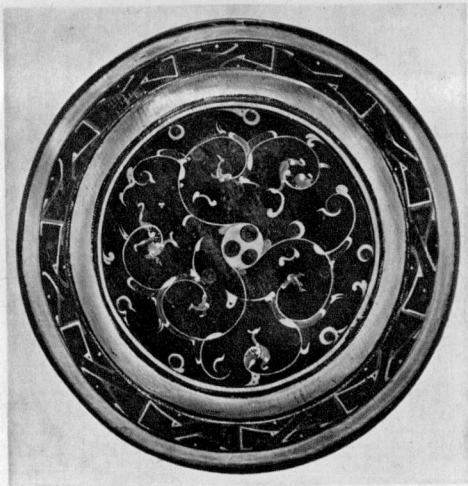

(A) Lid of a toilet box, *lien*, 3rd century B.C.; probably from Ch'ang-sha, Hunan. D 8¼ ins (p. 264)

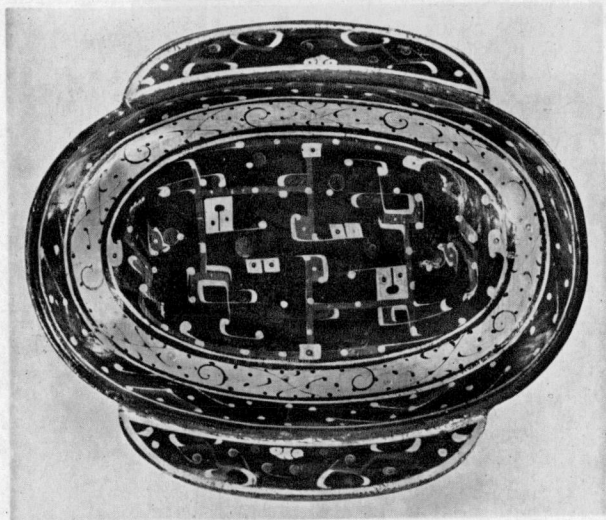

(B) Interior of a large cup, *pei*, 3rd century B.C ; probably from Ch'ang-sha, Hunan. L 9¾ ins (p. 264)

(A) Part of a table top, Han dynasty; probably from Lo-lang, Korea.
(p. 276)

(B) Part of a table top, Han dynasty; from Yang-kao, near Ta-t'ung,
Shansi. (p. 202)

(A) Exterior of a large cup, *pei*, Han dynasty, dated A.D. 4; from Lo-Lang, Korea. L 7 ins. (pp. 205-6)

(B) Toilet box, *lien*, Han dynasty; from Hai Chou, Kiangsu. H with lid 4 ins (p. 199)

(B) Part of a silk damask, Han dynasty; from Lou-lan, Chinese Turkestan. × c. 2 (p. 244)

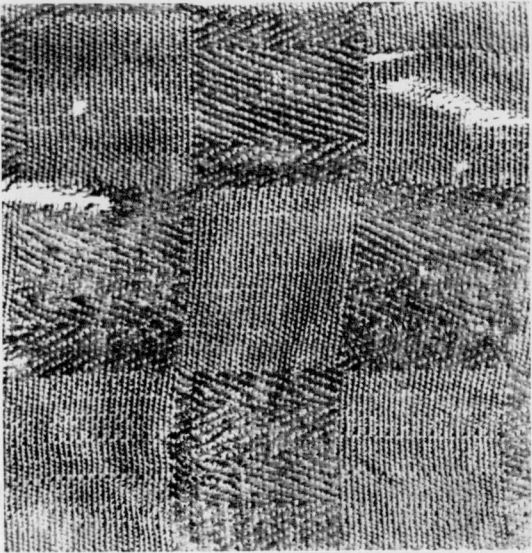

(A) Part of a silk damask, Han dynasty; from Palmyra, Syria. × c. 5 (p. 245)

20

Part of a silk damask, Han dynasty; from Palmyra, Syria. Area shown c. 2 by 2¾ ins (p. 276)

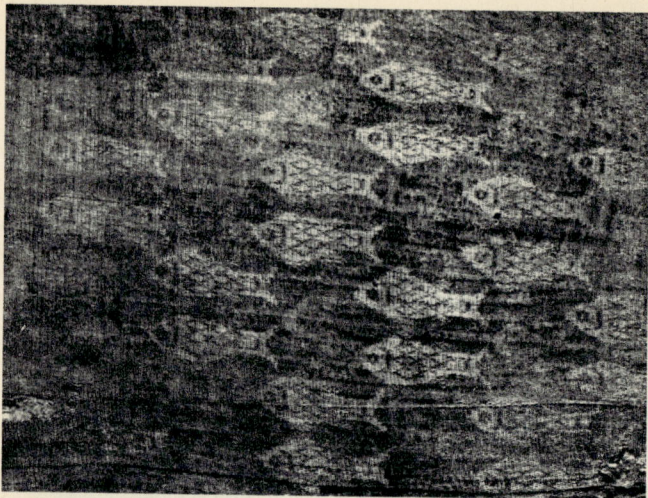

(A) Part of a silk polychrome, Han dynasty; from Noin-ula, northern Mongolia. About actual size (p. 286)

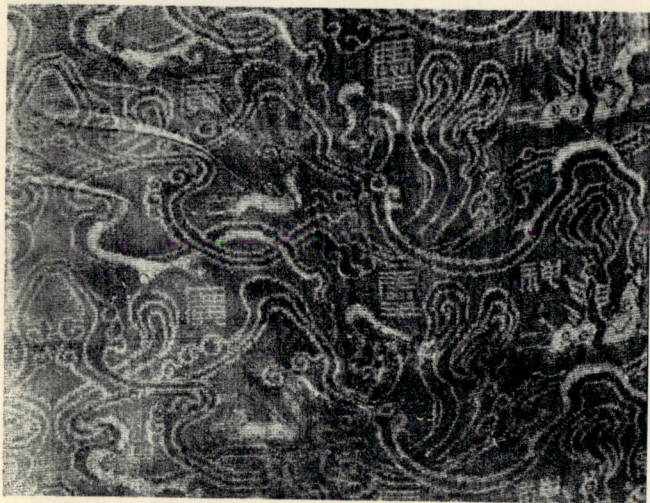

(B) Part of a silk polychrome, Han dynasty; from Noin-ula, northern Mongolia. Area shown c. 6 by 8 ins (p. 266)

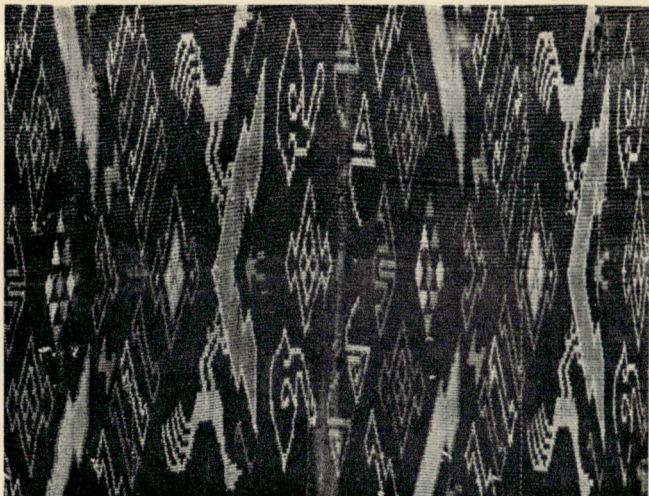

(A) Part of a silk polychrome, Han dynasty; from Noin-ula, northern Mongolia. W. *c.* 12 ins (p. 258)

(B) Part of a silk polychrome, Han dynasty; from Lou-lan, Chinese Turkestan. Remaining width *c.* 6 ins (p. 286)

Part of a silk polychrome, Han dynasty; from Noin-ula, northern Mongolia. Remaining width *c.* 15 ins (pp. 290–2).

long, have two shoots, one of which is removed and the other allowed to grow, reaching a height of about 6 feet by the autumn. In December the young trees are transplanted and spaced out, and cut back to some 18 inches in the following spring, that of the second year. Two shoots are now allowed to grow, and these are again cut back in the spring of the third year. Each autumn the tree reaches a height of 6 feet, and each successive spring it is cut back to 18 inches. In the third year four shoots are allowed to survive; in the fourth year, eight; and in the fifth year, sixteen. That year's growth provides the first crop of leaves actually fed to silkworms, and the tree is subsequently kept at a standard height of between five and six feet, being cut back whenever necessary. The wild mulberry, on the other hand, is neither headed down nor grafted, and grows to several times the size of the domestic variety.

Feeding lasts about thirty days, and it is a matter for careful calculation how many silkworms can be brought to maturity with the quantity of leaves available. Approximately a ton of leaves is needed to rear an ounce or so of newly-hatched worms, yielding eventually about twelve pounds of silk – from which only about half can be reeled – from 130 to 140 lb. of cocoons. A fully-grown tree will produce 80 lb. of leaves in a season, so that some thirty trees are needed to produce 6 lb. of reeled silk.

Hatching and Rearing Silkworms

Silkworms hatch out when the mulberry first breaks into leaf in mid-April. About ten days previously the eggs, enclosed in paper rolls, are brought into the house and allowed to develop at room temperature, or are placed in the clothing and kept warm by bodyheat. From about the sixth day, batches of eggs are daily examined for signs of hatching, a process that should be complete for each batch in the course of twenty-four hours. After hatching, the young caterpillars – then about a tenth of an inch long, and no thicker than hairs – are carefully brushed into bamboo baskets and fed with clean, fresh mulberry leaves chopped small on a straw chopping-pad. Every now and again, as they grow, the worms are distributed into more and more baskets, for which purpose a pair of fine bamboo forceps is used. Worms first feed for about five days, during which time – as during subsequent feeds – they are kept in light, dry, and warm surroundings, and are closely sheltered from draught. The first moult then occurs. When some worms have stopped feeding and become torpid, each batch is lightly covered with rice-husk ash, on top of which are placed more mulberry leaves; worms that are still feeding make their way on to this upper layer, *shang ma yeh*, or 'mount-horse leaves', whence they are removed to other baskets. This process of segregation is repeated at each moult, so ensuring that every batch develops at an even rate; the aim being, as we have seen, to secure absolute control over the life-cycle, so that all worms in a given batch spin their cocoons more or less simultaneously.

By the seventh day worms have cast their skins and are again fed at regular intervals for another five days. The second moult begins about the twelfth day, and is complete on the fourteenth. By this time worms are about half an inch long, and can be fed on more coarsely cut leaves. Further moults take place on the nineteenth and twenty-sixth days, or thereabouts, after which worms feed much more voraciously; and in a few days after the last moult they consume something like twenty times their body-weight of leaves. Whole branches are now fed to them, it being reckoned that at this stage a mouthful of leaves will yield its equivalent weight of raw silk. Worms are now about two inches long.

About thirty-five days after hatching, worms are ready to spin their cocoons. They stop feeding, take up a semi-erect posture, and are then transferred to straw trusses called 'silkworm hills' (*ts'an shan*), some sixty or seventy worms to a truss. Spinning lasts five days, the silk being extruded in a continuous figure-of-eight pattern. Cocoons are taken off the trusses in the order in which worms were put on. Selected hard white cocoons from the upper parts of the trusses are now put on trays and the moths allowed to emerge, which they do after eight to ten days; that is, after a life-cycle of about fifty days.[1] Moths are paired for eight hours in strictly controlled conditions, and the females all lay their eggs on the same day, upon sheets of thick paper; these eggs are to provide next year's crop of silkworms. They are washed, dried, and then hung up in folded papers on the walls of the house, away from smoke or damp. Towards the end of January,

1. The span of the life-cycle varies quite a good deal from place to place. In Japan it is sixty-three days, in central China fifty-four days, at Canton thirty-six days.

for no apparent reason, they are customarily steeped in an infusion of mulberry leaves or of tea, dried, and hung up again until ready for hatching.

In traditional Chinese manuals of silk-farming, one notices how finely detailed are the instructions given for each stage in the life-history. No pains are spared to secure uniform conditions for development. 'Silkworms', we are told, 'require to be equal in three things: the eggs should all be laid together, they must all be hatched together, and begin to spin together.' It also seems that silkworms are temperamental creatures, very easily affected by adverse conditions such as noise and vibration: 'They cannot bear to be near where people pound in a mortar,' the same authority tells us, 'neither do they like mourning, nor pregnant women.'[1] They also shun the smell of wine, of vinegar, smoke, musk, and oil. They refuse damp leaves, nor will they eat hot ones. It might appear from all this that successful rearing of a batch of silkworms is no simple matter; it *does* transpire that the outstanding quality of silk as a textile material, maintained throughout the whole of Chinese history, depended on a deep understanding of the need for uniformity at all stages of manufacture, and on an intimate knowledge, accumulated and handed down from time immemorial, of the problems peculiar to the craft of sericulture.

Filature or Reeling [2]

Of cocoons remaining after selection for breeding, some may be rejected as unsuited for reeling. These include *dupions* – double cocoons spun by two worms in close contact – cocoons damaged by escaping maggots of parasitic flies, those accidentally deformed, those spun by diseased worms, and so forth; all these are set aside to be spun into refuse silk. The rest are reeled.

Various methods of filature are, or have been, in use in China, but only one gives really satisfactory results. This is the 'water' method, now generally used wherever sericulture is practised. Immersing

1. Anon., 'A glance at the interior of China, obtained during a journey through the silk and green tea districts', being *The Chinese Miscellany*, no. 1, Shanghai 1849, p. 64.

2. The word 'filature' means also the machine by means of which, or the workshop in which, cocoons are reeled.

cocoons in very hot water serves several purposes. It kills the chrysalids, so that if cocoons cannot conveniently be reeled immediately they can be safely stored until required. On immersion, water also enters the cocoon and weighs it down, making for easy handling while the filament is being taken off. Finally, immersion in hot water, especially if a small amount of an alkali such as soda is added, partly dissolves the sericin binding the filament loops together; the silk can then be reeled off without difficulty once the end of the filament (Fr. *maître brin*) has been found. The traditional Chinese practice was to put cocoons in a pan of water placed on top of a wood-burning stove, near which was the reeling machine. Cocoons were stirred with a bamboo comb until the *maître brin* of each had been caught up. On lifting the comb from the water, each cocoon began to unreel. The operator then picked up a number of filaments, depending on the quality of the thread required.[1] Holding the filaments in one hand, he now, with the other, unreeled the cocoons to which they were attached by jerking them gently on the surface of the water, keeping them down by means of the comb, until a few yards of silk had been unwound. This was surface floss, filament of uneven thickness, lustreless and non-elastic, suitable only for making refuse silk after spinning; it was accordingly broken off and set aside. More silk was taken off until the operator was satisfied that it was unwinding clean and smooth. It was then led to the reeling machine, passed through an eyelet, over a roller, and under the hook of a horizontal 'pressing rod' or thread-guide, by means of which it was fed evenly on to the reel mounted at the back of the machine. This was set in motion by a treadle operating a driving-pulley attached to the front end of the reeling-frame. As the reel rotated, the silk filaments, drawn together and agglutinated into one as they passed through the eyelet, were wound on to it as thread. To dry out the thread – for it would tend to stick if wet – a small charcoal stove was placed under the reel.[2] The

1. Most Chinese threads are made of from six to thirty cocoon filaments, the finest type having six or seven filaments, followed by grades of eleven to twelve, fifteen to sixteen, eighteen to nineteen, and twenty and upwards. A fragment of a Han green taffeta found at Palmyra showed eleven to twelve filaments in the thread. One from Halebie-Zenobia showed a warp thread of fifteen to sixteen filaments, and a weft thread of twenty to twenty-five.

2. In modern power-driven filatures, which may have anything between twenty and three hundred reeling-basins, the threads are drawn together and

Chinese reeling-machine normally mounted two eyelets, rollers, pressing-rod hooks, and reels, so that the operator reeled two threads simultaneously.

Silk was reeled from cocoons until each became paper-thin and transparent (Fr. *pellette*), and as this stage was reached the operator had to break off the silk filament, remove the exhausted cocoon, replace it with a fresh one, and re-connect the filament. The remains of silk on the old cocoon went to join the surface floss and damaged cocoons to be made into refuse silk, while the chrysalids were either used for fertilizers or were sold as an article of human food.

The reeling-machine used in China before the coming of modern Western filatures, though efficient, was a comparatively simple affair, and there seems no reason at all why it should not have been known as early as Han times. On the other hand, it *is* strictly possible to reel silk using only one's hands and a reel; but in this case the silk is black and lustreless, and of inferior quality.

Silk as a Textile Fibre

Liquid silk is secreted in a steady stream from each of two silk glands running the length of the silkworm's body. These lead into a common duct, where the two streams come together and are enclosed in a coating of sericin produced by paired glands known as the Glands of Filipi. The strand emerges as a single filament from the spinneret at the head of the animal, and rapidly hardens on exposure to air. In cross-section two roughly triangular fibres can be seen lying in their common bed of sericin; and in longitudinal section the fibrils of which each is composed appear as striations, although these are far less evident in the *Bombyx mori* fibre than in those of wild silkworms. Sericin and the fibre substance, fibroin, have much the same chemical composition; but, since the sericin is sooner or later washed out, it is upon the properties of the fibre that the quality of silk as a textile depends.

Of the four main textile fibres, silk alone might seem to have been expressly designed by nature to serve the needs of man. It has three outstanding qualities. Staple-length is a good index of commercial

given a slight twist before being run over the reels. This, apart from binding them together as a single thread, also rinses them of excess water so that they reach the reel more or less dry.

utility, since the longer a textile fibre is, the more speedily and economically can it be converted into thread or yarn. The silk filament is several hundred yards long. Again, the tensile strength of a thread or yarn will depend in the first instance on that of the fibre. The tensile strength of silk, amounting to 65,000 lb. per square inch, is vastly greater than that of cotton, wool, or flax, and is equal to that of many engineering materials. Elasticity is the third important property of a good textile fibre. Silk can be stretched to between 1 and 2 per cent of its length, and it will regain its former length when the tension is released; it can be elongated to about 20 per cent of its length before breaking.

In converting any textile fibre into yarn suitable for warping, for weft, for sewing-thread, and so forth, account must be taken of all three of the above-mentioned properties, and the yarn produced will be a compromise in which factors such as degree of fineness, minimum tensile strength, and cost of production will play their part. But these limiting factors are of less account in the case of silk than in that of any other natural textile fibre; for a very strong and fine thread can be produced with the minimum of fibre-engineering and of expense of time and money. And in other respects the properties of the silk fibre augment those of the thread or yarn. It has the greatest affinity to dye of any known natural textile fibre, and a high affinity to mordants (pp. 241–2). It has a very low thermal conductivity, which makes it warm to wear. It is insoluble in water. It is supple to the touch and has a high lustre; and, when treated with weak acid to harden its surface, it emits a characteristic rustle, the 'scroop', if squeezed or pressed.

Fibre Engineering

Before raw silk thread is woven into fabric it may or may not undergo various forms of treatment designed to improve its natural qualities. Of these the most important is 'throwing'. Silk thread is 'thrown' – that is, twisted – so as to increase its tensile strength and elasticity, the better to undergo the rigours of weaving, and especially to produce a strong thread for warping.[1] But throwing, while increas-

1. Modern exported Chinese raw silk is customarily re-reeled, during which process the twist is inserted. Thus two or more raw silk threads twisted together with a few turns per inch produce a yarn suitable for weft, called tram

ing tensile strength, adds to cost of production; and besides, robs the silk of some of its lustre, makes it harder and stiffer, and tends to bring out any unevenness of the thread. The Chinese seem to have avoided it whenever possible. Certainly all experts agree that Chinese silks of the Han period, wherever found, show no perceptible twist in the thread. But in early Western silk fabrics, whether made from imported Chinese raw silk or no, the twisted thread is usually conspicuous. How are we to explain this difference in practice? If Western weavers found it desirable to throw their silk into yarns, why did not the Han Chinese?

To answer this question, I think we must first of all consider the qualities required of a good warping thread, and then take into account the difference between Eastern and Western weaving traditions. A warp thread must be long, strong, and elastic.[1] Long, because setting a warp, especially if an all-over pattern with complicated motives is required, is a laborious process; once set, the weaver does not want to have to re-set it – at any rate until a substantial length of cloth has been woven. Strong and elastic, because it has to withstand the strain of heavy and repeated blows from the reed (p. 233) as it beats up the weft at the 'fell', the point at which the cloth is being woven. Chinese silk makes an excellent warping thread, and seems always to have enjoyed the absolute confidence of Chinese weavers. Further, silk thread is stronger and more elastic if it is raw (p. 215, footnote 1). A thread still protected by its natural gum will stand up to weaving whether it has been thrown into yarn or not, and there is reason to suppose that Chinese monochrome silks of the Han period were not de-gummed ('boiled off') until after the cloth had been woven.[2] Left with its protective coating of sericin, unthrown silk thread makes a perfectly satisfactory warp.

With a first-class warping thread to hand, warp inevitably came to take precedence over weft in the Chinese weaving tradition. Its threads greatly outnumbered those of the weft in Han silk-weaves, so

(Fr. *trame* = weft); two tram threads twisted together with eight to ten turns per inch in the opposite direction, yield a warping yarn called organzine.

1. For the meaning of the word 'warp', and other terms used in this paragraph, cf. p. 231.

2. And not always even then. In the last century Chinese cloth made from wild silk (pongees) still held anything up to 20 per cent of its dry weight in the form of gum. (Raw silk thread contains 15 to 25 per cent sericin.)

that the latter played little visible part in the finished cloth. And when pattern-effects were sought, it was the warp which made them. It would probably be correct to say that the technical and artistic superiority of Chinese silk-weaving over all other known textile traditions until well on into the Christian era, stems from the supremacy of silk as a warp thread, and the consequent invention of looms and weaving-techniques capable of exploiting this natural advantage to the full.

In the West an entirely different tradition was at work, based on the short-staple animal or vegetable fibre, whether wool, cotton, or flax. Long, unbroken warp yarns of uniform strength and dimensions were rare.[1] Concentration upon weft effects, as opposed to those made by the warp, was the natural outcome of this deficiency. For the weft has only to pass across the width of the material. It can, in fact, be thought of as discontinuous, since a throw of the shuttle one way is followed by another in the reverse direction. Thus, although a long weft thread is an advantage, it is not strictly indispensable for good weaving.

In early Western weaves, weft greatly outnumbered warp; and when contrasting colours were required, wefts of different colours were introduced, whereas for the warp a single colour was generally used. The most characteristic expression of this tradition is found in the Syrian tapestry-weaves or gobelins, in which the pattern threads of the weft were woven into the ground-weave by hand. When Western weavers first began to imitate Chinese pattern silks, they naturally upheld their own earlier tradition, by which it was the weft that gave the pattern. The weave has very much the same appearance as its Chinese model (see footnote 3, p. 208); yet it witnesses to a diametrically opposite convention of weaving.

Trained in the tradition of weft-weaving, Western weavers did not recognize the intrinsic advantages of silk when it first became available to them in bulk; or, if they did, lacked the technical equipment to exploit them. They continued to cling to weft weaves, using a sparse and delicate warp. And – through force of habit, one imagines – they gave their silk warps a strong twist, as they had always done for their

1. Not until c. A.D. 1770 were English weavers able to produce a cotton yarn suitable for warping. Up to that time, fine cottons were woven with a linen warp. Presence of Chinese silk warps in Syrian mustered weaves (p. 215) is, of course, a testimony to the superior qualities of silk as a warp thread.

short-staple yarns.[1] They had not yet learnt to place confidence in the natural properties of silk as a textile thread.

Chinese Looms

We have little direct information about Chinese looms of Han times, and scarcely any about those of earlier periods. Technical treatises are missing, as they are for other crafts, since processes were either family or guild secrets, or else so widely known that no one thought it worth while to record them. As far as concerns silk-weaving, plain cloth could be made in every household of standing, and presumably was, on looms of no particular complexity. But weaving a complicated all-over pattern is quite another matter; it demands not only the expert attention of a specialist to set up the warp in accordance with a pre-selected pattern, but also elaborate and expensive looms. Professional weavers must have guarded their knowledge closely, and found employment only in the very wealthiest families; until, in Han times, silk ceased to be exclusively an item of family or clan prestige and became a factor in international trade.

On the other hand, something can be made out by inference from the textiles themselves, as well as from the construction of modern Chinese domestic looms. Craft traditions run deep in China, and the modern Chinese loom may not differ basically from similar machines in use during the Han period and earlier. Nor – and this opens up the possibility that Chinese methods of loom construction may have contributed to the development of the Western loom – is it significantly different from the frame-loom already in use in Europe by the thirteenth century A.D., but not, perhaps, much before.[2] We had better say a few words about its distinctive features.

1. Here and there one comes across a Western silk fabric in which the threads are not thrown. A damask found in Palmyra, and woven in Syria, is of this type. Pfister (see footnote p. 210), vol. ii, p. 35, concludes that the fabric was woven with raw threads and afterwards de-gummed in the Chinese fashion (cf. p. 227). But this piece is certainly exceptional.

2. Schaefer gives this date as a *terminus ante quem* for the introduction of the horizontal treadle-operated shaft-loom in Europe, his evidence being an illustration on a thirteenth-century MS at Trinity College, Cambridge. Cf. G. Schaefer, 'The hand-loom of the Middle Ages and the following centuries', in *C.R.*, vol. ii, no. 16 (Dec. 1938), pp. 554-5.

To begin with, the warp threads are stretched horizontally between two beams. One, the cloth-beam, confronts the weaver; the other, the warp-beam, is at the further end of the loom. Both beams can be rotated and locked at intervals by means of a ratchet at the side, or a crank braced against pegs. This allows the warp to be kept at the controlled and uniform tension necessary for even and close weaving, and at the same time provides a means of weaving long continuous pieces of cloth; since cloth can be taken up continuously by the cloth-beam, while a corresponding length of warp is let off by the warp-beam until the latter is empty. As we have said, silk provides a long, continuous, and regular warp-thread. One may assume that Chinese weavers quickly took advantage of this natural property to invent rotary beams by means of which the whole length of thread could be 'beamed on'.

In the West three main types of loom were known to antiquity. The oldest, as far as can be told from archaeological evidence in the form of drawings and models from graves, is the Egyptian horizontal loom made by driving four posts into the ground, sometimes connected by side and end-beams. One recorded example dates from predynastic times; most belong to the 12th Dynasty (2160–1788 B.C.). There is no indication as to how cloth was taken up on these looms, and no reason to suppose that either warp- or cloth-beam could be rotated. A modified version, in use among the Bedouin Arabs of to-day, has a very long warp pegged to the ground, and the weaver makes his way along it from one end to the other, so that a long piece of cloth can be woven although the beams are fixed. But according to Schaefer the size of preserved fragments of early Egyptian cloth does not exceed three yards by four, and in his view there were no roller appliances on the looms that made them.

Next in order of seniority is a vertical loom first known in Egypt and later introduced into the Roman Empire. This came in some time after 2000 B.C., but did not altogether supersede the horizontal type. Warp-threads, suspended between an upper and a lower cross-beam, stretched down towards the weaver, who beat the weft downwards at the fell so that the cloth gradually rose in the loom to a height beyond which he could not conveniently continue to work. Again there is a question, but no evidence, as to whether this loom was provided with a crank by means of which the cloth could be beamed on.

The third type of early Western loom was also vertical, but was operated on a rather different principle. The warp-threads hung downwards from an upper cross-beam, but tension was secured by gathering them into bunches at the lower end, and hanging a warp-weight on each bunch. The weaver beat the fell upwards, standing in what must have been an uncomfortable position, so that the cloth gradually grew downwards away from, not towards, the upper beam. A drawing on a *skyphos* in the Ashmolean Museum, Oxford, shows what seems to be a roll of cloth on the upper beam; and we have evidence from illustrations of Icelandic warp-weighted looms not long since in use, that the cloth could be taken up in this way, and that the threads continued beyond the warp-weights. Quite how the latter were adjusted as the cloth grew is not clear to me.

This last type of loom was used in antiquity for tapestry-weaving on a domestic scale, and seems to have originated in Greece. As we shall presently see, vertical looms, of whatever design, are unsuited for production of mechanically repeated all-over patterns. They are designed for hand-weaving of fabrics in which warp plays a minor role. Their structure permits of little mechanical development, and they have long been discarded by all but primitive weavers, and except for weaving certain special classes of textiles.[1] Advanced weaving techniques are bound up with the horizontal loom, use of which in China undoubtedly dates from the earliest period of recorded history, while invention of rotary cloth- and warp-beams may have followed not long afterwards.

Further Development of the Horizontal Loom

In all looms, of whatever type, means have to be provided for opening the 'shed'. As is well known, weaving is a process of inter-lacing longitudinal threads (warp) with cross threads (weft), each weft normally passing over one warp, under the next, over the next, and so on across the width of the cloth. If all alternate warp-threads can be simultaneously separated from their neighbours on each side – in a horizontal loom they would be raised – a space or 'shed' results through which the weft is thrown on its shuttle. On closing the shed

1. So in Chekiang an upright loom with fixed upper and lower cross-beams is still in use for making rush matting. An illustration of one appears in R. P. Hommel's *China at Work*, New York 1937, fig. 266.

it is evident that the weft-thread has interlaced with every thread of the warp. For its return journey, the weft must take a different path: it must pass through the contrary shed. Those warp-threads that were not previously manipulated must now be separated from their neighbours for the reverse throw; they, too, must be provided with a device whereby they can be simultaneously raised.

There are various means by which the two sheds can be made. A flat lath, or shed-rod, can be inserted through the warp, passing over one thread, under the next, and so forth, and kept in position during the whole process of weaving. This is a 'fixed' shed-rod. When the rod is turned through a right angle about its long axis, it will automatically raise one set of alternate threads and depress the other, thus creating the first shed through which the weft is thrown. With a fixed shed-rod in position, a second similar device cannot be employed to form the contrary shed. Instead, the second set of warp-threads must be raised at a point nearer the cloth by means of short strings – usually loops passing under each warp – all of which can be lifted simultaneously if attached by their upper ends to another stick, the rod-heddle. Notwithstanding the presence of the shed-rod, when the rod-heddle is lifted its string-loops will pull up the warps to which they are attached until they are well above the level of the rest, and the contrary shed is now open.

With shed-rod and rod-heddle the two alternating sheds can be quickly opened and shut. The weaver operates them alternatively with left or right hand, leaving the other free for throwing the weft across. Yet even so, the procedure is laborious and disjointed. The hands have to make several quite distinct movements, while after every few throws the weaver must suspend operations to beat the weft-threads into the cloth. The next stage in the development of the horizontal loom is to transfer some of this work to the feet. The heddle proper, or shaft, is a frame stretching across the loom at right angles to the plane of the warp, and provided with a large number of thin strings, or leashes, made of cord, wood, or metal, which are arranged vertically across its width. Each leash has a small loop or eyelet through which every other warp-thread is entered. On raising this apparatus, all alternate warp-threads will be raised and the shed made. To make two contrary sheds – the minimum number for weaving – we must, of course, have two heddles, one placed in front of the other, and the second heddle must be entered with the threads not entered through the first. If the heddles are connected by means of a top-frame of cords and pulleys (heddle-harness) to a system of two treadles, it is clear that on depressing the treadles alternately with the feet, the two sheds will be made one after the other without any movement on the part of the hands. These are left free for throwing the weft shuttle from one side of the weave to the other, and for beating in the weft. The weaver's 'comb', or 'beater-in', is a flat tool with a handle and a toothed outer edge. After a few throws it is brought down smartly on to the weft, the teeth forcing their way between the warps, thereby pressing the weft-threads into the cloth. At some stage in the history of the horizontal loom, the beater-in became incorporated in its construction. It became the reed, a long, rectangular frame with vertical strings lying between the warps and slung to the heddle-harness in such a way that its normal position was close to the front heddle. As soon as the shuttle had passed on its throw, the hand that released it swung the reed forward and up to the fell of the cloth, thereby beating it in. The reed then swung back under its own momentum to its original position against the front heddle, leaving the way clear for the return throw. Beating-in thus became semi-automatic.

These are of course basic features of most looms, and the reader must forgive me if I have described mechanisms with which he is already familiar. At the same time I have had in mind modern Chinese shaft-looms of traditional type, in the belief that they probably retain essential features of Han and even earlier looms.[1]

It seems more than likely that treadle-controlled heddles were a Chinese invention later introduced into the West. I do not know of any evidence for western use of treadles before about the sixth century A.D. Pictures of earlier western looms show nothing of the sort – indeed, since those we know about are mostly of the upright type it is hard to believe that the treadle principle could ever have been thought applicable to them.[2] Schaefer supports the view that treadle-weaving began in Asia. He says: 'As the European never made use of his feet to facilitate his work to the extent which the peoples of Asia,

1. For instance, the two looms photographed in Chekiang by R. P. Hommel (see footnote p. 231), figs. 263–4.

2. In fact it was. A reconstruction made in A.D. 1690 of a Roman upright loom shows it provided with an ingenious contraption of ropes, levers, and rollers, by which the sheds might be worked with treadles. As Schaefer says (see footnote 2, p. 229), p. 552, it shows how the seventeenth century, with its own treadle-loom, would have liked the Roman loom to be.

especially of the Far East, did, it seems probable that Asia was the original home of treadle-weaving.'[1]

There are in existence at least two Han representations of looms, both from the Hsiao-t'ang Shan series of bas-reliefs dating from the first century A.D. Treadles, heddle-harness, and heddles are clearly shown, although one is bound to admit that details of the mechanical connexions between these parts, and other vital details of construction of the looms, are in no way elucidated; this is partly because they are summarily executed, partly because the bas-reliefs on which they are figured are badly worn.[2]

Looms and Weaves

In order to find out more about the construction of Han Chinese looms, it will be appropriate at this point to begin studying remains of actual pre-Han Chinese silk weaves. In her article already referred to (p. 219), Dr Sylwan describes three sorts of silk textile which appear to be the earliest known silks in the world. Two would properly be called cloths, since in them each weft passes over one warp, under the next, and so on across the web as already described. In one example there are roughly as many threads in one direction as there are in the other; as many weft-threads, that is, as there are warps. Dr Sylwan counted thirty-seven, forty, and fifty threads in three selected centimetres in one direction, and thirty, thirty, and thirty-five in the other; the slight variation being due to 'drawing' of the fabric after it had been wrapped round the bronze. Such a cloth is a tabby or taffeta.

The other cloth was a warp-rep, by which is meant that threads were denser in what was considered the warp direction than in the direction of the weft. One example showed seventy-two threads per

1. Cf. G. Schaefer (see footnote 2, p. 229), pp. 544–5. Elsewhere Schaefer says: 'from the thirteenth century onwards European weaving is characterised by the use of the treadle-loom with horizontal warp. The links connecting this highly perfected type with the primitive hand-loom are missing. The treadle-loom appears in Europe as a perfected invention, and as its most highly developed form, the drawloom, certainly came from the East, the idea of the treadle-loom itself probably originated there, too.'

2. A rubbing of one of them is reproduced by S. W. Bushell (see footnote p. 3), vol. I, fig. 14. The other is reproduced by V. Sylwan (see footnote p. 208), fig. 104.

centimetre in the warp, and thirty-five in the weft; the other – a coarser material – had forty warps and seventeen wefts per centimetre. Here already we observe the ascendancy of warp over weft. It would be true to say that the majority of known Han silks are warp reps; and in these Shang-Yin textile remains we have striking evidence of the antiquity of the type. Not only this, but the ratio of threads in the two directions seems to have changed little if at all from the two/one ratio of the Shang-Yin reps. The same is true of their actual numbers. Thus the average count per centimetre for twenty-two Han silk rags from Palmyra – of each of which the selvedge remains to tell us which threads are warp and which weft – is sixty-eight and thirty-five for the two directions respectively. This average is noticeably similar to the thread density of the finer of the Shang-Yin cloths. Chinese silk cloths, we may say, were usually reps woven with about seventy warps and thirty-five wefts per centimetre, this being a more or less optimum density.

The third Shang-Yin textile, found on both axe and *chih*, is of quite different type. Instead of regular interlacing of warp and weft, some warps pass over three or even more weft-threads at certain points (warp-floats). Such warps are pattern-warps; for the effect of floating the warp over more than one weft in succession is to bring the warp out from the surface of the material at such points. And when warp-floats are massed together – that is, when nearby or adjoining warps behave in a similar way – a pattern is blocked in and appears as a distinct raised patch on the front face of the material (plates 20 and 21). In the Shang-Yin textile, adjoining warp-floats are arranged stepwise, so that the pattern effect is of diagonal bands.

The appended diagram (figure 30) is redrawn from Dr Sylwan's reconstruction of this weave as it appears on the axe. White squares represent points where weft crosses warp on the front face of the material, while black squares and rectangles are where warp crosses weft, the direction of the warp being vertical. The design, as far as can be told, consists of two concentric lozenges framed by a zigzag border; and Dr Sylwan says that it is woven on an ordinary over-under cloth, which appears on the left in the diagram. The design was almost certainly repeated along the length of the material (warp axis), but whether or in what manner it was repeated across the width (weft axis) is more problematical. However, given the basic form of the pattern-unit, almost any combination could be secured without adding greatly to the difficulty of weaving the cloth. The question is, how *was* it woven?

A moment's inspection will show that the wefts I have numbered 1–26 enclose one complete pattern-unit. Weft 27 passes through

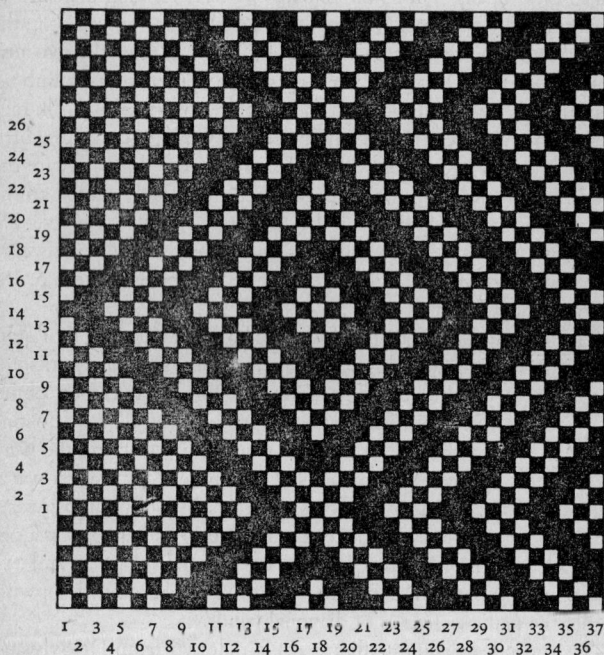

Figure 30. Reconstruction of pattern-units on a Shang-Yin 'twill', after Sylwan (warp runs up the page).

exactly the same shed as weft 1; weft 28 as weft 2; and so on. Once provision for the twenty-six sheds corresponding to wefts 1–26 has been made, weaving this pattern can be repeated indefinitely. But the mechanical problem is further simplified by the fact that the pattern-unit is symmetrical. At weft 14 it turns over on itself; weft 15 passes through exactly the same shed as weft 13; weft 16 repeats weft 12; weft 17 repeats weft 11; and so on. The number of different sheds needed to weave this pattern is therefore reduced to fourteen, corresponding to weft-throws 1–14.

Now it would be logically possible for fourteen sheds to be made by means of a shed-rod and thirteen rod-heddles, all being raised by hand. But it would be a tedious business. It is contrary to the observed conditions of weaving to have a large number of manually-operated heddles. Six is about the limit.[1] Alternatively, the sheds could be provided for by incorporating fourteen frame-heddles into the loom, all worked by means of treadles. But this also seems highly unlikely. Quite apart from the problem of securing efficient mechanical connexion between heddles and treadles, such a permanent contraption would be unnecessary for weaving the material now under discussion. It could be woven just as easily by means of two ground-weave heddles (p. 232), provided always that a special attachment were incorporated allowing each warp-thread to be raised individually as well. Such an attachment would be a form of drawloom (p. 209).

The drawloom is a device whereby a large number of different combinations of warp-threads can be made and secured at will. Every pattern-warp has a separate leash of its own, through which it is now entered. To each leash is attached one or more vertically-hanging draw-cords, the number for any given warp-thread depending on the number of combinations into which it enters. And these draw-cords are tied together in bundles each of which corresponds to, and operates, the particular group of warp-threads required to be raised for a given shed.

In weaving the fabric now being discussed, as reconstructed in figure 30, we should first enter all odd-numbered warps (1, 3, 5, etc.) through ground-heddle 1, and all even-numbered warps (2, 4, 6, etc.) through ground-heddle 2. Merely by operating these two heddles alternately, the two alternating sheds required for weaving an ordinary cloth would be opened one after the other; and cloth could be woven whenever we chose to do so. In making weft-throw 1, as marked on figure 30, we should operate ground-heddle 2; but it will be observed that warps 15, 21, 27, and 33 are also to be raised at this

1. As G. M. Crowfoot and J. Griffiths observe, in 'Coptic textiles in two-faced weave with patterns in reverse' in *J.E.A.*, vol. xxv, pt. 7 (1939), p. 46: 'There is little to be gained by multiplying heddles unless they can be controlled by treadles.' They also say: 'Primitive weavers rarely use many heddles; occasionally they use three, as in the case of the Navaho and other Indians, while up to six are used on the Mexican belt-looms. It is not impossible to use more, but it is difficult to manipulate many rod-heddles on the horizontal ground-loom, and still more difficult on the vertical loom.'

point, and they would therefore be connected up to a draw-cord bundle which would be pulled simultaneously with the opening of the shed. For weft-throw 2, ground-heddle 1 would be operated, and the draw-cord bundle controlling warps 14, 22, 28, and 34 would be pulled.

In our example it will be seen that each of warps 2, 3, 4, 5, 6, and 7 enters into one combination of warp-threads only; the greatest number of combinations into which any single warp enters is three, as is the case for warps 14, 15, 21, 22, 27, 28, 33, and 34; so that three is the greatest number of draw-cords that need be attached to any single warp. The total number of draw-cord bundles, corresponding to the total number of different sheds required to weave the pattern, is fourteen.

This patterned Shang-Yin weave is thus good evidence that a primitive form of the device by which complicated all-over patterns were woven in Han times (plates 21 to 24) was available to Chinese weavers a thousand or so years earlier; for a loom having some sort of drawloom attachment must have been used to weave it. One other feature of the traditional Chinese loom calls for comment here. Thread-density, as we have seen, was often as great as seventy per centimetre and more; so that in the case of a two-shaft loom, the heddle-leashes would have had to be set at a density of at least thirty-five to the centimetre. Moreover, the teeth of the reed would also have to be set fairly closely, and be sufficiently fine to pass through the warp-threads, and up to the fell of the cloth, without distorting them; draw-cords would also need to be fine. And for all these parts great mechanical strength in proportion to weight is essential. Under these conditions, I cannot imagine any material capable of being used for them in ancient China, other than silk itself.

Twills

The Shang-Yin textile was described by Dr Sylwan as a 'twill with a mixture of tabby weave'. A twill is a weave in which a given thread in one direction passes over several threads in the other before the binding-point – in this case the point where weft crosses warp on the front face of the material – is reached; and in which, as Dr Sylwan says, 'the binding points move diagonally in a step-like manner'. In this definition there is no stipulation as to how many threads are passed over before binding, nor whether it is warp or weft that is floated. Among Western twills recovered from Dura-Europos on the Euphrates, probably dating from the third century A.D., but certainly not later, we find such combinations as 2/1 – in which the *weft* passes over two warps on the front face of the material before binding – 2/2, and 4/2. All of these are weft twills.

Now the essence of a twill weave is that it is a distinct system of binding, no less *sui generis* than any other system – for instance, a tabby weave. It was not evolved as a means of patterning, but as a simplified method of weaving. And where employed, it normally extends throughout the weave. Early adoption of this system of weaving in the West was probably due to the fact that in such a weave the 'pick' – passing the weft through the warp by hand – did not need to inter-lace with all the warp-threads, but could miss some out. Weaving was thus speeded up.

The Shang-Yin fabric is not a twill in this sense, since warp-floats are introduced only to secure a decorative effect, and not as a simpli-fied means of binding. It does not provide evidence that twilling was a regular weaving practice in Shang-Yin times. And in fact true twills seem not to have reached China from the West until some fifteen hundred years later. There are, as we shall see, Han silks in which adjoining warp-threads do pass over several weft threads before bind-ing, and in which the binding-points do 'move diagonally in a step-like manner'. But again the weave is not employed throughout the entire fabric. It is used only to build up a pattern. The first evidence of genuine twilling in the Far East comes from a group of Chinese silks found by Sir Aurel Stein at Astana in Chinese Turkestan, dating from the second half of the sixth century A.D.

The Han Silk Weaves

The corpus of material now called Han silks has not been dated on internal evidence provided by the textiles themselves, but by means of other objects found with them, and from historical facts known about the sites. Thus Lo-lang is dated by presence of inscribed lac-quers bearing dates covering the period 85 B.C. to A.D. 102; Tun-huang by wooden slips bearing dates ranging between 53 B.C. and A.D. 137. From the sites near Edsin-gol have been recovered wooden slips with dates between 100 B.C. and A.D. 100, as well as a fragment of silk inscribed with a date corresponding to 56 or 58 B.C. A lacquer bowl found at Noin-ula has a date corresponding to 2 B.C., after which time the tombs there must have been furnished. Lou-lan provides dated documents of the early second century A.D., and there is other evidence that this place was abandoned by the Chinese no later than the beginning of the fourth.[1] Niya has associated documents dating from the second half of the third century A.D. The Oglakty burial is dated by Tallgren between 100 B.C. and A.D. 100, and the tomb near Kertch assigned by Rostovtzeff to the first century A.D. In the Middle East, Halebie-Zenobia was built between A.D. 266 and 270, and Dura-Europos fell in A.D. 256. The two Palmyra tombs were built in A.D. 83 and 103, and Palmyra itself was sacked in A.D. 273. There is thus overwhelming chronological evidence for grouping these textiles together, and assigning the majority to the first two or three centuries of our era. At the same time, technical and stylistic features give the group a remarkable internal consistency, and it would now be proper to use similar textiles as *points de repère* for dating sites in which they may henceforward be found.

By the end of the second century B.C. silk was being manufactured on a very large scale in China. There then existed a Government office called *chün shu*, which aimed at price stabilization by holding large stocks of consumer goods in reserve. In the year 110 B.C., we are told, the *chün shu* held no less than five million rolls of silk, each worth a thousand copper cash; the population was then about sixty millions. And in 16 B.C., when the Emperor went on a tour of inspection of the northern frontiers, he bestowed on members of the garrisons there, among other gifts, a million rolls of silk. A hundred or so years later silk seems to have gone down in price. Among remains at the Tun-huang *limes*, Stein made the happy discovery of a plain silk strip evidently at one time attached to a silk roll, and bearing an inscribed trade-mark. The inscription, translated by Chavannes, runs: 'A roll of silk from K'ang-fu in the Jen-ch'êng kingdom;[2] width 2 feet 2 inches; length 40 feet; weight 25 ounces; value 618 pieces of money.'

1. Lou-lan was plundered by nomads early in the fourth century A.D., and in A.D. 330 the Tarim River took a southerly course away from the outpost, leaving it waterless.

2. Jen-ch'êng was a kingdom established in A.D. 85, in part of what is to-day Shantung province.

Two wooden rules also found by Stein at Tun-huang show that the Chinese foot was then about 22.9 cm. On this basis, the width of the roll would have been 50.4 cm. The actual width, as can be told from another silk strip found together with the first and representing the full width of the piece, was 50 cm. The length would have been about 30 feet. The width of a third strip was just under 50 cm. These dimensions seem to have been more or less standard. Four plain silks found by Bergman at Lou-lan and one at Edsin-gol range from 40 to 47 cm. in width; one from Palmyra measures 53 cm.[1] As for length, another plain undyed strip, from Lou-lan, bears characters translated by Konow as: 'Sinduācārya's roll, forty (feet long)'. From a small bale of yellowish plain silk found by Stein at Lou-lan, it appears that Han silks were packed five in a bale, each being folded into two so that the bale appeared to contain ten rolls; their width was 47·6 cm.

Han Dyes and Mordants

Han silks show a fairly complete colour-range, including a bright and solid crimson, brown, yellow-brown and beige, bronze-yellow and olive-green, a brilliant green, bright blue, dark blue and violet, white and black. In the present condition of the silks, reddish-brown is the dominating shade; but this must often bear witness to some lost colour which has changed character as the result of contact with chemical reagents in the soil. Russian analysts, using both the spectroscope and ultra-violet light, have been able to plot some of the original colours of these fugitive dyes, including the brilliant green mentioned above. A dull white often masks the presence of indigo blue which has been oxidized by such common reagents in the soil as nitric acid. It can be restored by reduction with hydrosulphide.[2]

Most, if not all, of the Han dyes were extracted from plants.[3] And they were *adjective* dyes, in that they required mordants to bring out their colours and render them insoluble; as opposed to *substantive*

1. The average width of Han polychromes and damasks (pp. 243–53) was probably somewhat less, ranging from 35 to 45 cm.

2. A. A. Voskresensky and N. P. Tikhonov (Eugenia Tolmachoff transl.), 'Technical study of textiles from the burial mounds of Noin-ula', in *B.N.B.C.*, vol. xx, nos. 1 and 2 (1936), pp. 3–73.

3. Pfister mentions a red that may have been extracted from the Cochineal Insect (*Cartheria lacca*) of Indo-China.

dyes, which are applied direct and need no mordant. But the only dyes whose presence in Han silks has been definitely established are those produced from alizarine from the madder plant (*Rubia cordifolia*), which seems to have been used from time immemorial as a colouring agent in China, and indigo from *Polygonum tinctorium*, the indigo plant of north China.

We do not, of course, know the exact state of Han dyeing science. But effects of oxidation and reduction were familiar to Han glaze chemists, and one imagines that dyers had access to the same knowledge. And since almost any soluble metal salt used as a mordant will give a colour of some sort when brought into contact with alizarine, it may well be that dyers relied largely on madder as a dyeing material, and experimented more intensively with mordants to produce the various shades. The Russian analysts found abundant traces of iron in brown areas of their samples. This, in its reduced state, would give green in combination with alizarine; while if oxidized it would yield a range of browns. The Russians also found alum used as a mordant with madder. This combination was the one commonly used to give a range of bright and very stable reds. A blue could be got from alizarine by mordanting with copper, although, as far as I know, this metal salt has not yet been identified in tested samples.

Chinese silks seem to have been mordanted *after* dyeing, not before or during the process. French Jesuits in the eighteenth century were told that the Chinese anciently steeped already-dyed silk and cotton in cold concentrated solutions of the mordant for seven days at a time,[1] after which the latter was fixed by exposure to the sun or, more commonly, to steam heat. Their informants stressed the greater difficulty encountered in dyeing the vegetable fibre; and it is interesting to note, with Pfister, that steam heating is especially effective in fixing the mordants used in cotton dyeing, and that the ancient Chinese practice was taken up by French and English cotton dyers as late as the beginning of the nineteenth century, since when it has replaced the traditional Indian method of fixing with tannin.

1. 'The brilliancy and fastness of Eastern dyes', says Ethel Mairet in *A Book on Vegetable Dyes*, London 1917, p. 26, 'are probably due to a great extent to the length of time taken over the various processes of dyeing.'

De-gumming

We have already seen that at some stage in silk manufacture the material must be de-gummed (p. 218). That is, the sericin must be removed by steeping in almost boiling water, perhaps containing a little soap. By so doing, silk is made supple and lustrous. De-gumming, or boiling off, is best left until after the cloth has been woven, all else being equal, since sericin acts as a protective agent through the various stages of manufacture. On the other hand, silk that has not been de-gummed cannot satisfactorily be dyed, since sericin is highly absorbent of dyes, and its removal from the dyed thread would lead to much loss or patchiness of colour in the final article. Undyed silks can of course be de-gummed after weaving, and then either dyed or left self-coloured; but in the case of polychrome silks, where threads of several different colours were used as warps, de-gumming had to precede dyeing and weaving. It would be interesting to know how Han weavers compensated for loss of strength and elasticity in these differently-coloured de-gummed warp-threads. The Noin-ula polychrome silks analysed by the Russians show no trace of twist in the thread, by means of which tensile strength and elasticity can be improved for warping purposes. The weft-threads, we must add, were invariably of one colour, since it was not they but the warps that built up the pattern.

Han Damasks

Han silks fall into a number of categories, including taffetas (plain and embroidered), reps (plain and embroidered), patterned reps, gauzes, and even crepes. We are concerned here with the two classes of patterned reps, one or other of which has been found at every site yielding Han silk, and both of which have attracted much attention from textile historians. These are the damasks and polychrome weaves. Both show analogous methods of weaving and pattern-making, but the damask pattern-system is perhaps easier to understand, and possibly earlier. We shall deal with it first.

A 'damask' may be defined as a single-coloured textile in which the pattern is made by causing certain threads each to pass over more than one thread in the opposite direction before reaching the binding point, so that these passages stand out from the surrounding weave on the front face of the material. We have already encountered such a pattern-making system in the Shang-Yin 'twill' (p. 235), and it is one perfectly familiar to us in our own table linen. The term 'Han damask' is appropriate to name Han monochrome silks with this type of weave, despite the ambiguity of using a word originally coined to name a Near Eastern textile.[1] Henceforward we shall refer to them simply as 'damasks'.

A very rudimentary Han damask, analogous to the Shang-Yin 'twill', was found by Stein at Lou-lan but has not hitherto been described; and the present writer owes it to the kindness of Mr Charleston, who has supplied him with a small fragment of the weave, that he is able to do so here (plate 20b). It is nothing more than an all-over pattern of squares, occurring regularly at places where warp-threads follow an over-three under-one course, instead of the normal over-one under-one. Adjoining warps behave in exactly the same way, except that 'the binding-points move in a step-like manner'; and since there are only four alternative courses that the warps can follow – warp 5 repeating warp 1, and so on – only four different sheds are required, and the fabric can be woven on four heddles. Each square is made up of eighty adjoining warps, all of which interlace with twenty-eight wefts through the pattern area. As with the Shang-Yin textile (figure 30), we should note that this is not a twill in the true sense of the word, since the over-three under-one formula is employed not as a system of binding, but rather as the basis for pattern-making.

The typical Han damask incorporates far more elaborate pattern-units than that of the chequer-board damask described above and is also rather different in structure. Figure 31 shows part of such a weave in diagrammatic form.[2] The point to notice is that, unlike the Shang-Yin 'twill' and the Han chequer-board damask, the pattern-warps here alternate with ordinary ground-weave warps (2, 4, 6, etc.) following an over-one under-one course. Every other shed can therefore be made – that is to say, half the fabric can be woven – by entering every other warp-thread through a single heddle which is

1. The term was, I believe, first used in connexion with Chinese textiles by R. Pfister in his pioneer monograph, *Textiles de Palmyre* (see footnote p. 210). It is to M. Pfister that students of Chinese art must be chiefly indebted for what they know of the structural details of Han patterned silks.

2. As with figure 34, white squares represent passages of weft over warp on the front face of the material; black squares or rectangles, passages of warp over weft.

operated in making every other weft throw. The remaining warps, the pattern-warps, are entered through a second heddle, but must also be connected independently to a drawloom attachment. Thus, in the diagram, warps 1, 5, etc. must be tied together in a drawcord bundle which must be pulled when making weft throws 2, 6, 10, etc., while simultaneously operating the heddle raising the ground-weave warps

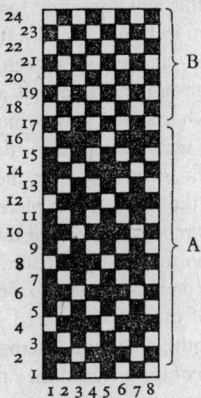

Figure 31.

Part of the front face of a Han silk damask, diagrammatic (warp runs up the page).

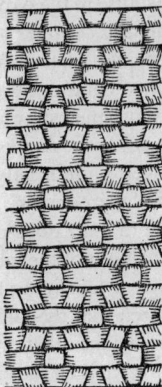

Figure 32.

Part of the reverse face of a Han silk damask inside a pattern-unit, semi-diagrammatic (warp runs up the page).

(2, 4, 6, etc.). Area A is the pattern area. From weft throw 17 onwards an ordinary ground-weave is woven through area B by means of the two ground-weave heddles.

Plate 20a shows the front face of an actual Han damask, magnified five times, in which this pattern-making system has been used; and figure 32 shows no less clearly the distinctive appearance of the reverse face of the fabric, where the ground-weave warps are pulled sideways at every fourth weft throw. The pattern, in fact, is intelligible only on the front face. Floating of the pattern-warps has carried the ground weave warps to the back of the material, creating what is virtually a double, or 'compound' fabric. No doubt the over-one under-one ground-weave was introduced to give structural solidity to the fabric in a way that pattern-warps alone, floated over three wefts, fail to do. But absence of perceptible pattern on the reverse face was probably felt to be a disadvantage which, as we shall see, was overcome in the polychromes by a somewhat different system of weaving.

Inspection of figure 31 will show that only four different sheds need be made in weaving this small section of fabric; the warp-threads could be entered through four heddles – a practical number – without having recourse to the drawloom. But this will not suffice for all-over pattern-units as complex as those shown in figure 33. This represents part of a typical Han damask from Lou-lan. It will be seen that the pattern, here comprising four complete units and part of a fifth, is bilaterally symmetrical about the mid-horizontal axis, which represents a line of weft. At this point in the weave the pattern turns over, being woven with exactly the same sheds, but made in the reverse order. The horizontal axis being along the width of the piece, we are to suppose that the double pattern was repeated over and over again down the length of the fabric; that is, in the warp direction.

The present remaining width of this damask is about 15 cm. And we have seen that the known width of other Han figured silks was somewhat less than that of the plain cloths, or about 45 cm. Assuming that to have been the original width of this piece, it may therefore have been made up of some twelve pattern-units. The fabric in its present state contains not quite a thousand warp-threads, giving sixty-six threads per cm. – a figure that agrees well with the observed average of about seventy threads per cm. for Han silks (p. 235). In the estimated width there would be somewhat under 3,000. Now in setting up the warp for weaving, half the number of threads can be entered through ground-heddle 1, since every other warp-thread behaves in exactly the same way. But of the remaining warps, each takes a different course.[1]

Figure 34 shows part of the courses of the ten pattern-warps that build up the backward hind leg of the 'dragon' and part of the lozenge border an inch or so from the left-hand edge of figure 33; between the pattern-warps lie the ground-warps. The first pattern-warp is floated over wefts 6, 32, and 36; the second over wefts 4, 8,

1. That is, assuming the pattern does not turn over on the warp axis. (We have already seen that it does so on the axis of the weft.) If in fact this pattern were to repeat about, say, the mid-vertical axis, then the number of different warp courses would be reduced by half.

Figure 33. Reconstruction of pattern-units on part of a Han silk damask from Lou-lan, drawn by R. J. Charleston. Lighter areas were reconstructed on the basis of the surviving pattern (darker areas).

247

30, and 34; the third over wefts 2, 6, 10, 28, and 32. Each behaves in a different way. Hence it follows that every other weft throw has to pass through an entirely different shed, as can be verified by referring once again to figure 34. In making the shed for weft 2, for instance, quite a different combination of warp-threads must be raised from

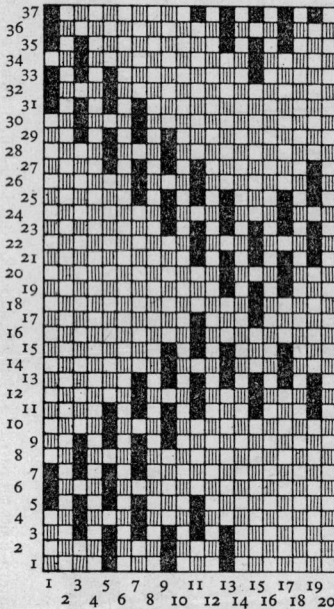

Figure 34. Weaving diagram of the backward hind leg of the dragon of figure 33 (warp runs up the page, and warp-floats are indicated in black).

that required for weft 4. In fact, for weaving this pattern, the number of different combinations of warp-threads will be half the number of weft throws, plus one for the ground weave represented by wefts 1, 3, 5, etc. In the fragment shown there are thirty-seven weft throws, of which eighteen (the even-numbered throws) require special sheds. The total number of sheds to be formed is therefore nineteen.

But, in fact, from the bottom of the design shown in figure 33 to the 'turn-over', there are eighty wefts. To weave this pattern, forty-one different sheds are therefore needed, of which one is opened by means of ground-heddle 1 – raising warps 1, 3, 5, 7, etc. – while the remaining forty all require drawcord bundles, in addition to ground-heddle 2, lifting warps 2, 4, 6, 8, etc. In the full width of the fabric there were probably some 1,500 pattern-warps (p. 246), each entering into at least one combination, and usually many. So in setting up the warp for weaving, the operator would have to determine in the case of each pattern-warp the number of combinations it had to enter, and for each combination ensure that it was correctly tied up with all the other threads, out of a possible 1,500, which entered that combination. Having done so he – or more probably his drawboy, sitting at another part of the loom – had to pull the forty different bundles in correct sequence at the precise moment when heddle 2 was being operated. On reaching the turn-over, the forty bundles had to be pulled in correct reverse sequence.

The scale and complexity of woven patterns of the type we have just discussed point unmistakably to use of a drawloom. Quite apart from the physical impossibility of picking a shed by hand through 3,000 different warps so closely set together, we have visible proof that these weaves were made mechanically. For when a mistake occurs, such as passage of a pattern-warp over one weft, over another, and under a third – instead of over all three – it is invariably repeated at corresponding points in the design throughout the weave. Such a mistake would be made if a warp were left out of a bundle into which it should have entered; it would be far too small to be noticed, and even if it were, almost impossible to rectify. But a mechanical arrangement of forty-one treadle-operated heddles, needed to weave the fabric in question, would be even more absurd than would the fourteen required to weave the Shang-Yin 'twill'. Once again we are forced back to some sort of drawloom.

It is not, of course, possible to say what was the actual arrangement of the drawcords. But lest the reader think that the complexity of such a system would put production of patterned silks on a commercial scale out of the question, we should perhaps view it once again in its whole context. Setting up a warp for pattern-weaving is, of course, an almost superhuman business. But, once having been done, the great length of fabric that could be woven, using silk as a warp, would quickly compensate for initial outlay. And, once the warp was set up, weaving of these superb silks would follow automatically, and would continue so for the whole piece. It may well have been the case that setting up a particular design was put in the hands of the same operative time and again; and that the weaver stuck to weaving it year after year, until pulling the drawcord bundles in proper sequence became second nature to him.

Han Polychrome Silks

Figure 35 shows part of the weave of a polychrome silk. In these, as we have said, the design can be read just as easily on the reverse as

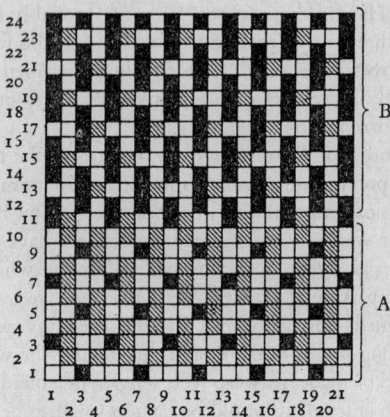

Figure 35. Part of the front face of a Han polychrome silk, diagrammatic (warp runs up the page).

on the front face. Every warp thread, in fact, is a pattern-thread, and the pre-selected design is set up with alternating warps of two different colours. In our example, area A appears as a red patch, area B as blue. In area A, red warps pass over three wefts, under the next, over the next three, etc., on the front face of the material. Meanwhile blue warps on either side of them are passing *under* three wefts, over one, under three, etc., so that the reverse face in area A appears blue. Between areas A and B the colour scheme changes. The red warp now goes to the back face; and in making this change it passes either *over two* wefts (in the cases of warps 2, 6, 10, etc.) or *under two* (in the cases of warps 4, 8, 12, etc.). From wefts 11 and 13 onwards, the red warp

250

appears only on the front face of the material at every fourth weft, and it is the back face that now appears red. On the other hand, the blue warps are now taken to the front face of the material, either by passing *over two* wefts (warps 1, 5, 9, etc.), or *under two* (warps 3, 7, 11, etc.); if the former, the warp continues under-one, over-three, under-one, etc., and if the latter, it continues over-three, under-one, over-three, etc. The front face appears blue.

From our figure it will be seen that successive warps in this weave follow four different courses. Warp 5 follows the same course as warp 1, warp 6 the same as warp 2, and so on. In figure 36 we have plotted the courses taken by these four successive warps through the weave, seen in side-view or longitudinal section.[1] It will be seen that warp 1 runs mainly on the reverse face as far as weft 9, where it

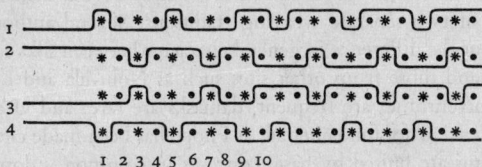

Figure 36. Courses of four successive warps in a Han polychrome silk (warps run across the page, wefts appear in cross-section).

comes to the front face. Warp 3, which is of the same colour, also lies mainly on the underside until weft 10, when it comes to the upper surface. These two warps, and all warps of the same colour, form a layer on the reverse face of the material in area A, while warps 2, 4, and their kindred form a layer on the front face. The cloth is therefore of the same double or 'compound' type as the damask. From figure 36 it will also be seen that binding takes place only around the wefts marked *, and never around those marked ●. In fact, if the four warps are imagined superimposed, it will be quickly seen that wefts marked ● *never* appear on either front or reverse faces of the cloth. They are completely enclosed by warp. In an analysis of a typical Han polychrome weave, Eleanor Sachs refers to this weft as a 'secondary weft' which, she says, 'is not interwoven with the warps,

1. Figure 35 only shows a fragment of the pattern-unit, of course. For purposes of weaving an all-over pattern of the sort shown in plates 22–4 each warp-thread would have to participate in drawcord bundles.

but lies between'.[1] She adds that its function was to reinforce the fabric and lengthen the warp-floats. This seems an unnecessary interpretation, since it suggests that the 'secondary weft' was introduced to serve these special purposes, whereas its role is already forecast in the oldest patterned silk we know, the Shang-Yin 'twill'. If we regard this early weave as a starting-point, then the damask may be said to represent an improvement on it, since a ground warp is incorporated for strengthening purposes. The polychrome patterned silk may well be regarded as a development from the damask, since the main drawback of the damask was that its pattern appeared on only one face. If this was the evolution, then the function of the 'secondary weft' in the polychromes is pre-determined by its earlier history in the other weaves.

Between damasks and polychromes we may have evidence of the existence of two separate weaving traditions. Several authors have pointed out the difference in general character between silks found at Palmyra, and those from other sites such as Noin-ula and Lou-lan. Where polychromes are frequent, damasks are rare; and vice versa. The difference is not fundamental, as I hope has been made clear. The two systems are united by basic concepts in common – dominance of warp over weft, pattern made by warp- not weft-threads, warp passing over three wefts and under one in the pattern areas – and the textiles are stylistically closely related. But the two weaves may be products of somewhat different generations, or of different parts of China.

We have already given one reason why the polychromes may perhaps be regarded as more highly evolved than the damasks. Of special interest in this connexion is the modification in the polychromes whereby, in leading the warps to and from the front face of the material, they are made to pass over, or under, only two wefts. This allows for a more gradual transition from one part of the design to the next than is possible in the case of the damasks. The result, as can be seen by comparing plates 21 and 22, is that the damask designs are 'squared off' and do not allow for much elaboration of detail; whereas the polychromes display much smoother edges to the patterns, and so favour the use of curvilinear design such as cloud scrolls. The division between damasks and polychromes therefore extends to the general character of the design. The polychrome pattern-system

1. Eleanor B. Sachs, 'Notes on the weaves of a group of silk fabrics from the burial mounds of Noin-Ula', in *B.N.B.C.*, vol. xx, nos. 1 and 2 (1936), p. 76.

is in fact more skilfully adapted for pattern weaving of all types of subject than is that of the damasks. So, perhaps, it is later. And this conclusion is also reached by Dr Sylwan, who points out that 'at least some of the patterns in these damask silks have their roots in an ornamental art older than Han'; she suggests that the damasks were no longer fashionable in metropolitan China in late Han times, but were very much to the taste of the Hellenistic countries of the Middle East, precisely on account of their more severe style.

The Décor of Han Lacquer and Silk

Han decorative design, as featured in lacquer and silk, displays astonishing imaginative resource and a catholicity of subject-matter unparalleled elsewhere in Chinese applied art. The range of motives is almost inexhaustible. Designers drew not only on those handed down by devious paths to Third Phase bronze art (p. 170), but also invented a whole set of new motives, and borrowed and adapted everything that came their way from abroad. Yet, in spite of the variety of its sources, Han decorative design has great integrity. Naturalistic birds and animals consort with stylized versions of similar beings; foreign motives are boldly planted in a purely Chinese *mise en scène*; rectilinear devices jostle alongside freely-executed forms with rounded contours, such as so-called 'cloud scrolls' and spirals; but through it all runs a common spirit, a verve that speaks of thorough assimilation, and a curious grasp of what can perhaps best be described as the inner life of its subjects.

This art would make a rewarding study for the art historian. But no one so far has attempted systematically to trace its multitudinous origins, or to explain the significance of its motives. Some are obviously decorative only. Others, equally clearly, are not. Both fantasy and menace are present, echoes of a rich mythology that only occasionally shows itself. Fleetingly we come on familiar ground, to the world of Taoist fancy found in *Lieh tzǔ* and *Huai nan tzǔ*;[1] then the mist descends, as it was wont to do over the elusive Taoist Isles of the

---

1. *Lieh tzǔ* is a compilation of literary fragments dating from the fifth to first centuries B.C., put together in final form at the end of the fifth century A.D. *Huai nan tzǔ*, attributed to the Prince of Huai-nan, Liu An, dates from about 120 B.C.

Blest in the Eastern Sea, and we are groping in a region of hostile pre-
sences, of beings that seem to belong to a more primitive, less codified
set of ideas. And if the reader should think this far-fetched, let him
turn to plate 17b, showing the inside of a lacquer *pei* from the Ch'ang-
sha find. This design seems to me dream-ridden. Would it be rash to
claim a kinship between it and the work, say, of Paul Klee – one that
involves not only style and presentation, but also its underlying
psychological purport? Do not the two rectangular cartouches with
their vacant but strangely compelling features – which must be meant,
I think, for masks – perhaps convey a hint of what that purport may
have been? The popular beliefs of the Ch'u tribes who lived in the
Ch'ang-sha region are preserved in poems belonging to the anthology
called *Ch'u tzŭ*, that had a profound influence on the forms of Han
poetry. Here is evidence of a cult of the dead, of spirit-journeys and
shaman go-betweens; of a pattern of thought quite distinct, as Waley
says, from that of magical Taoism.[1] Beyond doubt, exotic ideas and
beliefs not only from Ch'u but also from the northern steppe-belt and
elsewhere, helped to fashion the distinctive *Zeitgeist* of Han times, and
permeated its art.

To qualify himself for the task of elucidating Han art, a scholar
would have to be able to estimate the nature and strength of such outside cultural influences, and of their impact on the received native folk-
lore as recorded in Han and pre-Han texts, until he had reached the
point of being able to predict what elements in Han popular belief
might, because of their compulsive appeal, find their way into decorative design. Bushell, Chavannes, and Laufer, among others, made
successful attempts to do this in the case of episodes depicted on Han
bas-reliefs (p. 294). Some still resist identification; but the meaning of
others is quite clear, and this is because they illustrate more or less
familiar legends or historical events. Subjects favoured for portrayal
on objects primarily of utility, such as lacquerware, silk, pottery, and
mirrors, on the other hand, are not usually descriptive in this sense,
and it is less easy to say what meaning should be read into them. In
these circumstances we can do little more than indicate the general
character of Han decorative design and trace the continuity in time,
and from one material to another, of a few specially popular motives.
Our starting-point will be a stylistic analysis of Han and pre-Han

1. A. Waley, *Three Ways of Thought in Ancient China*, London 1939,
p. 77.

bronze mirrors made by Karlgren in his monograph, 'Huai and Han'.[1] We shall see how his findings can be applied to the décor of Han lacquer and silk.

Third Phase bronze art, as we have seen, is a hybrid that draws its vitality from the fusion of several distinct lineages. Most ancient and aristocratic is the First Phase art of Shang-Yin and early Chou times, which may have reached the Third Phase partly by direct descent and partly after modification due to intervention of the Second Phase. Nomad art is another ancestor whose features are discernible in the Third Phase, and a third influence undoubtedly entered it from the south. The question is, was Han art simply a continuation of what had gone before, or did it differ essentially in spirit, as did that of the Second Phase from that of the First? And if so, had this new spirit any connexion with the social and political upheavals of the third century B.C.? Was there a sudden break?

Karlgren answers these questions with a decisive 'yes'; he finds that there was indeed a radical difference between Third Phase and Han styles, the boldest expression of which is perhaps seen in the treatment of bronze *ting*, in which the all-over pattern is rejected in favour of an unornamented surface, and whose appeal resides in intrinsic form alone. The suddenness of the stylistic revolution, Karlgren says, is shown by the disappearance of certain categories of mirrors at the beginning of Han times; in particular, of a great group from the Shou Hsien region (category C), and of another from Lo-yang (category D). We had better quote his actual words. Of the mirrors he says that they 'confirm what the Ting tripods and big bells have already suggested: that the date *ca.* 200 B.C. is a real milestone, separating the Huai [*i.e.*, Third Phase] style from the Han style'. And when, after the death of feudal China and the rise and fall of Ch'in, 'China rose again to new power and health ... the Huai [*i.e.*, Third Phase] style that flourished between *ca.* 650 and *ca.* 200 was quite dead, and the Han art, though building on the foundations of the earlier epochs, had essentially acquired an entirely new style'.[2]

As a result of Karlgren's work, dating of mirrors belonging to the well-defined style-categories C and D need no longer be a matter of personal judgement based on style alone. Mirrors in these classes are never inscribed; the style of script of the many mirrors that do carry

1. B. Karlgren (see footnote p. 171).
2. See B. Karlgren (see footnote p. 171), pp. 115–16.

inscriptions is unquestionably Han, and it is thus a fair deduction that the uninscribed mirrors comprising categories C and D are pre-Han. Karlgren further claims that certain motives displayed by these mirrors – the 'comma' pattern, the line of granulations acting as filling for a band, and interlocked T's – fail to survive into the Han period whether as a complex or individually, and so can be used as criteria establishing the pre-Han date of objects on which they appear.

Now, a demonstration in which C and D mirrors were set beside the Han mirrors of Karlgren's categories F–L would immediately convince us of a fundamental difference between Third Phase and Han styles. But it would not be representative. Another category of mirrors, E, is dated by Karlgren to the period of 150 years before the beginning of the Han dynasty; yet these mirrors show close resemblances to the Han group F, while their differences could easily be explained as the result of a century and a half of slow stylistic change.

Moreover, are the above mentioned three style criteria valid also for art-forms other than mirrors? Karlgren believes that they are. My own impression is that other media reveal a more gradual stylistic transition from the Third Phase than do C and D bronze mirrors, and that presence of two, at least, of these three criteria does not necessarily preclude a Han dating in such cases. The 'comma', for instance, appears sporadically – not as an all-over pattern, it is true – on the lacquer cosmetic box of plate 19b, a piece that in other respects unmistakably proclaims itself Han.[1] And it might be held that the 'grain' pattern of Han jade and glass *pi* (plate 5b) is a natural descendant of the Third Phase 'comma' pattern.[2] As for the line of granulations filling a band, it surely reappears as a border ornament to the lozenge band on the lacquered table-top of plate 18a. This piece is beyond doubt Han. It almost certainly comes from the Lo-lang excavations, and probably dates from as late as the first century A.D.

In my opinion, then, facts do not warrant belief in a universal cataclysm of style at the beginning of the Han period. We have only to reflect that Ch'u, for example, was not finally absorbed into the Han

1. In respect, for example, of the 'Han curl border' on the 'cloud scrolls', adduced by Karlgren as a Han style criterion (p. 264).

2. A similar view is put forward by O. Karlbeck in 'Early Yüeh ware', in *O.A.*, vol. ii, no. 1 (summer, 1949), p. 4, who identifies the 'grain' pattern with the simple spiral which, he says, is 'likely to be a modified and simplified form' of the Third Phase 'comma' pattern.

Empire until 122 B.C. to appreciate how slight may have been stylistic changes corresponding to political events during the second half of the third century B.C. And whether or no the three style criteria cited by Karlgren disappeared with the coming of the Han dynasty, it is certainly true that other elements among the accumulated decorative wealth of the Third Phase were retained. We shall go on to examine a few of these.

FORMAL DECORATIVE MOTIVES

Of abstract, geometrical, or non-representational motives in Han art, the lozenge and its derivative, the zigzag band, are perhaps most widespread. The lozenge was known to the West quite as early as the fifth century B.C., when it appears as a textile design reproduced on Greek vases. But this motive is bound to crop up sooner or later in decorative design; as Pfister points out, primitive pottery with incised cross-hatching displays it in its simplest form, and there is no need to regard it as the special invention of any one part of the world. On the other hand, the Chinese seized on this element, and exploited it more thoroughly than did any other race of antiquity. It had, of course, been known in China at least as early as Shang-Yin times, but only towards the end of the Chou period did it begin to take on its characteristic diversity of form. Han designers used it in every

Figure 37. Simple and zigzag lozenges on Chinese silks: *a*, polychrome silk, Lou-lan; *b*, silk damask, Palmyra; *c*, polychrome silk, Noin-ula; *d*, polychrome silk, Kertch Peninsula; *e*, polychrome silk, Lou-lan; *f*, silk gauze, Noin-ula. (Not to scale.)

conceivable way. We illustrate a small series of variants taken from Han silks of various provenance (figure 37); and plate 23a shows another selection grouped together on a Noin-ula polychrome silk. It is obvious that the lozenge is particularly well suited for reproduction as a textile motive.

Its chief modification is that called 'lozenge with faulted angles' or 'zigzag lozenge', variants of which can also be seen in figure 37 as well as in plate 23a. This form may be claimed as distinctively Chinese. The question is, how did it originate? One obvious explanation is that it developed from three adjacent lozenges, linked or merged together (figure 38a). And from the zigzag lozenge a third element, the zigzag band, could easily be derived by placing such lozenges end to end (figure 38b), thus giving rise to an intermediate form represented in figure 38c, taken from one of several similar Shou Hsien mirrors dated to the third century B.C. by Karlgren;[1] subsequently, as Charleston supposes, the lozenges would be 'as it were, cut in two horizontally and the two halves separated by a small interval'[2] (figure 38d).

But Karlgren believes that the process worked in the opposite direction. He takes the all-over pattern called 'interlocked T's' as a starting-point (figure 39a) and finds a variant on a Third Phase *ting*, in which the horizontal top-stroke of one T – normally running straight into the vertical stem of another – is faulted to produce a zigzag effect (figure 39b). The half-lozenges thus created, if isolated from the rest of the pattern, would form a zigzag band like that of figure 39c; and Karlgren supposes that the complete zigzag lozenge was produced by bringing symmetrically confronted half-lozenges together. Karlgren provides examples of each stage from among his pre-Han mirrors, yet I find his explanation unconvincing. It does not take account of what is surely the logical starting-point for such a series, the simple lozenge, nor does it explain the popularity in Han times of the zigzag band, which on his theory is merely an intermediate stage leading to the fully-developed zigzag lozenge. He does not in fact so much as mention it. The zigzag band is, of course, not destined to reach full maturity on round objects such as mirrors, but comes into its own where a continuous linear border is needed, as in the damask of figure 38d. Once again we have to recognize a motive highly suited to the technical conditions of silk-weaving.

1. B. Karlgren (see footnote p. 171), examples C 80, a–e and C 81.
2. R. Charleston (see footnote p. 209), pp. 64–5.

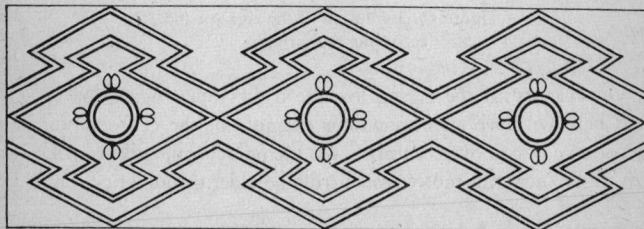

Figure 38. Possible evolution of the zigzag band: *a*, linked lozenges on a poly-chrome silk, Lo-lang; *b*, continuous zigzag lozenges on a silk damask, Palmyra; *c*, zigzag bands on a pre-Han mirror-back; *d*, zigzag bands on a silk damask, Palmyra. (Not to scale.)

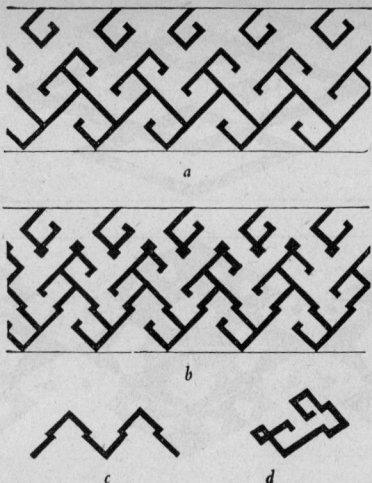

Figure 39. Evolution of the zigzag band
according to Karlgren.

One variety of the zigzag lozenge is the 'open zigzag lozenge';
and here we have an outstanding example of the conservation of
decorative design over centuries. On the polychrome silk from Lou-
lan (figure 40b) this motive can hardly be older than the first century

Figure 40. The open zigzag lozenge: a, on a Han
mirror-back; b, on a polychrome silk, Lou-lan.

A.D. Yet it is to all intents and purposes the same form as appears on a large number of Shou Hsien mirrors belonging to the third century B.C., part of one of which is shown in figure 40*a*. The resemblance is not limited to the lozenge: it extends to the curvilinear form with which it is merged, the 'cloud scroll' which we shall discuss presently. Figure 39*c* shows how ingeniously Karlgren has extracted the open zigzag lozenge from the all-over pattern of figure 39*b*.

The inlaid quatrefoil of the lacquer cosmetic box (plate 19*b*) has already been mentioned, as have later imitations in lacquer-painting from Lo-lang (p. 204). It, too, is a favourite Han motive, and goes to show the Chinese origin of the important damask found at Palmyra (figure 38*b*). But it is a constant feature of pre-Han C and D mirrors, on which it makes its first appearance, according to Karlgren, in the fourth century B.C. The leaf is identified by Pfister as that of *Trapa natans*, the water chestnut. Somewhat similar is a device called by Karlgren 'petal on a long stalk'. On pre-Han mirrors this has a heart-shaped blade indistinguishable from a single leaf of a quatrefoil, but on those of early Han times it sometimes bears three spines on its outer border, and then does not differ greatly from the type found on the Lou-lan silk of figure 40*b*.

Last among Han formal decorative motives is the so-called 'cloud scroll' (plates 19*b*, 22*b*). In broadest definition, this is a convoluted and curvilinear ribbon which encloses other more representational elements within its loops, thus binding them into an integrated design. Curves are deep, with strongly-marked changes of direction. Moreover, at various points along the curves, and especially at their apexes and where they change direction, excrescences of one sort or another are almost always to be found. In these lies a clue to the probable origin of all Han cloud scrolls. For the excrescences are vestiges of living tissue, and the cloud scrolls themselves are highly stylized and attenuated remnants of actual animals. In this sense the cloud scroll is not strictly 'formal' at all. We use the word only to stress its prevailingly decorative function in Han times.

Plates 17*a*, 19*b*, 22*b* and 23*b* show the cloud scroll, in a number of guises, upon objects made at intervals over perhaps four centuries between the third century B.C. and the first century A.D. Plate 17*b* shows a more angular version of what appears to be the same motive. The two Ch'ang-sha lacquers (plate 17) are undoubtedly the oldest in this series; and it will be noticed that upon them the motive is discontinuous and disposed with formal radial or bilateral symmetry, whereas on the lacquer box of plate 19*b* and on the polychrome silks it is a continuous linear band, tying other elements together but not disposed symmetrically in relation to a centre or single axis. In these later examples, designers have evidently freed themselves from the restrictions imposed when designing for a frame of fixed shape. Such a

Figure 41. Evolution of the cloud scroll: bird-dragon on an inlaid bronze ring in the Woods Bliss Collection.

frame is provided by the circular bronze mirror, and it is to pre-Han mirrors that we must turn to find immediate ancestors for the Ch'ang-sha scrolls.

Among pre-Han D category mirrors are some bearing a composite animal form, which Karlgren calls 'bird-dragon', disposed symmetrically in groups of four surrounding the central boss. It is, as Karlgren says, 'a curious creature, differing from an ordinary bird in having an embellishment on the head ... and often in having a dragon-like elongated body'.[1] A similar hybrid occurs twice on a flat bronze ring inlaid with gold and silver, in the Woods Bliss Collection (figure 41); and

1. B. Karlgren (see footnote p. 171), p. 78, and examples D 23–6.

Low-Beer, in his paper on the décor of Han lacquer,[1] takes this variant as the starting-point for the Han cloud scroll. We must add that on several C category mirrors, on the Woods Bliss ring, and on a lacquer box from Ch'ang-sha discussed by Low-Beer in a later article,[2] this vaguely naturalistic creature is fused at one of its extremities to an even more conventionalized bird-form. We thus have a sort of bi-polar organism, terminating at each end in a bird or head and neck of

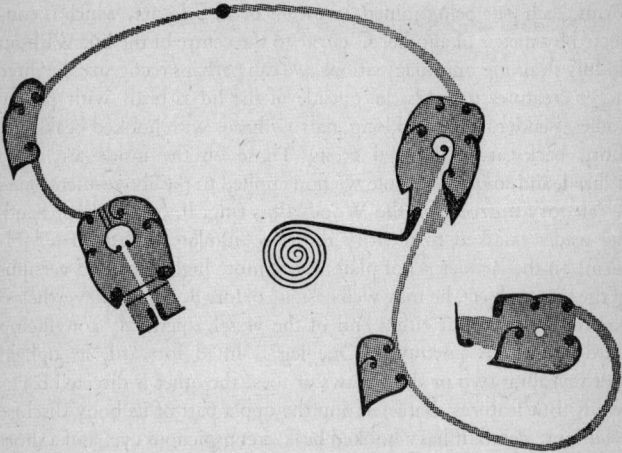

Figure 42. Evolution of the cloud scroll: part of the blue element on a lacquer box in the Low-Beer Collection. (Redrawn from Low-Beer.)

a bird. Even here the motive is not finally elaborated. On the above-mentioned lacquer box it appears four times: twice in dark blue lacquer, twice in vermilion. Each member of the blue pair consists of a long, straggling S-figure which proliferates at intervals along its curve no less than five cartouches (figure 42), of which the three main ones lie one at each end and one in the middle of the S-curve. The

1. F. Low-Beer, 'Zum Dekor der Han-Lacke', in *W.B.K.K.A.*, vol. xi (1937), pp. 65–73. Low-Beer here follows Rostovtzeff in assigning the Woods Bliss ring to the Han period. I consider that its resemblance to the C category mirrors mentioned above is close enough to place it, like them, in the pre-Han period.

2. F. Low-Beer, 'Two lacquered boxes from Ch'angsha', in *A.A.*, vol. x (1947), pp. 302–11.

two lesser ones are unrecognizable as parts of birds. Yet in fact they must be. We have in them obvious fore-runners of the little excrescences, called 'cloud-tips' by Low-Beer, which can be seen on the cloud scrolls of plate 19b. These, in turn, degenerate into the typical 'Han curl borders', seen so clearly in the Noin-ula polychrome silk of plate 22b as groups of three contiguous spirals proliferated off at various points on its long, meandering scrolls.

The lacquered lid of plate 17a shows three groups of two bird-forms, each pair being joined by means of an S-figure, which is connected by means of another C-curve to the centre of the lid. Without unduly straining our imaginations, we can perhaps recognize the three larger creatures towards the outside of the lid as birds with plump bodies, slender necks, and long, narrow heads with hooked beaks and short, backwardly directed crests. Those on the inside are more stylized, and so obey the rule we find applied to the above-mentioned C category mirrors and the Woods Bliss ring. If, on the other hand, the reader is asked to identify the two angular and attenuated H-forms on the lacquer *pei* of plate 17b as more highly stylized versions of the same subject, he may well hesitate before doing so. Nevertheless he will agree that at either end of the vessel a perfectly convincing 'bird-dragon' is portrayed. One leg is lifted forward, its upheld foot revealing two or three claws or toes; the other is directed backwards. But features characterizing the upper part of its body disclose even more detail. It has a hooked beak, a conspicuous eye, and a short backwardly directed crest, which continues as a fine, tightly-rolled spiral facing forwards.

With these features in mind, the two elements that lie in 'head to head' opposition almost in the centre of the dish may now be re-examined. We immediately see a bird head on a long neck, with hooked beak, prominent eye, and backwardly directed crest terminating in a forward facing spiral some distance behind it. At the other end of the H-form the design degenerates completely into a meaningless pattern which, by analogy only, we take to be a second bird form. Between the two lies the impressive rectangular cartouche of which we have already spoken (p. 254). It is perhaps a matter of opinion whether this is yet a third bird form or no, seen in frontal view and with its crest displaced to one side, or whether it represents a mask in the general category of *t'ao-t'ieh*. If the latter, it should probably not be thought of as part of the scroll.

Dating early uninscribed lacquers is a difficult business, but the date of these Ch'ang-sha pieces nevertheless needs some discussion. We have already made stylistic comparisons between their subject-matter and those of mirrors in Karlgren's C and D categories, specimens of which he dates to the third century B.C. They have this further feature in common – and in common, too, with the Woods Bliss ring – that the 'bird-dragon' is the principal subject of decoration. And when, as in the lacquers, 'bird-dragons' are joined together to compose a continuous scroll, this continues to dominate the composition. There is no question of its having merely an articulating function; one's eye is caught and held by the scroll itself. In the next phase of its evolution the scroll is no longer paramount. It begins to serve rather as an integrating band uniting other, representational, motives. The document cited by Low-Beer as typical of this stage is an inlaid bronze tube formerly in the Hosokawa Collection, undated save to the Han period. But closely comparable to it is a series of F mirrors which Karlgren dates to the second century B.C.[1] In all these bronzes, the cloud scroll forms a continuous band having the appearance of a mountain chain, a landscape peopled with fantastic trees, animals, and humans.

If the cloud scroll had acquired this secondary and subordinate role by the second century B.C., should we not be justified in assigning its primary phase at least to the hundred years preceding it? In that case the two Ch'ang-sha lacquers of plate 17, as well as the Woods Bliss ring, would be given dates in the third century B.C.

Here we propose to leave the 'bird-dragon', noting only that many of its bodily features are perpetuated in later and more naturalistic portrayals of birds called *fêng huang* (Phoenix) or *chu niao* (Scarlet Bird). Out of its *disjecta membra* designers built the typical formalized Han cloud scroll, such as we see on plate 19*b*. This version calls for no particular comment. Its bird ancestry is betrayed only by its 'cloud-tips' and the beginnings of 'Han curl borders'; its function is to support and link together into a co-ordinated design the fantastic animals that stand between its spirals.

The later history of the Han cloud scroll records two lines of evolution; one is easily described. Lo-lang lacquerware of the first century A.D. shows the motive in a state of partial or complete dissolution. Scrolls disintegrate and disappear, while 'cloud-tips' are progressively

1. B. Karlgren (see footnote p. 171), examples F 8 (a–c), F. 17.

elaborated until they form a virtually independent decorative device having the appearance of flames. Decomposition finally attacks the animals; in the last stage of decay they can be told apart from 'cloud-tips', spirals, and remains of scrolls only by the fact that they are painted yellow, while the shattered scroll and its derivatives are painted red.

To understand the second line of evolution we must return to the second-century B.C. mirrors mentioned above, and to the Hoso-kawa tube, which may date from the same period. We said that the cloud scroll on these formed a continuous mountain landscape peopled with fantastic beings. Perhaps the mountainous scenery of the Taoist Isles of the Blest is portrayed, and the beings are Taoist Immortals, *hsien jên*, and their weird familiars. Taoist the subject certainly is; but the setting may be China itself. Her Sacred Mountains, and especially Mount T'ai in Shantung (p. 367), were known to be resorts of Im-mortals no less than was the Paradise in the Eastern Sea, as inscriptions on these self-same mirrors testify. One, translated by Karlgren, runs: 'If you ascend the T'ai-shan, you will see the divine men; ... they yoke the Hornless Dragon to their chariot; they mount the floating clouds ...' Another goes: 'If you ascend the Hua-shan [in Shensi], you will see the immortals [*hsien jên*].' And a third: 'If you ascend the Hua-shan, the phoenixes will assemble [round you]; you will see the divine men; you may be preserved forever; may your longevity be of ten thousand years.'[1]

In a recent article Prudence Myer was able to show that a design embroidered on a silk shoe-sole found at Noin-ula is not, as was pre-viously thought, a stylized pair of animals, but is derived from a highly formalized and abstract mountain landscape. She concluded by saying: 'if this demonstration ... is accepted as valid, it may suggest a reinterpretation of certain other decorative motives; e.g. ... some of the so-called "cloud scrolls" in the woven textiles from Noin-ula and Lou-lan ...'[2] Thus encouraged, we can proceed to identify with con-fidence the meandering scrolls on the Noin-ula polychrome of plate 22*b* as representing a Taoist mountain landscape. Writing in 1926, Yetts had already recognized the winged horseman, who rides a

1. B. Karlgren, 'Early Chinese mirror inscriptions', in *B.M.F.E.A.*, no. 6 (1934), pp. 29–30.
2. P. R. Myer, 'A reinterpretation of the Noin-ula embroidered shoe-sole', in *A.A.*, vol. x (1947), pp. 108–20.

winged horse at 'flying gallop' on this textile, as a Taoist *hsien jên*.[1] In his hands he holds something, perhaps a gourd, from which issues a cloud of vapour.[2] Further left is another winged quadruped, which I am tempted to identify as that fabulous animal of good omen, the Heavenly Deer, *t'ien lu* (cf. plate 18*b*).[3]

Documents confirming the identification of this conventionalized mountain scenery, and its derivation from cloud scrolls, are plentiful. On the second-century B.C. mirrors and the Hosokawa tube, mountain peaks are quite obviously derived from 'cloud-tips' at the apexes of the scroll-curves, themselves descended from the lesser bird-forms of scrolls such as that shown in figure 42. Relief bands on the sides of Han 'hill-jars' – the conical tops of which are moulded into representations of the Taoist Paradise – confirm the descent even more emphatically. The most remarkable document bearing on our plate 22*b*, however, is an inlaid bronze tube in the Tōkyō School of Art Collection. In figure 43 the Taoist fauna has been dispersed in order to show more clearly how the mountains are disposed in two systems. Two scrolls meander across each other, in very much the same way as they do on the Noin-ula silk. Here is what I take to be final proof that the cloud scrolls of plate 22*b* are meant to represent a Taoist mountain landscape. But one tiny detail reveals their ancestry far away in the pre-Han 'bird-dragon'; it is, of course, the presence of the 'Han curl border'.

LIFE-FORMS

The words 'naturalistic' and 'representational' can be applied only in a limited sense to the repertory of life-forms in Han art; for most of the beasts, birds, and plants comprising it are highly stylized in

---

1. W. P. Yetts (see footnote p. 187), p. 181. As a matter of interest, the characters woven into this textile have been read by Professor Yetts as *hsin shên ling kuang ch'êng shou wan nien*, and translated by him as 'May this confer fresh spiritual vitality, so that longevity may be extended over a myriad years.'

2. In later Chinese art the Taoist Immortal Li T'ieh-kuai normally carries a gourd from which issues a cloud of vapour symbolic of his power to free the soul from the body.

3. For various Han and later references to the part played by portrayals of this animal in Chinese life, but not a description of it, cf. B. Karlgren (see footnote p. 266), pp. 50-1.

treatment, and at the same time belong to no single recognizable biological species. Individual traits drawn from several are combined in
the forms of Dragons, Phoenixes, Unicorns, and so on, while incon-
gruities such as wings on quadrupeds lift them altogether out of the
world of actuality into one of myth or fable. 'No one knows the
species of the Scarlet Bird', said the eleventh-century A.D. writer
Shên Kua, referring to a creature shortly to be discussed;[1] and no
further light has been shed on the matter since his day. For most subjects we have to be content merely to observe their family likenesses
to certain sorts of felines and other mammals, saurians and other reptiles, and birds.

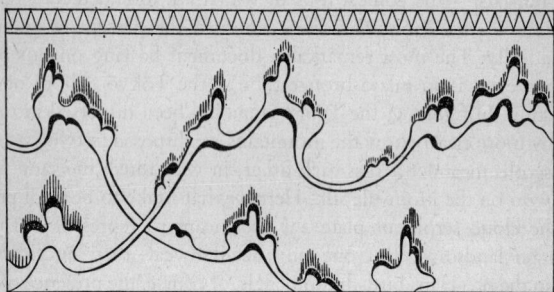

Figure 43. Evolution of the cloud scroll: cloud scroll in the form of
a mountain landscape on a Han inlaid bronze tube in the Tōkyō
School of Art Collection.

We face another difficulty in trying to determine just what the life-
forms portrayed in Han art meant to the Han Chinese. Unification of
China after the Ch'in conquest undoubtedly brought about some re-
adjustment of social and religious ideas among the people, just as it
changed the outlook of the intelligentsia. But the age-old religious
symbols – the zoomorphs of bronze art – survived essentially unchanged. Beliefs concerning them must have sunk deep in popular
imagination by the beginning of Han times, and probably needed a
good deal of dislodging. If they then acquired new cosmological
significance in the minds of philosophers, that is not to say they meant
anything different to ordinary people for centuries to come.

1. W. P. Yetts, 'Notes on Chinese roof-tiles', in *T.O.C.S.*, vol. vii (1927–8),
p. 35.

Again, the early history of cults and beliefs associated with these symbols has to be got largely from texts. It is quite clear that Han texts dealing with pre-Han folklore, religion, and ritual – and in some cases even with historical events – are by no means always impartial accounts compiled from extant historical sources, or even from hearsay, but are often products of doctrinaire minds seeking to stamp the past with thought-patterns of the present. Many alleged pre-Han texts are compilations of this sort. The dead weight of conjecture about pre-Han society and its beliefs would be greatly lightened, as Karlgren says,[1] if the fundamental distinction between 'free' and 'systematizing' texts in early Chinese literature were better preserved; meagre as the remnants might prove to be, they would at least give a less distorted picture than the one now generally current in the West. Thus, while archaeology allows us to trace a gradual evolution in the manner of portraying animal images through the Three Phases of bronze art and into the Han, no corresponding historical material is yet available to show the shift in religious ideas associated with them.

Within a short space one cannot possibly hope to present *all* the life-forms that appear in Han art. Those we propose to discuss are the ones appearing on lacquers and silks here illustrated. Outstanding among them are animals belonging to the two groups of four called Ssŭ Shên and Ssŭ Ling, involving five animals of which three appear on the silk of figure 33. In his article on Han damasks[2] Charleston was able to show that the motives remaining on this silk are entirely native to China, and that plausible claims for Western origins of some do not in the least disprove its Chinese provenance. Here we will take their Chinese ancestry for granted, and will proceed to describe their main characteristics, both as individuals and as groups.

THE SSŬ SHÊN

That human social order corresponds to a universal cosmic order seems to have been a belief innate in the Chinese over most of their history. So the first-century A.D. cynic Wang Ch'ung says: 'The destiny of the State is connected with the stars. Just as their constellations (*hsü*) are propitious or unpropitious, the State is happy or unhappy. As the stars revolve and wander, men rise and fall.'[3]

1. B. Karlgren, 'Legends and cults in early China', in *B.M.F.E.A.*, no. 18 (1946), pp. 199-365.   2. R. Charleston (see footnote p. 209).
3. W. P. Yetts, *The Cull Chinese Bronzes*, London 1939, p. 134.

Scarcely a class of observed phenomena failed to find its place in the system of fancied correspondences that grew up in Han times. North, East, South, and West, the Four Quadrants into which the vault of Heaven was divided, surrounded the circumpolar Central Palace of the supreme ruler T'ai-i,[1] just as upon Earth the Four Directions of terrestrial space (*t'ien hsia*, 'Under Heaven') surrounded the palace of the Emperor. They corresponded also with the Four Seasons – Winter, Spring, Summer, and Autumn respectively;[2] and the Four Cardinal Points corresponded with the seasonal solstices and equinoxes. Presiding over them were the above-mentioned Ssŭ Shên or Four Supernatural Beings, Tortoise, Dragon, Phoenix, and Tiger respectively; and these in turn symbolized the four classes into which animals were divided in Han times – shell-covered, scaly, feathered, and hairy creatures – and were brought into association with the Four Elements, Water, Wood, Fire, and Metal,[3] and the Four Colours, Black, Green, Red, and White.

If this cosmogony was arbitrary, the causal theory of two antithetical but complementary forces working it is a rudimentary scientific hypothesis analogous to modern theories of wave-motion. Indeed, their interaction can best be explained by means of a graph (figure 44). Associated with the name of the fourth-century B.C. scholar Tsou Yen, the dualistic concept of *yin* and *yang* explains all celestial and terrestrial revolutions as alternating phases of ascendancy and declension of these two forces. Under the *yin* character entry, *Shuo wên* has: 'south of a river, north of a hill', and the *Ku liang* commentary on *Ch'un ch'iu* says that *yang* means the north bank of a river, the south side of a hill. Yetts, from whom I gather this information, points out that in China the river-systems run mainly from west to east.[4] The south bank of a river running between high cliffs, and the north side of a hill, get very little sunshine. Shade is the essence of *yin*;

1. T'ai-i is regarded as the Han equivalent of the Shang-Yin Shang Ti (cf. p. 664).
2. So the fourth-century B.C. *Kuan tzŭ* says: 'The seasons appertaining respectively to the East, South, West, and North, are Spring, Summer, Autumn, and Winter.' Cf. J. J. M. de Groot, *The Religious System of China, Its Ancient Forms, Evolution, History, and Present Aspect*, 6 vols., Leyden 1892–1910, p. 660.
3. *Huai nan tzŭ* (cf. p. 253) says: 'The East pertains to Wood, the South to Fire, the West to Metal, and the North to Water.' Cf. J. J. M. de Groot (see above, footnote 2), p. 983.
4. W. P. Yetts (see footnote p. 269), p. 125.

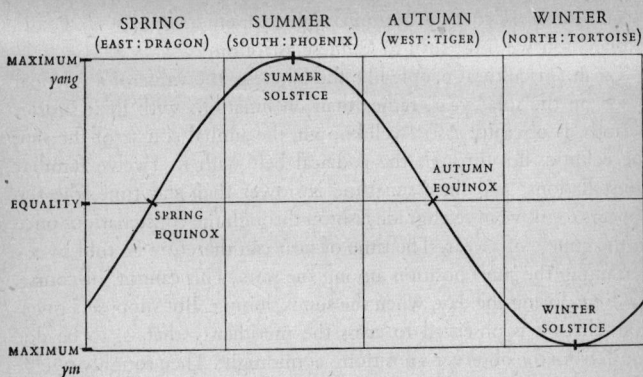

Figure 44. The alternation of *yin* and *yang* throughout the Chinese solar year.

hence the significance of the *Shuo wên* entry. And similarly, the north bank of a river and the south side of a hill will enjoy long hours of sunlight; light is the essence of *yang*. *Yin* manifests itself in other 'negative' qualities such as dampness, cold, weakness, femaleness, and so forth, while *yang* incorporates their opposites – dryness, warmth, strength, maleness.

Here was an explanation of seasonal, monthly, and daily changes. 'At the spring equinox', says *Shuo wên*, 'the dragon ascends to the sky; at the autumn equinox it enters the abyss.' In our graph, figure 44, *yang*, embodied in the Dragon, gains equality with *yin* by the time of the spring equinox. *Yang* reaches its climax at the summer solstice under the presidency of the Phoenix, quintessence of *yang*. Thereafter it declines, reaching equality with *yin* at the autumn equinox. The power of *yin*, manifested at first in the person of the Tiger, now waxes until it culminates at the winter solstice where rules the Tortoise, the epitome of *yin*.

But why did the Dragon suitably symbolize the coming of Spring? The view has been put that the conception of the Dragon was originally based on a species of alligator (*Alligator sinensis* Fauvel) still found in the lower Yangtze valley. If so, then as Yetts says: 'There is the significant fact that with the beginning of winter the alligator buries itself in the mud only to reappear with the warmer weather.'[1] But there is another sense in which 'at the spring equinox the dragon

1. W. P. Yetts (see footnote p. 268), p. 31.

ascends to the sky; at the autumn equinox it enters the abyss'. For an explanation we must turn to Chinese astronomy.

To an agricultural people like the Chinese, the value of a calendar based on the solar year, rather than on lunations with their shorter periods, is obvious. As is well known, the annual course of the sun, the ecliptic, lies through the zodiacal belt with its twelve familiar constellations; and since sun time is slower than star time, the sun appears to move in retrograde fashion through the constellations once in the course of a year. The time of year can therefore be told by ascertaining the sun's position among the stars. This cannot, of course, be done during the day, when the sun is shining. But suppose a given constellation is observed to cross the meridian – that is, to be due south from the observer's position – at midnight. Then roughly twelve hours later a constellation diametrically opposed to it on the celestial sphere will be crossing the meridian in its turn. But so will the sun, since at mid-day the sun is also due south. Stellar couples can be established with reference to a third, circumpolar star. Such a star never sets, and therefore may be seen to cross the meridian *twice* during one rotation of the earth round the celestial pole; that is, in the course of a sidereal day of rather less than twenty-four hours. Two stars or constellations will be diametrically opposed if each in succession crosses the meridian simultaneously with the circumpolar star.

What follows is extremely simple. In order permanently to establish, say, the date of the spring equinox, it is sufficient to observe that on its eve one member of the stellar couple is in a given position at a given time. For in all future years, when this star or constellation reaches the same position at the same time, the sun will be in the opposed constellation and it will be the eve of the spring equinox. And correspondingly, when the opposed constellation in turn takes up the observed position at the same time, the sun will now be in the first constellation and it will be the eve of the autumn equinox. The Chinese established two stellar couples to mark the two equinoxes and the two solstices. The asterisms containing them were among twenty-eight Stellar Mansions (*hsü*) analogous to our zodiacal constellations – although, in fact, on the celestial equator and not the ecliptic – seven of which lay in each of the Four Quadrants. We should add that the uranoscope was also divided into twelve groups corresponding to the divisions (*tzˁŭ*) of Jupiter's twelve-year cycle;

so that the seven Stellar Mansions of each Quadrant were distributed among three duodenary groups.

Exactly which stars in which asterisms formed the stellar couples in Han times is not relevant here. More important is the fact that the vault of Heaven was divided, as we have seen, into Four Quadrants presided over by the Four Supernatural Beings. When the sun entered the West Quadrant, presided over by the Tiger, the year was at the Spring. Then the seven Stellar Mansions among which lay the Dragon 'ascended to the sky' at evening. Each night they rose and set a little earlier until, as Autumn approached, they 'entered the abyss'. They were no longer to be seen in the night sky.

Just as in the West, the Chinese made attempts to trace the features of celestial beings in the configurations of their constellations. The tail of the Dragon (*lung tao*) was the Stellar Mansion *wei*, 'tail', corresponding to the tail of our Scorpio; its heart, the Stellar Mansion *hsin*, 'heart', was our Antares (α Scorpionis), together with σ and τ Scorpionis; and its head, the Stellar Mansion *chio*, 'horn', was in our Boötes far away to the south. Its first horn, our Arcturus (α Boötis) marked the eve of the spring equinox and the beginning of the year (*li ch'un*) when it rose above the horizon at dusk. Some hours later its second horn, our Spica (α Virginis) followed suit.

Indications are that the equinoctial stellar couple comprised stars in our Scorpio and Orion, the one corresponding to the Dragon, the other to the Tiger. Possibly, as Yetts suggests, the Greek conception of the constellation Scorpio as a tailed reptile may have found its way to China and led to an association between this constellation and the Dragon; and since to the Greeks Orion was a supreme hunter, the Chinese may have been under Hellenistic influence in choosing the Tiger, emblematic of war, as his counterpart. The concept of these two constellations eternally pursuing each other across the skies, day in, day out, year in, year out, is common to both traditions. In Greece it gave rise to the myth 'that Earth, terrified by Orion's threat to root out every wild creature from Crete, sent forth a scorpion to kill him with its sting'.[1] In China, the observed behaviour of this stellar couple accorded perfectly with the *yin yang* theory, and may even have played some part in developing it.

One other point should be noticed. Spring marked the beginning of the year and a period of ascendancy of *yang* under the beneficial

1. W. P. Yetts (see footnote p. 268), p. 30.

influence of the Dragon. Daybreak marked a similar beginning, a similar ascendancy of *yang*. In accordance with their notions of cosmic correspondences, the Han Chinese naturally associated the East Quadrant with Spring, since it was in the east that the sun rose at daybreak. The Dragon presided over both.

Origins of the formal categories Ssŭ Shên and Ssŭ Ling – the Four Efficacious Beings, in which *ch'i lin* (Unicorn) substitutes for Tiger – are obscure. *Li chi* mentions both groups; but *Li chi* is a Han compilation, and therefore unreliable evidence for the existence of either in pre-Han times.[1] A more reputable pre-Han text, *Chou li*, brings the White Tiger into association with the West in Chou rituals performed by the Master of Ceremonies (p. 91), and if this is an authentic record of third-century B.C. practice, then it may mark an early stage in the development of the Ssŭ Shên as a formal numerical category. Two other passages in *Chou li* serve to link the two stellar couples with four pairs of animals; namely, a pair of Dragons, a pair of birds (one a hawk), a bear and tiger, and a tortoise and serpent. The idea is germinating; but we are evidently still some way from the conventional Han group of four.

What *is* abundantly clear is that the Ssŭ Shên were fully fledged by Han times. Earliest mention of them in Han literature may be in the second-century B.C. collection *Huai nan tzŭ*, but references thenceforth are frequent. Equally clearly, the Ssŭ Shên cannot be found in pre-Han art. Even in Han times the group may not have made its appearance for a century or so; the earliest mirrors to feature it are dated *ca.* 100 B.C. to A.D. 100 by Karlgren. Other Han objects displaying it – walls of tomb chambers, sides of coffins, sides of memorial pillars (*ch'üeh*), lacquerware, bricks and tiles, domestic or ritual vessels, and perhaps silks – date preponderantly from the first century A.D. or later. Then may have been the culmination of the cult. The category Ssŭ Ling is even more difficult to place. It may have been a late modification of the Ssŭ Shên, but I know of no evidence bearing on its religious meaning, and few traces of its images as a set in Han art (p. 285).

With the coming of Buddhism both groups gradually lost ground until about the sixth century A.D. when the Ssŭ Shên, at least, had a brief new lease of life. Thenceforward they quickly disintegrated. The

1. B. Karlgren (see footnote p. 266), p. 26, believes that the *Ch'ü li* chapter of *Li chi*, in which reference is made to the Ssŭ Shên, is 'certainly a Chou time work'.

Tortoise became separately incorporated in new cults, while individual portrayals of the others seem to have had little more than emblematic meaning from the T'ang period onwards (cf. plate 36a).[1]

THE DRAGON

Having already dealt at some length with the varieties of Dragon portrayed in pre-Han bronze art (pp. 162–5), and with its cosmic role in Han times (pp. 270–4), let us quickly proceed to a short description of the form it takes in Han art. Monster as the Han Dragon

Figure 45. Dragon on a Han stone sarcophagus dated
A.D. 212 found at Lu Shan, Sikang.

undoubtedly is, it is a good deal more palpable than its predecessor on the bronzes. The Dragon which is featured above on this page as figure 45 is drawn from a rubbing taken from one side of a stone sarcophagus found at Lu Shan, just over the western border of Szechwan, in Sikang. The coffin is dated A.D. 212.[2] This exceptionally handsome creature has the top of his head turned towards us, so that it is not easy to make out facial details, which are usually best seen in profile. Other points of his anatomy are well shown. We remark a long

1. For post-Han portrayals of the Ssŭ Shên, cf. W. Cohn, 'The deities of the Four Cardinal Points', in T.O.C.S., vol. xviii (1940–1), pp. 61–75.
2. R. C. Rudolph and Wen Yu, Han Tomb Art of West China, Berkeley and Los Angeles 1951, pl. 73. Two other sides of this coffin are decorated with portrayals of Tiger and Tortoise, and the sculptor undoubtedly had in mind the Ssŭ Shên. But the fourth side, incongruously, has a portrayal of a human figure bearing what may be wings. Cf. also A. Waley, 'Life under the Han dynasty', in H.T., vol. iii, no. 2 (February 1953), pp. 89–98, for further comments on this portrayal.

and serpentine body with a crest of three spines, terminating in a long, slender, and sinuous tail. The belly is adorned with scales, and wings sprout from the shoulders. Legs are feline, feet are provided with three padded claws. The neck is long and slender, and so is the head. Two backwardly projecting horns are rather like those of antelope, while below the left horn can be seen a short, pointed ear. The forehead is marked by a massive crest, on either side of which are the eyes. The upper lip is fleshy and the gaping mouth holds what appears to be a ribbon.

The Dragon on a lacquered table-top, presumably from Lo-lang, has much the same anatomy in spite of his vaguely *folâtre* appearance (plate 18*a*). Mouth has a wide gape and fleshy upper and nether lips, snout is large and somewhat upturned, a massive forehead rises almost vertically and bears two sweeping, backwardly projecting horns. He on the damask from Lou-lan (figure 33) is a close relative. Legs are markedly feline, and fore-paw is uplifted in a gesture that has been claimed for Western Asia, but that is perfectly established in China by Han times.[1] The body is long, the tail long and convoluted. Unpatterned patches on the body represent scales; a single wing appears in profile, and the neck is long and arched.

The head of this Dragon shows features characteristic of the class. The muzzle is long and narrow, with a wide gape. From the fleshy nether lip depends what we know from other portrayals to be a beard or barbel, and the upper lip has a prominent upturned snout. The upright forehead terminates in a backwardly projecting horn, behind which is the ear, both these organs being presented in profile. The Dragons on the polychrome silk from Lou-lan (plate 23*b*) and the Palmyra damask (plate 21) show a somewhat different aspect, since they are in three-quarter view. But this type is also well attested in Han art; and once again we note long, serpentine body, convoluted tail, feline legs, wing, arched neck, horns, massive forehead, and mouth with wide gape – and equipped with powerful canine teeth.

The synthetic nature of the Han Dragon, which rapidly became standardized as a national and imperial symbol, did not pass unnoticed by Chinese antiquarians. Wang Fu (footnote 3, p. 133) dissects it

1. The uplifted fore-paw is featured, for example, on mirrors of Karlgren's C category, dating from the fourth century B.C. Remark it also as made by the 'bird-dragons' of plate 17*b*, a piece whose early date we have already discussed (p. 265).

thus: 'It has nine resemblances, or forms, viz.; the head of a camel, the horns of a deer, eyes of a rabbit, ears of a cow, neck of a snake, belly of a frog, scales of a carp, claws of a hawk, and palm of a tiger. There is a ridge of scales along its back, eighty-one in number. ... On each side of its mouth are whiskers, and a beard hangs under its chin.'

THE PHOENIX

The words used in Han texts and inscriptions on mirrors to name members of the Ssŭ Shên are binomes whose first character indicates the appropriate colour of each animal. *Ch'ing lung* is the Green Dragon; *pai hu*, the White Tiger; *shên wu*, Sombre or Black Warrior, is an unexplained designation for the Tortoise; and *chu niao* is the Scarlet Bird.[1] This last presided over the South Quadrant, corresponding to Summer. Hitherto in our discussion we have given this creature the name of Phoenix, as is customary; but in fact 'Phoenix' is the conventional translation, not of *chu niao*, but of another classical Chinese term, *fêng huang*. Can we justifiably equate *fêng huang* with *chu niao*? That is one question. Another is, can the name Phoenix be aptly applied to either?

Now Chinese and Westerners alike, when writing on the fabulous birds of Chinese antiquity, betray such confusion of thought, are so little in agreement, and arrive at such vague conclusions, that any attempt to answer the questions posed above, based on them, is almost bound to fail. *Chu niao* has been identified with *fêng huang*; but also with such real birds as quail, pheasant, and eagle (or falcon). Fabulous birds in Han art have been named *chu niao*, *fêng huang*, or *luan* – a classical name for yet another mythological species – according to the fancy of the writer, and often quite inconsistently;[2] while in seeking

---

1. In mirror inscriptions the Scarlet Bird appears, more often than not, as *chu chüeh*; the second character being that used for the bronze ritual vessel *chüeh* (p. 151).

2. Thus the authors of *Han Tomb Art in West China* (see footnote p. 275) describe their nos 60 and 61 as featuring the Red Bird or phoenix (the descriptions of these two rubbings seem to have got reversed). Essentially similar subjects of nos 62 and 63 are merely called 'mythological birds'. Having apparently made the equation Red Bird = Phoenix, they nevertheless describe nos 24, 49, and 99 as Red Birds simply, while no. 86 is identified as 'the mythological *fêng huang*, commonly called a phoenix in the West'. If there is a *rationale* behind this nomenclature, it is not evident from anything the authors have to say.

for ultimate ancestors for them, resort has been had not only to the actual birds named above, but also to peacock, crane, domestic rooster, and Burmese jungle-fowl. Here we must limit ourselves to a few general observations on the problem.

No serious attempt has yet been made to sort the fabulous birds of Han art into distinct categories. In calling them all 'Phoenixes' we no more mean to insist on an association between them and fire than that the Chinese Dragon should share the notoriously malevolent nature of his Western counterpart. The matter of names in what Charleston calls 'the Jabberwocky of Han art' need not be taken too seriously; a point of view to which Sowerby presumably cannot subscribe; for he strenuously protests against use of the word 'Phoenix', on the grounds that Chinese fabulous birds have nothing in common with the Western phoenix that 'is supposed to live for a hundred years, at the end of that period building a funeral pyre on which it cremates itself, a new phoenix rising out of the ashes of the old'.[1] Nor, presumably, can he subscribe to a suggestion made by Saussure, that it was on characteristics of the Chinese bird that the Western legend was based.[2]

Connexion between *fêng huang* and Fire is in fact extremely close if the Taoist Ho-kuan Tzŭ, writing about the fourth century B.C., is to be believed. He says: 'The phoenix (*fêng huang*) is the bird of the [duodenary group] "quail's heart" (*shun huo*, literally 'quail's fire'); it is the essence of the principle yang.'[3] The duodenary division 'quail's heart' corresponds to the middle asterisms of the South Quadrant, the abode of the Scarlet Bird, as does 'quail's head' to its eastern, and 'quail's tail' to its western asterisms. The significance of this did not escape Shên Kua (p. 268), who argued: '... the Scarlet Bird of the astronomers is a symbol based on the quail. Therefore they called the seven "mansions" (*hsü*) of the Scarlet Bird in the Southern Quadrant by the names "head", "fire" (='heart') and "tail" of the quail.'[4] Thus at a single stroke we have the probable equation *fêng huang*=quail=*chu niao* – in an astronomical context, at any rate.

1. A. de Carle Sowerby, *Nature in Chinese Art*, New York 1940, p. 21.
2. L. de Saussure, 'Les origines de l'astronomie chinoise', in *T.P.*, vol. x (1909), p. 264.
3. Translated and quoted by Yetts (see footnote p. 268), p. 37.
4. Translated and quoted by Yetts (see footnote p. 268), p. 35. A parallel to this division into 'head', 'heart', and 'tail' will be found in the case of Stellar Mansions in the East Quadrant, corresponding to the head, heart, and tail of the Green Dragon (p. 273).

The association between light, heat, and fire – aspects of *yang* – on the one hand, and the South and Summer on the other, is obvious to people living in northern latitudes. For just as by day the sun reaches its highest altitude, shines brightest, and is hottest at noon, so during the year it reaches its highest altitude, shines brightest, and is hottest at midsummer. At mid-day the sun is on the meridian, due south; and mid-day of the summer solstice brings the cycles of day and year into complete concordance. In choosing a bird to embody *yang* and represent the Southern Quarter, it would be proper to find one somehow associated with the above-mentioned elements. Shên Kua, pursuing his quail theory, points to the red colour of one species of quail, suggestive of fire. He also says that in settling, the quail will always perch on a tree (= wood); but the implied association with Fire in this case – that the bird settles on Wood just as Fire settles on Wood, Wood being the emblem of Spring, and Fire that of Summer – is surely a little contrived.

More important, I should say, is that the quail is a summer migrant to north China from the South, appearing and disappearing equally suddenly. Its arrival in the Yellow River region would be a proverbial portent of Summer, just as its departure would herald the approach of autumn. On the other hand, many actual birds mentioned by modern scholars in identification with the Phoenix – peacock, pheasant, and Burmese jungle-fowl – are also southerners, and might just as easily have been associated with the South Quadrant in popular imagination; the last named must have been introduced into the North from the South, since the domestic rooster of north China is almost certainly its descendant.

To sum up, I see no reason why Chinese artists of Han times should not have created, more or less capriciously, the Red Bird of the South as a sort of biological mosaic of parts taken from several sorts of birds. The *fêng huang*, which appeared out of nowhere as a herald of auspicious events, may also have been the fabulous offspring of a summer migrant from the South whose fleeting visits led to all sorts of rumours as to its actual appearance and habits. Whether or not Red Bird and *fêng huang* were one, in fact, Han artists would probably have recognized little or no difference between them as subjects for portrayal.

Turning to actual representations of Phoenixes in Han art, the symmetrically confronted pairs on the Noin-ula lacquer bowl of 2 B.C. (figure 46) give us a good idea of what they looked like, since the artist, with swift brush-strokes, has reduced their forms to bare essentials. We note that head is small, neck long and arched, body rather shallow. The pointed tail is continued in a long, thin, and soaring tail-plume which appears to curl forward in a tight scroll – a spiral being so placed in the angle between the upper edge of the decorative band and the tail-plume as to appear continuous with the latter. At the back of the head is a crest formed of three parallel-curving lines, also scrolled forward in a curve which repeats that of the tail-plume. And from the dorsal surface of the body rises a third scroll that may be meant either for wing or wing-plume. Legs are long and slender, one being raised in front of the breast with its lower leg-bone prolonged,

Figure 46. Phoenix on a Han lacquer bowl
dated 2 B.C. found at Noin-ula.

as Charleston observes, 'in an impossible curve and terminating in an arrangement reminiscent of an old-fashioned fruit-fork'.[1] In respect of all these essential features, resemblance to the 'bird-dragons' of the Ch'ang-sha lacquer bowl (plate 17b) is striking.

The west China bas-reliefs (cf. footnote p. 275) provide a whole repertory of Han Phoenixes, looking as realistic as fabulous birds ever can. Beak, head, neck, body, and legs are long and slender, tail is long and broad. Beak is usually open but empty; occasionally it holds a round object, no doubt meant for a pearl. From the back of the head rises a tall crest which is usually represented as a single broad plume curving forward so that its distal end is over the top of the head. At this end the plume bears an 'eye', much resembling that seen on peacocks' feathers. In a variation, the plume is long and reed-like, bearing at its distal end a knob like the head of a bullrush. Wings

1. R. J. Charleston (see footnote p. 209), p. 67.

are powerful-looking, and are usually raised as if for flight, the first primary flight-feathers being distinctly longer than the rest. Legs are long and slender like those of cranes, but they often bear spurs, as do those of gallinaceous birds, and talons suggestive of birds of prey.

But the most striking point of the Han Phoenix is its superb tail, which, perhaps more than any other single feature, has made the word *fêng* synonymous with elegance and sexual beauty. Occasionally this is abnormally long, trailing the ground, as does that of the Reeves Pheasant. More often its tail-plumes – usually three in number – sweep upwards and forwards in a graceful curve echoing that of the crest. Like it, they terminate either in 'eyes' or in club-like prominences.

The symmetrically confronted regardant birds on the Lou-lan polychrome silk (figure 33) have good claim to be recognized as phoenixes. Head is small; bill long, straight, and open. The long, flexible neck rises from a body that looks fatter than it actually is, because a single raised wing is silhouetted against it. The crest is long, and curls forward. Legs are long, with the plump thighs of cranes; and although only two tail-plumes are seen, these have the elegance and upward and forward sweep so characteristic of the class.

We have said enough to show that the Han Phoenix is very much of a hybrid, and perhaps need not make a final decision between the rival claims of one or other actual bird to be its true ancestor. Crest and tail both suggest one of the many species of pheasant, peacock, or pheasant-peacock indigenous to the border country between southwest China and Assam. Sowerby holds that this cannot be so, since peacocks and pheasants carry their tail-plumes stiff and straight; whereas those of the domestic rooster, which he regards as the main source of inspiration for the Phoenix, are flowing. But the curve of the Phoenix tail-plumes is forward, whereas that of the rooster curls backwards. Nor do I think the massive crest of the Han Phoenix is at all like the comb and wattles of the rooster or its ancestor, the Burmese jungle-fowl, as he asserts. Neck and legs distinctly suggest the crane. On the other hand, spurs on the lower legs support Sowerby's case for the rooster, while talons and an occasional hooked beak help to bear out Lo Chên-yü's theory that the prototype was an eagle.

In conclusion, we should perhaps say that the binome *fêng huang* reflects the belief that Phoenixes were bi-sexual creatures, needing no partners for mating, their male elements incorporated in *fêng*, their female in *huang*. Where in Han art we find two Phoenixes confronted – and especially where one carries a crest and the other does not – I think we may assume that the Han artist, unable to visualize the biological anomaly of a bi-sexual bird, intends the pair for male and female. In the case of our silk (figure 33) it would be difficult, for technical reasons, to show the signs of sexual differentiation.

TIGER AND TORTOISE

The *yin* animals, Tiger and Tortoise, call for no more than brief mention here. In particular, the Tiger seems to pose few problems. As represented in Han art he is a realistic-looking creature with a long – sometimes preternaturally long – body, and long, sinuous tail. The head with its open jaws is strictly naturalistic; so, too, are the feline legs. In fact, the only serious departure from anatomical truth that Han designers allowed themselves was to present him, as often as not, with a pair of rudimentary wings.

His cosmological status is also plain to see. The West Quadrant came to symbolize Autumn because of cosmic correspondence between day and year, the fall of the year being equivalent to sunset, just as Spring corresponded to sunrise. The Tiger symbolized Autumn in much the same way as did the Dragon Spring. *Shuo wên* observes of the Tiger: 'He is the king of mountain animals'; and the contemporary Wang Ch'ung comments as follows: 'Tigers emerge at a certain time just as dragons appear at their appointed season. The *yin* creatures come out in winter, the *yang* reptiles in summer.'[1] In the Autumn the tiger comes down from the mountain forests to ravage the plain, and with his coming the constellations of the West Quadrant rise in the night sky. We have seen how, in choosing a predatory animal to symbolize the West Quadrant, the Chinese may have been influenced by the Greek legend of Orion; and there are also certain correspondences between the Tiger and Metal, the Element associated with the West in *Huai nan tzŭ*, which I do not think need be discussed here. In brief the Tiger, well known in Chinese folk-lore and in bronze art for upwards of a millennium before the beginning of the Han dynasty, was an automatic choice for the position of ruler of the West Quadrant. Three of its Heavenly Mansions were made to

1. Both passages are translated and quoted by W. P. Yetts (see footnote p. 269), p. 142.

correspond to parts of his body. *Shên*, bordering the South Quadrant and containing the stars α, β, γ, δ, ε, η, and κ Orionis (the Shoulders, Belt, and Legs of Orion), is his torso; *tzŭ*, comprising λ and two φ Orionis (the Head of Orion), is his head; and *pi*, including six stars in Hyades and two in Taurus, is his mouth.

Nor, since she is not included among our illustrations, need we spend much time with the Tortoise, although the problems she presents are by no means easily solved. In referring to the creature as 'she', we have in mind the Chinese convention – it could scarcely have amounted to a belief – by which the Tortoise was thought of as female only. As Yetts says: 'This notion probably arises from the anatomical fact that, the genitals of the tortoise being hidden in a sort of cloaca, there is no visible organ to mark the sex.'[1] Thus the idea grew that the Tortoise could be fecundated only by another animal, the Snake. Han and later portrayals of the Ssŭ Shên – and perhaps of the Ssŭ Ling – show Tortoise and Snake coupled in a sexual embrace; and the same convention is observed when, from T'ang times onwards, the Tortoise became a deity of latter-day Taoism.

Use of tortoise plastrons for divination by oracle-bone technique in Shang-Yin times (p. 108) may explain why supernatural powers were attributed to the Tortoise very early in Chinese history, and account for legends in which she emerges from the waters of the Yellow River bearing magical writings on her back. Her association with the North is self-evident. Dark of hue, cold-blooded, slow-moving, and secretive of habit, frequenting low-lying and watery places, she is the very essence of *yin*. Her withdrawal from public affairs with the coming of Winter symbolized the slacker rhythms of human life in that season of death, return of the men from the fields, and the season of women's work inside the tightly-shuttered homesteads of north China; just as did the emergence of the Dragon from his winter sleep, the season of rebirth and release from the dominion of *yin*.

THE UNICORN

The *ch'i lin*, or Unicorn, is one of the Objects of Good Omen (*hsiang jui*), appearance of which was in Han times considered to be an auspicious sign indicating the birth of a virtuous ruler or a period of peaceful rule. The Ssŭ Ling seem to have been a group of this sort, for

1. W. P. Yetts (see footnote p. 268), p. 32.

we read in *K'ung ts'ung tzŭ* that 'when benefits shall be distributed over mankind by a Son of Heaven and universal peace shall obtain through him unicorns [(*ch'i*) *lin*], phenixes [*fêng* (*huang*)], tortoises [*kuei*] or dragons [*lung*] are the harbingers of it.'[1] A Unicorn is supposed to have appeared at the time of Confucius's birth.

Êrh ya (p. 89) says of the Unicorn that it has the body of an antelope, the tail of an ox, and a single horn; while *Shuo wên* remarks: 'The *ch'i lin* is an animal possessed of human-heartedness (*jên*). It has the body of a horse, the tail of an ox, and a horn [with a tip of] flesh.' A *ch'i lin* featured among the Objects of Good Omen from the

Figure 47. Unicorn from a Han bas-relief,
as featured in *Chin shih so*.

Shantung bas-reliefs, rubbings of which were reproduced in *Chin shih so* (p. 87), is very much like a horse indeed, except for its cloven hoofs and the single club-shaped and backward pointing horn (figure 47). It has a horse's robust neck, barrel chest, and rounded hindquarters. I am inclined to think that the model for this portrayal, and perhaps for other Han representations of *ch'i lin*, was the indigenous horse of the northern steppes and of ancient China, *Equus prjevalskii*. In particular, the tail bears a switch of long hair rising from its distal end and not from the root – an unusual and characteristic feature of this horse. *Equus prjevalskii* was of course well known to Han artists; a fine sculpture in the round is mentioned in the next chapter (p. 294).

1. J. J. M. de Groot (see footnote p. 270), vol. ii, p. 824.

Our animal featured on the Lou-lan damask of figure 33, it must be confessed, only vaguely resembles this horse. The forehead, for instance, is of the sort which commentators speak of when they say that the *ch'i lin*'s forehead is that of a wolf, and the tail shows no distal crop of hairs. But in its stocky build, massive neck, barrel chest, rounded hindquarters, and short legs the resemblance is a good deal more apparent. As for the horn, we cannot of course be certain that a single one was intended, since even if there were two, only one would be seen in profile; moreover, post-Han portrayals of the beast frequently show it with two horns. But, as Charleston says, representations of real animals with a single horn are not foreign to pre-Han art. One of these is the rhinoceros, and the suggestion has been made that *ch'i lin* inherit their single horns from this beast. On the other hand an upright mane is a peculiar feature of the steppe horse, one always emphasized in bronze inscription graphs standing for *ma*, 'horse'; I think we must therefore consider a possibility that the single horn of *ch'i lin* is simply a highly stylized rendering of the mane of *Equus prjevalskii*.

A final point calls for brief mention. Assuming the portrayal of figure 33 to be that of *ch'i lin*, then three of the four animals comprising the Ssŭ Ling group are represented on this silk. It seems hardly possible that the motive of which only a fragment remains on the right side of this cloth was the fourth member, the Tortoise. Yet one can reasonably assume that what remains of this silk is only about a third of the original width; and even allowing for a 'turn over' in the weft direction (p. 246) and a consequent repetition of surviving motives, there would still be room for one or two more. I think that Tortoise, accompanied by Serpent, may well have been among these.

DUCK AND CARP

Among the Objects of Good Omen depicted in *Chin shih so* are two somewhat enigmatic symbols, *pi i niao*, 'birds sharing wings', and *pi mu yü*, 'fish sharing eyes'. The portrayals show that in each case a pair of animals joined together like Siamese twins is meant – the birds with one pair of wings between them, the fish with one pair of eyes. They also reveal that the birds are a species of duck, the Mandarin Teal, and the fish some sort of carp, the fish *par excellence* of ancient China.

Duck and carp are among the most familiar denizens of the countryside, and of the larders, of north China, and for this reason alone must have recommended themselves as subjects for portrayal by the nature-loving Han designers. But their known habits also fit them as symbols of domestic happiness, and in particular of conjugal fidelity. Both go in pairs. Paired carp symbolize sexual union, while the tremendous reproductive powers of this fish help to associate it in popular imagination with abundant human progeny. The prodigality of its spawn sets a standard for human prosperity, a symbolism enhanced by the fact that the characters for 'fish' and 'superabundance' are pronounced as homophones (yü). So close is conjugal attachment between male and female Mandarin Teal that this bird is called yüan yang, the first character designating the drake, the second the hen. It is popularly supposed that male and female remain faithful to each other for life, and that they pine away and die if forcibly separated. Such ideas fully account for the happy invention of 'birds sharing wings' and 'fish sharing eyes' as Objects of Good Omen in Han folk-lore, and for presence of these creatures, united in flesh and blood, in Han art.

The polychrome silk from Lou-lan (plate 23b) bears a repeat design of a single flying duck. Clearly this is not the pi i niao motive, but its presence on a silk carrying a good-luck message (see footnote p. 267) strongly argues that the symbolism of conjugal felicity was in its designer's mind. Similarly, the gold carp that swim in pairs, one fish above the other, in the quiet waters of the lovely blue-green silk from Noin-ula (plate 22a) are not physically united, yet one can hardly doubt but that the same hope for domestic happiness is here expressed.

T'AO T'IEH

A good deal could be written about the Han t'ao t'ieh and its derivation from that found on pre-Han ritual bronzes (pp. 161–2 and figure 26). But we are nearing the end of a long and, I am afraid, almost intolerably discursive chapter, and detailed discussion of t'ao t'ieh would do little to enliven it. Moreover, an able analysis by Charleston convincingly traces continuity between this motive and its pre-Han forerunners, while admitting a possible modification in its iconography derived from the West.[1]

1. Cf. R. J. Charleston (see footnote p. 209), pp. 71–80.

The essential mask confronts us as a single motive – bilaterally symmetrical on the weft axis – on the extreme left of the silk shown in figure 33. We may perhaps sense its emblematic or talismanic purport, and see in imagination another identical mask at the other edge of this now incomplete silk. The cryptic dragons in profile forming left and right sides of a full mask, so characteristic of First Phase *t'ao t'ieh*, have altogether vanished. We are looking at a mask in full face, and nothing more.

Such a twist in presentation might perhaps argue in support of those who believe in a Western origin for the *t'ao t'ieh*, were we considering only Third Phase and Han versions. But analysis shows that 'every detail of the *t'ao t'ieh* of L.C. vii. 09 [figure 33] has a continuous history throughout the phases of Chinese art right back to the earliest times'; and the case for a totemistic origin of this mask among the Scythians, as Alföldi claimed, or a relation to 'nomadic motifs of Greek origins with Iranian modifications', which was Borovka's theory, remains as doubtful as ever.[1] Briefly, the details indicated are: the crest of five upright hairs (or feathers) on the forehead; the scrolled forms at the sides of the head which may be meant for horns or ears; the 'plumes' springing from upper arms and elbows; the large eyes; the broad nose terminating in flared nostrils; the open jaws with their conspicuous canine teeth; and the forelimbs with three, or possibly four, claws. More or less close parallels to all of them can be found in the First Phase mask – a circumstance which effectively disposes of Borovka's claim that the Han version derives 'from Western prototypes which cannot be dated before the middle of the first millennium B.C., and is therefore inconceivable in China before the Hellenistic period'.

What does seem to reveal the presence of a Western influence in the mask of figure 33 is the peculiar bowed and akimbo attitude of its forelimbs. It is as though the creature were holding something invisible in front of its face. Charleston drew attention to the general similarity between this type and a bronze ring-pendentive from north China comprising mask and ring (figure 48a); the mask is in full face, with shoulders hunched above the head, and with arms akimbo and clutching the ring on either side of the face. A Greek prototype of Gorgon-type is strongly suggested.

Now a variety of *t'ao t'ieh* in the form of a ring-handle in which the

1. R. J. Charleston (see footnote p. 209), p. 76.

Figure 48. *T'ao-t'ieh* masks: *a*, in the form of a Han bronze pendentive; *b*, from a Han bas-relief.

ring is separately cast and passes freely through an 'eye' made by the monster's projecting nose, is a familiar ingredient in Third Phase bronze art. Such ring-handles are attached to the sides of late Chou ritual vessels; and applied clay imitations of them, with decorative function only, are commonplaces, not to say clichés, of Han pottery. But much closer to our version on the silk is a now well-documented group of Han *t'ao t'ieh* in which the monster holds the ring in its two hands. This series, numerous examples of which are figured on the west China bas-reliefs,[1] was not known to Charleston at the time he compared the mask on the silk of figure 33 with that of the ring pendentive, a fact that makes the more impressive his recognition of stylistic connexions between the two. A typical example is shown in figure 48*b*, and its close similarity in form and presentation to the mask on the silk may be allowed to speak for itself.

Two features of *t'ao t'ieh* masks on the west China bas-reliefs call for brief mention. One is the talismanic air they have about them. They look as if they have been set down, carelessly almost, to act as seals of authenticity or authority for the motives with which they are associated. Whatever the meaning of this complex, it seems to be indissoluble. Perhaps it is worth pointing out, therefore, that when the main subject is one of cosmic or symbolic significance – such, for example, as the Ssŭ Shên – the mask is invariably this second type in

1. R. C. Rudolph and Wen Yu (see footnote p. 275), figs. 33, 60–3, 67, 69, 71.

which the ring is held by the hands; whereas when the subject is a tomb guardian in human guise,[1] the associated mask is of the familiar 'ring-handle' variety mentioned above.

THE 'PARTHIAN SHOT'

This name is given to a motive wherein a mounted archer, riding a horse at 'flying gallop', shoots backwards at a target in his rear. There has been much discussion as to its origin, which Gallois considers to be ultimately Phoenician, passing thence to Mycenae, to Greece, thence perhaps to Greek colonies on the Black Sea, and thence via Sarmatian and Scythian art to China.[2] It also makes its appearance on Parthian and Bactrian coins and, later, on Sassanian silverware (cf. p. 458).

I do not know of evidence to show that the 'Parthian shot' entered Chinese art before Han times. Earliest known portrayal may be on an inlaid bronze tube in the Imperial Academy, Tōkyō, perhaps dating from the beginning of our era;[3] the archer here shoots backwards at a tiger. It also occurs on the Shantung bas-reliefs, dating from the first century A.D.,[4] and on the decorative bands of a whole series of Han lead-glazed pottery vases.[5] On our cosmetic box (plate 19b) the archer is shooting at a fabulous beast in front of him – presumably a simple variant of the original motive.

The 'Parthian shot' is linked with the convention called 'flying gallop' – a position never assumed by a quadruped unless it is clearing an obstacle. There is no reason to associate this convention exclusively with any one part of the world. Artists naturally turn to it as a means of conveying an impression of speed; witness for instance the English sporting print. But it was certainly used in China before the coming of the 'Parthian shot', for Bachofer draws attention to its appearance on an inlaid bronze *chien* (p. 155) now in the Freer Gallery of Art.[6]

1. R. C. Rudolph and Wen Yu (see footnote p. 275), figs. 68, 70.
2. H. C. Gallois, 'Mutual influences between Chinese and Near Eastern ceramics in the T'ang period and before', in *A.R.*, vol. xxviii, no. 96 (October 1932), p. 648.
3. L. Bachofer, *A Short History of Chinese Art*, New York 1946, p. 88 and fig. xv.
4. É. Chavannes (see footnote p. 292), fig. 35.
5. B. Laufer, *Chinese Pottery of the Han Period*, Leiden 1909, pls. 48–51, and pp. 213–14.
6. L. Bachofer (see footnote above), p. 90 and fig. 83.

THE TREE OF LIFE

It was, I believe, Pfister who first suggested that a tree occupying the middle of the motive portrayed on a Noin-ula polychrome silk (plate 24) is derived from the ancient Mesopotamian Tree of Life.[1] In appearance very much like a conifer, it bears three pairs of symmetrically opposed branches from the upper edges of which rise short stalks bearing some sort of fruit, while other forms, coming off their lower edges, are more like leaves; the main trunk terminates above in a cluster or 'bouquet' of fruit around which are more leaves. Pfister notes a broad resemblance between this tree and another, embroidered on a silk damask from Palmyra, the branches of which are also disposed in three symmetrical pairs and bear slender and upright cone-shaped objects at their tips. From the top of the main stem arises a cluster of three more cones. He compared both versions with a tree featured on the Shantung bas-reliefs, having two symmetrical pairs of branches from each of which hangs a large, shapeless sort of fruit, and with a bifid terminal bouquet.

The notion of a Tree of Life, growing in a paradise inaccessible to ordinary mortals, and bearing fruit capable of rejuvenating, reanimating, or prolonging life when eaten, is part of the stock of world myth. Sometimes associated with a Well or Fountain of Life-giving Water, and varying in species according to its geographical setting, it crops up in Egyptian, Sumerian, Babylonian, Phoenician, Greek, Islamic, Siberian, Chinese, Japanese, Polynesian, Norse, and Gaelic folklore, and no doubt in that of many other cultures as well.

First mention of the Chinese and Japanese paradise, the Isles of the Blest in the Eastern Sea, may be in the book called *Lieh tzŭ* (p. 253). The paradise is gradually elaborated throughout the Han period. Its immortal inhabitants, their bodies transparent or wholly set aside, float in the air from island to island. All its animals are pure white. Its terraces and palaces are of gold and jade. Gay-plumaged birds fly through its groves, whose trees are laden with pearls and gems. Its flowers are sweetly perfumed, and they who eat its fruit are assured of youth and long life. Enormous rocks of jade exude a sweet water like wine, conferring longevity; and the *ling chih*, 'fungus of immor-

1. R. Pfister (see footnote p. 210), vol. i, p. 53. Yetts had previously drawn attention to the Iranian influence traceable in this scene. Cf. W. P. Yetts (see footnote p. 187), p. 176.

tality', is cultivated and harvested by the Immortals as ordinary people grow rice. Immortals, beasts, and birds, all feed on this fungus, and the birds sometimes carry it abroad in their beaks. Ssŭ-ma Ch'ien recounts that during the reign of the First Ch'in Emperor (p. 176) birds looking like crows or ravens appeared in China carrying *ling chih*. When they dropped the fungus on the faces of dead soldiers these sprang again to life.

Chinese accounts of the Isles of the Blest do not specifically mention a single Tree of Life; [1] and in depicting what I believe to be this tree – and this paradise – on the Noin-ula silk, the designer is making a more or less literal translation of the conventional Western Asiatic presentment. This art-motive travelled widely. Like the myth behind it, it is known in almost every ancient culture of the Old World, including Assyria and Babylonia, Palestine, Egypt, Mycenae, and India. The Arabs carried it to Spain, Sicily, and western Europe, while under Byzantine auspices it reached Russia and Italy.

All versions have the same heraldic air – a highly stylized, geometrical tree flanked by two figures. At Mohenjo-dāro, these are bulls; at Suza, lions; on Sumerian seals, mountains; on Sassanian silks, ducks or the Holy Ibis; from Assyria, figures with eagles' heads; from Cyprus, goats eating; from Crete, snakes; from a seventh-century A.D. relief at Venice, stylized trees; from a twelfth-century Sicilian textile, peacocks. And so on. In medieval Europe, the tree becomes the Tree of Knowledge, and the figures Adam and Eve.

The remaining width of the Noin-ula silk is about 35 cm., so that not more than some 7 cm. of its width can be missing, and we can therefore safely assume that almost the whole original motive is still present. [2] The photograph does not give its full lateral extension; but one published by Trever clearly shows that the curious fungoid growths on either side have each three main lobes or branches, beyond which the design repeats to left and right regularly along the warp. [3]

1. The Japanese version does. It grows on the highest mountain of P'êng-lai (Jap. Horaizon), the principal island, and has 'a trunk and branches of gold, roots of silver, and gem-leaves and fruit'. Cf. D. A. Mackenzie, *Myths of China and Japan*, London (no date), p. 116. The Altaic-Siberian myth also contains a Tree of Life in the form of a white seven-branched birch; a basin containing the Water of Life stands at its foot.

2. The width of this silk runs from top to bottom, as seen on plate 24, as is proved by a selvedge running along the top border.

3. C. Trever (see footnote p. 187), pl. 15.

Assuming the tree in the middle to be the Tree of Life, we are prepared to find figures flanking it on either side. They are birds, standing back to back, and apparently pecking at the plants that form the lateral limits of the motive. The birds stand on rocks treated in formal fashion as a number of more or less rectangular blocks, irregularly superimposed on each other. Can we plausibly read this scene as a Chinese adaptation of the Western Asiatic motive, by which to display the Chinese Isles of the Blest? In that case the plants towards which the birds bend may really be meant for fungi, the life-giving *ling chih*, and the birds may be the paradisial creatures who feed upon it, and sometimes carry it over the seas to ordinary mortals. They do not look very much like crows or ravens, it is true. Their general appearance is more like that of Mandarin Teal – a natural choice for the Han designer intending to portray paired birds. The crags on which they stand may, in accordance with the legend, be the jade rocks yielding the Water of Life whose taste is like wine.

One must admit that this identification is very uncertain. But parallels for the motive of tree flanked by animals can be found in Han art; for example, a tree with a horse on either side of it, among the Shantung bas-reliefs.[1] Its general air is so distinctive, its formal symmetry so thoroughly Western Asiatic in feeling, and its appearance in Han art so unprecedented, that its Iranian ancestry as the Tree of Life seems difficult to deny. In that case, what could be more natural than that the Western motive, linked with the Western quest for Immortality, should have been transposed by the Chinese designer of this silk as an appropriate condensation of the parallel Chinese myth?

1. É. Chavannes, *Mission Archéologique dans la Chine Septentrionale.* Text; vol. i, pt. 1, *La Sculpture à l'Époque des Han*, Paris 1913, fig. 24.

Chapter Five

SCULPTURE

Pre-Buddhist Sculpture in China

UNTIL the coming of Buddhism at the beginning of our era China had no consistent tradition of figure sculpture and, as far as we know, little enough of any other. Two recent discoveries make us modify the old view that sculpture was unknown before Han times. First are some marbles excavated at An-yang in 1934–5. They are impressive pieces, superbly executed and immaculately finished, measuring up to a yard or so in their greater dimensions. But the tradition to which they belong is that of bronze art. Favoured subjects are quasi-natural beasts and birds that remind us of animal *tsun* (p. 144 and plate 13), while surface-treatment echoes conventions of First Phase bronze décor. The art seems to have disappeared after Shang-Yin times.

A second discovery worth reporting is that of wooden sculptures, some of which show signs of having been lacquered, in the Ch'ang-sha tombs (p. 195). Men and women are portrayed, their features summarily rendered with bold linear cuts; others, better described as anthropomorphic, are grotesquely adorned with real deer's horns and long, protruding tongues. No doubt these figures served some magical purpose connected with the dead but no one, as far as I know, has attempted to explain just what.[1] Perhaps some were simply *ming ch'i* – burial furniture of a type similar to the pottery figures of attendants accompanying the dead man, so common in Han tombs. But until relations between the Ch'u tribes and the rest of China are better understood, it would be rash to claim these figures as ancestors of the Han funerary wares. The group has an unmistakable air of primitive art, and manifests a style that must surely have appeared exotic to metropolitan China.

1. A complete report on the Ch'ang-sha figures has now been made by A. Salmony, *Antler and Tongue. An Essay on Ancient Chinese Symbolism and its Implications*, Ascona 1954. For similar figures adorned with cervine horns, known to have come from the Altai region of Siberia, cf. R. D. Barnett and W. Watson, 'The world's oldest Persian carpet . . .', in *I.L.N.*, vol. cciii, no. 5960 (July 1953), pp. 69–71 and fig. 5.

Sculptures of Han times – I omit here the above-mentioned ceramic statuary – fall into two groups, bas-reliefs and figures carved in the round. The former served to illustrate mythological scenes and passages of Chinese history, real or imagined, and lined the death-chambers of Han nobility. Since personages depicted on these slabs are placed in a contemporary setting, they help to shed light on the details of Han daily life. They are, of course, simply translations into stone of a pictorial art in some less enduring medium, and their connexion with Buddhist figure-sculpture is slight; although certain decorative elements of this purely native Chinese glyptic art do re-appear among accessory motives of Buddhist votive steles.

We also have a very few examples of figures carved in the round from Han times. Best known is the portrayal of a horse of steppe type trampling down a nomad, which stands at the burial mound of Ho Ch'ü-ping (p. 178) in the valley of the Wei River in Shensi. Unkind words have been said about this group. To my mind, judging only from photographs, it is a most effective piece of secular monumental sculpture, having the odd vitality one associates with the Former Han period, to which I am quite sure it belongs. Other Han animal sculptures are known both at this site and elsewhere; but again, little stylistic or iconographic connexion with Buddhist art is apparent.

General Characteristics of Buddhist Sculpture in China

Chinese Buddhist sculpture is not, I would say, an outstanding art. It does, admittedly, display an austereness and sincerity befitting its hieratic purpose, especially during the early periods with which we propose to deal. And this, tempered by what Dr Cohn calls 'a visionary sweetness' of the features, lends it peculiar charm to Western eyes. But the symbolic content is confined almost entirely to the mask. Herein lies a real difference between Chinese and other great sculptural traditions. In both Greek and Indian sculpture the body, no less than the mask, helped to express certain mental and spiritual qualities or conditions. For the Greeks, beautiful or noble physical form was the counterpart of ideal character, intellect, and personality, such as they ascribed to their gods. The distinctive individuality of each was matched to a corresponding portrait type.[1] A naturalistic treatment

1. As G. Lowes Dickinson puts it, in *The Greek View of Life*, London 1941, p. 216: 'The statues of the various gods derive their distinguishing individual-

was employed to point these differences. The gown, for instance, gives the impression of an actual garment clothing a living wearer. It is a mode of expression one might call idealized realism.

Cult-images of early Indian Buddhism present a somewhat different case. The body is expressive, but not of an ideal ethical or intellectual type. Instead, it symbolizes the highly concentrated mystical state called *dhyāna*, in which mind and body are simultaneously implicated. The word is usually translated as 'meditation', but the practice by which *dhyāna* is attained involves putting the body into postures it would not normally assume, and the outcome is not a state of mind only. 'Every stage of it,' says Chanda, 'also permeates the whole body.' [1] We find pre-Buddhist images in *dhyāna* from sites as early as Mohenjo-dāro and Harappā (c. 2500–1700 B.C.), and they are habitual to early Buddhist and Jain sculpture. The rigidity of such poses places certain limitations on the sculptor, forcing him away from a strictly naturalistic treatment; while use of conventional signs such as the *uṣṇīṣa* (p. 327) carries him a stage further away from pure realism. With such a cult-image, in which the internal relations between various parts of the body assist at a technical demonstration, nothing must be allowed to distract attention from its essential nudity. Clothing is a hindrance; and Indian sculptors either discard it altogether, or mould it closely to the body of the wearer as a sort of second skin.

In Chinese Buddhist sculpture, on the other hand, the body usually plays a subordinate role. It expresses neither natural posture nor the rigidity and nervous tension of trance. Its organic relation with the head is not always easy to accept. Sometimes the head is disproportionately large, and the body suffers reduction – not of the sort we find, say, in Negro sculpture, which apparently results from a need to gain greater plastic effect than the human body normally offers – but rather due, one feels, to sheer failure to grasp its symbolic possibilities. Summary treatment of the body is often linked with an unconvincing rendering of drapery. It neither follows the natural rhythms of movement, nor does it reveal the underlying form. The gown is still recognizably a garment, but its folds are rendered schematically and there is a tendency for parts of it to develop into independent

---

ity ... from a concrete reproduction, in features, expression, drapery, pose, of the ethical and intellectual qualities for which they stand.'

1. R. Chanda, *Medieval Sculpture in the British Museum*, London 1936, p. 18.

decorative motives. This is especially evident in the treatment of its lower hem during the first part of the period we are to discuss.[1]

A second limitation of Chinese Buddhist sculpture – one that we find in that of Greece and Europe, and to some extent India, but from which Negro sculpture is free – is that its frontal aspect dominates all others; or, as Fry says when speaking of the European tradition, 'it approaches plasticity from the point of view of bas-relief'.[2] Indeed, this is a more constant feature of Chinese sculpture than of any of the other traditions I have named. Images in cave-shrines are obvious examples of objects meant to be looked at from one point of view only. The same is true of those adorning the niches of votive steles; while the stele itself is not conceived of *en ronde-bosse*, but is simply a two- or four-sided bas-relief. Free-standing images are comparatively rare, but even in these plastic feeling is not always strong. Few examples stand the test of being viewed from the sides, let alone the back, and if the reader will turn to plate 31 he will be able to see to what extent visual interest is concentrated in the frontal view.

Because of this reluctance to render form in three dimensions, we seldom find convincing accounts of complicated bodily movement or posture such as Indian sculptors delighted to attempt. Towards the end of its evolution, Chinese Buddhist sculpture did partly free itself from this inhibition, and in T'ang and later times much looser and more subtle postures may be met with. The sculptures have depth, and interest is not confined to the frontal plane alone. Yet even now the plastic formula is incomplete. The back is no more than a flat slab.

One is forced to conclude that the special qualities inherent in sculpture as an art-form are but poorly represented in that of China. The Chinese themselves appear never to have rated their sculpture very highly. Few names of individual sculptors have been preserved, and next to nothing of their work;[3] most of the others were what

1. Restriction of psychological interest to the mask in Chinese Buddhist sculpture helps to explain why we find so many heads in Western collections and so few complete statues. Dealers' agents, who during the first decades of the century steadily despoiled the great cave-shrines of north China, rarely bothered to take away more than the heads. What they left behind was not only more difficult to remove but also commercially far less valuable.

2. R. Fry, *Vision and Design*, London 1920, p. 66.

3. The Fêng family was famous for its sculpture during the fourteenth and fifteenth centuries. A wooden image of Avalokiteśvara (p. 364) now in the Metropolitan Museum, New York, is dated 1385 in its inscription, which also

we would call monumental masons, and the sensibility they express is not personal, but is a common quality of race and age. We are dealing with a 'primitive' art.

So much having been said by way of implied criticism, the reader may be wondering why one bothers with Chinese Buddhist sculpture at all. The answer is that its limitations – failure to conceive of human form in the round, and concentration of interest in the mask – do not as a rule detract from the imaginative appeal it exercises. That appeal may not be entirely aesthetic, but the same could be said of both Greek and Indian sculpture. All were arts pressed into the service of religion, and the distinctive form taken by Chinese sculpture was no less meaningful in its own way than that of the others. Moreover, I have stressed only its broad observable features. But so prolific is this art-form that scores of examples might be found to challenge, for example, the contention that the body is less powerfully expressive than the mask. It is only when we consider Chinese sculpture *en masse* that general laws governing its treatment become evident. For among this great bulk of material are many pieces so freely and wilfully conceived, and so brilliantly executed, that they transcend mere formulae and rank as works of high art. It is for their sake that we prize Chinese Buddhist sculpture. And for the sake, too, of countless thousands of lesser pieces – the sculptures of the cave-shrines, the gilt-bronze statuettes, and so forth – which do not pretend to be high art, but which have an unaffected charm and vigour and a happy air about them. This was a popular, journeyman art. Considerations of time and cost are often betrayed in the summary workmanship of these small votive pieces, and the repetitive nature of the work tends, as I have said, to obliterate personal sensibility. Yet it retains distinction and even majesty, owing perhaps to its simple and direct mode of expression, unmarred by overtones of sentimentality or the falsely dramatic.

The Period under Discussion

Buddhist sculpture began to be made soon after the beginning of our era in China. It has gone on being made ever since. Buddhism, of

gives its maker's name as Fêng Hsiao-chung. It names him *tai chao* (p. 517). A bronze Taoist group was cast by Fêng Chih-pao and Fêng Li in A.D. 1429. Cf. L. Bachofer (see footnote p. 289), pp. 83–4.

course, came to China from India, and the evolution of Chinese Buddhist sculpture has from time to time been affected by contact with Indian models. We can trace three main impulses of this sort, corresponding to the three chief stylistic phases into which Dr Sirén classifies Chinese Buddhist sculpture:

1. *The Archaic Period. From the beginning of the fifth to the middle of the sixth century* A.D.
2. *The Transitional Period. From about* A.D. *550 to 618.*
3. *The Period of Maturity. From the beginning of the T'ang dynasty in* A.D. *618 until about* A.D. *750.*

At the opening of the 'archaic' period China had acquired a sculptural style derived ultimately from the Indian Buddhist sculpture of Mathurā (p. 322), but bearing witness to complex interaction between this and the hybrid art of Gandhāra (p. 323). We do not know how far back before the fifth century this phase goes; but we can trace it by actual examples as far as A.D. 338 – at which date we start our account of it – and there are literary references to still earlier images which I shall mention presently. The two Indian schools mentioned above are, however, the earliest known to us in which the Buddha image appears. And, as we shall see, neither can be much older than the end of the first century A.D. It therefore seems unlikely that we shall ever have to account for any phase of Chinese Buddhist sculpture earlier than that called 'archaic' by Dr Sirén. The beginning of the 'transitional' period is marked by new influences coming from native Indian Gupta art (p. 375) and so is the beginning of the period of 'maturity'.

Exception might be taken to the use of words such as 'archaic' and 'mature' to distinguish between styles, and I prefer the less equivocal classification into numbered phases employed by Professor Yetts. Apart from the fact that descriptive labels are avoided, this system is much the same as Sirén's, except that Yetts brings his Third Phase to an end in A.D. 844, the year of the Third Great Persecution of Buddhism. A fourth Phase contains sculpture made between that time and the present day. It is one marked by steady loss of artistic integrity, and we omit it altogether here. Before going any further, the reader may like to look at plates 25, 30, and 32, which show typical examples from each of the three main phases, to assure himself that sculpture did undergo drastic changes of style within a fairly short period.

Against this stylistic background we propose to fit our account of Chinese Buddhist sculpture. It begins in the fourth century A.D. and ends at the beginning of the eighth. It includes the whole of the First Phase, covering the rule of the Northern Wei (A.D. 385–535), Eastern Wei (A.D. 534–50), and Western Wei (A.D. 535–57) in north China; the whole of the Second Phase, including the Northern Ch'i (A.D. 550–77), Northern Chou (A.D. 557–81), and Sui (A.D. 580–618) in north China; and the first eighty or so years of the Third Phase and of the T'ang dynasty (A.D. 618–906). We shall bring it to an end in A.D. 700, or thereabouts, mainly because of restrictions involved in our method of treatment as discussed in the Introduction (p. 7), but also because by the end of the seventh century A.D. the main stylistic and iconographic conventions had already been formulated. I think it would be generally agreed that the greatest masterpieces, and probably the bulk, of Chinese Buddhist sculpture were produced before that date. Sirén, for example, speaks of new styles and techniques which ushered in the period of 'maturity' and 'which became manifest during the second quarter of the seventh century (reaching their full development about the middle of the century).' [1]

Again, return of pilgrims armed with texts and images from India has always been the signal for outbreaks of devotional zeal in China. In A.D. 645 the pilgrim Hsüan-tsang arrived back in China after having spent sixteen years travelling in India and the Buddhist kingdoms of Central Asia. In India the religion was passing through its Golden Age, from about A.D. 500 to 650, and would soon abruptly decline; its fate, in Upper India at least, is linked with the Gupta dynasty (A.D. 320–c. 500), and with the mighty emperor Harsa, who died two years after Hsüan-tsang got back to China.[2] By Gupta times Indian Buddhist art was fully mature. Sculptors had long since freed themselves from the stylistic indecision we find in the Kushān art of Mathurā; and, throughout Central India from Sārnāth in eastern United Provinces to Ajantā and Ellura in north Hyderabad, were working with a verve and plastic freedom that seems to echo the spirit of Indian sculpture before the intrusion of the Buddha image

1. O. Sirén, 'The evolution of Chinese sculpture', in *B.M.*, vol. lxxii (1938), pp. 106–21.

2. Strictly speaking, Harsa's brilliant reign falls well outside the Gupta period; but it is convenient and appropriate, for art-historical purposes, to disregard that fact.

(p. 321). Hsüan-tsang, the story goes, brought back seven statues of Buddha[1] to serve as models for Chinese sculptors. An immediate, though short-lived, spate of image-making now occurred in China, as inscriptions at the Lung-mên cave-shrines clearly attest (p. 349). These shrines are only a few miles away from Lo-yang in Honan, a sort of secondary capital during most of the T'ang period, and their contents may therefore be taken as reflecting the condition of Buddhist sculpture, and of the religion, while the caves were being built. Of a total of 111 dated dedicatory inscriptions for the entire T'ang period, no fewer than fifty-three cover the fifteen years immediately following Hsüan-tsang's return. The middle of the seventh century A.D. was evidently a climax in the history of Chinese Buddhist sculpture.

Sculpture was not, of course, the only art-form alive during the period now under review. But little else of its material culture, except pottery, is known to have survived. In particular, almost all trace of architecture and painting – forms that must have passed through phases of development no less strongly marked – has vanished. Use of perishable materials and the unsettled state of the times must be blamed for this. Yet so abundant are sculptural remains in stone, so vigorous is the artistic tradition they manifest and – as inscriptions testify – so closely are they linked with the aspirations of people of all classes, that we are probably not mistaken in regarding Buddhist sculpture as the outstanding art-form of the early medieval period in China.

This chapter is concerned with two main topics: the subject-matter and styles of the sculptures. But if these are to be made intelligible, we must first touch on a number of cognate themes. They are, firstly, political conditions in China from the end of the Han period to the middle of the seventh century; secondly, the beginnings of Buddhism and of Buddhist sculpture in China; thirdly, the early history of Buddhist sculpture in India and countries between it and China; and lastly, the development of Buddhist doctrine in as much as it affected choice of motives for portrayal.

1. By 'Buddha' we mean the historical Buddha, Śākyamuni, unless otherwise specified.

Political History of China from A.D. 220 to 700

For a detailed account of this period may I refer readers to chapters 7 and 8 of Eberhard's *A History of China*.[1] Here we present only its main features. Until A.D. 580 the political pattern is, to say the least, confused. One petty dynasty follows another in quick and dismal succession, dates overlap maddeningly, and the pattern of states, kingdoms, and empires on the map is kaleidoscopic. Apart from struggles between native dynasts, serious inroads were made by nomads from the North. In fact, no fewer than four foreign powers controlled north China during this time. But from A.D. 580 to the end of the period, China enjoyed national unity of a sort, and peace, after a fashion.

Out of the confusion one salient fact emerges. The South now becomes an area of colonial development, and soon acquires political and cultural independence. Already during the last hundred years of Han rule more and more people had been moving south of the Yangtze to escape the unrest round the Throne, where rival cliques headed on the one hand by Court eunuchs and on the other by Confucianist ministers contended for the right to control the succession. Real power lay in the hands of provincial generals, who alone were capable of putting down intermittent peasant revolts, such as that of the Yellow Turbans which began in A.D. 184. By about A.D. 150 the country was already divided into three blocks, each controlled by military factions. War-lords got into the habit of reinforcing their armies with foreign man-power, and the most powerful general in the north, Ts'ao Ts'ao, had actually settled a number of Hun tribes in Shansi between A.D. 180 and 200 in return for armed help. It was the thin end of the wedge. From this time forward northern Shansi became a base, although not the only one, for nomad aggression in north China.

(a) THE THREE KINGDOMS (A.D. 220–65)

Ts'ao Ts'ao's son, Ts'ao Pei, was able to force the last Han Emperor to abdicate, and in A.D. 220 founded a new dynasty, the Wei,[2] which

1. W. Eberhard (see footnote p. 110), pp. 110–206.
2. This dynasty must not be confused with that of the Northern Wei (p. 305), under which China saw the first great outburst of Buddhist sculpture. The latter is generally called the Wei dynasty for short.

controlled all China north of the Yangtze watershed. The period known as the Three Kingdoms (*San Kuo*) now ensued. In the north, its main capital at Lo-yang, was Wei. To the south-east, enclosing the basin of the lower Yangtze and reaching everywhere to the coast as far south as Tongking, was Wu. Its capital was Chien-yeh, on the site of modern Nanking. And in the south-west was Shu, its capital at Ch'êng-tu, in what to-day is the Red Basin of Szechwan.

The forty-five years of the Three Kingdoms was, as one might guess, a time of protracted struggle. But most of the actual fighting was between Wei and Shu. It was they who were aiming at control of all China, while Wu sought only to consolidate its position by diplomatic means. As a result Wu enjoyed comparative security and became a haven for refugees from the North. Buddhism was able to make important gains in south-east China during the third century A.D.; and the great ports of Nan-hai on the site of modern Canton and Chiao-chih at the head of the Gulf of Tongking became centres of missionary enterprise.

(b) NORTH CHINA (A.D. 265–385)

In A.D. 263 Shu was overthrown by Wei. No doubt an attack on Wu had also been planned, but Wei was facing internal difficulties, and in A.D. 264 a member of the powerful Ssŭ-ma clan,[1] rival to that of the Emperor, declared himself 'king'. His successor founded the Western Chin dynasty in north China in the following year. Wu survived until A.D. 280, when it was absorbed by the Western Chin dynasty, which then exercised at least nominal control of all China until its collapse in A.D. 317. It had no internal stability to speak of. Between A.D. 299 and 306 at least seven major political murders occurred; and the Huns, who had made themselves independent, promptly moved south from their base at Tai (modern Ta-t'ung in north Shansi) and attacked and captured Lo-yang (A.D. 311) and Ch'ang-an (A.D. 312) in quick succession. The Former Chao, a Hun dynasty in north China, dates from A.D. 316.

Chapot speaks of the 'melancholy third century' in Europe. In China it had been no less miserable, but the fourth was even worse. Map 6 shows the approximate dispositions of the nomad groups now investing China along its northern frontiers. But it would be impossible

1. A collateral branch of the family of the historian Ssŭ-ma Ch'ien.

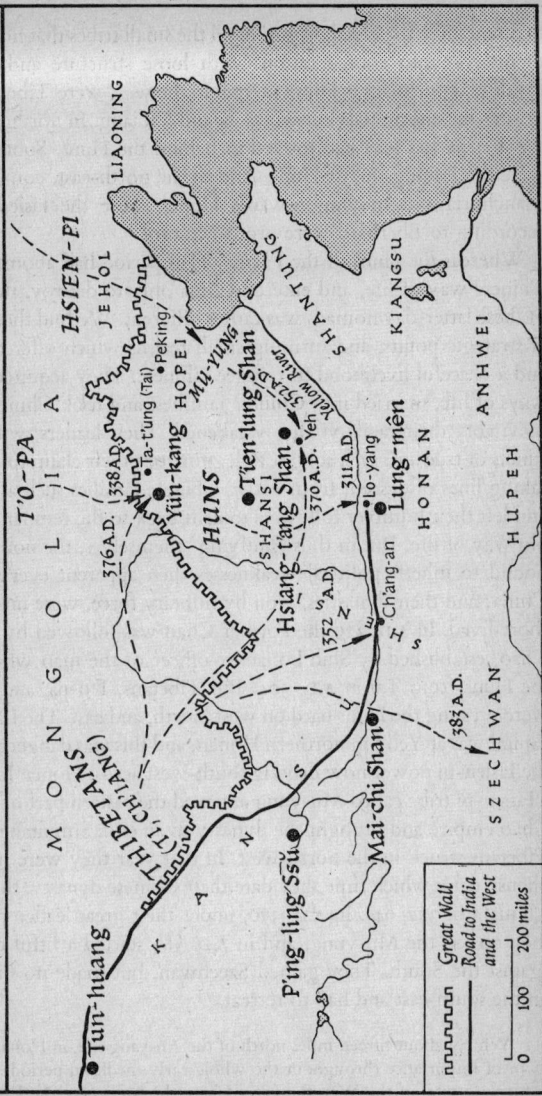

Movements of nomadic tribes into North China (4th century A.D.)
Buddhist cave-shrines (•) in North China (5th–7th centuries A.D.)

Map 6.

to disentangle the racial origins of all the small tribes that now banded themselves into confederations with loose structure and uncertain loyalties. Four main groups emerge. In the west were Tibetans, comprising the aboriginals known as Ti and Ch'iang. In northern Shansi, the T'o-pa (p. 305) had moved in behind the Huns. South of them were the Hsiung-nu, or Huns. And to the north-east, coming out of Manchuria and moving towards Hopei, were the Hsien-pi, who according to Eberhard were proto-Mongol.

Whereas the Huns of the Former Han period had abominated the Chinese way of life, and entered China only to destroy, the attitude of these latter-day nomads was rather different. We find them settling at strategic points, and forming small realms which offered security and a peaceful livelihood to refugee Chinese. They acquired Chinese ways of life, married into Chinese families, and took Chinese names. Inevitably their racial vitality weakened. Their leaders, with the instincts of true *arrivistes*, sought to legitimatize their claim to power by faking lines of descent from native Chinese families such as the Han, and left their humbler followers to drift back to the remnants of their old way of life. But in thus 'sinifying' themselves, the nomads were bound to inherit political weaknesses then apparent everywhere in China; and their dynasties, won by military force, were unstable and short-lived. In A.D. 329 the Former Chao was followed by the Later Chao, established by Shih Lo, an ex-officer of the man who had led the Huns from Tai in A.D. 304. But Tibetans, T'o-pa, and Hsien-pi were pressing the Huns hard on west, north, and east. The Later Chao capital was at Yeh [1] in northern Honan, and this was dangerously near the Hsien-pi power now driving south-west across Hopei. In A.D. 352 a Hsien-pi tribe called Mu-yung annexed the eastern part of the Later Chao empire and brought the dynasty to an end. Simultaneously the Tibetans struck in the north-west. In that year they were masters of Shensi, from which time they date their Chinese dynasty, the Former Ch'in (A.D. 352–94). In A.D. 370, under their great leader Fu Chien, they ousted the Mu-yung, and in A.D. 383 started a fitful campaign against the South. They gained Szechwan, but made no impression on the south-east and had to retreat.

1. Yeh lay about fifteen miles north of the An-yang site, in Honan. It was a town of importance throughout the whole early medieval period, becoming in turn a capital of the Wei, the Later Chao, the Mu-yung, the Eastern Wei, and the Northern Ch'i.

Although the Former Ch'in dynasty officially ended in A.D. 394, the North had been disintegrating for ten years before that time. It was a period of utter confusion. Half a dozen petty régimes date from the year A.D. 384, Hsien-pi in Hopei – and, surprisingly, in Shensi and eastern Kansu – and Tibetan in Shensi and western Kansu. But at this point the fourth nomadic power, the T'o-pa, make their appearance; and the dynasty they founded in A.D. 385, the Northern Wei, proved much less transient than any of which we have yet spoken. It was to become, in fact, the first great patron dynasty of Chinese Buddhist sculpture.

(c) THE T'O-PA DYNASTIES (NORTHERN WEI, A.D. 385–535); EASTERN WEI (A.D. 534–50); WESTERN WEI (A.D. 535–57)

The T'o-pa, a tribe of Turkic stock with Mongol and Tungusic admixture, seem to have left their original home near Lake Baikal and entered north China in the third century A.D. on the heels of the Huns, founding a small State around the old Hun base of Tai in northern Shansi (A.D. 338–76). In the latter year they were defeated by the Former Ch'in, who placed part of their territory under Hun administration. But they were by no means destroyed and, as the Former Ch'in empire collapsed, were able to gather many petty Shansi tribes beneath their banner. At the time of the upheaval of A.D. 385 there were no fewer than 119 of these, including a good many Hun and Hsien-pi groups, all giving allegiance to the T'o-pa, who were fast becoming the most important single power in north China.

From the outset the new dynasty, called Northern Wei, adopted Chinese manners and modes. Long contact with Chinese settlers who sought refuge under T'o-pa administration had given them a taste for civilized life. And when greatness was thrust upon them, they established at Tai an imperial court modelled strictly on Chinese lines. More and more Chinese officials found employment at this northern capital, which had been re-named P'ing-ch'êng in A.D. 376. As they extended their conquest eastwards, the Northern Wei found the task of governing far-distant territories and millions of Chinese peasants altogether beyond them. Administration could not be put in the hands of tribal chiefs, whose loyalties were uncertain, and regional government was left, willy-nilly, to local Chinese gentry. Thus, from quite early on, both central and provincial government was largely in

Chinese hands. By the middle of the fifth century, Chinese at Court were beginning to press for removal of the capital to a more central site. Campaigns against the southern Liu Sung dynasty (p. 309) gave the Northern Wei control of north China down to the Yangtze, and in A.D. 494 they were able to transfer the capital to Lo-yang. The Buddhist cave-temples at nearby Lung-mên were begun soon afterwards.

From the very first the T'o-pa, who seem to have had no written language of their own, were using Chinese. But between A.D. 490 and 499, Edicts were issued banning the use of any sort of foreign language, whether written or spoken; and in A.D. 496 the Emperor took the Chinese family name of Yüan. The leading T'o-pa families had by this time married into wealthy Chinese households, and the disaffected remainder, in the words of Eberhard, 'grew visibly poorer and poorer'.

This policy of 'sinification' was to be the downfall of the Northern Wei. Outlying T'o-pa tribes went into revolt about A.D. 530, invested the whole of Shansi, captured the capital, and massacred its inhabitants. By the time the dust had settled, in A.D. 534, the Chinese had taken themselves off to their eastern stronghold, together with a puppet Emperor whom they installed as the first ruler of the Eastern Wei dynasty (A.D. 534–50), with his capital at Yeh. The T'o-pa had moved westward with another figure-head, whom they placed on the throne of the Western Wei dynasty (A.D. 353–557) with its capital at Ch'ang-an in Shensi.

(d) THE NORTHERN CH'I DYNASTY (A.D. 550–77); THE NORTHERN CHOU DYNASTY (A.D. 557–80)

Political and racial rivalries in north China now set in the old familiar pattern – the Chinese in the east, upon the Plain; and various foreign remnants, T'o-pa, Hsien-pi, and Huns, with a very few Chinese, on the Plateau in the west. The two puerile dynasties, Eastern and Western Wei, were followed by the no less impotent Northern Ch'i and Northern Chou, respectively, in the same regions. But north of them a new and dangerous tribal league had formed. Its peoples, whose core seems to have been Hunnish, became known to the Chinese as T'u-chüeh. They inherited the age-old vitality of the eastern Asiatic nomads, and quite soon began to make important gains in Central

Asia and to the east. For the next four centuries the T'u-chüeh were to occupy the traditional position of a nomadic power dominating the northern steppes. They were the people we in the West know as Turks. Already, in the middle of the sixth century, the Turks were campaigning independently against the Northern Ch'i, who were also being attacked by the south Chinese and the Northern Chou.

There is little to be said in favour of the Northern Ch'i dynasty, whose rulers, remarks Eberhard, 'were thoroughly repulsive figures, with no positive achievements of any sort to their credit'. And yet some of the loveliest of all Buddhist sculpture was produced under its patronage (plate 28b, 29b). Perhaps this was because it was the true inheritor of the cultural traditions of the Northern Wei, grown up under Chinese guidance, and because nearly all the old centres of north Chinese Buddhism lay within its territory.[1] For whatever reason, Northern Ch'i sculpture has an air of refinement and sophistication that contrasts sharply with the rather primitive work done under the Northern Chou, as far as we can tell from the few surviving pieces assignable to that dynasty.[2]

For about four years after the downfall of the Northern Ch'i in A.D. 577, the Northern Chou controlled all north China. Then a new Chinese ruling family, the Yang, came into prominence through marriage alliances with influential Northern Chou leaders. For, as Eberhard clearly shows, the Northern Chou had been deteriorating in much the same fashion as had the Northern Wei, except that in its case 'sinification' was involuntary. Cut off from their life-giving nomadic roots by more than two hundred years of settled livelihood, the T'o-pa and their like had no choice but to lose their identity among the ever-present Chinese. In A.D. 581 a scion of the Yang family called Yang Chien managed to make himself Emperor of a new dynasty, the Sui, after killing off members of the Northern Chou imperial house. With the Sui, China was once more united under Chinese rule.

1. For example, T'ien-lung Shan, well within range of the capital, in T'ai-yüan Hsien, Shensi; North and South Hsiang-t'ang Shan in Hopei; Shên-t'ung Ssŭ in Shantung; Ting Chou in Hopei; and Lung-mên in Honan.

2. In A.D. 555 the Northern Ch'i Emperor became officially Buddhist. In A.D. 573 the Northern Chou Emperor became Confucianist and disbanded Buddhist and Taoist foundations in his territory. This was the so-called 'Second Great Persecution'.

(e) THE KANSU STATES

Kansu lies directly across the main route to Central Asia and India. Control of the Kansu Corridor, or at least access to it, was therefore always a paramount Chinese interest; and in the period under discussion, much energy was spent by both northern and southern dynasties in endeavouring to secure it. Buddhist enterprise was now flourishing everywhere from Kansu to the Pamirs; and the tiny and more or less autonomous oasis kingdoms that spanned the route all gained great economic benefits in consequence. In Kansu, a rather anomalous Chinese kingdom, the Former Liang, had somehow managed to survive while Huns, Tibetans, Hsien-pi, and T'o-pa in turn were crowding into north China. Between A.D. 313 and 376 this little realm had grown in strength, and at one time extended into Central Asia as far as Turfan. Like the south-eastern kingdom of Wu a hundred years earlier, it became a place of refuge for many native Chinese, attracted by its good and peaceful administration. Within its borders the first great Buddhist architectural enterprise in China proper, the cave-temples at Tun-huang, was begun in A.D. 366. Then, ten years later, the régime gave way to that of the Former Ch'in (p. 304), which was in turn ousted by a succession of Turkic, Tibetan, Hsien-pi, and Hun hordes between A.D. 386 and 439. In the latter year the Northern Wei gained control of the whole corridor as far west as Tun-huang, where a Hun dynasty, the Later Liang, had been in possession since A.D. 397. The Wei drove them from the district, and evacuated 39,000 Tun-huang families to their capital at P'ing-ch'êng. This event is of some importance because sculptors were among the persons moved. Work on the second great group of Chinese cave-temples, at Yün-kang not far from the Wei capital, had begun as early as A.D. 414; but not until the middle of the century was any real progress made, no doubt with the help of craftsmen from Tun-huang.

From A.D. 439 to the end of our period the political history of Kansu is of no particular interest, since it always lay within the jurisdiction of the dynasty controlling the plateau; that is to say, of the Northern Wei, Western Wei, Northern Chou, Sui, and T'ang.

(f) THE SOUTH

The history of the South during 250 years, between the collapse of the Western Chin in A.D. 317 and reunion under the Sui in A.D. 581, is fortunately far more pedestrian and uneventful than that of the North. There were, of course, social disorders. Just as the last years of the Han dynasty had seen extensive colonization of the South by northern Chinese, so the downfall of the native Western Chin in the north led to a new mass migration to the south of the Yangtze. The latest arrivals were scarcely welcome. Their thoughts turned always to the re-conquest of the North, where they still had ties, whereas the older generation had long since given up any such idea. Furthermore, the newcomers had no land, and very little money. Yet for the South this period was one of prosperity and cultural achievement. Shipping routes to India from south China ports lay open, and access to the north-western land-route by way of Szechwan and southern Kansu was from time to time gained, so that Buddhism was able to entrench itself securely.

Had the nomad invaders of north China not been forever at each other's throats, the picture might have been very different, But, in the event, scarcely a serious threat of invasion ever came from the North; and, indeed, the south Chinese were able to take advantage of their neighbours' disaccord to mount an occasional offensive on their own account. With the exception of these, of a rather serious peasant revolt that broke out in the south-east about A.D. 400, and of one or two sporadic attacks from the North, armed conflict seems to have been limited to the *coups d'état* that occurred every few years as one family clique after another made its bid to control the succession.

There were five dynasties: Eastern Chin (A.D. 317–419); Liu Sung (A.D. 420–78); Southern Ch'i (A.D. 479–501); Liang (A.D. 502–56); and Ch'ên (A.D. 557–88). They were remarkably undistinguished. 'Nothing happened at court', says Eberhard, speaking of that of the Liu Sung, 'but drinking, licentiousness, and continual murders.' Succeeding rulers seem to have been no better; although the fact that average expectation of rule was less than eight years could have afforded them little encouragement in their task. Only one is at all well known outside China – namely, Emperor Wu, first ruler of the Liang dynasty (reigned A.D. 502–50). He became an enthusiastic Buddhist, and retired to a monastery some years after reaching the Throne, no doubt in the hope of atoning for misdemeanours committed in getting there. It was he who first officially welcomed to China the Indian Bodhidharma (p. 618), reputed founder of the Ch'an Buddhist sect in that country. He was eventually given the complimentary rank of Bodhisattva (p. 341), in which guise he is occasionally portrayed in later Buddhist sculpture.[1]

(g) THE SUI DYNASTY (A.D. 589–618); THE T'ANG DYNASTY (A.D. 618–906)

The military, political, and social history of the long and culturally renowned T'ang dynasty is dealt with in a general way in chapter six. Here we are concerned only with the Sui and the first four reigns of the T'ang, a period of about a hundred years during which Buddhism prospered as never before or since.

Yang Chien (p. 307) had declared himself Emperor in A.D. 581, but the Sui dynasty did not officially begin until eight years later, by which time the last southern dynasty, the Ch'ên, had been disposed of and all China brought under one rule. It was a period of national reconstruction on a grand scale. Ch'ang-an, capital during the reign of Yang Chien (Emperor Wên, reigned A.D. 589–605), and Lo-yang, capital during the reign of his son (Emperor Yang, reigned A.D. 605–18), were extensively laid out and rebuilt. New fortifications were put up along the line of the Great Wall; and vast canal works were completed by which Ch'ang-an, Lo-yang, and the lower Yangtze region were linked by water. All this led to social unrest, and hastened the fall of the dynasty, but helped to put its successor on a solid footing. For the greatness of the T'ang dynasty rested largely on administrative reforms and public works which had been begun during this short transitional period, much as did that of the Han upon Ch'in statecraft.[2]

The Sui Emperors were great patrons of Buddhism. For purely practical reasons, as Eberhard points out, Emperor Wên opposed Confucianism, yet he seems also to have had a positive hankering for the elegance and grandeur with which Buddhism and its works could ennoble daily life. He introduced laws protecting Buddhist property. And we are told that he ordered the construction of nearly 4,000

1. For instance, on the eastern of twin pagodas at Chüan Chou (Marco Polo's 'Zayton') in Fukien, dating from the thirteenth century. Cf. G. Ecke and P. Demiéville, *The Twin Pagodas of Zayton*, Cambridge, Mass. 1935, pl. 49.

2. A fair comment is perhaps that made by a Chinese administrator of the sixteenth century, who wrote that Emperor Yang had 'shortened the life of his dynasty by a number of years, but benefited posterity unto ten thousand generations'. Cf. L. C. Goodrich, *A Short History of the Chinese People*, London 1943, p. 114.

temples; old images to the number of a million and a half were to be repaired, and over 100,000 new ones made of materials such as gold, ivory, bronze, sandalwood, lacquer, and stone.[1] This Imperial patronage is reflected by the large number of known sculptures bearing Sui dynasty dates, and by a perceptible development in their style and execution (plate 30).

Along the northern frontier the Turks had meanwhile split into two factions and Sui foreign policy was to keep them apart. It was not unsuccessful; nevertheless, in A.D. 615, the Turks launched an attack and managed to surround Emperor Yang and his troops in the Ordos. He was extricated by a young Chinese commander called Li Shih-min, but this was the effective end of Sui rule. Emperor Yang retired to his pleasure palace at Yang Chou (the modern Chiang-tu) on the lower Yangtze; and Li Shih-min, his prestige greatly increased, overran the whole country and founded the T'ang dynasty three years later, making Ch'ang-an its capital.

For the first nine years of the new dynasty, during which Li Shih-min placed his father on the Throne, Buddhism was under a cloud. The Emperor, Kao-tsu, was a Confucianist who listened approvingly to a memorial presented by his minister, Fu I, pointing out that seclusion of monks and nuns was contrary to the tenets of Confucianism.[2] Buddhism was proscribed in A.D. 626. Only three Buddhist and two Taoist temples were to be allowed in the capital, and one of each in each province; monasteries and nunneries were to be disbanded and their occupants sent out into the world to marry. The regulations were never enforced. Nevertheless, Kao-tsu's reign was a bad time for Buddhist enterprise, and not a single known piece of sculpture can be dated to it.

With the accession of Li Shih-min as Emperor T'ai-tsung (A.D. 627–50), the pendulum swung again in favour of Buddhism. It was the period of Hsüan-tsang's travels, and of a great spate of image making at Lung-mên. On his return, Hsüan-tsang installed himself at Ch'ang-an and set to work translating Indian Buddhist scriptures.

1. Cf. O. Sirén, *Chinese Sculpture from the Fifth to the Fourteenth Century*, 1 vol. text, 3 vols plates, London 1925, vol. i, p. lxiii.

2. The gist of the Confucianist case put by Fu I appears in his statement: 'We say that life and death, riches and poverty, are at the disposal of Heaven; they say that it is the idol which has control of this.' For reference to this and other material contained in the above paragraph cf. O. Sirén (see footnote above), vol. i, pp. lxxxvi–lxxxvii.

Others joined him, and for the next hundred years or so Ch'ang-an became a great centre of Buddhist scholarship, visited by pilgrims from Japan, Korea, and other countries of Far Eastern Buddhism. Texts were translated into Chinese, and thence into Uighur Turk, Tibetan, Korean, and Japanese.

Patronage of Buddhism was continued by the third T'ang ruler, Kao-tsung (A.D. 650-83), and by his successor, Empress Wu (A.D. 684-705). This extraordinary person, daughter of a provincial governor, had been a concubine of Emperor T'ai-tsung at the age of fourteen. Following brief retirement to a Buddhist monastery upon his death, she became in turn Kao-tsung's concubine and Empress, after murdering her own daughter by the Emperor and causing the rightful Empress's hands and feet to be cut off. When Kao-tsung died in A.D. 683 – probably poisoned by his consort – she manœuvred one of her sons on to the Throne and thenceforth ran the country as she chose. In A.D. 689 she openly proclaimed herself 'Emperor', changed the name of the dynasty to Chou, drastically altered the calendar, and introduced a dozen or so new characters into the written language. In the meantime she carried on an intrigue with a disreputable Buddhist monk for whom she built a temple, and whom she eventually had murdered.

The Empress strongly favoured Buddhism. In A.D. 672, for example, we find her giving 20,000 strings of cash towards making a colossal image of Amitābha Buddha (p. 382) at Lung-mên. Vast sums were now spent in endowing Buddhist temples, and more images were made than at any other time during the T'ang period. They were not always approved of. The famous Buddhist priest Tao-hsüan complained that the sculptors made them indistinguishable from dancing-girls 'so that every court wanton imagined that she looked like a Bodhisattva'.[1] Empress Wu, who seemed to be aiming at becoming religious as well as secular head of the Empire, certainly believed that she herself was one. By dexterous interpolations in one of the scriptures she managed to pose as a reincarnation of the Bodhisattva and Future Buddha Maitreya (p. 341).[2] And it is interesting,

1. O Sirén (see footnote p. 311), vol. i, p. xcii.
2. A. Waley, *A Catalogue of Paintings recovered from Tun-huang by Sir Aurel Stein, K.C.I.E.*, London 1931, Introd., p. xxix, says that in A.D. 690 she ordered the translation of *Mahāmogha* or 'Great Cloud' *sūtra* (*Ta yün ch'ing yu ching*) in which passages were inserted to prove that Maitreya would one day descend to earth and rule China as a woman.

although almost certainly coincidence, that about this time the forms of Bodhisattvas in sculpture, hitherto represented as male, begin to wear a decidedly feminine air (plate 32). There was a strong element of truth in Tao-hsüan's assertion.

The Beginnings of Buddhism and of Buddhist Sculpture in China

We have now to go back on our tracks to notice a few early literary references to Buddhism in China, and to the making of Buddhist images in the period before the first known dated examples. These records, when combined with information yielded by yet earlier surviving Indian images, are invaluable in helping us to trace the stages by which style and iconography in Chinese Buddhist sculpture grew away from their roots in native India. They have been ably summarized by Yetts.[1]

The date officially given by the Chinese for the coming of Buddhism to their country is A.D. 64. In that year, they say, Emperor Ming of the Latter Han dynasty (reigned A.D. 58-76), dreamt that a divine personage appeared before him emitting a holy light, his head encircled by a halo that glowed like the sun and moon. The Emperor's wise men then told him that such a one had lived in India and was called Buddha. He thereupon despatched a mission to the Ta Yüeh-chih, who by this time had established the Kushān Empire in north-west India (p. 180). A Buddhist scripture (sūtra) was brought back in A.D. 66.

The story, which first appeared in the second century A.D., received various glosses during the fourth and fifth centuries. These added, among other things, that Indian monks accompanied the mission on its return, bearing a copy of a famous image of Buddha on a white horse. But Henri Maspero has been able to show that the whole account is a pious fraud.[2] In fact, the first genuine known reference to Buddhism in Chinese literature, though made at a later date, refers to an earlier event. Wei lüeh (p. 214) records that an ambassador from the

1. W. P. Yetts, *The George Eumorfopoulos Collection Catalogue of the Chinese and Corean Bronzes, Sculpture, Jades, Jewellery, and Miscellaneous Objects. Vol. 3, Buddhist Sculpture*, London 1932, pp. 1-8.

2. H. Maspero, 1, 'Le songe et l'ambassade de l'empereur Ming', in *B.E.F.E.O.* vol. x (1910), pp. 95-130.

Ta Yüeh-chih was giving oral instruction to a Chinese official in China on the tenets of Buddhism in 2 B.C. The stories, it will be noticed, agree that contact with the new religion came by way of the Ta Yüeh-chih, by land along the Silk Road from the West.

In the light of present knowledge it seems most improbable that any image of Buddha was made in China at this time. Indeed, we have no reason to suppose that such a thing was then to be found any-where in the Buddhist world, India included. All evidence suggests the first century A.D. as the earliest possible date for the first Indian Buddha image; and making allowance for time taken to reach China, one could scarcely expect to find it in that country before, say, the beginning of the second century A.D.[1]

The oldest reliable reference to actual Buddha images in China re-lates to the year A.D. 166, when an anti-Buddhist memorial, the first of its kind, was delivered to the Throne by an astrologer named Hsiang Ch'iai. He criticizes its preoccupation with mystical religions, and mentions statues of Taoist personages – the mythical Huang Ti and the quasi-historical Lao Tzŭ – and also of Buddha.

Maspero has shown that by the end of the second century A.D. a Buddhist community was flourishing at Lo-yang. It seems that the first Chinese Buddhist monk was ordained there in A.D. 180. His name was Yen Fou-t'iao, and he is best known because of the translation bureau he set up at Lo-yang in partnership with a certain An Shih-kao. This man, the story goes, had been a prince of Parthia who gave up his throne to become a Buddhist priest, and who made his way to China in the middle of the century, bringing with him a number of texts. An Shih-kao is credited with translations of 176 books, by no means all of them scriptures.[2] The languages in which these books – the first foreign texts to be translated into Chinese – were written, included not only Sanscrit and other Indian languages but also Iranian dialects such as Parthian, Sogdian, and Khotanese. Many traders and early

1. *Mou tzŭ li huo*, the book which first mentions Emperor Ming's dream, is unreliable; and no confidence can be placed in its statement that the Emperor had a Buddha image made to surmount his tomb. Even more unlikely must be the conjecture by a sixth-century commentator on the biography of Ho Ch'ü-ping (p. 178) in *Hou han shu*, that the 'gold [image of a] man', *chin jên*, cap-tured by the young general from the king of the Hsiu-t'u (a tribe occupying the site of modern Liang Chou in Kansu), in his campaign of 121 B.C., was a Buddha image.

2. Cf. L. C. Goodrich (see footnote p. 310), p. 87.

Buddhist missionaries to China were Sogdians; and their tongue was now a lingua franca throughout Central Asia.

In the Three Kingdoms period (A.D. 220–65) Lo-yang continued to be a centre of Buddhist activity. The first set of monastic rules (Sanscrit *vinaya*) was issued there by an Indian named Dharmakala (Ch. Fa-shih) some time towards the middle of the century; and we are also told that he made a Buddha image 'as its sixteen feet had been displayed in the Deer Park, as glorious and heroically beautiful as if it had been (really) the adamantine (body) under the twin trees'; [1] and that various relics of Buddha as well as images and *sūtras* from the West were deposited in the Fa-yün Temple which he built at Lo-yang.

About this time the South first heard of Buddhism. A foreign priest called K'ang Sêng-hui, whose ancestors had evidently been Sogdians living in India, and whose father had come to the southern port of Chiao-chih (p. 302) as a trader, 'was anxious to propagate the religion in the South and to set up icons and temples there on a grand scale'. [2] He accordingly set out overland for the Wu capital of Chien-yeh and arrived there in A.D. 247. The officials were at first inclined to be suspicious, for 'this was the first time that a monk had been seen in Wu', but after he had demonstrated his supernatural talents by performing a miracle or two, the Emperor allowed him to stay. He founded the first Buddhist temple in south China.

During the third century Buddhism spread triumphantly to every corner of China. Its progress is well documented, not only in dynastic histories, but also in special works on Buddhism such as the biographies of Buddhist priests *Kao sêng chüan* (below, footnote 2) and its

1. This passage is quoted from a sixth-century A.D. description of temples and palaces at Lo-yang called *Lo-yang ch'ieh lan chi* by Yang Hsüan-chih. Pious enthusiasm seems to have led this author to merge together two separate episodes in the life of Buddha, both popular subjects for portrayal. The 'Deer Park' (at Vārāṇasī, the modern Sārnāth near Benares) is where Buddha first preached; the 'twin trees' are the *sala* trees at Kuśinārā (probably modern Kasiā on the Gandak River in Nepal) where occurred his death or *parinirvāṇa*. The 'sixteen feet' was a canonical height for Buddha images in the Far East. Cf. A. C. Soper, 'Literary evidence for early Buddhist art in China. I. Foreign images and artists' in *O.A.*, vol. ii, no. 1 (summer 1949), p. 29.

2. Passage translated by A. C. Soper (see footnote above), p. 28, from *Kao sêng chüan*, 'Lives of Famous Priests', written in A.D. 519 by the monk Hui-chiao. From this source are taken the other details of K'ang Sêng-hui's life recorded above.

sequel *Hsü kao sêng chüan* by Tao-hsüan (p. 312), the encyclopaedia of Buddhist lore *Fa yüan chu lin* by Tao-shih (A.D. 668), and the general history of Chinese Buddhism *Fo tsŭ t‘ung chi* by Chih-p‘an (*ca.* A.D. 1270). Such texts often speak of early Buddhist images – either imported or manufactured in China – but usually not in terms that allow us to visualize them in the absence of surviving examples. Nor do they as a rule specify which Buddhist personages were represented; so that, since we should not be justified in assuming that the subject was in every case Śākyamuni (Ch. Shih-chia), the historical Buddha, they are not much use as guides to early Buddhist iconography or the state of the popular religion. The sculptures they mention seem to have attracted attention because of their associations with famous personalities of Chinese Buddhism; or because of miraculous powers with which they were credited; or because they passed as genuine portraits of Buddha and his satellites, or close copies of them. But of popular Buddhist sculpture not a thing is said.

One of these portraits, or portrait-types, is worth a little attention because chance survivals give us some idea of what it may have looked like. It is a figure of Śākyamuni Buddha, generally known as the 'Udyāna' image. The story of how the first 'Udyāna' image came to be made is told in a scripture called the 'King Udyāna *sūtra*'.[1] Śākyamuni had gone to preach to his mother in the Tuṣita Heaven, the abode of the Future Buddha Maitreya. He had been away so long that Udyāna, King of Kauśāmbī, despaired of his ever coming back to earth. At last the king sent thirty-two craftsmen, with sandalwood for making an image, to the disciple Maudgalyāyana (Ch. Mu-lien) and begged him to transport them miraculously to the Tuṣita Heaven. This the disciple did. When the portrait was finished it was installed in the Jetavana monastery; and there, says the *sūtra*, it can be seen to this day. Kauśāmbī, it should be noticed, was a small state on the Jumna River near its confluence with the Ganges in eastern Uttar Pradesh, and the Jetavana monastery lay in the kingdom of Śrāvastī in modern north-west Nepal. Whatever was the original image that gave rise to this legend – and it is so persistent that one can scarcely doubt such a thing existed – the geographical locations suggest that it was of native Indian type made in Mathurā style (pp. 325–34), no

1. This is probably the *sūtra* of which a late seventh-century translation exists entitled *Ta ch‘êng tsao hsiang kung tê ching*. Cf. A. C. Soper (see footnote p. 315), pp. 31–2 and footnote 39.

doubt during late Kushān or early Gupta times; that is, in the third or fourth century A.D.

This image was to become the most famous icon of Far Eastern Buddhism (table 4). The story goes that a copy reached China as early as A.D. 66, brought by the mission sent by Emperor Ming to the Ta Yüeh-chih. But apart from the unreliability of the source for this statement (p. 313), there is, as we shall see, little likelihood of any prototype existing at so early a date. Scarcely more plausible is the statement in *Hsü kao sêng chüan* that the famous translator Kumārajīva, captured at Kucha in a campaign undertaken between A.D. 383 and 386 by the forces of Fu Chien (p. 304), brought with him to China in A.D. 405 the original image – 'that made in the Master's life-time by order of King Udyāna of Kauśambi' – and installed it at Ch'ang-an. The later history of Kumārajīva's statue, whatever it may have been, is obscured by conflicting accounts of its whereabouts. One says it was taken south when Ch'ang-an was captured by the Western Ch'in Emperor, An, in A.D. 417–187, and placed in the Lung-kuang Temple at T'an-yang (modern Ch'ang-sha in Hunan).[1] On the fall of the Ch'ên dynasty in A.D. 588 it was shifted to the Ch'ang-lo Temple at Chiang-tu, and later to Pien (modern K'ai-fêng in Honan), which was the capital of the Northern Sung dynasty. There it was seen in A.D. 987 by a Japanese priest who had a copy made of it for the Seiryō Temple at Kyōto. This image is still extant. The original was meanwhile kept in the Sandalwood Temple at Peking, finally to disappear during the Boxer Rising of 1900. It was the subject of the inscription on a stele dated A.D. 1721 in the same temple, which recorded its miraculous transportation to China and its subsequent wanderings there. Our notions of what the 'Udyāna' image may have looked like are based on the Seiryo copy (figure 52*d*), and other similar Japanese examples traditionally linked with Kumārajīva's statue.

Other reports say that the original 'Udyāna' image never left India, or that it did, but never reached China. At this point accounts become impossibly confused. The pilgrims Hsüan-tsang and Sung-yün, the latter travelling in India in the early sixth century A.D., tell of a colossal image in a monastery of Khotan which they both visited. But they disagree as to its height, and as to the material of which it was made. Hsüan-tsang quotes the local Khotanese story that this was the true 'Udyāna' image that had flown of its own accord from

1. Cf. A. C. Soper (see footnote p. 315), p. 30, footnote 26.

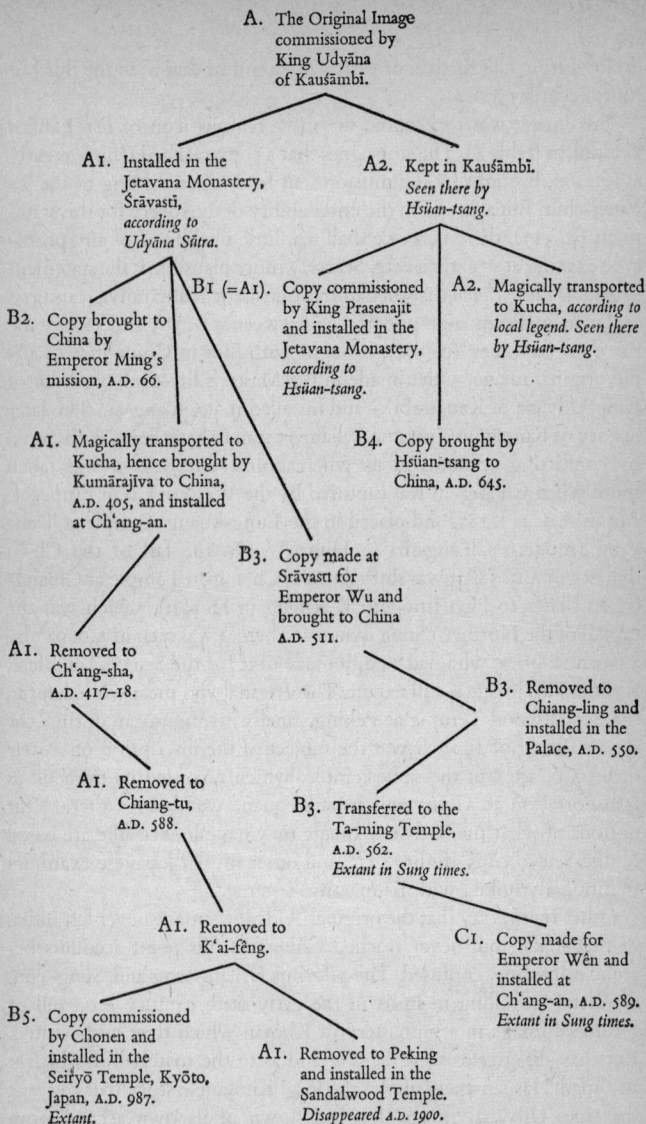

A. The Original Image commissioned by King Udyāna of Kauśāmbī.

A1. Installed in the Jetavana Monastery, Srāvasti, *according to Udyāna Sūtra.*

A2. Kept in Kauśāmbī. *Seen there by Hsüan-tsang.*

B1 (=A1). Copy commissioned by King Prasenajit and installed in the Jetavana Monastery, *according to Hsüan-tsang.*

A2. Magically transported to Kucha, *according to local legend. Seen there by Hsüan-tsang.*

B2. Copy brought to China by Emperor Ming's mission, A.D. 66.

A1. Magically transported to Kucha, hence brought by Kumārajīva to China, A.D. 405, and installed at Ch'ang-an.

B4. Copy brought by Hsüan-tsang to China, A.D. 645.

B3. Copy made at Srāvasti for Emperor Wu and brought to China A.D. 511.

A1. Removed to Ch'ang-sha, A.D. 417–18.

B3. Removed to Chiang-ling and installed in the Palace, A.D. 550.

A1. Removed to Chiang-tu, A.D. 588.

B3. Transferred to the Ta-ming Temple, A.D. 562. *Extant in Sung times.*

A1. Removed to K'ai-fêng.

C1. Copy made for Emperor Wên and installed at Ch'ang-an, A.D. 589. *Extant in Sung times.*

B5. Copy commissioned by Chonen and installed in the Seiryō Temple, Kyōto, Japan, A.D. 987. *Extant.*

A1. Removed to Peking and installed in the Sandalwood Temple. *Disappeared A.D. 1900.*

Table 4. The 'Udyāna' image in the Far East.

Kauśāmbī to Khotan. He could not have believed it, since he himself claimed to have seen the original, although not at the Jetavana monastery in Śrāvastī which he visited, but at Kauśāmbī, where it had been all the time! The image at the Jetavana, he says, was a copy made on the orders of King Prasenajit of Śrāvastī. Yet even this eye-witness account is disputed. *Fa yüan chu lin*, quoting an earlier work on famous Buddhist temples and icons written by Tao-hsüan in A.D. 664,[1] says that in A.D. 502, Emperor Wu of the Liang dynasty dreamt that the sandalwood ('Udyāna') image had come to south China, and thereupon sent an expedition to India under General Ho Ch'ien to bring it back. They found it at Śrāvastī – and according to Hsüan-tsang this would have been King Prasenajit's copy – but the ruler refused to part with it, saying that it was 'the principal image in Central India, and could not be sent to an outlying land'. Instead, he ordered thirty-two craftsmen (the same number as were said to have made the original) to carve another image in purple sandalwood; and with this copy the expedition returned to China, arriving at Ch'ien-yang in A.D. 511.[2]

I have touched on a mere fraction of the 'Udyāna' legend; for several versions exist, and still other images have at one time or another been claimed as true originals. These stories, emanating from different sources and relating to different pieces of sculpture, have in common a mere name and an unsubstantial legend. Yet they disclose an important fact. It is that from the early days of Buddhist sculpture in China the Chinese were importing, or trying to import, images direct from India. They were trying to get at the source of Buddhist iconography. The reason for this is quite obvious. To the believer the

1. Cf. A. C. Soper (see footnote p. 315), p. 32 and footnote 38.
2. This image also had a chequered career. On the death of Emperor Wu it was transported to Chiang-ling (on the site of modern Chiang-ling on the Yangtze in Hupeh) and housed in the Palace. Then, in A.D. 555, the Northern Chou attacked Liang and took the capital. For thirty years Liang became a Northern Chou dependency. During the first part of this period the image was hidden by a pious monk, but in A.D. 562 it was brought out and placed in the Ta-ming Temple. When, in A.D. 589, the Sui Emperor sent an emissary to secure it, a copy was again made and sent to Ch'ang-an in its stead. This copy was still at Ch'ang-an when the reports concerning it were gathered together in Sung times; the other image, at Chiang-ling, had been lacquered, and the lacquer later removed. These details are taken from a Japanese history of Chinese Buddhism by Omura Seigai, published in Tōkyō in 1915. Extracts from it form the substance of Soper's important paper. Cf. A. C. Soper (see footnote p. 315), pp. 32–3.

efficacy of an icon is measured by the closeness of its historical connexion with the being it symbolizes; constant duplication reduces that of ultimate copies almost to nil. What merit was there in merely multiplying images whose models, as everybody knew or suspected, had reached their final form in China worn and rubbed after continual local comings and goings between the Buddhist communities of the 'Western regions'? That Chinese sculptors could take up the Central Asiatic style and coax out of it altogether new and compelling aesthetic qualities did not in the least alter the fact that their works were palpably inferior as icons. Aesthetic considerations were not uppermost in donors' minds. They wanted simply to be brought into the full presence of Buddha and his fellow-beings.

The effect of importing single images was, of course, to infuse new life periodically into Chinese Buddhist sculpture as a whole. And since it was in India that envoys naturally sought authentic relics, China was able to tap native Indian sources direct. Gupta art (p. 299) is one of the most satisfying embodiments of religious feeling the world has ever seen. By the middle sixth century A.D. Chinese sculpture was being directly affected by it. One of the statues brought by Hsüan-tsang to China in A.D. 645, an alleged copy of the 'Udyāna' image seen by him at Śrāvastī, was almost certainly a Gupta original. Whether or no we accept reasons for linking an early T'ang torso of Śākyamuni in the Victoria and Albert Museum (plate 31) with the 'Udyāna' type, there can be no doubt that it was closely inspired by a Gupta model (p. 389). Willy-nilly, therefore, direct contact with India forced Chinese sculptors to work out new problems of stylistic synthesis, and led to the creation of the Second and Third Phases. In my opinion these problems were satisfactorily solved and native Indian influences on Chinese sculpture proved entirely beneficial. This, then, was the effective outcome of Chinese obsession with the 'Udyāna' image.

Having said so much, and anticipated the question of early stylistic influences on Chinese Buddhist sculpture which we shall now discuss, we must add that the 'Udyāna' tradition is not entirely bound up with importation direct from India. Kumārajīva, as we have seen, is supposed to have brought an image from Kucha; and we might therefore expect that this alleged 'Udyāna' image – the one said to have been copied for Japan (figure 52d) – was of Central Asiatic workmanship. That may have been so; in which case it still need not have differed essentially from the type represented by the Śākyamuni torso of plate 31. It would have displayed, that is to say, a visible likeness to the same ultimate Indian prototype, whatever its own later stylistic history may have been.

The Beginnings of Buddhist Iconography in India

For hundreds of years after the life of Śākyamuni (taken as 563–483 B.C.) his image, as far as we know, was never portrayed in Indian Buddhist art. Did worship in any sense corresponding to that understood by the West form part of Indian Buddhist practice during that time? And if so, may we assume that it needed no external symbol to fix on? It is hard to say. We read that on the death of Buddha his cremated remains were divided among the chiefs of eight tribes, and domed burial-mounds (stūpas) built to house them. We also know that the first great patron of Buddhism, the Mauryan Emperor Aśoka (264–227 B.C.), erected polished sandstone pillars, some of which still stand, to advertise Buddha and the Law throughout his realm; but quite what significance attached to such works is not clear. We also have remains of three major Indian Buddhist enterprises in stone dating from before the beginning of our era. Bhārhut, between Allahābād and Jabalpur in Nagod State, is the earliest (c. 150 B.C.); next is Bodh-Gayā in central Bihār (c. 75–25 B.C.); and latest is Sāñchī in Bhopal State (c. 50–10 B.C.). Sāñchī is to-day best preserved and, to judge from photographs, is still a strangely lovely place. But all must have had a disarming gaiety about them, breaking out in the freely-carved figures of female deities – such as form brackets to the architraves of the Sāñchī gateways – that are surely among the most amiable religious images ever made.

Such local godlings, yakṣas, yakṣīs, nāgas, and so forth, have no particular connexion with Buddhism; they are the immemorial creations of village India. Apart from the stūpa itself, wholly symbolic in character, the only reminders of Buddha at these early sites are friezes and medallions carved with scenes from his life and with illustrations to incidents in his former lives (jātaka stories). But in these anecdotal bas-reliefs the central figure of Buddha never appears. A stūpa, a lotus, a wheel, footprints, and other symbols intrude incongruously where we should expect to see his image. A scene leads with mounting dramatic intensity to the culminating experience – and then, instead of the climax, comes only an oblique reference to the object of our thoughts.

This apparent reluctance to portray Buddha, or else this superb understatement, may have resulted from actual prohibition; for in the monastic rules of the Sarvāstivādin sect (p. 340), as Yetts emphasizes, a disciple asks Śākyamuni, 'World-honoured One, if images of your body are not allowed, pray may we not at least make images of Bodhisattvas in attendance upon you?' [1] Or it may simply have been what Foucher, one of the first Western students of Indian Buddhist iconography, called 'custom elevated to a law'; or because, in Gangoly's view, it was felt that neither god nor man could conceive of the Buddha's appearance now that his body was decayed, and that no conceivable aesthetic form could ever be found worthy of embodying it. Or again, as Coomaraswamy held, because the Indian mind is deeply aniconic and does not need external aids to focus on the object of contemplation.

The Origins of the Buddha Image

For nearly thirty years scholars have been arguing the question which of two schools of sculpture should be awarded priority for the introduction of the Buddha image. In eastern Uttar Pradesh, part of the Kushān Empire during the first three centuries of our era, was Mathurā. At the outset Mathurā sculpture was purely Indian in feeling and tradition. But I have spoken of its 'stylistic indecision' (p. 299), and in fact the Mathurā *ateliers* seem to have been at work for centuries both before and after the Kushān era, during which periods their work underwent such changes of style and served such a variety of patrons that one can hardly call it a 'school' at all. The earliest known Mathurā Buddha image, found not long before the war at Kauśāmbī, bears a dedicatory inscription of the second year of the Kushān king, Kaniṣka; a similar standing figure in the museum at Sārnāth is dated in his third year.

To the north-west, across the Punjāb, in the Peshāwar and Rāwal-pindi districts of North-west Frontier Province, was Gandhāra. A

1. Cf. W. P. Yetts (see footnote p. 313), p. 2. But perhaps this text merely underwrites an already existing convention rather than proclaims an official prohibition.

reliquary casket taken from the remains of King Kaniṣka's *stūpa* near Peshāwar features images of Buddha and attendant beings in what is almost certainly early Gandhāra style. The casket is supposed to date from the first year of Kaniṣka's reign.[1]

This handful of dates provides poor evidence with which to judge the case for priority. Nor are matters helped by profound dispute among scholars as to when Kaniṣka reigned. Dozens of different opinions have been voiced since Edward Thomas proposed, in 1874, the two alternative dates 45 and 9 B.C. for the beginning of his reign. To-day there is a very definite tendency to place it in the first part of the second century A.D.[2] And, if we stick to the view that Kaniṣka's casket is a primitive and not decadent example of Gandhāran art, we must abandon the commonly-held idea that Gandhāran sculpture was flourishing in the first century A.D. and even earlier.

Gandhāran art gained a good deal of publicity when specimens first came to light a hundred or so years ago. Striking resemblances to Greek sculpture were noted. The Buddha mask conformed closely to that of an Apollo. And the heavy outer garment was treated after the fashion of a Greek *himation*, its deeply undercut folds stylized to a set formula, yet giving the impression of belonging to an actual garment. It was taken for granted that Gandhāran art was part of the Greek cultural legacy inherited by the Middle East after Alexander's conquests, and the term 'Greco-Buddhist' was found to name it. Bactrian coins of the late third and early second centuries B.C. do carry the Greek impulse in undiluted form, and may be presumed to be the work of Greek craftsmen; Gandhāran art was seen as a direct continuation of this colonial Greek work.[3]

1. This is disputed. According to Deydier, the original reading of its inscription by Konow can no longer be sustained. The best we can say is that the date of the casket is directly connected with that of Kaniṣka's reign. See H. Deydier, 'L'Inscription du bas-relief de Kāpici-Bēgrām et la chronologie de l'art du Gandhāra', in *O.A.*, vol. ii, no. 3 (winter 1949–50), p. 112.

2. Recent figures have been: Konow (1928), A.D. 127–8; Ghirshman (1946), A.D. 144; Konow (1947), A.D. 138 (and later, A.D. 200); Lohuizen-de Leeuw (1949), A.D. 78 (that proposed in 1880 by Fergusson).

3. And still is, in some quarters. Tarn, who holds the view that the earliest Buddha images were of Greek type and date from the beginning of the first century B.C., writes that 'the Gandhāran school ... *must* from its date be in the line of development of the Greeks who came to India from Bactria'. If this is a minority opinion to-day (p. 324), his comment that 'you may search these suave faces in vain for what should have been there, the inner spirit of the great

One can understand the enthusiasm, and indeed relief, with which Western classical archaeologists greeted this apparent triumphal entry of the Greek spirit into the dark world of Indian thought. Gandhāran sculpture was eulogized in extravagant terms. 'Your European eyes', said Foucher, speaking of what he considered the most beautiful specimen of the style (figure 52a), 'have in this case no need of the help of any Indianist, in order to appreciate with full knowledge the orb of the nimbus, the waves of the hair, the straightness of the profile, the classical shape of the eyes, the sinuous bow of the mouth, the supple and hollow folds of the draperies.'[1] Foucher believed that Buddhist hostility to the idea of image-making fell before so exquisite a plastic formula, and concluded that the first Buddha images were made in Gandhāra and conformed to the classical canon. It was a view perfectly suited to the reigning philhellenism of the nineteenth century. For if some distress was occasioned by the thought that the West might unwittingly have introduced means of idolatry to north-west India, it was at least reassuring to feel that Buddhist sculptors had rejected the debased values of native Indian sculpture in favour of something altogether better.[2]

But unfortunately the matter has not ended there. On the one hand is a distinct likelihood, bordering on certainty, that the Buddha image was invented at Mathurā and not in Gandhāra. And on the other, it is by no means evident that the stylistic affinities of Gandhāran art as a whole are exclusively with the Hellenistic world. Thus, according to Rowland, the earliest pieces display 'an incised drapery technique not markedly different from that of the ancient national schools of India as represented by the sculptures of Bhārhut and Sāñchī'. Later, in the heyday of Gandhāran art, which he puts in the second and third centuries A.D., a pronounced Western influence is visible. Finally, during the fourth and fifth centuries A.D. there is 'a return to Indian models, with special emphasis on the transparency of

Reformer' will be shared by many. Cf. W. Tarn, *The Greeks in Bactria and India*, Cambridge 1938, pp. 404–5.

1. A. Foucher, *The Beginnings of Buddhist Art and Other Essays in Indian and Central Asian Archaeology*, Paris and London 1917, p. 120.

2. Cunningham, for example, held that 'the art of sculpture ... in India ... deteriorated more and more the further it receded from the Greek age, until its degradation culminated in the wooden inanities and bestial obscenities of the Brahmanical temples', Sir A. Cunningham, *Report for the Year 1871–2*, being *A.S.I.A.R.* (old series), vol. iii, Calcutta 1873, p. 100.

the robe'.[1] A point of slighter interest for us is that the Western influence, when present, is probably not Greek, but Roman. The word 'Hellenistic' is of course valid for any style ultimately derived largely from Greece, and perhaps one should not try to specify more exactly the Western influence at work in Gandhāran art. On the other hand, close parallels have been claimed between certain elements in Roman art of the first and second centuries A.D. and that of Gandhāra, in the light of which the term 'Greco-Buddhist', with its old associations with the art left behind by Alexander, becomes definitely misleading.

The Buddha Image at Mathurā

It now seems probable that the Buddha image first originated at Mathurā some time early in the first century A.D., perhaps as much as a hundred years before it appeared in Gandhāran art. If so, it was not created out of nothing. There had long been a flourishing Jain community at Mathurā. Now Jainism shares with Buddhism not only fundamental doctrines of transmigration of souls and final liberation from the cycle of rebirth (p. 340), but also the same sacred symbols and decorative motives in sculpture, and in architecture the practice of building *stūpas* surrounded by railings and gateways. Indian art, as has often been remarked, is non-sectarian; one looks especially for free iconographic intercourse between two Indian religions so closely similar and so intimately connected as were Buddhism and Jainism at Mathurā at the beginning of our era. Since seated images of the Jinas in the form of relief medallions (*āyāgapaṭa*) can be dated about that time,[2] and since Jina is exactly the Jain equivalent of Buddha – each being on occasion called by the other's name (p. 344) – we need not look beyond a Jain image for the prototype of the seated Buddha: Not only this but, rooted in both religions, less articulate cults of tree-spirits, of *nāgas*, of *stūpas*, and of *yakṣas* constantly seek expression and irresistibly burst through into the sculpture. One type of standing

1. B. Rowland, 'Notes on the dated statues of the Northern Wei dynasty and the beginnings of Buddhist sculpture in China', in *A.B.*, vol. xix (1937), p. 94.

2. The earliest known dated Jain image, that of the Goddess Āryavatī, was dedicated by the lady Āmohinī in 57 B.C. Cf. J. E. van Lohuizen-de Leeuw, *The 'Scythian' Period*, Leyden 1949, pp. 147–8.

Buddha image, according to Coomaraswamy, is based on a *yakṣa* model. We will deal with this type first.

Figure 49a and b shows a *yakṣa* image of Mathurā type found at Patna, together with an early standing Mathurā Buddha, now in the Musée Guimet. The Patna piece probably dates from the second cen-

a   b

Figure 49. Two standing images: *a*, *yakṣa* from Patna in the India Museum, Calcutta; *b*, Buddha from Mathurā in the Musée Guimet, Paris.

tury B.C., while the Buddha image resembles in point of style that dedicated in Kaniṣka's third year (p. 322) and so can be assigned to the end of the first century A.D. or rather later. Apart from the somewhat ungainly monumentality shared by the two figures here illustrated, they have a number of finer points of resemblance. Both are inclined to corpulence, with prominent breasts and deep navels. Both stand in strict frontal pose, the weight evenly distributed between the two feet. In both, as far as can be told, the right arm is uplifted and the left lowered to the hip with its hand clenched.[1] Both wear an under-garment (*antaravāsaka*) tied at the waist with a girdle, the lappets of which hang down between the legs or on to the right thigh. The standing Buddha has also an upper garment (*sanghāṭī*) of some thin material (p. 333) draped over the left shoulder, its top hem crossing the chest diagonally to the opposite side, its bottom hem carried up to fold over the left wrist. The folds of this garment are summarily drawn as a fan-tracery of delicate, incised pleats on the left shoulder and across the thighs; and it is closely moulded to the body of the wearer, so that it in no way conceals the underlying contours. In the *yakṣa* image it takes the form of a roll of material, or shawl, thrown over the left shoulder and passing across the body in the usual way. Not too much need be made of this discrepancy, since a time interval of over three hundred years may be involved. And Mme Lohuizen-de Leeuw claims to have partly bridged the gap by identification of Buddha images which she takes to be earlier than the first dated examples, and whose upper garment is, in fact, a shawl.[2]

A further point of comparison must be noticed. Many of the *yakṣa* figures wear turbans; and others have what appears to be a top-knot of hair arranged in a distinctive snail-shell coil (*karpada*). Figure 50a shows the top-knot as it appears on the head of a seated Buddha of this 'karpadin' type found at Katra near Mathurā, an image that is probably quite as early as the first dated standing Mathurā Buddhas. Now a prominent cranial protuberance is a feature of Buddha images everywhere, and much speculation has gone into trying to explain it. The word *uṣṇīṣa*, in late Buddhist texts, signifies 'cranial bump'; but that is certainly not its original meaning. There exist much older lists of auspicious signs (*lakṣaṇa*) by which a Great Man (*mahāpuruṣa*) or Universal King (*cakravartin*) can be told. In such lists, *uṣṇīṣa* means simply a turban, symbol of kingship in ancient India. Now, since the popular idea of a heavenly ruler was much the same as that of an

1. The Patna figure, which is minus its left hand, may be compared with that of another standing *yakṣa* illustrated by Lohuizen-de Leeuw (see footnote p. 325), pl. xxii, the left hand of which clenches a purse at the hips.

2. For instance, a Mathurā relief found at Kankālā Tīlā, discussed and illustrated by Lohuizen-de Leeuw (see footnote p. 325), pp. 158–61 and fig. 10.

SCULPTURE

earthly monarch and vice versa,[1] the iconographic type of *yakṣa* – and hence of standing Buddha – was inevitably inspired by conventional notions of what kings should look like. Compare, for instance, the Mathurā standing Buddha of figure 49*b*, with a description of auspicious signs betokening kingship in a text of the sixth century A.D., one based on earlier lists: 'Kings have rounded legs ... and excellent thighs similar to an elephant's trunk, and fleshy, equal knees. Kings have elevated middle part of the belly. Kings and happy men have thick fleshy and low nipples. ... One whose neck is marked with three folds like shells is a king.'[2] *Yakṣas*, in accordance with this line of thought, would appropriately be portrayed wearing a turban. The *karpaḍa*, according to Lohuizen-de Leeuw, was a foundation of hair for the turban since 'a long piece of material can very easily be draped on the head, if there is something to drape it around.'

But why are the early Buddhas represented with a top-knot, yet never with a turban? Simply because such a portrayal would not have accorded with the known facts of Buddha's life; for when he renounced the world to gain Enlightenment, he discarded the trappings of princely rank. Here a complication arises. According to legend, when Buddha became a monk he also shaved off his hair; and it is usually understood that the smooth surface of the head in the 'karpadin' type of Buddha, looking rather like a skull-cap, represents a fully-shaven tonsure. The cranial protuberance in that case could not have been meant for a top-knot of hair, and this inclined scholars to see it as an *uṣṇīṣa* in the late meaning of the word – a cranial abnormality.

But the truth seems to be that these images are *not* intended to display fully-shaven heads. In the first place, there was no canonical compulsion to do so. *Nidanakatha sūtra*, for instance, says only that Buddha cut off his hair to a height of two inches, and that it remained that length throughout the rest of his life. Secondly, in some Mathurā free-standing images and bas-reliefs – both of Buddha and other personages – hair is positively indicated by incised lines on the otherwise

1. Cf. K. de B. Codrington, 'The minor arts of India', in *Indian Art*, a series of essays edited by Sir R. Winstedt, London 1947, who says (p. 178): 'The development of the ideals of Indian kingship and of devotion to a personal god, which Indian religious feeling clings to despite the cold metaphysics of the schools of philosophy, are closely interwoven.' 'They did not distinguish between the God and the Rajah,' says E. M. Forster in *A Passage to India*, 'both were too far above them.'

2. R. Chanda (see footnote p. 295), p. 15.

smooth surface of the scalp. But even if the rest of the head of the 'karpadin' Buddha was meant to be shown shaven in accordance with a strict Buddhist canon, the top-knot of hair would probably still have been retained for iconographic purposes. For it was an essential part of the convention by which Buddha was portrayed with kingly attributes.

Figure 50. Development of the Buddha's head-dress: *a*, 'karpadin' type on the Katra Buddha; *b*, Gandhāra type; *c*, Gandhāra type as modified by Mathurā; *d*, 'native Indian' type; *e–h*, the corresponding Chinese versions.

In Gandhāran sculpture the Buddha is made to have flowing tresses, and the top-knot becomes a chignon often encircled by a fillet which marks it off from the rest of the head (figure 50*b*). Here no attempt at all is made to conform to the description of closely- or fully-shaven hair. Starting from the axiom that the *uṣṇīṣa* was thought of as a cranial protuberance at this time, Coomaraswamy suggested that Gandhāran sculptors piled up the hair so as to cover the abnormality, which they could not tolerate for aesthetic reasons. This view also seems mistaken. Gandhāran sculptors were simply making their own translation of the Mathurā top-knot, having as their starting-point the Apollo type of mask with its full head of wavy hair. There was no abnormality to cover up.

When Mathurā sculpture eventually came under Gandhāran influence (p. 333), the heads of Buddha images began to feature this Gandhāran formula, but with certain modifications. The hair appears as rows of vertical, crescentic lines, disposed in horizontal gores that continue over the surface of what was previously the single coiled top-knot – thus again disguising its true nature (figure 50c). But this phase did not last long. The hair along the horizontal gores was now broken up into rows of short 'peppercorn' curls (figure 50d), and this has remained the most popular formula for the Buddha head ever since. Starting at Mathurā, the convention spread to the eastern centres of Gupta art and to Gandhāra. Thence it travelled to Central Asia and China.

In First Phase Chinese Buddhist sculpture we meet all four types. First, the smooth 'karpadin' type of the early Mathurā Budda (figure 50e); second, the version with flowing hair and conspicuous chignon typical of Gandhāra (figure 50f); third, the Gandhāran formula as modified by Mathurā (figure 50g); and lastly, the new national Indian type, in which scalp and uṣṇīṣa alike are covered with 'peppercorn' curls (figure 50h). It will be observed that in all these versions except the first, the true nature of the uṣṇīṣa is so concealed by hair piled on top of it, that one can hardly wonder it was mistaken for a cranial abnormality. Here is a case where change in meaning of a word in the texts probably results from an altered iconographic convention.

While on the subject of lakṣaṇa, two others, typical of Buddha images, should be mentioned. One is the elongated ear-lobe. This is an obvious token of kingly rank, since it represents a distortion due to the aristocratic practice of wearing heavy jewelled ear-rings. The second is the ūrṇā, an incised circle or concavity between the eyebrows. In lakṣaṇa lists it is described as a circle of hairs or 'a hairy mole white and soft like soft cotton down'.[1] Its connexion with royalty is not apparent, but the suggestion has been made that the ūrṇā perpetuates a belief that thick eyebrows, continuous over the root of the nose, were signs of great wisdom such as was credited to a mahapurusa.

1. Cf. R. Chanda (see footnote p. 295), p. 14.

Let us now turn to the seated Buddha image. This has features in common with the standing type, and the question which was first used for portraying Buddha remains open. But the seated image, unlike the standing, is essentially that of a being in *dhyāna* or *yoga* posture; and the image in *dhyāna*, as we have noticed (p. 295), is much older in Indian art than the beginnings of either Jain or Buddhist iconography. It has none of the popular appeal of the ruler-type of *yakṣa* from which the standing Buddha descends; we are here at the opposite pole of Indian religious experience, that of personal physical and psychological discipline as a means of emancipation from cosmic laws (p. 339). Images in *yoga* posture, especially in the seated pose usually called *dhyāna-āsana*,[1] portray not kings or gods with kingly attributes, but ascetics and those who have gained Enlightenment by following the path of asceticism.

So invariable an element in Indian religious practice is the subjective discipline represented by *dhyāna*, that Chanda prefers to regard the image in *dhyāna* whether Buddhist or Jain as a generic type, which he calls the image of the Yogi, or Dhyānayogi. Jain *āyāgapaṭa* of the beginning of our era show it in quintessential form, nude, expressionless, shorn of all emotive content (figure 51*a*). Such images point the way to the type of seated Buddha. A Buddha image in the Boston Museum of Fine Arts (figure 51*b*) has features derived from it, married to others borrowed from the early Mathurā standing Buddha. Thus it does not have quite the unrelenting severity of the Jain image, and stylistically its relations are closer to the standing images. An upper garment is draped over the left shoulder leaving the right shoulder bare in exactly the same way as appears in the standing Buddha of figure 49*b*; and the arms and hands are not in orthodox *dhyāna* position, but make the gestures found in *yakṣa*- and standing Buddha-images. Yet in other ways the resemblance is striking. The internal tensions of the body are the same, and so are the proportions and general shape of the torso and its relation to the right arm.

The nude seated Jain image has a long history at Mathurā, extending right through the Kushān period. We cannot doubt that its existence helped pave the way for the ineffably beautiful and all-but-nude seated and standing Buddhas of the Gupta period such as we find at Sārnāth (figure 51*c*).

1. See Note p. 391 for the meaning of Sanscrit terms used to name the positions of the hands (*mudrā*) and of the legs (*āsana*) of Buddhist images.

Figure 51. Three seated images in *dhyāna*: *a*, Jain *āyāgapaṭa*; *b*, seated
Buddha from Mathurā; *c*, seated Buddha from Sārnāth.

With this wealth of stylistic and iconographic ancestry for the standing and seated Buddha image of Mathurā, the claims of Gandhāra to have invented either recede almost to vanishing point. Its influence came later. Probably during the second century A.D.,[1] Buddhist sculpture at Mathurā became strongly affected by mannerisms emanating from Gandhāra. Perhaps patrons were asking for images made in Gandhāra style. At all events, the outcome was a distinctly new type of Mathurā image, in which nominal adherence to the Gandhāra formula was observed, while allowing the true spirit of Mathurā art to shine through. In Gandhāra the mantle covered both shoulders and the whole body. It was meant to look like an actual garment. According to Lohuizen-de Leeuw it did not even represent the same material as that depicted on the early Mathurā images; for the former was wool, the latter a delicate stuff called kāśi-tissue.[2] In executing images based on Gandhāran originals, Mathurā sculptors still treated the gown as though it were made of this lighter material. It was effectively reduced to a succession of light parallel-curving incisions, representing folds falling symmetrically from both shoulders and enclosing the body, as Rowland says, 'as though nude in a mesh of cords'. The volumes that emerge are those of the body, not of the gown. Nipples, navel, pudenda, the inner planes of arms and thighs – features that a heavy gown would obscure – are distinctly suggested; and the lappets of the girdle beneath the gown are plainly visible, as though the latter were transparent (figure 52b).

The aesthetic result of this compromise between native Indian and Hellenistic conventions can hardly be acclaimed. Yet the new style quickly took root and began to filter back into Gandhāra, passing thence to Central Asia and China. The standard type of seated and standing Buddha images of the Far East thus stem more or less directly from this hybrid presentment, originating at Mathurā in the second century A.D.

1. Lohuizen-de Leeuw places the first stage of Gandhāra influence between A.D. 120 and 130. But this is based on the date A.D. 78 as the beginning of Kaniṣka's reign. General consensus of opinion would put it about fifty years later.
2. Lohuizen-de Leeuw (see footnote p. 325), p. 184.

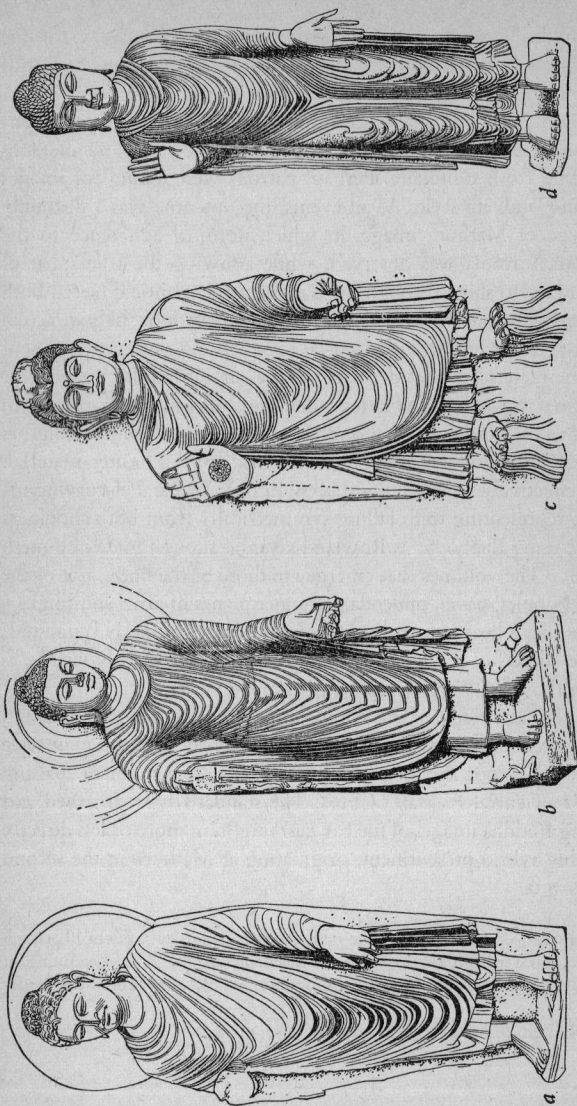

Figure 52. Four standing Buddha images: *a*, Gandhāra type; *b*, Mathurā type from Sārnāth; *c*, Gandhāra type as modified by Mathurā; *d*, 'Udyāna' image in the Seiryō Temple, Kyōto, Japan.

The Spread of the Mathurā-type of Buddha Image

We have already seen that an early Mathurā statue has been found as far east as Kauśāmbī, the very place where the 'Udyāna' image is supposed to have originated (p. 322). Since sculptures in the characteristic mottled pink sandstone of Mathurā dating from the fourth century A.D. have also been found at such widely-spaced sites as Bodh-Gāyā and Patna in the east and Taxilā in the north-west, it becomes apparent that the Mathurā image was capable of affecting style and iconography in Buddhist sculpture throughout the whole northern Buddhist world. It did. When Rowland talks of Indian models influencing Gandhāran art in its last phase, he is referring to images in late Mathurā style. Gandhāran Buddhist sculpture, originating in the Taxilā area and employing the soft blue talcose schist and green phyllite of the Swāt River valley, spread north into Afghānistān during the third and fourth centuries A.D. to areas where, perhaps owing to shortage of suitable stone, various sorts of lime composition were used for image-making.[1] In this later phase, called by Sir John Marshall 'Indo-Afghan', the Mathurā idiom is very conspicuous. Especially prominent is the uncovered right shoulder of many seated images, the gown being draped in a manner similar to that of the early seated and standing Mathurā images. Again, the gown is treated as though it were of far lighter material than that of earlier Gandhāra sculptures. Several standing Buddhas demonstrate this tendency, which has the effect of partly revealing the body contours in a way analogous to the work of Mathurā (figure 52c). Thirdly, its folds tend to be treated as though they were a series of padded ridges, forming a schematic pattern on the surface of the body; and this, too, is typical of late Mathurā style. A number of other features, including the conventional 'peppercorn' curls and the position of the hands known as *dharmacakra* (see Note p. 391), have also passed into Gandhāran art via Mathurā.

A bizarre image of the goddess Hāritī found at Skārah Ḍherī (figure 53) bears a date corresponding to A.D. 270, and is therefore late in the tradition. Here the conventions of Gandhāra and Mathurā seem to have got thoroughly out of hand, although the Mathurā spirit is still

---

1. It may equally have been due to the Sassanian invasion of Gandhāra in 242 A.D. Use of stucco for architectural ornamentation seems to have originated in Iran.

plain to see. The mantle is nothing but a tight pattern of meaningless channels, and the modelling is appallingly summary judged by the assured standards of Hellenistic art. Yet the image has a vitality rare in

Figure 53. Image of the Goddess Hāritī
found at Skārah Ḍherī.

Gandhāran sculpture. The mask, with its boldly-cut eyebrow ridges and wedge-shaped nose, is no longer the emasculated portrait of some Greek youth. It is a bare 'concept-symbol', as Fry would put it, expressionless, betraying nothing of any interior psychological state; and it foreshadows that of images such as the fifth-century Yün-kang colossus of plate 25. The colossal stone Buddhas at Bāmiyān in Afghānistān are of the same sort. Here the mantle folds are reduced to sharp ridges, built on to the surface of the figure by moulding mortar along the lines of light cords stretched between wooden pegs which are socketed into the stone.

Various stages in the later treatment of the Mathurā-type image, with its thin, clinging gown, can be traced in sculptures at Buddhist sites between Afghānistān and the north-west frontier of China at Tun-huang. At the Rawak *vihara*, Khotan, and at Kharashahr between Kysil and Turfan in western Chinese Turkestan, the folds of the mantle on the thighs no longer run across from one to the other in an unbroken curve, but fall in almost vertical ridges. At the knee this pattern is interrupted by a curious oval boss which seems to be an attempt to render the smooth patch formed by pressure of the knee on the gown; if so, it is singularly unconvincing. Between the legs the folds form a series of crescentic pleats not obviously connected with the vertical folds upon the thighs (figure 54). One further characteristic of Central Asiatic Buddha images should be noticed, for it is apparently distinctive, and it found its way to China. In the region between Kucha and Turfan, on the north side of the Tarim basin of Chinese Turkestan, von le Coq found seated Buddhas in which a fold of the mantle covers part of the otherwise bare right shoulder. Perhaps this reflects an unwillingness to leave the upper parts of the body exposed in an region of severe climate. At any rate, the feature was copied in early Chinese sculpture, and appears on the Yün-kang colossus of plate 25.

From these indecisive Central Asiatic treatments, the final step taken by the Mathurā standing and seated Buddha image in its transformation to the Chinese type is a short one. The First Phase Maitreya of plate 26, now in the Metropolitan Museum, New York, bears a date corresponding to A.D. 477.[1] Let us briefly run over the lineage of

---

1. Unfortunately this inscription is probably a modern Japanese fake. Doubts have also been cast on the genuineness of the image itself; I personally do not share them. As regards both style and iconography, the New York Maitreya closely resembles another in a private collection at Tientsin, cast in A.D. 443, the more polished appearance of the New York piece being no doubt due to the fact that it was intended for a major work. Genuine or no, it undoubtedly faithfully reproduces a type of cult-image popular in the late fifth century, and the date attributed to it is as plausible as any. Cf. H. Munsterberg, 'Buddhist bronzes of the Six Dynasties period', in *A.A.*, vol. ix (1946), pp. 275-315.

this superb end-product of a long stylistic evolution. It originates from the earliest type of standing Buddha images, probably made at Mathurā during the first century A.D., based upon *yakṣa* models. In common with these, it stands with feet well spaced, weight borne equally by each; right hand is raised, left outstretched at the level of the waist; the head carries a top-knot; the volumes of the gown are

Figure 54. Lower part of the robe of a stucco Buddha image from the Ming-oi site, Khara-shahr, Chinese Turkestan.

not allowed to obscure those of the body. It next reflects the Hellenistic influence of Gandhāra. The top-knot is hidden under a high chignon; the gown covers the whole body and is hung from the shoulders. But it is treated in the style evolved by late Mathurā sculptors working from Gandhāran models, for its folds are reduced to schematized ridges. Lastly, it shows the impress of late Gandhāran art and of the schools of Central Asia; the mask is of the abstract type we saw on the Hāritī image of Skārah Ḍherī, and the mantle folds follow the system elaborated at such centres as Kharashahr and Rawak, falling in vertical lines down the thighs, and being broken up into lunulate pleats between them.

One might think it well-nigh impossible that an image embodying such varied stylistic influences could have any vitality or authenticity left. Yet the Chinese sculptor has given it a new lease of life. We may have here a legacy of the 'Udyāna' tradition that stemmed from Kumārajīva's alleged image brought from Kucha.

The Development of Buddhist Doctrine and Its Effect on Chinese Buddhist Sculpture

We have so far dealt only with the image of Śākyamuni Buddha and of those non-Buddhist beings whose images seem to have played a part in establishing it. The reader must now make the acquaintance of a number of other personages long since attached to the body of Buddhism, yet whose presence might be thought supernumerary to the religion as preached by its Founder. What are these beings, and how did they get incorporated?

There was not really anything revolutionary about the Noble Fourfold Truth by which Śākyamuni Buddha summarized his doctrine. Its roots were in Hinduism. For untold generations religious minds had been facing the same metaphysical impasse, and resolving it by similar practices. Even among Buddha's contemporaries there must have been hundreds upon hundreds whose influence died with them, yet who had experienced the same sort of spiritual crisis as he, and whose gospel was fundamentally no different. Belief in reincarnation, part of the workings of the cosmic law, *dharma*, was universal. Moreover, a retributive principle was at work. For as one life spent itself in action, *karma*, a new life automatically took shape as a result of what it did. *Karma* determined the condition of every living soul throughout eternity, and every incarnation followed an identical path of birth, existence, and death. There were differences of degree; a being might be born in a higher or lower form, depending on the merits of its former lives. But there was no difference in kind. All sentient life was shackled to the wheel of rebirth, and orthodox theology offered no reason to suppose that it could ever free itself. The problem was whether a being could, by personal effort, accumulate such store of purpose as to conquer his craving for existence and so annihilate *karma*. Could he escape its gravitational pull, so to speak, and enter some new dimension outside its orbit, from which there would be no subsequent change? The question had been answered affirmatively. Vedantism, Jainism, Buddhism, Shaktism, Vaishnavism, among other creeds, all announced final liberation as their message. The means was asceticism, leading to a state of perfect understanding and recollection called *sambodhi* by the Buddhists, and *kevala* by the Jains. The goal was what the Buddhists called *nirvāṇa* and the Jains *Siddha*-hood. Buddha himself passed through successive stages of renunciation (his flight from his father's palace), asceticism (his six years privation and self-examination), and *sambodhi* (his Enlightenment beneath the *pippala* tree at Bodh-Gāyā). Assured of Buddhahood, he devoted the remaining period of his final incarnation to preaching his message, and then entered *nirvāṇa*.

During the following three centuries the Buddhist community gradually split into a number of sects, traditionally said to have been eighteen. Poor communication between one district and another sufficiently accounts for this. But it does not follow that there was no regional interpenetration at all between the sects, or that they at first differed doctrinally or had different scriptures. Yet in them we can trace the germ of a later split that was to divide the Buddhist world both geographically and doctrinally – that between Mahāyāna and Hinayāna. It should be observed that the term 'Hinayāna' ('Lesser Career') is simply one of disparagement by which the followers of Mahāyāna ('Great Career') grouped together all Buddhists who were not to their way of thinking. Of these latter sects, most can be traced back to the great school called Theravāda, but as far as Theravādins were concerned, the expression 'Hinayāna' was without meaning as applied to them.

The roots of Mahāyāna lie in another great school of early Buddhism, the Sarvāstivāda. The Sarvāstivādin school dominated northwest India from Mathurā to Kashmir, whereas the Theravādins flourished in the middle Ganges basin; it is therefore no historical anachronism that Mahāyāna should have become the religion of northern Buddhist countries, disseminated from north-west India across Central Asia to the Far East.

Theologically, the difference between Theravāda and Sarvāstivāda in the few centuries before the beginning of our era lies in the development of the Bodhisattva doctrine in the latter. To the extent that the early religion as practised had any sort of metaphysical content, and was not simply a way of living, it taught personal salvation for the individual, unaided except for his own efforts. Such a perfected disciple was called an *arhat*. Between him and final deliverance lay a path that only Buddha before him had travelled; and Buddha was no longer here to point the way. The Sarvāstivādins now taught that Buddhahood was a possible goal for everyone. Help in bringing its seeds to flower came from the Bodhisattvas, beings who had attained to Enlightenment, ripe for Buddhahood, but who were deliberately delaying its onset in order to help ordinary mortals along the same path. In elaborating the Bodhisattva doctrine during the first and second centuries A.D., Mahāyānism made itself a religion of universal appeal, authoritarian and ultramontane.

But where did the Bodhisattvas come from? Many, no doubt, were invented. But others seem to have been gods of alien faiths, requisitioned by Buddhism as it broadened its geographical range. An identification has been proposed, for instance, between the Bodhisattva Maitreya, the Vedic Sun Mitra, and the Iranian Sun God, Mithras.

At the same time the conception of Śākyamuni alters. He has not passed forever from human ken. Indeed, the historic Buddha is now only the earthly shadow, the *avatār*, of an absolute and unvarying principle, a Buddha of infinite duration eternally dwelling on the Vulture Peak, whence his messages carry to mankind. Nor is he alone. Infinite myriads of Buddhas have preceded him into Buddhahood, and all now dwell in their respective Paradises, surrounded by multitudes of worshippers. The present dispensation, a *kalpa* containing inconceivable aeons of years, has seen seven earthly Buddhas of whom Śākyamuni was the last, and is presently to welcome an eighth. This is to be Maitreya. And the Final Phase of the present *kalpa*, in the course of which Maitreya is to descend from the Tuṣita Heaven to undergo his last human incarnation, was reckoned to begin a thousand years after the death of Śākyamuni. The advent of Maitreya was expected daily by Chinese Buddhists after the year A.D. 433. It is not surprising, therefore, to find that during the fifth and sixth centuries his popularity out-rivals even that of Śākyamuni in China, as is witnessed by the great number of images dedicated to him (figure 56); or that a favourite vow of Buddhist devotees was to be reborn in the Tuśita Heaven, thence to descend to earth in his company.[1]

All these elaborations of Buddhist cosmology find expression in the most widely-read Mahāyāna *sūtra* of all, the *Saddharma-puṇḍarīka*, or

Figure 55. The earliest known Chinese Buddha image: a gilt-bronze statuette of Śākyamuni Buddha dated A.D. 338.

'Lotus of the True Law' (Ch. *Miao fa lien hua ching*), written early in our era, perhaps in the second century A.D. Here Śākyamuni preaches the message of salvation, the Mahāyāna, on the Vulture Peak. He tells

1. This vow was made as early as the fourth century A.D. by the priest Tao-an (A.D. 314–85) who with his followers worshipped before an image of Maitreya. It was still being made as late as the tenth century.

various parables illustrating the superiority of the 'Great Vehicle',
Mahāyāna, compared with the 'Small Vehicle', Hinayāna, and the
'Middle Vehicle', Madhyamayāna, in bringing souls to Buddhahood.
He forecasts the coming Buddhahood of a great many attendant persons. A miracle follows, when the Buddha Prabhūtaratna (Ch. To-
pao), believed to be extinct, appears in the heavens enclosed in a *stūpa*
and voices his approval of Śākyamuni's discourse. Śākyamuni now
miraculously summons from 'the ten directions of space' an infinite
multitude of Buddhas with their Paradises and 'then it was', says the
sūtra, 'that those Lords, those Buddhas, attended by one or two satellites, arrived at this Saha-world and went one after the other to occupy
their place close to the foot of a jewel-tree'.[1] Śākyamuni then takes
his place in the *stūpa* beside Prabhūtaratna so that both Buddhas are
'seen as meteors in the sky, sitting on the throne in the middle of the
great Stūpa of jewels'.[2] Discourse and demonstration continue. Towards the end of the *sūtra* the Bodhisattva Avalokiteśvara (Ch. Kuan-
yin) is introduced, and his hymn of saving grace is sung. Another
Bodhisattva, Samantabhadra (Ch. Pu-hsien) then charges himself
with the task of protecting all who shall preach the Law after the
nirvāṇa of Śākyamuni.

'Lotus' is an attempt to synthesize theories and cults assimilated into
this latter-day Buddhism. Its effect, as its English translator remarks,
is that of a dramatic performance; and as the various Buddhas and
Bodhisattvas make their appearance, one after the other, we get the
feeling that they are being officially presented for the first time. Its
influence on the Chinese popular religion and its iconography was profound. Motives such as that of the 'Thousand Buddhas' – those for
whom Śākyamuni foretold Buddhahood in the course of his sermon –
Śākyamuni and Prabhūtaratna sitting together in the *stūpa*, and
Śākyamuni's Paradise, are all directly inspired by this text; and, inci-
dentally, are original creations of Chinese Buddhist sculptors.

One cannot read 'Lotus' without noticing how well it sings its
own praises. It is forever exhorting devotees to cause it to be copied,
thus ensuring for themselves 'an accumulation of pious merit the
term of which is not to be arrived at even by Buddha-knowledge'.
Donors hastened to take advantage of this offer. At the Lung-mên

1. H. Kern, *The Saddharma-pundarika or the Lotus of the True Law*, being vol.
xxi of *S.B.E.*, Oxford 1884, p. 236.
2. H. Kern (see footnote above), p. 233.

caves, for example, we find such inscriptions as this of the T'ang period: 'The youngest daughter of Liu Tê-jên has respectfully caused … to be engraved a copy of *Fa hua ching* ('Lotus'). … May it be her good fortune, the fruit of this pious act, to gain merit both for herself and her dead father, and to attain to that wisdom than which none is greater.'[1] But 'Lotus' also encourages the making of images and memorial *stūpas*. Enlightenment now becomes virtually automatic, provided only that the mind of the devotee is set on good works. We read:

And those who erected Stūpas from marble, sandalwood or eagle-wood; constructed Stūpas from deodar or a combination of different sorts of timber;

And those who in gladness of heart built for the Ginas Stūpas of bricks or clay; caused mounds of earth to be raised in forests and wildernesses in dedication to the Ginas;

The little boys even, who in playing erected here and there heaps of sand with the intention of dedicating them as Stūpas to the Ginas, they have all of them reached enlightenment.

Likewise have all those who caused jewel images to be made and dedicated, adorned with the thirty-two characteristic signs, reached enlightenment. …[2]

Here is a religion of the familiar contractual, deontological kind. Mahāyāna Buddhism, at this level, was not difficult for the ordinary man to grasp, even when it offered him nothing more tangible than Enlightenment to aim at. And it was soon to promise much more attractive rewards.

Although Chinese Buddhism has produced sects and disciplines of the utmost austerity, and some of the most subtle of metaphysical speculation, the popular religion has remained throughout at this simple level of *do ut des*. You received a blessing, or you had one to ask. You therefore dedicated a statue to the appropriate Buddha or Bodhisattva, mentioning in the inscription your reason for doing so. A certain Li Chün-chêng, we read in a Lung-mên inscription, 'has made with respect a statue of Maitreya while formulating the hope that his son, Tê-kang, will recover from his illness'. A disciple called

1. É. Chavannes (see footnote p. 292), vol. i, pt. 2, *La Sculpture bouddhique*, Paris, 1915, p. 358.

2. H. Kern (see footnote p. 343), p. 50. The word 'Ginas' (= Jinas) is, as I have said (p. 325), employed as a synonym for 'Buddhas'.

Fan-ch'ing 'for the benefit of his much-loved elder brother, Hsüan-tao, has had made with respect a life-size statue of Avalokiteśvara who delivers from suffering; may [his elder brother] be reborn in the Pure Land (the Paradise of Amitābha) thanks to this pious work'. And sometimes – since popular belief did not concern itself with theological hair-splitting – one gets wholesale mix-ups of this sort: a lady causes a statue of Śākyamuni to be made for the benefit of her dead father and mother, thanks to which pious work 'she hopes to secure for her dead parents a rebirth in the Western Region (the Paradise of Amitābha), in the kingdom of perfect joy, and that they may meet Buddha and hear the Law; and that from existence to existence they may see Maitreya; and that all living beings may enjoy the same good fortune'.[1] The three chief Buddhas of early Chinese Buddhism are all involved in this dedication. Yet each belongs to a different stage in its growth, and a distinct facet of its popular cosmology.

The early and continued popularity of Śākyamuni as a subject of Chinese Buddhist sculpture needs no particular explanation, since he had the prestige of being the Founder of the Faith and since his image had long been established in the art of Gandhāra and Mathurā. Publication of texts such as 'Lotus', in which he is the central figure, must have done much to ensure the multiplication of his image in every part of the Buddhist world.

Nor is the Chinese cult of Maitreya difficult to understand. The first translation of the *sūtra* foretelling his approaching Buddhahood, *Maitreya-vyākarana* (Ch. *Fo shuo mi lo hsia shêng ching*) was made as early as A.D. 303 by Dharmaraksha, and it was followed about A.D. 400 by an extremely popular version done by Kumārajīva. Among the earliest known dated Chinese Buddha images, those of Maitreya preponderate. Wegner records no less than eighty-five named examples of Northern Wei date,[2] and Chavannes identifies thirty-seven from Lung-mên inscriptions covering that period.[3] After Northern Wei times, numbers begin to fall off, perhaps because of disappointment caused by his failure to appear on earth, but more

1. These three inscriptions are translated by É. Chavannes (see footnote p. 344), on pp. 399, 398, and 415 respectively.
2. M. Wegner, 'Iconographie des chinesischen Maitreya', in *O.Z.*, vol. xv (1929), pp. 156–78, 216–29, 252–70. This is probably the most detailed monograph on the iconography of a Buddhist personage ever to have been made.
3. Cf. É. Chavannes (see footnote p. 344). This huge work includes a full translation of all the Lung-mên dedicatory inscriptions known to Chavannes.

probably because another Buddha, Amitābha, has come into the lime-light. Yet the Maitreya cult by no means disappeared; we have seen (p. 312) how the T'ang Empress Wu tried to pass herself off as an in-carnation of the Buddha as late as A.D. 690.[1]

The third member of this great trinity is Amitābha. His origins are obscure. Apart from the scriptures, we have no record of his presence in Indian Buddhism until towards the end of the seventh century A.D., when the Chinese pilgrim I-ching mentions his cult there. Neither Fa-hsien, travelling in India between A.D. 399 and 414, nor Hsüan-tsang speak of it. What is more, no image definitely identifiable as Amitābha has ever been found in India, with the exception of a minia-ture figure that regularly appears in the head-dress of the Bodhisattva Avalokiteśvara (p. 364). The authors of an encyclopaedia of Buddhist terms, Hōbōgirin, therefore say: 'Outside the world of Chinese civil-ization the existence of Amida [i.e. Amitābha] does not seem to be attested by a single other iconographic or epigraphic document or monument'.[2] Everything points to the fact that Amitābha is of Iranian ancestry.

Amitābha is mentioned in 'Lotus' as a Buddha presiding over the Western Paradise called Sukhakara (Sukhāvati). Not much is said, and perhaps his personality is here only just beginning to make itself felt in Buddhist dogma. Fuller descriptions of his Paradise are found in the Greater and Lesser Sukhāvati sūtras,[3] both translated for the first time into Chinese during the third century A.D. It seems a delectable place, with its gardens, rivers, palaces, pavilions, jewel-bearing trees, flowers, and fruits; with swans, curlews, and peacocks performing every night a concert 'each uttering his own note', and with the blessed company of souls reborn into it, who by happy inspiration

1. The last person to have made the attempt seems to have been a vagabond monk of the Ch'an (Jap. Zen) sect called Pu-tai (d. A.D. 916). He was also by far the most successful. His seated image, that of a cheerful and corpulent monk, is best known to us as the 'Laughing Buddha', but to the Chinese he is Mi-lo (Maitreya). Among ordinary Buddhists, at least, the identity of the true Maitreya image, usually relegated to the back parts of Buddhist temples, has been forgotten.

2. S. Lévi, J. Takakusu, P. Demiéville, 'Amida', in Hōbōgirin, 1st fasc., Tōkyō 1929, p. 25.

3. M. Müller, The Larger Sukhāvati-vyūha and the Smaller Sukhāvati-vyūha, in Buddhist Mahāyāna Texts, Part 2, being vol. xlix of S.B.E., London 1894, pp. 1–85 and 89–107.

are said to rise from the calyces of lotus flowers. Here is a final concession to popular taste. The idea of Enlightenment, of Buddhahood and of *nirvāṇa*, was all very well for a saint. But it was cold comfort for lay believers. Whereas prospect of a more or less indefinite period of felicity in a Paradise was one to fire the imagination and rouse the senses. The Amitābha cult in China comes nearer to worship in our sense than any other branch of Chinese Buddhism.

The first record of Amitābha Buddhism in China seems to relate to the year A.D. 386, when the monk Hui-yüan had a temple built on Lu Shan in Kiangsi, and established the Community of the White Lotus (*Pai lien shê*), whose ceremonies took place in front of an image of Amitābha.[1] Out of it there grew one of the most famous sects of Chinese Buddhism, the Pure Land (*Chʻing tʻu*) School, whose beliefs centred entirely around the Western Paradise and ways of getting there. In the fifth century the Amitābha cult was much encouraged by translation into Chinese of the 'Meditation on Amitāyus' *sūtra*, in which Śākyamuni discloses means whereby an ordinary layman may by meditation have a foretaste of the paradisial bliss. From this time, donors constantly voice the wish to be reborn in the Western Paradise. The earliest I can find dates from the year A.D. 518 when a donor at Lung-mên, in dedicating a statue to Amitābha, hopes 'that her husband may be reborn in the Western Regions'.[2] The number of dedications to Amitābha now rapidly increases, and a century or so later he has become by far and away the most popular personage in Chinese Buddhism. During the Tʻang period no less than 110 Lung-mên inscriptions name him as the object of dedication, as against sixty-one for Avalokiteśvara, eighteen for Śākyamuni, and only twelve for Maitreya.

To illustrate the rise and fall of the three great Buddhas, Śākyamuni, Maitreya, and Amitābha, I have put into graph form (figure 56) the distribution of dedicatory inscriptions naming them at Lung-mên during the period of its greatness, from A.D. 494 when nearby Lo-yang was made the capital, to A.D. 760 when Lo-yang was

1. The name given to this image in the description is in fact Wu-liang-shou, which is a translation into Chinese of the word Amitāyus, or 'Boundless Life'. But, without going into detailed argument, one can say with assurance that in Chinese eyes Amitāyus and Amitābha ('Boundless Light') are two synonyms for the same personage. He had many others.

2. É. Chavannes (see footnote p. 344), p. 388.

pillaged. By far the bulk of them, we observe, fall into two great groups, one Northern Wei, the other T'ang. And the starting-point of each series coincides with an historical event. For the Northern Wei group it is the founding of Lo-yang; for the T'ang it is the return of Hsüan-tsang in A.D. 645. We see also that in the earlier period Amitābha (under the name Amitāyus) is far less popular than are Śākyamuni and Maitreya; at this point Maitreya, indeed, is slightly ahead of the rest of the field. But in the T'ang group quite another order is disclosed; Amitābha has come to the front and Śākyamuni and Maitreya have fallen away almost completely.

A fourth personage, the Bodhisattva Avalokiteśvara (p. 343), has always found favour among lay worshippers. His popularity during the Northern Wei period is only exceeded by that of Śākyamuni and Maitreya, if we rely on the evidence of dedicatory inscriptions, and is second only to that of Amitābha in T'ang times. Over the period of image-making with which we are here concerned, Avalokiteśvara is in fact the most popular Buddhist personage after Amitābha; but if we include later periods not surveyed here, we shall not hesitate to say that more images of Avalokiteśvara have been made in China – and indeed throughout the Far East generally – than of any other single personage of Buddhism.

The Iconography of Chinese Buddhist Sculpture

Iconography is a dull topic. But as soon as people realize that beings other than Śākyamuni are portrayed in Buddhist sculpture, they naturally want to know how these can be told apart. Moreover, gradual extension of iconographic range in Chinese Buddhist sculpture is a visible counterpart of developments in the theology of the religion. If, therefore, means can be found of identifying subjects favoured by donors at various periods for image-making, we have a powerful instrument by which the progress of Chinese Buddhism can be charted. Its history ceases to be a mere academic abstraction, but takes on substance and immediacy from contact with actual documents. Lastly, I take the view that pleasure in a piece of sculpture depends, indirectly perhaps, on knowing what it represents. Knowledge, in this sense, offers no bar to appreciation; whereas unsatisfied intellectual curiosity may greatly reduce one's capacity for aesthetic response.

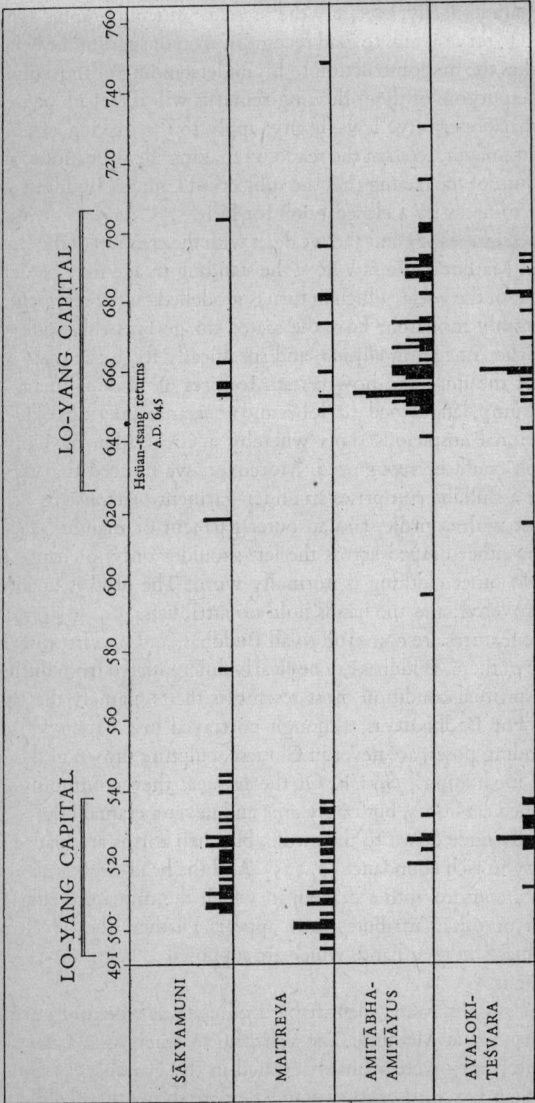

Figure 56. Distribution of dedicatory inscriptions to Śākyamuni, Maitreya, Amitābha, and Avalokiteśvara at Lung-mén, Honan, between the years A.D. 494 and 760. The smallest units represent single images.

349

It is, paradoxically, precisely the presence of iconographic symbols intended to serve as aids to glad recognition on the part of the beholder that makes the first obstruction to his understanding of the sculptures. Thus the purpose of the following remarks will therefore be to consider what prescriptive laws, if any, apply to the making of Chinese Buddhist images; to assist the reader in making identifications; and to relieve him of the feeling that the subjects of Chinese Buddhist sculpture are of necessity a closed book for him.

Between pages 325 and 330 we dealt with the creation of the Buddha image at Mathurā. We saw how the standing image may be derived from that of the *yakṣa*, which in turn is modelled on the representation of an earthly monarch; how the seated image probably took shape from earlier images in *dhyāna*, and specifically from the nude seated image of the Jina; and how certain features of Buddha images, the cranial bump, lengthened ear-lobes and *ūrṇā*, are renderings of *lakṣaṇa*, conventional auspicious signs whereby a Great Man or Universal Monarch could be recognized. Moreover, we noticed that the costume of a Buddha comprises an under-garment (*antaravāsaka*) tied at the waist with a girdle, and an outer garment or mantle (*sanghāṭi*), which is either draped across the left shoulder only, or hangs from both. No other clothing is normally worn. The head is unadorned and uncovered; and the hands hold no attributes.

These features are common to all Buddhas, and by virtue of them, or some of them, Buddhas can be clearly differentiated from the beings whose spiritual condition most resembles theirs, namely the Bodhisattvas. For Bodhisattvas, although portrayed in a variety of seated and standing poses, are never in Chinese sculpture shown in the 'posture of meditation', *dhyāna*. Of the *lakṣaṇa*, they commonly carry lengthened ear-lobes, but rarely *ūrṇā* and never a cranial bump. They are usually nude down to the girdle, but their torsos are loaded with jewellery in rich abundance (p. 375). And the head-dress is always an elaborate coiffure with a diadem in which the miniature effigy of a Buddha or other attributes may appear. Further, they very often carry objects in their hands which are supposed to be means of identifying them.

As far as I am aware, identifiable Bodhisattvas were not portrayed in Kushān art at Mathurā. The first two to emerge – Maitreya and Avalokiteśvara – were probably created in the Gandhāran school not earlier than the third century A.D. They are shown in attendance on

Śākyamuni, one on either side, in many Gandhāran sculptures of that period.

From our present knowledge of Buddhist iconography it is hardly possible to say what were the models upon which these first Bodhisattvas were based. The Buddha trinity itself can plausibly be derived from the Brahmanist idea of the *trimurti* – Brahmā, Viṣṇu, and Śiva. Its earliest Buddhist counterpart seems to have comprised Buddha attended by Brahmā and Indra – the trinity appearing on the Kaniṣka casket, for instance – but this does not mean that our two Bodhisattvas are descended from the Hindu pair, as many people claim. Indeed, the identification is directly contradicted by Gandhāran reliefs in which two major and two minor beings are in attendance on Śākyamuni, the lesser pair beyond doubt being Brahmā and Indra. The chief attendants, as their attributes show, are Maitreya and Avalokiteśvara.[1] The two Bodhisattvas naturally displace the interlopers Brahmā and Indra in all but the earliest Buddha trinities; and, as the distinctive personality of each becomes known, they also come to be portrayed as single images. These, too, we find in late Gandhāran art, while they also make an appearance in Gupta sculpture dating from about the beginning of the fifth century A.D.

The three personages, Śākyamuni Buddha and the Bodhisattvas Maitreya and Avalokiteśvara, were the only major Buddhist beings individually portrayed in Indian Buddhist sculpture up to the sixth century A.D. Foucher long ago warned us that the iconographic range and accuracy of Gandhāran art were strictly limited. He wrote: '... Greco-Buddhist art is still far from having elaborated the complicated and precise formulae of later iconography ... we have no definite reason to suppose that the names of Avalokiteśvara and Mañjuśrī were any less strange in the thought of the early Indo-Grecian sculptors than to those of the compilers of the *Mahāvastū* and the *Lalitā-vistara*.'[2] And the name of Maitreya should be added to these.

This being the case of Gandhāran iconography, one could scarcely expect a better state of affairs to have existed in China at that time. The truth is that over the whole Buddhist world there never has been a universally accepted and applied canon for image-making, least of

1. Cf., for instance, a relief in the Peshāwar Museum illustrated by Lohuizen-de Leeuw (see footnote p. 325) pl. xvi.

2. A. Foucher, *L'Art Gréco-Bouddhique du Gandhāra*, 2 vols, Paris 1905 and 1922, vol. 2, p. 238.

all in the early days. The distinction between Buddha and Bodhisattva is usually plain to see. But between one Buddha and another, or one Bodhisattva and another, there is often no outward visible difference. One might almost imagine that sculptors had no more than two models in their *ateliers*, one for the Buddhas and one for the Bodhisattvas; and that a purchaser who wished to dedicate an image to a particular Buddha or Bodhisattva would be supplied from stock with one of appropriate type, space being left for a suitable inscription to be added after purchase. Matters were not always perhaps as bad as that. Haphazard as may have been the procedure of the sculptors, and unexacting the demands of donors, *some* attempt was probably made, even in early days, to find conventional formulas for portrayals of individual beings. In Gandhāran art Maitreya is usually shown holding an ambrosia flask, *amṛta kalaśa*, whereas Avalokiteśvara holds either a lotus on a stalk or else a water-pot, *kuṇḍikā* (p. 467). This convention passes into Chinese practice. Where, in a Chinese Buddhist trinity, we find one Bodhisattva holding the *kalaśa* and the other a lotus we may be reasonably sure that these are the two Bodhisattvas the sculptor had in mind.

One method, then, of building up the Chinese Buddhist iconography was to adopt conventions practised in India. But this did not take Chinese sculptors very far, because the personages of early Indian Buddhist sculpture, as we have seen, are so few. The essence of Mahāyāna Buddhism is the multiplication of its gods.[1] But this process never went so far in India, or the intervening countries of northern Buddhism, as it did in China. The culminating personality, and the most popular cult-image, is always that of Śākyamuni; until we get to the Far East. As Mahāyānist scriptures spread to China and Japan, a demand arose for images of beings never before portrayed in India. The iconographic range of Chinese Buddhist sculpture between the fifth and eighth centuries A.D. is thus perceptibly wider than that of its Indian parent. How were the new subjects worked up?

Scriptures, although not text-books of iconography, do often have something to say about the physical characters of the beings they feature, and we come across conscientious attempts to follow their

---

1. I use the word 'gods' against my better judgment; strictly speaking, the higher personages of Buddhism are not gods, nor are they divine in any conventional sense. In Buddhist cosmology gods (*dēvas*) are inferior beings, whose store of merit is unquestionably less than that of Buddhas and their kin.

guidance when making images. 'We examined the scriptures and investigated literary sources in arranging the figures and depicting the scenes,' runs part of the inscription on a stele dated A.D. 776 found at Tun-huang.[1] And Waley stresses this role of *sūtras* when he says, 'As regards iconography, then, it is to the texts and not to an oral tradition that the Buddhist turns. Very instructive in this respect is the *Higashi-yama Ōrai*, a correspondence between a Buddhist abbot and his parishioners written early in the twelfth century. By intending donors he is again and again consulted concerning the proper method of representing the various Paradises and divinities. In each case he replies by citing a text.' [2]

Sculptures obviously inspired directly by the scriptures are those that illustrate, in summary or extended fashion, episodes and scenes taken *en bloc* from them. Among Mahāyānist *sūtras*, 'Lotus', the Amitābha *sūtras*, and the very popular *Vimalikīrti-nirdeśa* (Ch. *Wei mo ch'ieh so shuo ching*) or 'Vimalikīrti's Discourse on Emancipation', come quickly to mind; and the motives chosen are in nearly every case distinctive to China. From 'Lotus' are taken such subjects as Śākyamuni's Paradise, the Thousand Buddhas, and Śākyamuni together with Prabhūtaratna in the *stūpa* (p. 343). The Amitābha *sūtras* provide material for countless representations of that Buddha's Western Paradise, in which a charming and diagnostic feature is the presence of naked infant souls emerging from lotus blooms to be reborn in his company (p. 361).

The Vimalikīrti *sūtra*, a lively and even satirical essay, seems to have been expressly designed for the laity, and is addressed particularly to wealthy patrons of Buddhism. It tells how the rich man Vimalikīrti, credited also with miraculous powers and supreme wisdom, is lying on his sick-bed wondering whether Śākyamuni will send a messenger to inquire after his health. This the Buddha intends to do, but can find no one willing to undertake the mission, since all are afraid of Vimalikīrti's powers as a disputant. At last the Bodhisattva of Wisdom, Mañjuśrī (Ch. Wên-shu), overcomes his reluctance and sets off to visit the Sage with a company that includes some of the most celebrated of Buddha's disciples. The scene changes to Vimalikīrti's residence. The Sage, wishing to speak on Emptiness, has removed every

1. É. Chavannes, *Dix Inscriptions Chinoises de l'Asie Centrale, d'après les Estampages de M. Ch.-E. Bonin*, Paris 1904, p. 264.

2. A. Waley (see footnote p. 312), Introd., p. xix.

article of furniture; and the venerable disciple Śāriputra (Ch. Shih-li), who is made to feature as Aunt Sally in the proceedings, remarks that there is nowhere for people to sit. Vimalikīrti thereupon miraculously calls up 32,000 lion-thrones (*simhāsana*). A heavenly maiden next appears, scattering flowers; and 'when those flowers touched the Bodhisattvas they fell from them, but when they touched any of these disciples they clung to him and did not fall. All the disciples strove to remove the flowers with their supernatural power, but in vain.'[1] Śāriputra rashly asks the divine being why she chooses to appear in the lowly form of a woman and she, to illustrate the thesis that 'all things are neither male nor female', changes herself into his likeness and him into hers. This leads to a discussion on the doctrine of Non-duality. Asked to define it, Vimalikīrti preserves silence; thus causing Mañjuśrī to exclaim that silence, indeed, describes it best. Śāriputra now wonders whether food will be forthcoming to feed the congregation; and Vimalikīrti, reading his thoughts, conjures up a Bodhisattva and sends him to the Buddha-field of the Buddha Gandhakūṭa. The Bodhisattva returns with a bowl of perfumed rice wherewith all are fed, and the fragrance attracting the wealthy men of the district to the number of 84,000, these, too, are satisfied. Vimalikīrti then miraculously transports the entire company to the Amrapālī Grove, where Śākyamuni is preaching. The apotheosis is reached when Vimalikīrti makes manifest the Abhirati world and its Buddha, Akṣobhya, with his congregation of Bodhisattvas, saints, and disciples.

This sort of thing made an immediate appeal to the Chinese. They were quite at home in a world of Wise Men and magicians – their own *hsien jên* (p. 266) were of the same quality as Vimalikīrti, who was 'a dragon among men' – and subtle disparagement of the priesthood flattered their vanity. The scene at Vimalikīrti's house appears many times in the cave-shrines and upon steles of the sixth century A.D., significantly, perhaps, in proximity to portraits of the rich donors whose prestige Vimalikīrti was no doubt intended to symbolize.

The impressive version of plate 28a, which comes from the reverse side of a stele dated A.D. 543 now in the Metropolitan Museum, New York, is more full of descriptive detail than any other presentment known to me. To the left, on a lotus throne (*padmāsana*) beneath an

1. I. Hokei, *Vimalikīrti's Discourse on Emancipation*, in *E.B.*, vols ii–iv (1923–8), vol. iii, p. 345.

Colossal seated Buddha, probably Amitābha, with attendant Bodhisattva,
Northern Wei dynasty; the Yün-kang Caves, Shansi. H c. 45 ft (p. 337)

Maitreya Buddha, Northern Wei dynasty, dated A.D. 477. H 55¼ ins (pp. 337-9)

Celestial Musician, *gandharva*, Northern Wei dynasty; probably from the Lung-mên Caves, Honan. H 25¾ ins (p. 373)

(A) Part of a Buddhist stele, Eastern Wei dynasty. w of shaft 44⅛ ins (pp. 354-5)

(B) Seated Maitreya Buddha with two attendant Bodhisattvas, Northern Ch'i dynasty; the T'ien-lung Shan Caves, Shansi (pp. 378-9)

(A) Bodhisattva, perhaps Avaloki-
tesvara, Northern Chou dynasty.
H 37 ins (p. 377)

(B) Bodhisattva Avalokiteśvara,
Northern Ch'i dynasty.
H 61 ins (p. 364)

Colossal standing Amitābha Buddha, Sui dynasty, dated A.D. 585; found at Hsiang-pei, near Ting Chou, Hopei. H 18 ft (p. 381)

Three views of a standing Buddha, perhaps Sākyamuni, T'ang dynasty;
found at Chü-yang, near Ting Chou, Hopei. H 57 ins (pp. 388-90)

Standing Buddha, perhaps Amitābha, accompanied by two attendant
Bodhisattvas and two Guardian Kings (of which one only can be seen), Tʻang
dynasty; the Pʻing-ling Ssŭ Caves, Kansu (p. 388)

enriched canopy, sits Mañjuśrī. He wears the princely costume of a
Bodhisattva and his head is adorned with a circular halo. His right
hand makes the gesture 'freedom from fear' (*abhaya*) and in his left is
an attribute, the *t'an ping* or 'wand of discussion'. He is attended by
some thirty persons. Towards the centre appears the dignified figure
of Śāriputra, also with a halo, engaged in dispute with the heavenly
maiden who stands on the far side of a pair of Ginkgo trees. Vimalikīrti sits in a decorated house on the right, with fourteen attendants.
He wears a heavily-padded gown and holds his attribute, a fan, in his
left hand. Above the house can be seen a Bodhisattva bearing one of
the 32,000 lion-thrones; and to the left and right above the Ginkgo
trees are other flying Bodhisattvas with bowls of food. Beneath the
panel two lines of donors in separate niches can be seen, each accompanied by an attendant bearing an umbrella.

But if scriptures were means of introducing a new range of pictorial
motives to Chinese Buddhist art, there is little to show that they were
habitually used to provide blue-prints for individual Buddhas and
Bodhisattvas. And this was just where the likelihood of confusion lay.
For example, the two Bodhisattvas attendant on Amitābha, as we
read in the Greater Sukhāvati *sūtra*, are Avalokiteśvara and Mahāsthāmaprāpta (Ch. Ta-shih-chih). The text says, hopefully, that 'all
beings can recognize either of the two Bodhisattvas by simply glanc-
ing at the marks of their heads' – meaning the attributes that appear in
the head-dresses. It also speaks of a turban worn by Mahāsthāma-
prāpta, in which is 'a jewel-pitcher, which is filled with various brilliant
rays'.[1] Well and good. But in practice, nothing of the sort is ever
shown. Indeed, in these Amitābha trinities we are fortunate if we can
so much as tell the two Bodhisattvas apart. In 'Meditation on Amitāyus' we are told that the Bodhisattva on Amitābha's proper right is
Mahāsthāmaprāpta, and he on the left Avalokiteśvara, but there is no
evidence that Chinese sculptors ever took advantage of this hint when
portraying the pair.

Now it is perfectly true that certain attributes were generally agreed
to be distinctive of particular Bodhisattvas. Thus a miniature figure
of a Buddha seated in *dhyāna* often appears in the head-dress of
Avalokiteśvara (plate 29*b*). This is Amitābha, who as well as presiding
over his Western Paradise was also one of a canonical set of 'spiritual'
or Dhyāni-Buddhas, corresponding to five 'human' or Mānuṣi-

1. M. Müller (see footnote p. 346), p. 184.

Buddhas.[1] Amitābha is the Dhyāni-Buddha corresponding to the
'human' Buddha Śākyamuni, and is also the 'spiritual father' of
Avalokiteśvara. Hence his presence in the latter's head-dress. Yet
sculptors very often left him out. The 'spiritual father' of Maitreya,
when portrayed as Bodhisattva, is the Dhyāni-Buddha Amoghasiddha, who sits in *dhyāna* with the right hand upheld in the gesture of
'freedom from fear'. It would be strictly correct, and very helpful,
always to introduce this Buddha in the head-dress when portraying
the Bodhisattva; yet he is rarely found in Chinese versions, and even
then, not in orthodox *mudrā*. The same is true for the Bodhisattva
Mañjuśrī, whose Dhyāni-Buddha is Akṣobhaya, distinguished by
the fact that his right hand makes the 'earth-touching' gesture
(*bhūmisparśa*); the Buddha is omitted in Chinese portrayals. As far as
concerns this type of attribute, therefore, its presence is a sure means of
identification; but since it is usually missing we have to fall back on
other evidence.

A lotus in the form of a bud held in the hand or on the end of a long
stalk, is *generally* carried by Avalokiteśvara and not by other Bodhisattvas. Yet almost any Bodhisattva featured in Chinese art may, in
one portrayal or another, be found holding a lotus. The same is true
of the fly-whisk, usually associated with Avalokiteśvara, but occasionally put into the hands of Maitreya. As for the vessels held by this
pair, Coomaraswamy has tried to show that the ambrosia flask
(*amṛta kalaśa*) is the special attribute of Maitreya and the water-pot
(*kuṇḍikā*) belongs to Avalokiteśvara.[2] The former vessel has a short
neck and decorated body (figure 71*c*); whereas the *kuṇḍikā* is undecorated, has a long spout and a tall neck (plate 37*a*). In Chinese portrayals
of Avalokiteśvara, the Bodhisattva often holds a curiously flattened and
pear-shaped object which has been variously identified as a small halo,
a palette, and a pointed bag, but which according to Coomaraswamy
is simply a debased version of the *kuṇḍikā*. Yet in spite of his authority,
I should hesitate to say that every Bodhisattva carrying the *kuṇḍikā*
was thought by its maker to be Avalokiteśvara, or vice versa.

1. The Five Dhyāni-Buddhas are, by name, Vairocana, Akṣobhya, Ratna-
saṁbhava, Amitābha, and Amoghasiddha; and their equivalent Mānuṣi-
Buddhas are Krakucchanda, Kanakamuni, Kāśyapa, Śākyamuni, and Maitreya
respectively. The category seems to have come in during the third century A.D.
2. A. Coomaraswamy and F. Kershaw, 'A Chinese Buddhist water vessel and
its Indian prototype' in *A.A.*, vol. iii (1928–9), pp. 122–41.

When we come to the Buddhas, matters are even worse. For they carry no attributes at all. Apart from accessory elements not on the person of the Buddha himself, which may or may not be present, all we have to go on are the positions of the legs (*āsana*) and of the hands (*mudrā*). And more often than not these are useless as guides to iconography. Amitābha is a glaring instance of iconographic caprice. As the Buddha of meditation *par excellence* he is properly portrayed, when seated, with hands and legs both in *dhyāna*. But it would be unsafe to identify every image in *dhyāna mudrā* and *āsana* as Amitābha, or to suppose that a Buddha not in such a position must necessarily be some other. Amitābha's *āsana* is always *dhyāna*; but so, for that matter, is Śākyamuni's. And named images of Amitābha belonging to one and the same period show him indifferently in *dhyāna mudrā* or with the right hand held in *abhaya*, the left in *vara*.

The upshot seems to be that individual images were not habitually made according to fixed iconographic rules. This being so, how are we ever to identify an unnamed image with any confidence? The answer is that we must rely on an accumulation of evidence pointing in one single direction. A large number of named images exist. While we certainly cannot assert that names were *never* given to images at random, and without taking into account the distinctive features they presented, the fact remains that when named images are grouped on the basis of their names, a tendency becomes evident for members of each group to show the same sets of features in common. Let us take the case of the Bodhisattva Maitreya. Inscribed images in the cave-shrines show him seated with lower legs pendent, the ankles crossed. This is an unusual pose, one that immediately catches the eye; and, by what seems a singularly fortunate hazard, no other Bodhisattva ever sits in it as far as can be told from inscriptions. We should therefore be justified in identifying an unnamed image of this type as portraying Maitreya.

But the identification can, in given circumstances, be made even more certain. Wegner, in his brilliant monograph on Maitreya,[1] gives dates for the innovation of a number of accessory features, culminating in a full presentation of Maitreya Bodhisattva with his entourage by the middle of the sixth century A.D. Each feature can be established by means of named and dated examples. Thus, seated Bodhisattvas of the so-called 'meditating' type (p. 362) accompany the portrayal until

1. M. Wegner (see footnote p. 345), p. 175.

about A.D. 510, when they are replaced by standing Bodhisattvas. Up to that date, and beyond, Maitreya's feet are held aloft by an Earth Goddess and lions support his Throne. Between A.D. 510 and 520 pairs of adoring monks are added. Two Guardian Kings appear after A.D. 520; and another feature of the series is the presence of the Seven Buddhas of the Past portrayed above the Bodhisattva's niche, quietly directing him to his own Buddhahood. Here, then, is a complex of features brought into association with the same being. Pendent legs with crossed ankles, 'meditating' or standing Bodhisattvas, lions supporting his Throne and an Earth Goddess his feet, adoring monks, Guardian Kings, and the Seven Buddhas of the Past – all characterize this distinctive portrayal of Maitreya and serve to identify dozens of unnamed examples in which some or all of them appear.

This series, one has to admit, is exceptional. Other presentments known to be of Maitreya are not so amenable to identification by cumulative evidence, and those of other personages are even less clear-cut. The same procedure must nevertheless be followed for all; and when this has been done, enough evidence can usually be brought to bear on a given unnamed image to make its identification virtually certain.

The example of Maitreya in the form of Bodhisattva does go to show that sculptors worked their way towards conventional portrayals over a period of years, and did not lift them ready-made from the scriptures. It also shows how iconographic consistency may be expected over a short period only; and, equally, how the manner of portraying a particular being may change markedly during a comparatively longer time.

The iconographic notes that follow relate only to Chinese images made during the period under survey and take no account of Gandhāran and other forerunners; although if a portrayal is distinctive to China, I mention that fact. For reasons of space I have had to eliminate all but the most important personages of Chinese Buddhist sculpture. But the Buddhas Śākyamuni, Maitreya, and Amitābha, and the Bodhisattvas Maitreya, Avalokiteśvara, Mañjuśrī, Samantabhadra, and Kṣitigarbha certainly cannot be excluded, whether we have in mind the sculptures or the popular religion that sponsored them. Two words of warning are necessary. In offering these notes I inevitably make a good deal of summary statement which would take too long to prove by citing actual instances; secondly, as the reader must by now be well aware, it is imprudent in the extreme to make any generalization about Chinese Buddhist iconography and pass it off as law. No guide to a subject so clouded with present uncertainty can claim to be definitive. The best one can hope for is to avoid having to fall back invariably on such confessions of failure as 'Buddha attended by two Bodhisattvas' – so exasperatingly frequent in museum galleries – in making our identifications.

I. ŚĀKYAMUNI BUDDHA (Figure 59)

(a) Āsana. Standing pose kayotsarga; sitting pose dhyāna.
(b) Mudrā. If standing, (1) right hand in abhaya, left in vara or holding loop of gown; (2) vitarka.
    If sitting, (1) right hand in abhaya, left in vara; (2) dharma-cakra; (3) dhyāna; (4) bhūmisparśa; (5) vitarka.
(c) Vehicle. If standing, lotus pedestal.
    If sitting, (1) lotus throne (padmāsana); (2) lion throne (siṁhāsana); (3) diamond throne (vajrāsana).
(d) Attributes. None.
(e) Halo. The Seven Buddhas of the Past sometimes feature in miniature.
(f) Attendants. Either the Bodhisattvas Maitreya and Avalokiteś-vara (standing), or the Bodhisattvas Mañjuśrī and Samantabhadra (standing or on their vehicles). Sometimes the disciples Ānanda and Kāśyapa (the former young, the latter old) accompany the Buddha trinity.
(g) Remarks. Since Śākyamuni is the first Buddha to be portrayed in Buddhist sculpture, features of his iconography have naturally perme-ated that of later Buddhist images. On the other hand, images of Śākya-muni display a much wider range of mudrā than do those of other Buddhas. Bhūmisparśa, 'earth-touching', seems to be distinctive of Śākyamuni portrayals.

As for attendant Bodhisattvas, all four mentioned above are associated with Śākyamuni in 'Lotus'. Possibly the former pair, together with Śākyamuni, symbolized a 'popular' concept; that of the Buddha of the Past (Śākyamuni), of the Present (Avalokiteśvara, who despite the fact that his spiritual condition was that of Bodhisattva, was regarded as a 'stand-in' until Maitreya should have reached his nirvāṇa) and of the Future (Maitreya). Equally, Mañjuśrī and Samantabhadra together with Śākyamuni are held by some to symbolize the Triratna or '3 Precious Ones' namely Buddha (Śākyamuni), Dharma or Law (Samantabhadra), and Sangha or Congregation (Mañjuśrī) – a 'philosophical' concept.

In one portrayal distinctive to China, Śākyamuni is seen sitting beside the extinct Buddha, Prabhūtaratna, in the *stūpa* miraculously sprung from earth at Vulture Peak on the occasion of the preaching of 'Lotus'. Often the two Buddhas are indistinguishable; if one is in *dhyāna mudra* and the other in *abhaya* and *vara*, as sometimes happens, the latter is more likely to be Śākyamuni.

A very popular subject of Gandhāran sculpture was the *nirvāṇa* of Śākyamuni, who is portrayed reclining on his deathbed in the *sala* grove at Kuśinārā (p. 315, footnote 1). It is rare in Chinese Buddhist sculpture.

2. MAITREYA BUDDHA (Plate 26)

(*a*) *Āsana*. Standing pose *kayotsarga*; sitting pose *bhadrasana*.

(*b*) *Mudrā*. If standing, right hand in *abhaya*, left in *vara*, unless holding attributes or loop of gown.

       If sitting, right hand in *abhaya*, left in *vara* or on own knee.

(*c*) Vehicle. If standing, lotus pedestal.

       If sitting, (1) lion throne; (2) lotus throne.

(*d*) Attributes. Usually none, but some early images carry alms-bowl (*pātra*) and/or ambrosia flask (*kalaśa*).

(*e*) Halo. Sometimes the Seven Buddhas of the Past feature in miniature.

(*f*) Attendants. Two Bodhisattvas of uncertain identity, either standing or sitting in 'meditating' pose (p. 362).

(*g*) Remarks. Chinese sculptors freely portrayed Maitreya as if he were already a Buddha, and these portrayals are distinctive to China. Images of the standing Buddha, usually in the form of gilt-bronze votive statuettes (plate 26), are an early and compact group, with eleven known examples dating between A.D. 486 and 588. In one of these he holds an alms-bowl and an ambrosia flask. The significance of the former is obvious. When Śākyamuni became a Buddha, each of the Four Heavenly Kings offered him a begging-bowl. Those they first presented he rejected as being unsuitably luxurious, but finally accepted four earthenware bowls which he transformed into one. It became a sacred relic. Fa-hsien tells that when Maitreya reaches Buddhahood this vessel will fall apart into the original four bowls. They will be presented by the Heavenly Kings to Maitreya, who will again transform them into one. Thus the *pātra* is a direct symbol of Buddhahood.

First Phase seated images of Maitreya are usually associated with portrayals of the Buddhas Śākyamuni and Dīpaṅkara (the latter who foretold the Buddhahood of Śākyamuni, who in turn foretold that of Maitreya).

Although the popularity of Maitreya was offset by that of Amitābha after the First Phase, later images of the former are by no means rare. A colossal image of Maitreya at Yün-kang is probably of Sui date and another, at Lung-mên, is T'ang.

3. AMITĀBHA BUDDHA (Plates 25, 30)

(a) *Āsana*. Standing pose *kayotsarga*; sitting pose *dhyāna*.

(b) *Mudrā*. If standing, right hand in *abhaya*, left in *vara*.

If sitting, (1) *dhyāna*; (2) right hand in *abhaya*, left in *vara*.

(c) *Vehicle*. If standing, lotus pedestal.

If sitting, lotus throne.

(d) *Attributes*. None.

(e) *Halo*. Presence of five Buddhas (presumably the Five Dhyāni-Buddhas) in the Buddha's halo or above his niche, points to a portrayal of Amitābha.

(f) *Attendants*. The Bodhisattvas Avalokiteśvara and Mahāsthāma-prāpta, standing.

(g) *Remarks*. Portrayals of this Buddha are distinctive to China. Up to T'ang times he is known as Wu-liang-shou (Amitāyus), after which he is called O-mi-t'o (Amitābha). There seems to be no iconographic difference between named standing images of Wu-liang-shou and of O-mi-t'o. The sitting Wu-liang-shou is always seated in *dhyāna*, the hands usually in *dhyāna* but sometimes in *abhaya* and *vara*. The sitting O-mi-t'o is always seated in *dhyāna*, and the hands are always in *dhyāna* except in Paradise scenes where they are usually in *abhaya* and *vara*. Presence of reborn souls sitting on lotuses, and of less fortunate beings who 'entertain doubt about being born in the world Sukhāvati' still enclosed in lotus buds, are diagnostic of Amitābha's Paradise. Accessory features of Paradise scenes are: Buddhas in the halo of Amitābha ('in that halo there are Buddhas miraculously created'); the *bodhi*-tree of Amitābha with Seven Buddhas mentioned by name in the Chinese version of Lesser Sukhāvati *sūtra* (*O-mi-t'o ching*)[1]; masks representing heavenly children who live 'quite naturally' in such trees; a banner hung from four posts and covered with jewelled veils; the monks Ānanda and Kāśyapa (the former young, the latter old), who were present when Śākyamuni expounded the 'Meditation of Amitāyus' (p. 347); a pair of lay devotees; a pair of Guardian Kings; flying *apsaras*; lions; a *yakṣa* holding aloft a *stūpa*; and birds that 'three times every night and every day ... come together and perform a concert'.

1. This is the opinion of K. Tomita, 'The Tuan Fang altarpiece and the accessories dated A.D. 593', in *B.M.*, vol. lxxxvii (1945), p. 163. The possibility that they are the Seven Buddhas of the Past remains open.

SCULPTURE

4. MAITREYA BODHISATTVA (Figure 60)

(*a*) *Āsana*. Standing pose, (1) *kayotsarga*; (2) *tribhanga*. Sitting pose, (1) *lalitā*; (2) both lower legs pendant, the ankles crossed.

(*b*) *Mudrā*. If standing, frequently carries *kalaśa* (ambrosia flask) in right hand. If sitting in *lalitā*, left hand rests on own knee, forearm raised and tips of fingers held against right cheek. This is the 'meditating' pose (figure 60).

If sitting cross-ankled, (1) right hand in *abhaya*, left in *vara* or more usually upon the knee; (2) *dharmacakra*.

(*c*) Vehicle. If standing, lotus pedestal.

If sitting in *lalitā*, jewel throne. If sitting cross-ankled, feet are held aloft by Earth Goddess. Lion supporters accompany either seated posture.

(*d*) Attributes. The standing Bodhisattva frequently carries a *kalaśa* (ambrosia flask). A Dhyāni–Buddha often appears in the head-dress of the cross-ankled Bodhisattva. In portrayals where the 'meditating' Bodhisattva is the central figure, a *stūpa* symbolizing forthcoming Buddhahood regularly appears on the aureole, supported by a grotesque mask (figure 60).

(*e*) Halo. The Seven Buddhas of the Past frequently appear in miniature.

(*f*) Attendants. If sitting in 'meditating' pose, the Bodhisattva may be attended by standing Bodhisattvas and Guardian Kings; lion supporters; a *yakṣa* holding aloft a censer; flying *apsaras* bearing a jewelled garland; a grotesque mask supporting a *stūpa*. If sitting cross-ankled, he may be accompanied by two Bodhisattvas, usually in the 'meditating' pose but sometimes standing; two Guardian Kings; two kneeling monks in *añjali*; lay figures worshipping a censer in the pediment.

(*g*) Remarks. The iconography of Maitreya Bodhisattva is complex, and the above list of variant types could be extended. Standing and cross-ankled images identified with reasonable certainty as Maitreyas are known in Gandhāra; and I can think of one Gandhāran relief in which two attendant persons sit in 'meditating' pose, though they are not necessarily Maitreyas. But China is the home of Maitreya Buddhism as a popular religion, and it was here that presentment of Maitreya first underwent detailed elaboration.

The standing Maitreya is a cult image pure and simple. But the 'meditating' image which so often forms the main theme on front or reverse face of votive steles, is the counterpart of images of Śākyamuni in the same pose, which undoubtedly served to symbolize his Enlightenment. This event was associated in Chinese minds with the moment when Śākyamuni, having left his father's palace, sent his horse home riderless. Thus the inscription on a Chinese stele mentions an 'image

362

representing the Heir-Apparent [Śākyamuni] at the moment when he becomes a Buddha and the white horse licks his feet'.[1] This presentment shows Śākyamuni in 'meditating' pose, and the dedication speaks of an 'image representing the Heir-Apparent meditating', using for 'meditating' the expression *ssŭ wei* by which images in this pose are commonly named in China. Moreover, portrayals of Maitreya in the same pose often show him seated under a tree; and it is perfectly clear, I think, that a *bodhi*-tree is meant, and that the moment of Maitreya's future Enlightenment and accession to Buddhahood is referred to.

The third type of presentment, the cross-ankled portrayal, shows Maitreya sitting in the Inner court of the Tuṣita Heaven waiting to be reborn on earth as the son of Subrahman, minister of the King of Ketumatī, here to become a Buddha. The inscription on a Chinese stele of A.D. 670 wherein Maitreya appears in this pose says: 'On the front face has been carved an image of Mi-lo (Maitreya) exactly as he is, sitting in the Tuṣita Heaven'.[2] Although images in the pose are known from Gandhāra, it is not evident that they were meant specifically to represent Maitreya in the Tuṣita Heaven. Perhaps they were. But more probably it was the Chinese who first made the portrayal a conventional illustration, perhaps as the result of a story told by the returned pilgrim, Fa-hsien. Speaking of an image seen by him in a small kingdom of northern Kashmir he says: 'In this kingdom there was, formerly, an Arhat, who, by his spiritual power, transported a sculptor up to the Tushita Heavens, to observe size, colour, and general appearance of Maitreya Bodhisatwa ... he finally completed the image. It was 94 ft. high, and the length of the foot of the image was 9 ft. 4 in. On festival days it always emits an effulgent light.'[3]

Identity of the two Bodhisattvas attendant upon Maitreya in Chinese portrayals cannot be proved. But since they are usually in the 'meditating' pose, I think we must assume that Śākyamuni and Maitreya himself are meant. We have seen that Chinese sculptors *did* portray both Śākyamuni and Maitreya in this way. Further, 'meditating' Bodhisattvas at the moment of their Enlightenment are wholly appropriate symbols of Maitreya's coming Buddhahood, just as are *bodhi*-tree, alms-bowl (p. 360), and *stūpa*. The Chinese sculptor found no psychological difficulty in representing Maitreya as Buddha before the event, and duplication of the same personage in a single presentment need not have been thought more of a paradox.

1. Cf. É. Chavannes, 'Six monuments de la sculpture Chinoise', being *A.A.*, vol. ii (1914), p. 30.
2. Cf. É. Chavannes (see footnote above), pp. 34–7.
3. S. Beal (transl.), *Travels of Fah-hian and Sung-yun, Buddhist Pilgrims from China to India (400 A.D. and 518 A.D.)*, London 1869, pp. 18–20.

5. AVALOKITEŚVARA BODHISATTVA (Plate 29*b*)

(*a*) *Āsana*. Standing pose, (1) *kayotsarga*; (2) *tribhanga*. Sitting pose, (1) *lalitā*; (2) *dhyāna*; (3) *mahārājalila*.

(*b*) *Mudrā*. Occasionally right hand in *vitarka*, left in what appears to be *vara*. More often the hands hold attributes, the one arm lowered, the other flexed at the elbow and the forearm raised.

(*c*) Vehicle. If standing, lotus pedestal.

If sitting, lotus throne.

(*d*) Attributes. The object most commonly held in the hand is the lotus bud. Second comes a vessel which Coomaraswamy identifies as a *kuṇḍikā*. Other attributes are: fly-whisk (commonly described as a wil-low-branch); a flattened purse-like object, considered by Cooma-raswamy to be a distorted *kuṇḍikā* (p. 467): the *dhyāni*-Buddha Amitābha in the head-dress.

(*e*) Halo. Five (*dhyāni*-?) Buddhas, or the Seven Buddhas of the Past often feature in miniature.

(*f*) Attendants. In early Chinese portrayals Avalokiteśvara is, more often than not, himself an attendant on Śākyamuni or Amitābha. As a cult image he is almost always portrayed alone. A presentment on a stele dated A.D. 575, considered by Fernald to be of Avalokiteśvara, shows him attended by two Bodhisattvas, two monks, and two persons in long gowns.

(*g*) Remarks. The history of Avalokiteśvara in China is long and com-plicated. He appears in a good many different guises, and after the eighth century seems generally to have been thought of and portrayed as female. The principal early form, derived from India, is that called Padmapāṇi, 'Lotus Bearer', in which the Bodhisattva holds a lotus bud and very often a *kuṇḍikā*. This is the type favoured for reproduction in the form of small gilt-bronze statuettes. First Phase examples show the Bodhisattva in a rigid *kayotsarga* stance, but during the Second Phase a tendency towards a freer posture, approximating to the Indian *tribhanga*, begins to assert itself and reaches a climax in T'ang times. At least as early as the eighth century A.D. Avalokiteśvara is being represented in a number of Tantric forms, of which the Eleven-headed (Samantamukha, 'All-sided One') is probably commonest (figure 62). This version is distinguished by the presence of ten miniature heads of the Bodhisattva in the head-dress of the main portrayal.

Avalokiteśvara's change of sex in Chinese art is not really our con-cern here, since there is no evidence that it took place until after the end of the Third Phase. A number of factors may together have accounted for it. First is the natural tendency to think of a saviour deity as being a woman, especially in a case such as that of Avalokiteśvara whose name – as we learn from 'Lotus' – barren women were invited to invoke as a means of getting children. Next is the estimated effect of new styles imported from India during the sixth and seventh centuries; the *tribhanga* posture has a suggestively feminine air about it. To the Indian mind the idea of an effeminate-looking male deity was not incongruous, but the Chinese might well be excused for mistaking the sex of Indian images in this pose of fluid *déhanchement* – of what Professor Beasley calls 'a devilish elegance'. Third, I think, must be the felt need for a female deity in any religion claiming popular support. Fourth, and probably most important, was the development of *śaktism* – of female emanations of male deities – inside the framework of Tibetan and Indian Tantrism. A T'ang woodcut from Tun-huang representing Avalokiteśvara bears, according to Waley, an invocation to his *śakti*, Tārā. Specifically it refers to Tārā in her 'mild' aspect, to White Tārā called in Sanscrit Pandaravāsini. The Chinese term Pai I, 'Clad in White', is often used adjectivally in reference to Avalokiteśvara; and both Waley and Maspero conclude that the female Avalokiteśvara in Chinese art is in fact descended from White Tārā. The centre of her cult is the sacred 'mountain' of P'u-t'o, actually an island in the East China Sea.

6 AND 7. MAÑJUŚRĪ AND SAMANTABHADRA BODHISATTVAS

These two Bodhisattvas can be dealt with together because of a series of close and obvious correspondences between them, and because in Chinese sculpture as we know it they are an inseparable pair, rarely being portrayed as single cult images.

That Mañjuśrī and Samantabhadra are the standing Bodhisattvas attendant on Śākyamuni in many trinities is an assumption for which iconography provides no proof. Distinctive *āsana*, *mudrā*, and attributes are lacking. Indeed, only when the former rides a lion and the latter an elephant, can we be sure that we are dealing with images of Mañjuśrī and Samantabhadra. How a lion came to be associated with Mañjuśrī I do not know – possibly because one of his many epithets was Simhanāda, 'Lion's Roar'; but Samantabhadra and his elephant have been famed as long as 'Lotus' has been read. In the twenty-sixth chapter, the Bodhisattva makes a long series of vows to safeguard the True Law and its exponents in times of danger ('... then, O Lord, will I mount a white elephant with six tusks, and with a train of Bodhisattvas betake myself to the place where that preacher is walking, in order to protect this Dharmaparyāya.'). The motive is distinctive of Chinese Buddhist sculpture.

Origins of both Bodhisattvas are obscure but both are exclusively bound up with Mahāyānism and play no part in the Hīnayāna tradition. Neither seems to have had much popular appeal. Neither is so much as mentioned in the Lung-mên inscriptions. Yet the pair seems to have been better known in China than anywhere else in the Buddhist world. Two of the Four Sacred Mountains of Chinese Buddhism were dedicated to them – Wu-t'ai Shan in Shansi to Mañjuśrī, and O-mei Shan in Szechwan to Samantabhadra. And by a strange irony, in the eleventh century, long after Buddhism had disappeared from India generally, it was believed in the little Buddhist kingdom of Nepal that both Bodhisattvas were Chinese in origin; a Nepalese miniature of Samantabhadra is inscribed with words meaning 'Samantabhadra of China'; and one of Mañjuśrī is similarly inscribed. But as early as the seventh century the Chinese pilgrim I-ching was noting that the Indians then believed Mañjuśrī to be Chinese, and in A.D. 720 the Indian Vajrabodhi came on a pilgrimage to China to get a glimpse of him, as did Prajñā eight years later.

We have already seen that portrayals of Samantabhadra and Mañjuśrī attendant on Śākyamuni may be interpreted as symbolizing the Triratna – Buddha, Dharma, and Sangha (p. 359); according to some authorities, the trinity has a more popular signification, namely the Preaching on the Vulture Peak. But the two Bodhisattvas are also portrayed in company with yet another Buddha, Vairocana, and are linked with that final sophistication of Mahāyānist doctrine, the concept of the Dharmakāya in which one supreme Buddha, Vairocana, out-Buddhas all the rest. Development of this doctrine was in the hands of the Hua-yen sect and was based on the *Avataṃsaka sūtra* (Ch. *Hua yen ching*), first translated into Chinese in A.D. 420. In it Mañjuśrī and Samantabhadra are the chief Bodhisattvas, representing *prajñā* (Wisdom) and *caryā* (Practice) respectively, two phases of the stride taken by the believer into Enlightenment.

8. KṢITIGARBHA BODHISATTVA

(a) *Āsana*. If standing, *kayotsarga*; if sitting, *lalitā*.

(b) *Mudrā*. If hands are free, *abhaya* and *vara*.

(c) Vehicle. If standing, high lotus pedestal.
       If sitting, high lotus throne.

(d) Attributes. Monk's staff (*khakkhara*); Precious Gem (*cintāmani*) emitting rays. Kṣitigarbha is invariably portrayed with a monk's shaven crown, the most important aid in identifying images of him.

(e) Halo. Dhyāni-Buddha (Amitābha?) sometimes appears in miniature.

(f) Attendants. Kṣitigarbha is usually shown unattended. But paintings and steles exist in which various accessory beings, including those symbolizing the Six Ways of Existence (p. 367), are incorporated.

(g) Kṣitigarbha, the last great Bodhisattva to join the popular religion, is largely a creation of Chinese Mahāyāna Buddhism. Several of his scriptures supposedly translated into Chinese from Sanscrit are probably Chinese apocrypha; and his separate cult image also seems to be an invention of Chinese iconography. His is the sacred mountain of Chiuhua Shan in Anhwei, famous as a resort of Taoist refugees from the first century B.C. onwards. Later it became a Buddhist sanctuary, associated with Kṣitigarbha ever since the end of the eighth century A.D. when a Korean prince turned monk, who died there, was claimed as an incarnation of the Bodhisattva.

In genuine Sanscrit texts translated before the seventh century, Kṣitigarbha appears as a compassionate Bodhisattva, who, in the guise of a monk with shaven crown, rescues the soul from rebirth in the three lowest of the Six Ways of Existence (*gātis*); namely those of Hell, Animals and Hungry Ghosts. But by the end of that century his powers have increased. He now becomes a saviour deity pure and simple, with authority extending into the recesses of the 'Dark Palace' (*ming fu*) where is decided which of the Six Ways of Existence the reborn soul shall enter; he is able to reverse judgment on those sinners who invoke his name. In that dismal abode his Precious Gem shines so bright, we are told in an undated apocryphal text, that it is transformed into Paradise. As part of the inscription on a Tun-huang painting dated A.D. 963 puts it: '... may his merit cause (Kṣitigarbha's) Golden Staff to shake so that in Hell lotus buds grow; and may his *mani* (Radiant Gem) shine forth in the Dark Ways, till they be turned into the semblance of the Pure Land.'[1] He is therefore appropriately portrayed on steles and in paintings holding one, or two, Precious Gems from which emerge six rays bearing at their extremities beings representing the Six Ways of Existence.

The idea of an underworld court to pass judgement on sinners and presided over by Yama (Ch. Yen-lo) has no counterpart in native Chinese belief. The nearest equivalent was probably the sacred mountain of T'ai Shan, near where the souls of the dead were believed to congregate. T'ai Shan was first used by Chinese Buddhists as the equivalent of the underworld court, and later as the name of one of the Ten Kings who ruled it. Yama became another. Quite when this category came into being one can hardly say; it is certainly a Chinese notion, and I believe it was already current well before the end of the T'ang period. Certainly it was completely mature by A.D. 903, in which year an apocryphal text popularly called 'Sūtra of the Ten Kings' made a first appearance.

The Kṣitigarbha cult seems to have reached its *floruit* in China by the middle seventh century. The first Lung-mên inscription mentioning him by name is dated A.D. 667. A votive stele in which he appears seated in *lalitā* on a high lotus throne, with shaven head and holding two

1. A. Waley (see footnote p. 312), p. 34.

Precious Gems each emitting three rays, bears a date corresponding to A.D. 670.[1] The first alleged translation of the scripture in which he announced his saving mission to mankind was made in A.D. 695.

A series of wooden images in Japanese temples, dated between A.D. 800 and 1300, must, I think, predicate Chinese models of the middle T'ang period. They show the Bodhisattva standing in *kayotsarga* on a high lotus pedestal, holding the Precious Gem in his upheld left hand, his right apparently in *vara*. Treatment of the gown is highly reminiscent of the 'Udyāna' type of Śākyamuni portrayal; and this is particularly true of the arrangement of padded ridges, representing folds of the gown, at the back (plate 31). My personal opinion is that the makers of these images borrowed the treatment of the gown from Śākyamuni images of 'Udyāna' type extant in T'ang times. On this assumption we have no means of knowing whether such an image as that shown in plate 31 was originally intended to portray Śākyamuni or Kṣitigarbha.

Types of Chinese Buddhist Sculptures made during the First, Second, and Third Phases

Known Chinese Buddhist sculptures of the fifth to eighth centuries fall into four main typological groups. Earliest are small gilt-bronze votive statuettes[2] popular during the whole period under survey and later. Evidently they answered a need for cheap, standard domestic cult-images; yet they are conspicuously free from the shoddy workmanship, summary design, and sentimental treatment that often spoil such merchandise. Indeed, although seldom on a large scale, they include some of the noblest pieces of Chinese sculpture we know; and throughout the whole period they sensitively reflect prevailing stylistic trends.

Next, and coming rather later, are large rectangular votive steles (plate 28a). This form, according to Sirén, arose from the inscribed memorial slab of Han and later periods which, he says, was 'originally made to be raised at both sides of the tomb of prominent men, at the time of their burial'.[3] Two such slabs, each with a single perfora-

1. Doubts have been cast on the genuineness of this relief. On stylistic grounds I see no reason why the image should not be mid-T'ang.

2. Of 54 dated sculptures made between A.D. 390 and 500 listed by Rowland (see footnote p. 325), pp. 106–7, 35 are of this class and only 15 are made of stone.

3. O. Sirén (see footnote p. 311), vol. i, p. xlix.

tion near the top, could be used to support a pole between them, whereby the coffin was lowered into the grave. Unornamented in Han times, they later acquired a pair of intertwined dragons disposed over their rounded tops; and this decorative element persisted when the slabs were taken over by Buddhists and transformed into votive steles.

A third class includes the sculptures of the cave-shrines, by far the fullest and most impressive corpus of surviving material. Although a dozen or so of these sites are known to-day, they are mostly in ruinous condition and only a few need be mentioned here (map 6). They are Tun-huang in western Kansu; the newly-discovered caves at Ping-ling Ssŭ and Mai-chi Shan near the borders of that province and Shensi; Yün-kang in northern Shansi; Lung-mên in Honan; T'ien-lung Shan in central Shansi; and Hsiang-t'ang Shan in Hopei. The earliest, Tun-huang, is also the most western; and in fact the Chinese cave-shrines are simply the eastern termination of a series that begins in the *chaitya*-caves of India (p. 370), and continues across Afghānistān and Central Asia into China.

In none of the above-mentioned classes of sculpture is the subject conceived *en ronde-bosse*. Images were almost invariably set against some sort of background, and all had to be looked at more or less from the front. But about Sui times free-standing stone sculptures begin to appear, planned on the sort of scale and given the same individual treatment we associate with the works of European master-sculptors. These may be thought of as constituting a fourth typological group. They are, however, few and far between. One of the leading production-centres for them was Ting Chou, in northern Honan, where a fine-grain micaceous marble was to be had; the pieces illustrated in figure 61*b* and plates 30 and 31 are with good reason claimed as products of Ting Chou *ateliers*.

THE FIRST PHASE

Models for the manufacture of small gilt-bronze statuettes probably found their way into China through ordinary trade-channels during the fourth century A.D., no doubt imported direct from Gandhāra. The earliest known Chinese Buddhist sculpture, a gilt-bronze statuette now in the C. T. Loo Collection, was perhaps modelled on such a piece. It portrays Śākyamuni Buddha, seated in *dhyāna* (figure 55).

With its Apollo-like mask, this image is strongly reminiscent of Gandhāra style; and the possibility that it is not Chinese at all, although unlikely, must be taken into account.[1] It bears a Later Chao (p. 304) year-name corresponding to A.D. 338.

Sculptures of the cave-shrines, although showing much the same stylistic affinities, are rather the result of steady diffusion across the oasis-kingdoms of Central Asia. The Tun-huang caves, few of whose First Phase sculptures now survive, clearly imitate Indian ancestors in their mode of construction. The latter were chapel- or *chaitya*-caves, part of rock-hewn Buddhist monasteries (*vihara*) dating from the second century B.C. to about A.D. 750, at plates like Karli, Nasik, Kanheri, Ajaṇṭā, Ellura, and Elephanta.[2] And these were in many respects no more than translations into solid stone of free-standing wooden buildings, the assembly halls of the secular guilds.

Among features imitating wooden originals is the horse-shoe arch, framing doorway or sun-window, with outer 'ace of spades' moulding and a deep porch lined with replicas in stone of wooden supporting ribs. Details of wooden post-and-beam construction, even down to the heads of nails by means of which beams were tied in the wooden originals, are reproduced in stone in Cave 10 at Ajaṇṭā. In Cave 9 at Ellora, dating from A.D. 600, is a rendering in stone of the characteristic 'lantern-roof' still found to-day in wooden domestic architecture of the Middle East from Armenia to the Hindu Kush, Kashmir, and the Pamirs.[3] It is a pyramidal vault made by piling up wooden frames in such a way that the four corners of each rest on the mid-sides of the one beneath; the top frame is left open as a chimney aperture.

Another feature of the Indian chapel-caves should be noticed. The Karli *chaitya*, dating from 150 B.C., has at its apsidal end a free-standing *stūpa* (p. 724) which was circumambulated by the devotee just as

1. B. Rowland (see footnote p. 325) illustrates (fig. 4) and discusses (p. 98) a gilt-bronze statuette in Gandhāran style, now in a Japanese collection, which he thinks may be an imported piece. Munsterberg (see footnote p. 337) cites several Gandhāran pieces closely resembling the A.D. 338 Śākyamuni in point of style, but he is convinced that the latter is truly Chinese.

2. Earliest seems to be the Lomas Rishi Cave in the *vihara* of the Ajivika sect, cut into the Barabar hills near Bodh-Gāyā. This work was begun by Aśoka (p. 321), who may have instituted the practice generally. Cf. H. Rawlinson, *India, A Short Cultural History*, London 1948, pp. 85-6.

3. Another rock-cut imitation of the lantern-roof is at Bāmiyān. Cf. B. Rowland (see footnote p. 386), pl. 56a.

though it stood in the open air. In later Indian *chaityas* – for instance, those at Ajaṇṭā and Ellora – the *stūpa* is still present, but it now enshrines an image of Buddha and is no longer itself the principal object of adoration.

All these features are found at the Tun-huang and Yün-kang cavetemples. At Tun-huang we notice horse-shoe arches and 'lanternroof', the latter rendered in rich variety as a painted ceiling-design simulating a coffer and framing a gigantic lotus. A scheme of painted rectangular panels enclosed by painted wooden beams – of which the 'lantern-roof' with central lotus is one element – imitates the wooden beam-and-coffer ceiling of native Indian architecture. And in Cave 3 at Yün-kang the central pillar, fashioned to look like the lower storeys of a pagoda, and with niches enclosing Buddha images, is the Chinese version of the apsidal *stūpa* of Indian *chaityas*. It, too, could be circumambulated. In doing so, the devotee passed by a series of scenes from the life of Buddha cut in bas-relief on the nearby cave-walls.

The Chinese cave-shrines reveal their parentage in other ways. At Yün-kang, for example, debased Hellenistic and Iranian decorative motives adorn tops and sides of niches, frames of doors and windows, and roof-vaults. Indeed, as Sirén remarks, sculptors seem to have been more familiar with Western Asiatic than with native Chinese decorative motives, which are almost entirely missing. Among the former Sirén mentions conventionalized acanthus-stem patterns, garlands held aloft by flying genii, heraldic lions, pseudo-Ionian pillar-capitals, 'egg-and-tongue' patterns forming borders, and tripartite arches divided into trapezoid panels above niches. And accessory beings, celestial musicians (*gandharvas*), guardians (*dvārapālas*), and 'angels' (*apsaras*), belong to the world of Indian fancy and have their counterparts in the sculptured godlings of Bharhut and Ajaṇṭā.[1]

Interiors at Yün-kang and Lung-mên (p. 369) are crowded with a solid mass of images lining the walls and set against a background of decoration so profuse that scarcely an inch of wall-space has escaped the sculptor's chisel. Judging from photographs and paintings, these interiors look to-day like nothing so much as the scene in some Victorian opera-house, noisy, colourful and overcrowded. But much

1. Two images in bas-relief at the embrasures of Cave 8, one with six arms and five heads, the other three-headed and eight-armed, seem to be unique portrayals in early Chinese sculpture of Hindu gods, one a Garuda-raja, the other a form of Śiva.

haphazard restoration has gone on, and the garish effect of ill-matched pigments on sculptures daubed with gesso may not have been quite what their original makers intended. Only when we look at them one by one, and strip them of their adventitious make-up, do they disclose their deeper aesthetic qualities. It then becomes apparent that sculptures made at Yün-kang between A.D. 450 and 500, and at Lungmên during the following half-century, are at the very heart of the strange and spiritually moving First Phase of Chinese Buddhist sculpture.

The First Phase is by no means stylistically one. There was a grand style and a lesser style, as well as several provincial schools and, as one would expect, a number of pieces that lead into the transitional Second Phase. Yet all convey the same impression of a feverish energy and high nervous tension. It is hard to say what impulse drove their makers so hard. But several writers have commented on what seems to be an emotional kinship between this Phase and early medieval Christian sculpture. I mention the comparison only because it may help us to recognize a definite quality pervading all First Phase sculpture, its primitiveness. The word 'archaic' is, as I have suggested, misleading. But when we look at photographs of the Lung-mên caves with their row upon row of curiously animate occupants – bodies long and angular, waists slender, shoulders sloping, necks exaggeratedly tall and supporting long, narrow heads that look like heavy flowers swaying on thin stems – we cannot help feeling that a communal emotion is being discharged, that a whole *Volksgeist* is expressed and not merely the verve and sensibility personal to the artist.

The grand style need scarcely detain us, for we have already dealt with it and its stylistic antecedents (pp. 335–9). It is well exemplified by the Maitreya of plate 26 and the Amitābha of plate 25. These were major works, and their makers seem to have held closely to the Mathurā recipe in designing them, no doubt taking it for the *sans pareil* of authenticity. Typical of the style is a somewhat mechanical and abstract modelling of the mask, broad forehead, a wedge-shaped nose with semicircular eyebrow-ridges springing from its root, a small mouth with corners turned up in an 'archaic' smile; and a convention by which mantle-folds are rendered as raised double ridges, so that the gown appears padded (p. 335). No attempt is made to give the mask the characteristics of an ordinary human face. It offers no clue to racial identity, mental disposition, psychological state, or emotional mood, as does that of classical European sculpture. Yet, as Rowland says of it: 'the very absence of the qualities that make for what we call naturalistic representation raise the idol beyond and above the classical standard, whereby the gods are made anthropomorphic to accommodate the limitations of the worshipper in imagining the object of devotion'.[1]

The lesser style is more personal. A happier illustration could hardly be found than the gracious little study of a celestial musician (*gandharva*) from Lung-mên, shown on plate 27. Apart from the air of friendly intimacy it radiates, the piece manifests an objective interest in decorative composition for its own sake, in the beauty of its formal layout. This cool detachment underlies all the impassioned lyricism of the First Phase, whose sculptors sought not only to satisfy the bare requirement for mass-produced cult-images, but also to create miniature essays in tectonic design. With minor pieces such as the *gandharva* we are as far away from the hieratic immobility of the grand style as is possible to imagine; far nearer, I think, to the purely Chinese spirit present in, say, bronze and lacquer décor.

This does not mean that the lesser style was altogether free from clichés and mannerisms: the conditions under which it was made neither called for nor encouraged individual treatment. Images had to be produced quickly, cheaply, and in enormous numbers. What the less style *does* consistently display is that genius for creating dynamic tensions, by the interplay of related parts inside a compositional framework, so typical of Chinese art. Within such formal limits sculptors experimented freely with decorative detailing, nowhere to better effect than in the sides and lower edge of the gown (figure 57), which falls like an evening skirt over the throne in a cascade of pleats ending in stiff, pointed 'swallow-tail' projections, elaborated beyond reason and with the most brilliant effect. We are reminded – as so often in Chinese decorative design – of suddenly-arrested movement; perhaps of a great bird's wing still arched and vibrating from its recent flight. The full development of this motive occupies a hundred years or so, and culminates at Lung-mên in the first decades of the sixth century. Some sculptures from the very end of the First Phase foreshadow, in the rounding and softening of their mantle-folds, the more plastic and relaxed treatment of the Second. But on the whole the stiff, linear, and angular convention that gives the First Phase its heightened dramatic power continues to prevail.

1. B. Rowland (see footnote p. 325), p. 92.

Like that of the grand style, the mask of the lesser style is of abstract type. Its proportions vary from a preternaturally long and narrow shape to one that is almost square (plate 27); but all exhibit the same facial features. The 'archaic' smile is here more pronounced than in the case of the large hieratic pieces, and the mouth is small. Eyes are reduced to elongated slits. High, arched eyebrow-ridges spring from the root of the nose, and are emphasized by incised lines. Ear-lobes,

Figure 57. Sides and lower hem of the robe of a First Phase Buddha image, probably from Lung-mên, now in the British Museum.

of course, are conventionally lengthened; and the chin is pointed. This is a slight, evasive sort of beauty. And it creates the impression of a pristine innocence, of a child-like purity that permeates the whole of First Phase Chinese Buddhist sculpture.

One other feature is to all intents and purposes distinctive of the First Phase. This is the large leaf-shaped aureole or nimbus that forms a backing to seated and standing images of both Buddhas and Bodhisattvas. It is almost always present, and where it is not I think we can assume it originally was. Bronze examples are adorned with an outer zone of flame-ornament, partly cast and partly engraved, within which is a circular halo backing the head. Corresponding versions in stone are incised and/or carved in relief, or the aureole may form a painted background for a stone image.

Something similar to the First Phase aureole is known from sixth-century A.D. India; but among the sculptures of Mathurā and Gand-hāra we find only the circular halo. In view of the fact that the earliest known Chinese Buddhist sculptures are gilt-bronze votive statuettes, this feature may have originated in bronze as an answer to the technical problem of giving support to the image while casting it.

● THE SECOND PHASE

Although occupying only some seventy years between the fall of the Eastern and Western Wei dynasties and the beginning of T'ang, the Second Phase marks a real advance in the history of Chinese Buddhist sculpture. First Phase styles rapidly became demoded; and the original Mathurā formula that had groped its way across Afghānistān and Central Asia to China, and that formed the starting-point for all First Phase developments, lost ground. But the Mathurā formula had also travelled east to the great centres of Buddhism in central and eastern India. And there it had flowered into a new native Indian art, Gupta. The gravely beautiful standing and seated sandstone Buddhas of Sār-nāth belonging to the fifth century A.D. (figures 51c and 52b) are, as we have seen, stylistically related to nude Jain images of the late Mathurā school (p. 331). Though clothed, these Buddhas were given an appearance of nudity by reducing the gown to a few incised lines, so leaving the eye free to explore every significant passage of the underlying form. The Buddha image was thus successfully transfigured to accord with age-old Indian conceptions of the naked body as an expressive symbol.

Having once divested the body, Gupta sculptors proceeded to fetter it again with every conceivable article of accessory ornament. Canonically, a Buddha may not be personally adorned; but he is given a delicately carved circular halo bounded by a beaded border, within which is a luxuriant plant-trail, and within which again is a lotus rosette backing his head (figure 58a). Bodhisattvas, entitled to princely regalia, positively drip with jewellery – high and ornate diadems, necklaces and girdles both hung with pendants, armlets, bracelets and wristlets, ear-rings, jewelled chains, and a long scarf hung from the

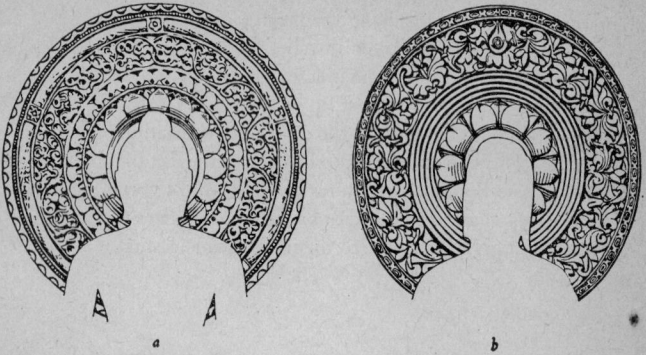

Figure 58. Two circular halos: *a*, from a standing Buddha image found at Sārnāth, India; *b*, from a seated Chinese Buddha image, probably of the Sung period, but reproducing the style of the Second Phase.

shoulders and looped through a large ring at the mid-riff. But their bodies remain essentially nude; and the *tribhanga* posture in which they stand (p. 391), a legacy from earlier Indian schools represented by Sāñchī, Barhūt, and Bodh-Gayā, contributes to the impression of a purely physical *élan*.

The new style was now absorbed into Second Phase Chinese Buddhist sculpture, but not in its entirety. Decorative motives were accepted without question. The carved floral halo, for instance, is faithfully imitated in sculptures of the Northern Ch'i dynasty, as comparison between Indian and Chinese examples makes clear (figure 50, *a* and *b*). In other and more fundamental respects, the Second Phase clung for a time to First Phase conventions, and only gradually succumbed to the intrusion of the new Indian school.

So far apart in fact had the two national traditions grown by the middle sixth century A.D. that in point of style they now had little or nothing in common. Each had turned for strength to its own native aesthetic genius – the Indian striving to recapture the full plasticity and rhythm of bodily movement so convincingly rendered by its oldest schools, the Chinese following the path of linear conventionalization. But fashions in Buddhist sculpture were still being dictated by India; and import of a few Gupta images now forced Chinese sculptors, willy-nilly, to begin making over the entire native tradition in obedience to India's decree. It is scarcely surprising that a long transitional

376

period should have ensued, or that the Second Phase should manifest active experimentation – and pronounced local differences – in style.

Very rarely in the Second Phase a piece of sculpture, recognizably within the older linear tradition, manages to catch the true spirit of Gupta art without apparent effort. Such is the delicate Bodhisattva of plate 29a. This image, wrought in the grey limestone of Shensi, is one of a number, several of which bear Northern Chou dates. Now as Sirén remarks, Northern Chou sculpture as a whole shows far less trace of Indian influence than does that of its neighbour, Northern Ch'i. Its rhythms, although forceful, are ponderous; its execution is often clumsy; and its general air is distinctly provincial. Yet this piece is a delightful, indeed feminine, counterpart of the best contemporary Gupta work. The restrained eloquence of its treatment is in striking contrast to the nervous agitation of the First Phase, and to the fussy rhetoric of other sculptures in its own series, that succeed in reproducing little more than the outer magnificence of their Gupta models. Upon it, the distinctive marks of a Bodhisattva are almost obliterated; indeed, the piece is less Bodhisattva than Buddha, and of Buddhas it recalls most vividly the standing images from Sārnāth. This notwithstanding its evident First Phase characteristics – rigidity of pose, anatomical disproportion, and the linear renderings of its mask.

First Phase and Gupta Buddhist sculpture differ radically in respect of four interdependent features – treatment of mask, and of gown, and the degree to which plasticity of form, and bodily movement, are rendered. In reducing the gown to a system of incised lines, Indian sculptors reaffirmed the supremacy of the nude body with its inherent plastic values. Chinese sculptors knew of no such tradition; and the gown, however subordinated to the body of its wearer, is always an appreciable entity in First Phase sculpture. Indeed, the very way in which its folds are schematized, in accordance with the Mathurā formula, tended in Chinese hands to diminish the plasticity of the image itself; for it encouraged sculptors to work the folds into an independent decorative pattern, such as is best deployed upon a flat surface. This irresistible instinct for pattern-making effectively prevented First Phase sculptors from ever emancipating their work from its original condition of relief-carving meant to be seen from front view only. The tendency in Second Phase sculpture was to deprive the gown of its decorative interest, with a resulting gain in plasticity.

In its treatment of mask and of bodily movement, a step towards Indian standards taken by Second Phase sculpture was a step nearer realism. For whatever symbolic meaning earlier Indian sculpture possessed, it was superficially a naturalistic art in respect of these features. Under Gupta inspiration, the mask in Second Phase sculpture no longer retains its earlier abstract quality; features and expression begin to resemble those of actual faces. Such characterization is of course only relative. A hieratic mask must never be allowed to look too human; and Chinese sculptors of the Second and Third Phases distinguished in treatment between the abstracted other-worldliness of Buddhas and Bodhisattvas, and the portrait-realism of lesser beings. Yet, compared with that of the First Phase, the Second Phase mask is fuller and more rounded, the 'archaic' smile less evident, and the execution of eyebrows, eyes, nose, and lips less perfunctory. At the same time images begin, ever so slightly it is true, to stir to life.

As a rule all we can discern is a slight movement away from absolute rigidity of pose, a slackening in tension of one leg so that the body tilts somewhat at the hips, again in the opposite direction at the waist, and again in the first direction at the shoulders. This is the *tribhanga* posture of which Indian sculptors made so much. But not even in the Third Phase could Chinese sculptors see wholly through Indian eyes; there is nothing in Chinese sculpture to match the wilful and emphatic dance that Indian sculpture makes in its less inhibited moods. Only rarely does Second Phase sculpture suggest rhythmic movement such as Sirén describes, when speaking of images of which plate 30 is representative, as 'quite slow – gliding and perfectly balanced – rising and falling with about equal strength'.[1]

All these tendencies are conveniently illustrated by the white sandstone cave-sculptures of T'ien-lung Shan, a few miles south-west of T'ai-yüan in Shansi. This master-work was begun soon after the founding of the Northern Ch'i dynasty, and was continued into the T'ang and beyond. A particularly strong Indian impulse, it seems, was being directed towards T'ien-lung Shan – indeed, Sirén suggests that Indian sculptors may have worked there – and its contents represent the *avant garde* of Chinese Buddhist sculpture during much of the Second and Third Phases.

Plate 28*b* shows one of the oldest parts of T'ien-lung Shan, the west wall of Cave 3 dating from A.D. 560. A simple and orderly arrange-

1. O. Sirén (see footnote p. 311), vol. i, p. lxxix.

ment is adopted in this and other early caves at the site; a trinity of which Śākyamuni Buddha is central figure on the north wall, an Amitābha trinity on the east, and a Maitreya trinity – shown here – on the west. There are some accessory figures in very low relief, and walls and ceiling were once brightly painted, yet the contrast between this sober layout and the unplanned profusion of First Phase sculpture at Yün-kang and Lung-mên leaps to the eye. Moreover, the carving of the main images, judged by First Phase standards, is in surprisingly high relief. The treatment of the gown is still linear, but its folds are far more deeply undercut; they still project in wing-like lobes from the sides and lower hem of the skirt, but their whole appearance is softer and more rounded, and the emotional tension drops in consequence.

The Bodhisattvas, as Sirén says, present rather flatter surfaces, but even they gain in plasticity by being brought away from their background and made to stand on substantial circular lotus pedestals. The leaf-shaped aureole persists, but it, too, no longer occupies one plane only; it is brought forward and outward so that its tip projects above the top of the niche. The entire composition shows a new feeling for sculptural form, of which the plasticity of the main image is an inseparable element.

Sculptures in Caves 10 and 16 at T'ien-lung Shan are rather later, and are more directly modelled on Indian prototypes, than are those of Caves 1, 2, and 3. Indeed, the critical swing in favour of Gupta conventions probably occurred some time between the making of these two groups. For whereas in the Maitreya trinity the treatment of the gown – original as it is – has as its starting point the decorative linear formula of the First Phase, in this second set of sculptures all attempt to work out a satisfactory treatment for it, based on First Phase conventions, has been abandoned. The stark Gupta formula – body a rounded and monumental mass, gown a series of light incisions upon its surface – is peremptorily commandeered. A large Śākyamuni seated in *dhyāna*, right hand in *abhaya* and left in *vara*, in Cave 16, resembles seated Buddhas of the fifth and sixth centuries A.D. from Sārnāth closely enough to persuade us that its maker, whether Chinese or Indian, worked directly from a Gupta model (figure 59).

Here, for a moment, Chinese and Indian traditions seem to meet. But towards the end of the Second Phase the former again begins to diverge. Sui pieces at T'ien-lung Shan are of inferior quality and in poor state; and the best-known examples of late Second Phase work come from various sites in Hopei and Shantung.

The school of Ting Chou in south Hopei (p. 388), working in the local white micaceous marble, begins to be prominent towards the end of the Northern Ch'i. Like the sculptures of Caves 10 and 16 at

Figure 59. Image of Śākyamuni Buddha in Cave 16, T'ien-lung Shan, Shansi. Second Phase.

T'ien-lung Shan, Ting Chou work has a monumental massivity – from which the lightly etched mantle-folds in no way detract – but the mass has grown stylized and abstract. We are now asked to admire not so much the surface brilliance of carved drapery, or the evocative beauty of an underlying body, as a certain type of abstract volume for its own sake. The favoured shape is ovoid, and the plastic mass grows in volume from the feet and culminates in the weighty, rounded shoulders. Sirén observes that this movement is directly contrary to that preferred by First Phase and early Second Phase sculptors, in which the mass grows downwards from a small head and narrow, sloping shoulders, to culminate in the peacock magnificence of the skirt.

Pride of place among these images must be given to the colossal standing Amitābha of plate 30, now in the British Museum. This piece, nearly 18 feet high, bears a date corresponding to A.D. 585, four years after the founding of the Sui. Until 1918 it stood in a village [1] in Wan Hsien, a district between Ting Chou and Pao-ting Fu, so that it is beyond doubt a product of the Ting Chou school. In every respect it is a masterpiece. As Sirén says of it: 'The beautiful white marble has been chiselled and rubbed in a way similar to that found on archaic Greek sculptures and has taken on a remarkably smooth tactile beauty.' [2] Mantle-folds, we observe, are reduced to lightest possible relief, and the wave-like band at the lower hem is all that is left of the multitudinous pointed lobes so distinctive of First Phase treatments. A Second Phase characteristic is presence of three horizontal creases on the neck; and a mannerism seemingly confined to the Sui period is the double-curved eyelid.

Among its minor features, the Second Phase exhibits great wealth of floral and other accessory ornament on halos, above niches, above doorway arches, as decorative bands on steles, and on carved or incised lunettes and balustrades. Nearly all this art is exotic. The lotus, as rosette or as plant-trail, in which it seems to be crossed with the Western acanthus, comes ultimately from India, as do various types of bodhi-trees, apsaras bearing garlands, yakṣas holding up censers, and grotesque masks supporting stūpas. Of Iranian and Hellenistic ancestry is the vine-trail (p. 498); and an oval jewel enclosed in a beaded border, distinctive of the Phase, is Sassanid Persian. All this decoration, and especially plant-trail and lotus rosette, is carved with great care and precision; something of its quality can be gauged from the Vimalikīrti scene shown on plate 28a.

The atmospheric, vaguely Baroque, effect of layouts such as the Maitreya group of plate 28b is reproduced in the forms of elaborately carved and pierced stone lunettes, balustrades, and steles, distinctive of the Phase. The steles are especially interesting (figure 60). Twin bodhi-

---

1. Presumably that mentioned in the image's inscription as Han-ts'ui, for whose Ch'ung-kuang Temple it was made.

2. O. Sirén (see footnote p. 299), p. 117.

trees stand erect, forming the sides of a massive aureole, and project upwards a luxuriant canopy of leaves. Against this backcloth are pinned flying *apsaras* bearing jewelled garlands. Often the *stūpa* of Śākyamuni and Prabhūtaratna (p. 343), held aloft by a *yakṣa* and festooned with garlands, closes the design above. Through irregular perforations of varying size, light falls on to the forms of the main personages seated or standing in their formal group beneath the trees. The scene has a vivid, theatrical quality; and the figures, like persons in a tableau, create an impression of actuality, the direct outcome of that feeling for three-dimensional space which was the greatest single acquisition of the Second Phase.

THE THIRD PHASE

By the end of the Second Phase, Chinese sculpture had deviated quite perceptibly from the stylistic standards of Gupta art. Images such as the Amitābha colossus of plate 30 have little in common with contemporary Indian work, despite direct descent from Gupta-inspired models such as the Northern Ch'i Buddha of figure 59. During the Third Phase a decided revulsion in favour of Indian standards set in. This renaissance does not coincide with the beginning of the T'ang dynasty. It gets properly under way only about the fourth decade of the seventh century A.D., and flourishes for less than a hundred years. By the end of the century the creative stream is already beginning to run dry. There is no new infusion of style or subject-matter; modelling becomes clumsy and workmanship inferior. We therefore close our account of Chinese sculpture at the end of the seventh century.

A few dates will help localize the period of vital achievement. After many decades during which inscriptions are silent, that of a famous stele dated A.D. 641 records the restoration of certain old caves at Lung-mên, and the building of new. In A.D. 645 Hsüan-tsang returns to China, bringing seven Gupta images with him (p. 300). He is followed three years later by the imperial envoy, Wang Hsüan-tze, terminating the last of four missions to the Gupta court, and bringing with him a copy of the famous Maitreya image at Bodh-Gāya. The greatest number of Lung-mên inscriptions lie around A.D. 660. The largest Lung-mên cave and the greatest Lung-mên image – that of Amitābha Buddha – were hewn between A.D. 672 and 675. Making of images culminated during the reign of Empress Wu (A.D. 684–705),

Figure 60. Stone stele showing Maitreya Bodhisattva in the Tuśita Heaven.
Second Phase.

when the important Ch'i-pao Terrace was constructed for the K'uang-chai Temple at the capital, Ch'ang-an. Many pieces originally belonging to this building have survived, and are of great value in helping to fix dates for others stylistically related to them (figure 62).

The Phase is marked by unprecedented interest in the human form. Chinese sculpture now surrenders, momentarily but completely, to the seductions of the mature Gupta style. Not many late Gupta images survive to-day, but enough remains both of sculpture and of painted frescoes in rock-cut temples, dating from the sixth and seventh centuries A.D., to show how irresistibly they must have appealed as models to foreign craftsmen. T'ang sculptors carry a stage further the trends already manifest in Second Phase style – naturalistic treatment of mask, reduction of gown to a tracery of lines so that it forms a *drapérie mouillée* over the naked body beneath, and modelling of figures in the round and as though in movement.

The *tribhanga* posture now reaches full accentuation. In India, it is well shown in the figures of Avalokiteśvara and Tārā (p. 365) that decorate Cave 10 at Ellura, dating from *c.* A.D. 590; in the case of Tārā it is exaggerated into a stance of almost aggressive femininity. Third Phase Chinese examples are not quite so outspoken, but the Bodhisattva image of figure 61b effectively shows how far the native tradition had been revolutionized and vitalized by contact with India during the seventh century A.D.

We mentioned, as leading centres for the manufacture of Second Phase sculptures, schools in Shensi (p. 377), Shansi (T'ien-lung Shan), and Hopei (Ting Chou); important works were also made at Lung-mên in Honan. These four regional schools remained active during the seventh century. One of the earliest Third Phase pieces known, made for the official Ma Chou at Ch'ang-an in A.D. 639, shows several characteristics distinctive of the Phase – the gown covering both shoulders of the seated image, the skirt falling in a trifid pattern over a lotus throne on a high-pillared pedestal; but in other respects, for instance of ovoid mass and stiff posture, it is reminiscent of the Second.

The highest refinements of Third Phase style are best exhibited by Bodhisattva images. That illustrated in figure 61b, reported to have come from a temple at Lung-yen Shan near Pao-ting, Hopei, has been recommended as 'perhaps the finest example of Buddhist sculpture in existence'.[1] It stands in a pronounced *hanche* posture. The weight rests

1. L. Ashton and B. Gray, *Chinese Art*, London 1951, p. 136.

upon the left leg, which is somewhat advanced, while the right, a little behind, is slightly flexed and poised on the ball of the foot as if about to step forward. This movement swings the left hip outwards so that the trunk inclines at an angle to the legs, the right shoulder rising to restore the balance; were head and neck present their axis would

Figure 61. Two Bodhisattva torsos: *a*, from Sāñchī, India; *b*, from Lung-yen Shan, Pao-ting, Hopei.

be parallel to that of the legs. Modelling is naturalistic, skilfully suggesting the texture of firm and supple flesh, while well-developed chest, narrow waist, and broad hips give the image an unmistakably feminine air.

Various opinions have been expressed as to the date and stylistic connexions of this piece, and even as to the material of which it is made. An Indian counterpart is not far to seek. For in posture, modelling, and decorative detailing the Chinese image closely resembles a famous Bodhisattva torso found at Sāñchī, now in the Victoria and Albert Museum (figure 61a). Almost inevitably, the date of this latter is also in dispute. The Museum authorities assign it to the sixth century A.D.; and it is generally accepted as Gupta, although one more recent opinion claims it as Pala work, done between the seventh and ninth centuries A.D.[1] But assuming it to have been made before the middle of the seventh century A.D., close connexion between India and China would still allow us to date the Chinese piece before the beginning of the eighth. I personally believe it may be several decades earlier.

The images originally installed on the Ch'i-pao Terrace at Ch'ang-an, transferred thence to the Pao-ch'ing temple in the same city and thence to various Japanese and American collections, are stylistically so closely akin as to lead one to suppose that they were all made in one *atelier* and within a fairly short space of time. These sculptures, as we said, were made during the reign of Empress Wu (p. 384) at the turn of the century. They consist of Buddha trinities, and single images of the Eleven-headed Avalokiteśvara which compare stylistically with a free-standing statue of the same divinity dated A.D. 691. A characteristic specimen is shown in figure 62. Comparison between it and the Lung-yen Shan Bodhisattva is instructive. For the former would appear to be a deliberately 'sinified' version of the latter. Note a close similarity in treatment of the lower garment below the girdle and a broad resemblance in detailing of necklet and scarf upon the chest. Yet what a world of difference in style and execution. The modelling of the Lung-yen Shan Bodhisattva is free and naturalistic. That of the Ch'ang-an image has become strictly methodized; the roll of flesh forced up by pressure of the girdle, for example, is quite clearly rendered according to a formula. Moreover, graceful and infinitely dignified as this image appears, it has lapsed into a rooted Chinese immobility of posture. There is only the barest suggestion of *tribhanga*. The foot of the slightly flexed left leg is advanced a mere inch or so, while the comparative slimness of the hips corrects what Chinese sculptors may have felt to be an unduly profane feature of Indian prototypes.

All this suggests that the Lung-yen Bodhisattva preceded that from

1. B. Rowland, *The Art and Architecture of India*, London 1953, pp. 155-6.

Figure 62. Image of an Eleven-headed Avalokiteśvara from Ch'ang-an, Shensi. Third Phase.

Ch'ang-an.[1] We have already noticed an instance of reversal to a Chinese manner towards the end of the Second Phase; something similar probably occurred around the beginning of the eighth century A.D. when the Ch'ang-an images were made. Two other groups of sculptures are available for stylistic comparison. Those made at T'ien-lung Shan, in the early part of the T'ang period, are as freely-modelled, as close to Gupta style, as anything we know in Chinese sculpture. Others at the shrine show a deterioration in execution, and Sirén believes that twenty years or so may separate the two series. Unfortunately, none are dated. Nevertheless, Sirén's assumption that the first series dates from the middle seventh century A.D. carries weight, and supports an early date for the Lung-yen Shan piece, with which they have obvious stylistic affinity.

The second group is that recently re-discovered at P'ing-ling Ssŭ in southern Kansu. Of these lovely sculptures, none is better preserved than the Amitābha group shown on plate 32; and of this group the image third from the left, strictly that of Avalokiteśvara, shows all the verve and sensitivity of the Lung-yen Shan Bodhisattva. Note the fully developed *tribhanga* posture in which the divinity stands. I would date it about A.D. 670, contemporary with the colossal Amitābha group at Lung-mên.[2]

Provenance and material both indicate that the Lung-yen Bodhisattva came from a Ting Chou workshop. The last Chinese sculpture with which we deal, the headless torso of plate 31, is undoubtedly a product of this school, for it was found at a place only some seventeen miles north-west of Ting Chou and is made of the local white mica-ceous marble; its great weight suggests that it could only have been transported with difficulty. This piece raises several questions, of which the first of course is that of its date. The fact that a nearby temple was founded in the eleventh century is probably not important unless we assume the sculpture to be an archaistic work of the Sung

1. We can point to no evidence for a fresh impulse from India, such as might have promoted the free and vigorous treatment of the Lung-yen Shan Bodhi-sattva, at any time after the close of the seventh century A.D.

2. Reasons for identifying the Lung-mên colossus as Amitābha, and not Vairocana as named in an inscription at the site carved soon after A.D. 723, are given in my article, 'Superb Chinese Buddhist Sculptures from newly revealed cave shrines in north-west China. . .', in *I.L.N.*, vol. ccxxiv (1954), pp. 185–8. Diagnostic of both portrayals is the *yakṣa* king Vaiśravana, supported on a dwarf *yakṣa* and holding aloft a *stūpa* in his right hand.

period. More rewarding are stylistic parallels with other works, such as an image of Maitreya in Cave 4 at Lung-mên, bearing a date corresponding to A.D. 648.

A second question concerns its connexion with the 'Udyāna' portrait-type (pp. 316–21). We have seen that the 'Udyāna' tradition terminates in China with a sandalwood image of Śākyamuni which was in the Sandalwood Temple, Peking, until 1900; and in Japan with an extant sandalwood image in the Seiryō Temple, Kyōto. Figure 52d reproduces the front view of the Seiryō image, the copy of the claimed original made in A.D. 987. It shows striking similarities to our torso, especially in respect of the bilateral symmetry of the mantle folds. The back of our torso also shows a distinctive arrangement of the mantle-folds, which spread towards the ground in a succession of gradually widening loops. The convention by which they are rendered as a series of padded ridges is, as Yetts says when describing the piece, 'a poor plastic expedient and far from realistic', yet in this case it is used 'with vital economy and significance'.[1] Comparison with the back view of the Seiryō image shows that in the latter the treatment is exactly the same. The torso of plate 31, in fact, conforms strictly to the stylistic type associated with the 'Udyāna' image.

We can now return to the question of its date. The third of the images brought back to China by Hsüan-tsang, in A.D. 645, was claimed as a copy of the original 'Udyāna' image seen by him at Kauśāmbī in India. This copy was undoubtedly a Gupta image. Yetts cites two Śākyamuni images from Mathurā which seem to him sufficiently close to our piece in point of style, and particularly in respect of the bilateral symmetry of their mantle folds, to demonstrate its direct descent from an Indian original; and he concludes by saying 'possibly the third among the images brought back by Hsüan-tsang may have been a factor in standardizing and popularizing the conception [of the "Udyāna" portrait-type] both in China and Japan'.[2]

Our torso may well have been made not long after his return. To my mind it has none of the overtones of an archaistic product, while the spontaneity and verve of its workmanship would not have been possible, I think, before the Third Phase. In short, this image is a rare individual masterpiece, dating from the last great burst of creative achievement in the history of Chinese sculpture.

1. W. P. Yetts (see footnote p. 313), p. 56.
2. W. P. Yetts (see footnote p. 313), p. 55.

One slight point remains to be discussed in connexion with this image. Is it of Śākyamuni? The conventional gestures made by the 'Udyāna' type, as we know from the Japanese image, are *abhaya* and *vara*. Those certainly seem to have been the gestures made in the present case, as far as can now be told. But by mid-T'ang times the cult of Kṣitigarbha was well under way, and reasons have been given on p. 368 for assuming that images of this Bodhisattva were based on the 'Udyāna' image. Since the torso lacks its head we cannot be absolutely sure that Kṣitigarbha – with his monk's shaven crown – was not represented. But bearing in mind the scale and importance of this piece it is more reasonable to assume that it portrayed Śākyamuni, the Founder of the Faith.

NOTE

Positions of the hands (*mudrā*), and of the legs (*āsana*),
in Chinese Buddhist sculpture

MUDRĀ

1. *Bhūmisparśa:* 'Earth-touching'. Right arm pendent, hand turned palm inwards, touching the ground.
2. *Abhaya:* 'Freedom from fear'. Right arm flexed, hand shoulder-high, palm turned outwards.
3. *Vara:* 'Giving'. Left arm pendent, hand turned palm outwards.
4. *Dharmacakra:* 'Preaching'. Arms flexed, hands held before breast. Tip of thumb and of one other of one hand touch one finger of the other.
5. *Vitarka:* 'Discussion'. One arm flexed, hand held before breast, palm outwards. Tip of thumb touches that of one other finger.
6. *Añjali:* 'Adoration'. Arms flexed, hands held before breast, fingers pointing upwards, palms pressed together.
7. *Dhyāna:* 'Meditation'. Many variants. In all, arms are flexed, hands lie on lap, one on top of the other, or with fingers interlocked.

ĀSANA

A. *Seated*

1. *Dhyāna (Padma, Paryanka):* 'Meditation', 'Lotus', etc. Legs flexed and interlocked, feet resting on opposite thighs, soles upwards.
2. *Bhadra:* Sometimes called 'European'. Both legs pendent, separate, or with ankles crossed.
3. *Lalitā:* One leg pendent, other flexed, its foot resting on opposite thigh.
4. *Mahārājalila (Ardha-paryanka):* 'Royal ease'. Both legs flexed, one vertical, other horizontal, feet touching.

B. *Standing*

5. *Kayotsarga:* Feet symmetrically placed, weight equally balanced between them.
6. *Tribhanga:* 'Thrice bent'. Weight rests on one leg. Other knee is bent, foot slightly advanced. Thus the line of the hips is oblique, and that of the shoulders slopes in the opposite direction.